THE PRACTICE OF
HUMAN RESOURCE
STRATEGY

Using appraisal to fulfil strategic
Objectives p166

THE PRACTICE OF
HUMAN RESOURCE STRATEGY

Edited by
Shaun Tyson

FINANCIAL TIMES
Prentice Hall

An imprint of **Pearson Education**

Harlow, England · London · New York · Reading, Massachusetts · San Francisco · Toronto · Don Mills, Ontario · Sydney
Tokyo · Singapore · Hong Kong · Seoul · Taipei · Cape Town · Madrid · Mexico City · Amsterdam · Munich · Paris · Milan

Pearson Education Limited
Edinburgh Gate
Harlow
Essex CM20 2JE
England

and Associated Companies throughout the world

Visit us on the World Wide Web at:
http://www.pearsoneduc.com

First published in Great Britain in 1997

© Pearson Professional Limited 1997

ISBN 0 273 62824 0

British Library Cataloguing in Publication Data
A CIP catalogue record for this book can be obtained from the British Library

9 8 7 6 5 4 3 2
04 03 02 01 00

Typeset by Phoenix Photosetting, Lordswood, Chatham, Kent
Printed and bound in Great Britain by Redwood Books, Trowbridge, Wiltshire

The Publishers' policy is to use paper manufactured from sustainable forests.

CONTENTS

v

LIST OF CONTRIBUTORS

Shaun Tyson	Cranfield School of Management
Eva Lauermann	King's Fund
Noeleen Doherty	Cranfield School of Management
Keith Cameron	Burton Group
John Lloyd	Amalgamated Engineering and Electrical Union
Don McClune	Watson Wyatt
Alan Fell	T-Three Consultants
Tom Davies	T-Three Consultants
Zoe Gruhn	Berkshire Consulting
Andrew Kakabadse	Cranfield School of Management
Andrew Myers	Cranfield School of Management
Siobhan Alderson	University of Leeds
Lola Okazaki-Ward	Cranfield School of Management
Martyn Sloman	Ernst and Young
Randall Schuler	New York University
Mark Huselid	Rutgers University
Toshitaka Yamanouchi	Niigata University
Michel Domsch	Universtät der Bundeswehr Hamburg
Martina Harms	Universtät der Bundeswehr Hamburg
Frank Bournois	Université Jean Moulin Lyon III
Jaap Paauwe	Erasmus University Rotterdam
Magnus Söderström	IPF Institute Uppsala

ACKNOWLEDGEMENTS

We would like to thank a number of individuals who have contributed ideas and who have commented on earlier drafts of the various chapters. In particular we would like to thank Barbara Smolarz and Elizabeth Warwick (Chapter 7), County Natwest, Graham Chambers, Dick Bresland, Neil Coulbeck, and Beverley Webster (Chapter 10); Susan Jackson, Fred Lane, Marty Plevel, Sandi Nellis, John Fulkerson, Bill Reffett, Bill Maki, Mike Mitchell and Horace Parker (Chapter 11); Marc Vogel, Harriet Macke, Christiane Strasse, Ariane Ladwig, Peter Sticksel, Uta Lieberum, Klemens Kleiminger and Erika Blum (Chapter 13).

We would also like to thank Professor Chris Brewster for permission to quote from his work in Chapter 10, and Professor John Storey, Editor of *Human Resource Management Journal*, for permission to reproduce part of an article originally published in Vol. 6, No. 3 (1995), in Chapter 15.

Finally, but not least, we would like to thank Jayne Ashley, for her patience and hard work in compiling the final manuscript.

Shaun Tyson

PREFACE

We know much about the theory of strategy making, but what do we know about the practice? The rationale behind this book is the belief that people management strategies are integral within organisational strategy and that strategy implementation entails performing practical management tasks aimed at making things happen in the organisation. The notion that 'strategy making' is a practical activity may seem contradictory. The creation of a business or organisation strategy requires both a long-term vision, and a set of achievable objectives which can be operationalised into practical plans.

In our fast moving global economies, the planning horizon is shortening, and the constraints and opportunities are increasingly international. The speed of change encourages managers to be driven by current issues. What is remarkable is the extent to which these issues are shared: downsizing, reorganisation, flexibility, new reward approaches, culture change, and sustaining employee commitment for example, are topics which find a resonance in large and small organisations, in both the public and private sectors of the economy. In my regular contact with managers from other countries, it has become apparent to me that there are also similar issues faced in other parts of Europe, in the USA and Japan. This book is intended to offer insights into the strategic human resource management themes in the UK at the organisation level of analysis, and to discover the major people management themes in the USA, Germany, France, Japan, Sweden and Holland, as countries broadly representative of the developed economies.

While the universality of these themes may suggest we are facing common economic and social change, that is only a half-truth. Organisational change is very much a consequence of the particular circumstances and historical developments which result in the context for change. The values, beliefs, attitudes and ultimately behaviour of employees, are formed by the institutional and cultural conditions of their societies. From the perspectives of international comparisons therefore, we may be able to understand better how the economic forces sweeping through our organisations produce human resource strategy responses, by understanding the institutional frameworks and the cultural influences on organisations.

My role as editor has been to offer a platform for the authors who have kindly written chapters, looking at these issues, seeking to link theory to practice. I have assembled chapters from authors with wide-ranging experience and knowledge of human resource management who are sharing here an understanding of the issues and their perspectives on the changes in human resource management. The authors have been chosen for their expertise as researchers, senior practitioners, and high-level consultants. They bring the depth of awareness which only comes from living through the events described, indeed from often having to take responsibility for the events, together with a deep interpretation of the trends in their own societies: a lived truth which relies not just on research based evidence, but also on a demonstrable empathy and the interpretative understanding so essential to sociological analysis.

By concentrating on the practical aspects of HR strategies we have sought to bring new ideas and approaches to solving problems, and the reformulation of issues using theory where there is a beneficial consequence for our long-run thinking. The book was born out of a desire to contribute to the debate on how human resource strategies are being deployed to address the major themes in human resource management: themes which centre on the management of strategic change. Our hope, collectively as authors, is that our readers will recognise the themes we have discovered, and will benefit from the practical descriptions we have made.

Professor Shaun Tyson
May 1997

HUMAN RESOURCE MANAGEMENT COMES OF AGE: STRATEGIC INTEGRATION

Shaun Tyson

This book concentrates on the practical, strategic issues of managing people at work. The study of human resource management (HRM) has attracted increasing attention, following the definition of HRM as an activity which seeks above all else to bring a strategic focus to people management, in order to gain and sustain high levels of organisational performance.

The strategic role of HRM

The study of this subject seems to be falling under the influence of three different perspectives. First, there are those who believe HRM represents a recognition that certain special policies, mostly concerned with employee development and the treatment of people at work as assets, bring improved organisation performance. There is thus a normative argument in favour of this view, and a human asset accounting reason for supporting investments into knowledge workers from whence long-term financial returns will flow (Guest, 1987; Huselid, 1995). The second position shares some of these ideas. This position accepts that HRM is a more strategically oriented version of personnel management, with a strong emphasis on change management, but HRM is seen as another model of personnel management, neither better nor worse than other models, its appropriateness being entirely dependent on organisational contingencies (Purcell, 1989, 1995; Storey, 1992; Tyson, 1987). Third, there is a further group of researchers who now believe any paradigmatic shift in management which did occur in the 1980s to have been largely a theoretical construction of academics themselves, who, drawing on a few well-known company examples, have been engaged in a bid to find a new 'cause' on which to base research publications and career advancement (Blyton and Turnbull, 1992; Legge, 1995).

This book takes the second position. From the contingency perspective, the study of

HRM is axiomatically at the organisation level of analysis: HRM is performed in organisations, on behalf of those who control the organisations, and to experience HRM one normally has to be an organisation member, or to be in some way associated with the organisation.

However, taking this view does not negate the argument that employees are resources, and the perspective that their knowledge and skills are the main source of competitive advantage, which derives from the resource-based view of the firm, is entirely consistent with acknowledging that contingent variables determine organisational action (Barney, 1991; Wright and McMahan, 1992). For example, Knudsen (1995) shows through an analysis of Selznick's (1957) theory how economically rational action and 'rule following' social norms are not mutually exclusive, because there is an extended behavioural foundation to Selznick's theory. 'Selznick's introduction of an institutional analysis of organisations can therefore be understood as an attempt to introduce a process perspective within organisational theory that would make the processes per se (not just their outcomes) the object of the analysis' (Knudsen, 1995, p. 161). Human resource strategy creation and implementation is a process of adjustment for organisational members. The adjustments are to societal, political, and technological environment pressures, and to the expectations (expressed through their perceptions) of organisation members (Tyson, 1987, 1995).

Influences at the organisation level include the history and culture of the firm, the national culture and the institutional framework in which HRM exists, as well as the decision-making habits and the trade union relationships in the organisation, the labour markets in which the firm operates, and the perceptions of these variables and of HRM by the people who work in the organisation (Tyson, 1995). These variables also influence the kinds of personnel policies pursued, and there is therefore no set pattern or bundle of HR policies which will deliver successful organisation performance.

The creation and implementation of an HR strategy is a practical managerial activity, which takes place as a consequence of an analysis of what is happening in the organisation currently, and of senior management's strategic intentions. Human resource strategy may be defined as the philosophies, policies and practices which management adopt in order to achieve business-related people management objectives.

Since strategy is often given the image of a long-term, senior management (and therefore 'important') activity, concerned with such august documents as 'mission statements' and 'value statements', to suggest that strategy is a practical activity may appear to underestimate its significance. But management is a practical task. The pragmatic, action-oriented decisions needed to increase revenue, to improve quality and to generate greater efficiency may be regarded as everyday requirements for modern managers: this is nevertheless what is meant by implementing strategy. Indeed, there is a new acceptance within the strategy literature that business strategies are always emergent, and are speculations about possible future actions until realised (Bailey and Johnson, 1992; Mintzberg and Waters, 1985). The involvement of HR managers within strategic implementation provides opportunities for HRM to make a strategic contribution therefore, irrespective of whether or not HR issues were key concerns when strategic plans were made. This contribution is acknowledged to be most visible as a consequence, when change management activity is a major part of the strategy. The 'implementation' process becomes therefore the method by which managers in organisations come to adjust the organisation members to a new rationality.

The considerable degree of social, economic, technological and political change we have experienced throughout the 1990s has produced a paradigmatic shift to managerial thinking. To say that organisations are now in a constant state of change is to understate the obvious. The old certainties of organisational life have only existed for around a century. Our changing corporations are just reflecting the normal life cycle process: change, development, decay and metamorphosis into new forms, where boundaries shift between supplier and customer, where ownership is a complex of interlocking corporations, with franchises, alliances, joint ventures, and international collaboration. Lean production and the formula of organising around processes of production or customer relations rather than functions were guiding principles for the many businesses which restructured with the intention of becoming more competitive on price, and quality of product or service, during the 1990s (Womack et al., 1990). The old certainties had their own rationalities. In our post-modern era there are no certainties anymore.

The degree of change and disruption to working people caused by the recessions of the early 1980s and the 1990s are evidenced by the disappearance of 46 per cent of the 'Fortune 500' companies during the 1980s. In the five years up to 1992, 70 per cent of UK companies had been affected by mergers and acquisitions, 62 per cent by closure of existing sites and 65 per cent by investment in new locations (Sisson, 1995a). At the same time there have been substantial changes to occupational structures, with a massive increase in part-time working in the UK, the rest of Europe and the USA (Brewster et al., 1996), increases in self-employment and increases to around 50 per cent of the workforce in female employment in the UK. There are also trends towards home working 'telecommuting' and variations to shift patterns, working hours and other contractual arrangements.

The extensive changes to our social and occupational worlds brought about by all of this restructuring have provided a strategic role for HRM. New organisation structures require new ways of managing: from bureaucratic and functional controls to flat structures and business processes, from hierarchies to networks. The relationship between culture and structure gives HRM a significant opportunity to match formal reporting relationships to working styles and decision-making norms. The strategic HR role is partly within visible, pragmatic people management actions such as selection, pay system design and training initiatives and partly in sustaining abstract concepts such as 'commitment', 'empowerment' and 'organisational learning'. HR managers therefore, wittingly or not, come to manipulate organisational symbols, and to institute roles and rituals, and to sustain the organisational norms on which culture is based.

Strategic objectives

Competitive business strategies in a global economy have typically been based on differentiation according to price, innovation and/or quality of product or service (Porter, 1980). The pressure from Pacific Rim competitors has driven change both through direct competition (as in the car industry) and through indirect competition between EU States for investment in greenfield sites (as in consumer electronics).

One direct consequence from freeing up the movement of capital around the globe is that in seeking the best return, capitalists pay no respect to national boundaries. This has put cost pressures on the western economies which find the low wages and the phenomenal growth rates of the Far East tigers impossible to match. Competition from the Far East arose at a time when European social benefits were also under discussion, as the entry criteria for entering the European Monetary Union (EMU) impinged upon economies in general and social policy in particular. The realisation that many Far East economies can compete on the same basis of technological sophistication has now dawned. The forces for change experienced in the USA and Western Europe have also produced change in Japan. The complexities of these economic, political, social and technical changes have different effects in different countries, but are principal drivers for the human resource changes described in this book. Strategic objectives influence the organisation structures of enterprises; for example the great multinational enterprises have strategic objectives which also transcend national boundaries with global branding reflected in more complex organisation structures, which may require reporting through local managers, regional managers, and product managers as well as functional managers.

For larger organisations, especially the conglomerates, corporate strategies are followed for the whole group of companies. Corporate strategy is usually considered separately from business strategy since corporate strategic objectives are usually financial ratios, the broad narrative account being a description of such aims as growth, and the portfolio of businesses desired. Business objectives for particular companies or business areas are also usually a mixture of quantitative and qualitative targets. For example from a study undertaken in 1993, Vickers, the arms and car conglomerate, had, in addition to its financial objectives, diversification aims, and issues around the achievement of a significant order for battle tanks from the British Army, and the progress towards the launch of a new model for Rolls Royce cars, together with the related questions about investment and partnership with other car manufacturers (Tyson, 1995).

Related to the question of strategic objectives is the issue of whether these should be generated from below, in the subsidiary companies, or passed down from the centre. Strategy formation is an iterative process. Usually, broad outline frameworks are created by the Board, and there is an element of bottom-up involvement in the agreement and discussion process in each company or division. Issues also change, as does strategy in response.

The time frame over which strategic plans are made is shortening. Planning horizons are down to two or three years from the norm of five years in the 1970s. The uncertainty in the business environment has prompted a reappraisal of long-term planning. The need for flexible planning produces the need for the flexible organisation. Strategic objectives such as growth or expansion are particularised into 'growth by acquisition if a suitable target can be found in the next few years'; survival or 'steady progress' to 'look out for some collaborative venture of a size to keep the city and the shareholders happy'. The element of opportunism as seen in the Glaxo acquisition of Wellcome and the takeover by US and French companies of the recently privatised utilities in the UK shows how significant size is to organisation survival. Our discussions on corporate objectives raise the question of how can we expect employees to understand, or do more than give tacit agreement to the objectives? This leaves management with problems of employee commitment, and how to help employees to cope with change. The whole planning process with its opportunism and swiftly changing focus is inimical to employee involvement, we might assume.

The human resource strategy process

There is an extensive prescriptive literature on the way HR strategies should be formed, for example Armstrong (1992), Fishman and Cherniss (1990). The ideal typical model of HR strategy is represented as a linear flow as shown by Fig 1.1.

The argument is that HRM issues should be considered at each stage. From the time that companies start to consider or reconsider their missions, the questions from HRM are pertinent. For example, what are the corporate values about people at work, are there social and personal objectives which are consistent with corporate objectives, what is happening in the labour markets, both internal and external, and what HR strategies should be followed to achieve corporate objectives? For those who take the resource-based view of the firm, for whom the starting point would be the existing human resources, the arrows would point the opposite way, and the ordering of the stages would be different, with a feedback loop from the corporate mission and values into the kinds of resources (competencies, personal aspirations) and the commitment of

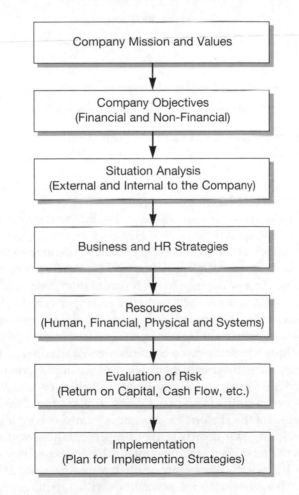

Fig 1.1   Flow chart of strategy process

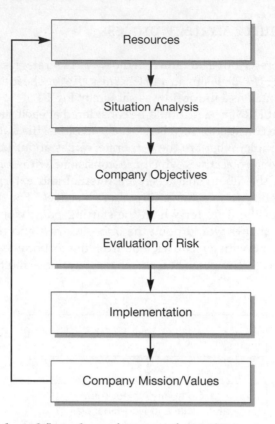

Fig 1.2   Resource-based flow chart of strategy formation

the people to the organisation goals, which would be a part of the situation analysis periodically undertaken (Fig 1.2).

Whether or not HRM issues are seen as integral to business strategies would seem to be a variable, dependent upon the model of HRM which the company is enacting. The evidence on HRM main board representation gives a figure in the UK of around 47 per cent, Germany 19 per cent, Sweden 87 per cent and France 83 per cent (Hegewisch and Brewster, 1993). These figures are open to a number of interpretations. In the case of the UK, Millward et al., 1992, came up with a figure of 40 per cent in 1990, and there are possibilities that respondents interpret questions about HR representation at board level to include the representation by non-specialists at board meetings, which might account for higher figures in some cases. Some aspects of the disparities between countries may also be explicable by structural differences, such as Germany's codetermination laws. Sisson (1995b) comments that the failure in British organisations to accord the personnel function board status in so many cases, and the trend away from specialist representation, in spite of the rhetoric to the contrary, means both a lack of integration of personnel policies, and that boards without representation would be less likely to take account of HR matters when making strategic business decisions.

In the study of 30 high-performance large British companies, specialist representation was often 'one step' below board level, sometimes with a requirement to attend board meetings when a significant HR issue was likely to arise (Tyson, 1995). The picture is further complicated by divisional structures. If major strategic decisions are to be taken at divisional level in highly devolved structures, them some of the corporate HR function must move to that level also, so the need for the old centralised function with a high strategic profile may disappear. There are also companies such as Marks and Spencer and Hewlett Packard where it is claimed that HRM has become so much a part of all managerial work that there is a reduced need for HRM specialists at the centre.

In order to unpick this tangle of mixed messages we need to understand what happens in the strategy formation process. Our definition of business strategy, as a long-term perspective on the way the organisation should position itself in the planning environment to achieve competitive advantage, makes a number of assumptions. There is the notion that strategy is 'forward thinking' and that organisational strategy is a process of flexible positioning. All commentators on strategy stress its emergent nature, and the tendency for management to rationalise often disconnected, short-term measures after the event as 'strategy'. The way that HR strategies are emergent, often unwritten and susceptible to rapid change must also be acknowledged.

There are often good reasons for avoiding formal statements of HR strategy. First, strategy creation is a complex interpersonal process, in which the power position of senior individuals and their egos become enmeshed with strategy creation. The very ambiguity of the strategy is a benefit, not just for directors to avoid being held accountable for its successful conclusion, but to allow for the reconciliation of the conflicting interest groups. Second, the degree of change in the business environment demands a flexible strategy response. The need to respond quickly to threats from competitors, and the pressure to bring out new ideas rapidly, exploiting opportunities, encourage the making of strategy 'on the hoof'. Thus even if there are formal written statements and policies they are likely to be framed in the most general terms. Third, all studies of decision making have shown how managers 'muddle through' (Lindblom, 1959), making the best of what is known at the time: formal strategy statements fail to acknowledge this awkward fact.

However, the paradox which is central to understanding HR strategy is the need for agreement upon and a degree of coherence and consistency within the management process. It is not exceptional for managers to change strategic objectives, and to manipulate these, but constant reorganisation and change to management systems bring heavy costs. While rapid changes do occur in processes, these are a consequence of organisational learning: the adaptation essential for survival.

Employee commitment can be gained by creating suitable management processes, even though everything else is changing. This requires a stable management process, and a stable decision-making infrastructure designed to give datum points for action. For example, broad agreed and published accountabilities and the reporting relationships which go with them provide a command structure through which different strategic objectives can be prioritised. Employee commitment can only be maintained if managers are able to sustain their own credibility with their staff.

Strategic integration

The rising levels of uncertainty in the HR environment accorded increased influence to the personnel functions of the 1980s (if we follow contingency theory) thereby giving rise to the HRM paradigm. What is not so clear now is the extent to which human resource management as a set of specific beliefs ever existed, or whether the phenomenon we were observing was a shift in attitude which could be characterised as placing HRM at the centre of business strategy. The evidence is that we were observing both, but in varying amounts, depending on organisational circumstances and history (Storey, 1992).

The evidence now is that the shift in the focus of the HR function has brought line managers to the fore, as policy creators as well as implementors of policy. HRM has returned to line managers the administration of policies. For example, Poole and Jenkins (1996) reported that line managers had greater responsibility than personnel/human resource managers for the main types of employee involvement, on most training and development issues, and for changing work practices. Their study of members of the Institute of Management showed that there had been more decentralisation of the function to the line in the private sector than in the public sector.

A further trend noted in the UK and the USA is the split in the function between a high level strategy consultancy role, reporting to the Board, and an operational role, reporting to line management (Hope-Hailey, 1996; Tyson and Fell, 1986; UCLA, 1995). Many large organisations are now divisionalised. The divisional HR role must be engaged in strategic HR activity, if the delegation to division is to deliver any benefits. Typically policies within the purview of divisional management are in areas such as industrial relations, communications, rewards and training, whereas at the centre there is responsibility for management development, fast track selection, senior level succession planning, and corporate initiatives such as profit share schemes and pension arrangements.

The outsourcing of HR function activities is part of a wider movement towards reducing overheads, gaining value for money and the establishment of the HR function as a profit centre in its own right. The shift towards outsourcing begins by charging for services internally – the move from cost centre to profit centre is easy to make. The 'customers' are the line managers, and the 'consumers' of HR policies are the employees. Outsourcing was encouraged in the late 1980s by the competitive tendering requirements of public organisations and by the cost-cutting reorganisations of companies facing the deepest recession since 1945. A US survey carried out in 1995 showed that 91 per cent of the responding HR departments outsourced one or more of their functions. Sixteen per cent outsourced more than $1 million annually, favoured areas for outsourcing being outplacement, training delivery, relocation and compensation planning/surveys (Harkins et al., 1995). The idea that HRM could trade internally and externally as a business has gained credence. IBM's outplacement department became independent of the company and set up in business with redundant IBM executives to run it, for example. Training departments are also prime examples of this process, reducing overheads and utilising spare capacity by selling courses to other organisations.

The picture painted so far is of an HRM function disintegrating, fragmenting and subdividing – a prey to consultancies, and to line managers' demands for authority to match their accountability, and to the short-term cost cutting of the early 1990s. This tendency to balkanization was noted in the 1980s (Tyson, 1987), when the effects of consultancies on the central HR role were a cause for concern (Torrington and Mackay, 1986). However, the growth of HR strategic interest frees the HR role from techniques and the operational methodologies of the function. These can often be delivered by specialists – communication consultants, reward consultancies, head hunters, training advisors and hired-in experts of various kinds. The outsourcing of these aspects of the operational role only strengthens the need for co-ordination, and for integration. Integration does not necessarily require a specialist, and we may see more executives from other specialisms assuming the most senior HR role, as a part of their general management remit.

There are three types of HRM integration:

1. between HR and business strategies;
2. integration between policies themselves; and
3. the integration with line management.

The move towards greater integration within these three areas is the sign that HRM is coming of age. The need felt by members of a self-conscious, insecure specialism constantly to seek reassurance of their importance has dissipated. Self-evident to line and senior management, the strategic focus makes HRM a responsibility for all managers. Once the message that successful competition for business rests on superior quality human resources, and superior people management practices, so that quality and cost effectiveness are of a high order, is accepted, then HRM becomes too important to leave to a specialist activity, unconnected to business strategy, and unaccountable for business results.

A close 'fit' between business strategy and human resource strategy is taken to be synonymous with the strength of the HRM contribution to business success. The argument put forward by a number of academic commentators is that without human resource strategies and policies linked into strategic business objectives, high levels of organisational performance are not likely (Huselid, 1995; Miles and Snow, 1994). The suggestion is that more is demanded than just a written business strategy with a linked human resource strategy. In addition, there must be an overall HR system which ensures an integration between HR policies and processes themselves:

> **An even larger advantage, however, is enjoyed by those firms that first put together the new strategy–structure–process package demanded by major changes in markets and/or technology.** (Miles and Snow, 1994, p. 23)

Guest and Peccei (1994) made a similar point when they drew out evidence on the effectiveness of human resource management as a function of the management processes applied to people management. Huselid's research into over 1000 US companies shows how HRM can accelerate performance improvement, the argument being that HRM practices were able to take performance into a higher level only if productivity improvements and technically advanced systems had pushed organisational performance up to the threshold of competitiveness. The point here is that on their own, HR policies and practices will not result in high levels of profitability or improved shareholder value, but combined with appropriate organisation structures, integrated processes and systems, and management styles which are supportive, HRM policies can create conditions which are inimitable, and thereby achieve a competitive advantage for the firm.

The worthy intentions expressed here can be found in the hoped-for benefits from business process re-engineering (BPR), if not in the reality of its delivery. Successes and failures in BPR have been attributed to causes which are indicative of the significance of people management policies, and the importance of taking people issues seriously in the management of change. There are positive stories to be told, such as at the Royal Bank of Scotland, where HR staff worked with the technical change, seeking to create the behavioural skills necessary through role definition which described the new way work was to be done, and through selecting and building the new teams (Wellins and Rick, 1995). A similar account comes from the Union Bank of Switzerland UK Group, in which BPR was used to re-engineer HR processes with wide ranging effects on the competency system, the performance review scheme, and employee communications (Timms and Finn, 1996).

However, re-engineering failure in the USA and the UK is almost equally well documented. Mumford and Hendricks (1996) quote evidence that re-engineering has become identified with cost-cutting 'slash and burn' exercises, which destroy employee commitment and team working, and produce dramatic reductions in morale. They quote survey evidence that 40 per cent of US and UK companies undertaking re-engineering projects reported poor results, while 25 per cent reported failure. The causes included failure to take the social system into consideration alongside the technical system; the tendency to copy others in a management fad without sufficient attention to the context or to any theoretical foundation; and crass consultancy interventions which failed to involve employees in the changes. Some of the consequences for individuals are found in the 'survivors' syndrome' problems for those who remain after downsizing, who have to cope with all the extra work and psychological distress occasioned by the departure of their colleagues (Doherty and Horsted, 1995).

If applied with attention to all the interlinking policy issues, organisation-wide interventions such as BPR or TQM can have the effect of forcing a review of people management practices and result in a more coherent, themed policy portfolio. Although such initiatives usually originate from outside the HR function the strength of the senior line management commitment helps to sustain change and to deepen the involvement of all parts of the organisation.

Organisation culture, underpinned by strong management ideologies, is one further integrative mechanism. Well-known examples of this approach can be found in companies such as Johnson and Johnson, Marks and Spencer, John Lewis Partnership, IBM, and Hewlett Packard. The feature of all these companies is the strong belief in the approach to people management, developed over many years, based on explicit values delivered from their founders. These act as 'litmus tests' of policy initiatives, as filters for new policies and for reviewing existing initiatives. Cohesion therefore comes from two directions, from the underlying values, and from the integration of policies. The latter approach can be seen in the use of competency frameworks, and in the overarching policy initiatives such as TQM and empowerment.

Policies in HRM are a product both of societal influences and of needs at the organisational level. Trends from the national context include moves towards family-friendly policies on one hand and moves towards the 'hard' contract, the privatisation of public services, and changes to competitive rules on the other. These trends are translated into management ideologies through the influence of stakeholders, which ultimately leads to restructuring, outsourcing, and new HR policies and practices.

The integration of HRM into line management roles was the subject of extensive comment as a feature of HRM in the late 1980s and 1990s (Hope-Hailey, 1996; Storey, 1992). The belief is that the reductions in overheads and delayering were achieved by pushing more responsibility down to supervisors and to line managers, and by creating more strategic business units and semi-independent divisional structures.

The strategic role of line managers in creating HR strategies was discussed earlier in this chapter, from which one may conclude that HRM is too important to be left to specialists. Changes to structure and to information processing have also encouraged the trend to devolution. Access to information on employees and to policy rules obviates the 'gatekeeper' role of specialist HR staff. Simple software packages can be widely distributed allowing managers to construct reward and development solutions within the boundaries of agreed policy. For example, Liberty Insurance, a US 21 000 employee insurance group in Boston, developed a Windows-based support system called SMART (Survey, Market, Analysis and Reporting Tool) with automated access to employee and labour market data to be used by line management and HR staff on job evaluation and compensation and benefit decisions.

Much more is possible for individual employees, for example relocating employees at Apple Computer Incorporated could house hunt on the Internet, and could use the in-house 'Intranet' called Applelink to provide access to company relocation policy details. Open learning using computer-based training, for example at British Steel and the Body Shop, enabled employees to access centres for learning where multimedia methods of learning were available, so employees could move their knowledge forward at their own pace, and keep up to date. The integration of HRM within the working environment means more than line managers taking over HRM roles: the HRM roles are changing rapidly. If we assume a desire by managers to engage their teams in a psychological bargain which includes openness of style, learning opportunities, and challenging work this is a redefinition for many of the management roles and brings consequential employability for employees whose commitment and innovation are key to organisational performance.

We may conclude therefore that the HR role is changing and that organisations are changing. The need now seems to be for high level strategic consultancy, or for specialised expertise in such fields as expatriate rewards, communication techniques and psychometrics. There also exists the Organisation Development role, either as a consultant or in a senior change agent role within the organisation. Jac Fitz-Enz, president of the Saratoga Institute in California which specialises in the evaluation of HRM, sums up the view from the USA:

> There will be no need for 90 percent of the positions in today's HR department. So, if you are less than 50 years old and you intend to make a career out of human asset management, listen to what your customers are saying. We must be responsible for preparing both ourselves and our successors for the marketplace of 2001. (Fits-Enz, 1996, p. 88)

More confirmation comes from this side of the Atlantic by a survey by Hewitt Associates which found that only 7 per cent of chairmen and chief executives thought HR experience was important for non-executive directors on remuneration committees, and 32 per cent said HR experience had no relevance (*People Management*, 16 May 1996, p. 6). The picture is not clear, however, as the HR role still claims a substantial presence in large corporations. Board membership is steady, and the profit centre concept, together with new technology applications, has given the HR function flexibility and the senior HR staff the capacity to act entrepreneurially. Some senior HR staff have risen to chief executive level: Len Peach from IBM to the Health Service, Mike Betts to a senior level at BT, Mike Bowlin from a labour relations career to President and CEO of Atlantic Richfield (ARCO) are examples. As with other functional areas, HR specialists can take their chances in the corporate jungle, and the new post-modern organisation provides flexible, changing interfaces with the environment where the action is fast, and the possibilities for developing new models are considerable.

Integration and national context

The rationale for this book comes from a desire to explain the ways new trends are influencing HRM, and a need to show how strategic integration is occurring. In view of the societal impact on policies we need to understand how variables at country level affect these trends through international comparisons of HRM. What is important is to understand how different histories, cultures and traditions are shaping management theories and actions in different countries. In this chapter the argument has been developed around different levels of analysis. Previous work on a general theory of HRM set out a framework for understanding how national contexts at a societal level are translated into organisational realities, and the processes by which meaning is negotiated with employees to establish that organisational reality (Tyson, 1995).

In this book, the HRM theory task is taken further. The interplay of societal and organisational characteristics is explored in the chapters which use the UK context as a basis for explaining the key trends in HRM. The first chapters are concerned with change – starting with the fascinating cases of the National Health Service and British Airways, whose approach to change is compared and contrasted by Eva Lauermann, who held senior positions concerned with strategic change in both organisations. 'Downsizing', that euphemism of the 1990s, which captures the main strategic thrust for many organisations in the heavy recession of 1989–95, is examined by Noeleen Doherty where she looks at the mechanisms utilised to implement this particular form of change, and the consequences for those who remain. In the words of Keith Cameron, managing the change process has become a dominating feature for HR departments. His insider account shows how a major organisational change was managed at the Burton Group where he is Personnel Director, and how the strategic reasons for change prompted HR policy changes which contributed to improved efficiency and were critical to business success.

Following this section there is a set of chapters which describe in turn the main HR policy areas. John Lloyd, a senior official with the AEEU and an accomplished academic commentator, reviews industrial relations in the UK as a primary field where the trade union movement and the employers' strategies form the arena where societal influences enter into organisational life. As a sub-set of industrial relations, Don McClune, a director of Wyatt, the world famous reward consultancy, then examines employer reward strategies and shows from a case study example how even the apparently narrow confines of a reward policy are integrated into HR strategy as a whole. Alan Fell, a consultancy partner, and Tom Davies of the NHS take the debate a stage further by discussing the results of their research into strategy formulation and the contribution of management development to organisational objectives. Zoe Gruhn then takes up the case of business education as a mechanism for carrying through changes to values and to the competencies of senior managers from a description of a major intervention in one of the main clearing banks drawing from her experience as a management development advisor to a major British bank. Andrew Kakabadse et al. take their research into executive competencies internationally as a platform for a sensitive and careful analysis of top team strategic behaviour – the very stuff of major OD interventions, an understanding of which is a critical factor in strategy formation and consultancy. From his experience at County Natwest, Martyn Sloman brings the debate in this section to a stage where the issues described so far are clearly set out – in particular the linkage into business strategy, the significance of change management, the integration of HRM and the role of line managers.

The final chapters translate our issues-led discussion into the international dimension. From each of the major economies distinguished academics have summarised the main issues in HRM, relating their comments to the organisational situations where companies are seeking to adapt societal trends into organisational realities. From the USA, Mark Huselid and Randall Schuler have set out a comprehensive guide to that vast country and have pulled out the key issues showing how universal is the concern for the new role of HR and the need to link it into business strategy. This theme is found throughout all the chapters – as is the universal picture of fundamental change, as demonstrated by Toshitaka Yamanouchi and Lola Okazaki-Ward in their picture of Japanese HRM turning away from lifetime employment. The changes and the strategic pressures in German HRM are set out by Michel Domsch and Martina Harms, with the European scene being explored from the perspective of a country now playing the major role in the EU, where personnel now has not only a strategic role but increasingly an independently orchestrated marketing strategy. HRM in France is similarly central to the changes experienced there, as Frank Bournois explains: 'In France as in other countries, each in its own way, the role of the human resources managers is developing from a functional role into a strategic type role.'

The HRM strategic issues in the Netherlands are shown by Jaap Paauwe to be again centred upon the linkage of HRM to corporate strategy, and Professor Paauwe is able to demonstrate how from the human resource based theory of the firm, the HR contribution interlinks with the societal level into HR processes, the outcomes from which feed into new emerging organisation forms, new product market technology dimensions and changed socio-cultural and legal dimensions. The Swedish strategic issues again bring us back to the HRM role, and Magnus Söderström draws a number of threads together, by showing how by meeting the strategic challenge, HRM is able to integrate economic service quality, new organisation structures, ideology and ethics. The final chapter in the book summarises these trends, and draws conclusions on the universality of the themes we have all addressed in this book. The depth of analysis is intended to give to our readers more than simple prescription. Although the messages are simple, they arise from the complexity of the human condition, as we experience organisational life where HRM as a subject is devoted to the study and the practical evolution of solutions.

REFERENCES

Armstrong, M. (1992) *Human Resource Management Strategy and Action*, London, Kogan Page.

Bailey, A. and Johnson, G. (1992) 'How Strategies Develop in Organisations', Chapter 8 in Faulkner, D. and Johnson, G. (eds) *The Challenge of Strategic Management*, London, Kogan Page, pp. 147–78.

Barney, J. (1991) 'Firm Resources and Sustained Competitive Advantage', *Journal of Management*, 17, pp. 99–120.

Blyton, P. and Turnbull, P. (eds) (1992) *Reassessing Human Resource Management*, London, Sage Publications.

Brewster, C. et al. (1996).

Doherty, N. and Horsted, J. (1995) 'Helping Survivors to Stay on Board', *People Management*, 12 January, pp. 26–31.

Fishman, D.B. and Cherniss, C. (eds) (1990) *The Human Side of Corporate Competitiveness*, London, Sage Publications.

Fits-Enz, J. (1996) 'On the Edge of Oblivion', *Human Resources Magazine*, May, pp. 85–8.

Guest, D.E. (1987) 'Human Resource Management and Industrial Relations', *Journal of Management Studies*, 24 (5), pp. 503–21.

Guest, D.E. and Peccei, R. (1994) 'The Nature and Causes of Effective Human Resource Management', *British Journal of Industrial Relations*, 32 (2), pp. 219–42.

Harkins, P.J., Brown, S.M. and Sullivan, R. (1995) 'Shining New Light on a Growing Trend', *Human Resource Magazine*, December, p. 75–79.

Hegewisch, A. and Brewster, C. (eds) (1993) *European Developments in Human Resource Management*, London, Kogan Page.

Hope-Hailey, V. (1996).

Huselid, M. (1995) 'The Impact of Human Resource Management Practices on Turnover, Productivity and Corporate Financial Performance', *Academy of Management Journal*, Vol. 39, No. 3, pp. 635–73.

Knudsen, C. (1995) 'The Competence View of the Firm: What Can Modern Economists Learn from Philip Selznick's Sociological Theory of Leadership?', in Scott, W. and Christensen, S. (eds) *The Institutional Construction of Organisations*, Thousand Oaks. Cal. Sage. pp. 135–63, Ch. 7.

Legge, K. (1995) *Human Resource Management and Rhetorics and Realities*, London, Macmillan.

Lindblom, C.E. (1959) 'The Science of "Muddling Through"', *Public Administration Review*, 19, Spring, pp. 79–88.

Miles, R.E. and Snow, C.C. (1994) *Fit, Failure and the Hall of Fame*, New York, The Free Press.

Millward, N., Stevens, M., Smart, D. and Hawes, W.R. (1992) *Workplace Industrial Relations in Transition*, The ED/ESRC/PSI/ACAS surveys, Aldershot, Gower.

Mintzberg, H. and Waters, J.A. (1985) 'Of Strategies, Deliberate and Emergent', *Strategic Management Journal*, 6, pp. 257–72.

Mumford, E. and Hendricks, R. (1996) 'Business Process Re-engineering RIP' *People Management*, 2 May, pp. 22–9.

Poole, M. and Jenkins, G. (1996) *Back to the Line? A Survey of Managers' Attitudes to Human Resource Issues* Institute of Management Research Report.

Porter, M. (1980) *Competitive Strategy*, New York, The Free Press, Macmillan.

Purcell, D. (1989) 'The Impact of Corporate Strategy on Human Resource Management', in Storey, J. (ed.) *New Perspectives in Human Resource Management*, London, Routledge.

Purcell, J. (1995) 'Corporate Strategy and Human Resource Management' in Storey, J. (ed.) *Human Resource Management: A Critical Text*, London, Routledge, pp. 63–86.

Selznick, P. (1957) *Leadership in Administration: A Sociological Interpretation*, New York, Harper and Row.

Sisson, K. (1995a) 'Organisational Structure', Ch. 3 in *Strategic Prospects for HRM*, Tyson, S. (ed.), IPD, London, pp. 56–80.

Sisson, K. (1995b) 'Human Resource Management and the Personnel Function', Ch. 4, pp. 87–109 in Storey, J. (ed.) *Human Resource Management – A Critical Text*, London, Routledge.

Storey, J. (1992) *Development in the Management of Human Resources*, Oxford, Blackwell.

Thatcher, M. (1996) 'Chief Executive Seems to Undervalue HR Skills,' *People Management*, 16 May, p. 6.

Timms, S. and Finn, R. (1996) 'Banking on a Wise Investment', *People Management*, 22 February, pp. 32–5.

Torrington, D. and Mackay, L. (1986) 'Will Consultants Take Over the Personnel Function?', *Personnel Management*, February, pp. 34–7.

Tyson, S. (1987) 'The Management of the Personnel Function', *Journal of Management Studies*, Vol. 24, No. 5, September, pp. 49–53.

Tyson, S. (1995) *Human Resource Strategy: Towards a General Theory of Human Resource Management*, London, Pitman.

Tyson, S. and Fell, A. (1986) *Evaluating the Personnel Function*, London, Heinemann.

UCLA (1995)

Wellins, R. and Rick, S. (1995), 'Taking Account of the Human Factor', *People Management*, 19 October, pp. 30–32.

Womack, J.P., Jones, P.T. and Roos, D. (1990) *The Machine that Changed the World*, New York, Macmillan.

Wright, P.M. and McMahan, G.C. (1992) 'Theoretical Perspectives for Strategic Human Resource Management', *Journal of Management*, 18 (2), pp. 295–320.

2

MANAGING CHANGE: THE NHS AND BRITISH AIRWAYS

Eva Lauermann

During the 1980s the scale of change in the public sector forced unprecedented challenges upon managers whose task was to change the hearts and minds of employees – indeed the very ethos of their organisations. These organisational change programmes present an invaluable example of how new ways to manage people become central to organisational strategy. No better cases could be found than those of British Airways and the British National Health Service (NHS), the former having been privatised, while the NHS remains as an evolving public institution.

This chapter will propose that there are many interesting parallels between British Airways and the NHS and valuable insights can be gained from comparing the changes that the two organisations have made over the past 10 to 15 years. In summary, it will be suggested that both organisations have achieved considerable change, but that one significant key to success has failed to be turned – more so in the case of the NHS than in that of British Airways. Finally we will consider the reasons for these outcomes.

This chapter is necessarily a personal and somewhat idiosyncratic view of the changes as it is written by someone recruited into British Airways to assist with change, who now finds herself similarly attempting to facilitate the continuing change process in the NHS. However, advice has been received from Gina Shakespeare, who has joined the author at the King's Fund after a career as a senior executive in the NHS.

The chapter will start by exploring the similarities between the organisations and then will offer a very abbreviated historical perspective. The stages in the culture shift will be charted, beginning with where the organisations were starting from and the nature of the overall objectives for the changes. We will then consider the process by which the vision was set; the strategy for achieving the changes, the part played by the human resource strategy and the role of the HR and finance functions will all be compared.

Other issues that will be compared are the effects of changing purchaser and provider relationships, issues of quality, and the way customer expectations have been handled. In addition, organisational and structural questions, especially as they affect power relationships, will be explored. The final section will assess where each organisation is today and what can be learned from the relative successes and failures.

It will be argued that both organisations have made substantial progress but that in one significant respect, namely the degree of success in capturing the hearts and minds of the most powerful professional groups, the NHS still has considerable ground to make up to catch up with British Airways but that the nature of the change has been much more complex in the NHS than in British Airways and that one has to be careful of using simplistic analogies to produce solutions for the public sector from private sector experience.

Comparing British Airways and the NHS

First, the parallels between British Airways and the NHS can been seen from the following comparisons.

Both organisations can be characterised as being highly professional, populated by technically qualified experts, in a business where safety is of major concern as is customer or patient care. At the commencement of this period, both were in the public sector and many employees joined them through a sense of public service.

Both organisations have a wide number of stakeholders and occupy a special position in the population's psyche. However, the NHS occupies a particularly sensitive position in the UK. On becoming involved with the NHS, it was startling to observe the parallels between pilots and doctors. This included their backgrounds, their allegiance to their profession rather than to their employer, the strong tribal culture, the fact that much of the job is routine although requiring great concentration, their tendency to be business people as well as professionals. Other parallels were observed in the area of relationships – those between doctors and nurses being perfectly echoed in those between pilots and cabin crew.

In both organisations, the doctors and the pilots wield enormous power and have considerable industrial muscle. Both groups are extensively socialised by lengthy training – much of which is outside the employer's control – and there is a strong sense of hierarchy. These professional groups appear to hold the key to the ultimate achievement of the changes. Both entities are, in their different ways, subjected to a regulatory framework and have strong external bodies laying down such things as limits to flying hours or the accreditation of hospitals as medical training establishments.

There are, of course, major differences, the prime of which relate to size and independence. British Airways, even at its largest, was only 100 000 employees strong whereas the NHS is the largest employer in Europe with one million employees. Although at the time of the commencement of these changes British Airways was in public ownership, the responsibility for achieving the change was handed over to the chairman and chief executive. Political interference was kept to a minimum and, provided the objective of preparing for privatisation was successfully met, the airline was left to operate within the overall regulatory framework.

The NHS on the other hand has always played a key political role. There have been a number of new chief executives during the period of the changes and they have been accountable to many different ministers. It is interesting to note that Virginia Bottomley was one of the longer servers, with about six years, first as Minister and then as Secretary of State. Both organisations are in a type of managed market in that deregulation of airlines has not yet occurred and the NHS cannot countenance closing hospitals purely on grounds of inefficiency if it leaves a population unserved.

The changes in the NHS towards a service more sensitive to patients' needs and the service culture shift in British Airways were both initiated in order to move the organisations away from an operational focus, where aircraft flew, or medical interventions were practised, according to the priorities of the professional groups who dominated the organisation, to a situation where the needs of the customer determined the service offered. Another way to view this is as a power shift in favour of the customer.

The background to change

Second, it is worth briefly recounting the environment and circumstances that the two organisations found themselves in at the beginning of the 1980s.

British Airways was still in public ownership and was making operational losses of about £300 million per annum. It has a labour force of 100 000 and very powerful trade unions. The merger of British Overseas Airways Corporation (BOAC) and British European Airways (BEA) had not really taken place; although on paper it had occurred several years earlier, employees still divided themselves according to the old company cultures into BEA and BOAC. The pilots were in a very powerful position, as were the engineers. The business was one of flying aeroplanes, not transporting passengers. The dominant positions were held by the directors of flight crew and engineering. The government had made it clear that it wished to prepare the airline for privatisation some years hence, and in practice the decision was delayed several times, before the airline was finally launched on the market in 1987, several years after it had become profitable.

The NHS was, and still is, the largest employer in Europe. Before the Griffiths reforms in the early 1980s the NHS was described as a classic example of an administered public sector bureaucracy spending £230 000 million per annum (Best, 1987). This was characterised by uniform structures and procedures, an internal focus with consequent insensitivity to the consumer, an administrative rather than managerial approach to change and a reactive stance in relation to the external environment. The power of the trade unions was still very high and, in particular, the positions of the consultants and the British Medical Association (BMA) were immensely influential. The government had made it clear that it wished to see greater accountability.

Hospitals were administered by District Health Authorities and GPs by Family Practitioner Committees. These latter bodies were superseded in 1990 by Family Health Services Authorities. Administration, rather than management, was the order of the day. There was little sense of financial accountability. Hospital consultants felt themselves to be considerably superior to GPs and considerably more powerful.

In driving through change, in British Airways, the role of the chairman and the CEO were vitally important, especially in setting the vision: Colin Marshall (now Sir Colin) and John King (now Lord King) joined British Airways in the early 1980s specifically to bring about the change to a customer service ethic. There has been a single-minded adherence to this objective, with every step of the way, every stage of the change being constantly driven by this goal.

Leadership was also significant in the case of the NHS. The late Sir Roy Griffiths began the process of trying to professionalise management by the introduction of General Management in 1983. He also wished to involve doctors and other health professionals in the management of resources, but this does not appear to have been a shared vision.

The fundamental objective had been very clear and, just as in the British Airways case, the vision was to move from being operationally focussed to being customer led, so the vision in the NHS was to move from being hospital driven to being patient led. One major and early step towards achieving the culture shift required in the NHS by this objective was the Resource Management Initiative. This was an attempt to improve the accountability for the use of resources by clinicians, to understand what was actually being delivered so that the service could be managed, not administered, and to get the doctors and nurses involved in management. A secondary objective was to bring about closer scrutiny of financial and other aspects of NHS performance. The overall need was to encourage a shift away from an organisational culture in which professionals determined what patients received and administrators organised at their bidding. Because of the size of British Airways, it was possible to involve most of the senior managers in developing the vision there, whereas the debate with major groups in the NHS had been carried out through the medium of white papers and articles in the *British Medical Journal*.

The change programmes

In British Airways, a series of seminars called 'Putting People First' for all employees was launched in the early 1980s, in order to communicate the new vision to everyone and to enable all staff to understand their role. During a week-long management programme, all managers were invited to create their view of the vision. This certainly helped to achieve greater ownership of the changes although it has to be admitted that it was more difficult and took longer to gain the commitment of the professional groups – in particular pilots and engineers.

Since the original series of events aimed at getting all employees involved in understanding the new vision, there had not been any time without further initiatives. Once the process was begun, it proved very difficult not to continue with new initiatives. For example, after several years of 'Putting People First', another corporate event followed and then another. When a year occurred without one, staff felt that management no longer cared.

However, one challenge was that, with the increasing sophistication of staff and perhaps also their increasing cynicism, future events had to be more and more sensitive to employees' needs. The most significant requirement was to ensure that the rhetoric was matched by the deed of senior management. This had implications for all aspects of human resource strategy.

In the NHS the initiatives came in the form of a series of papers which were published to lay out the vision, in particular 'Caring for People' and 'Working for Patients' in 1989. These were followed by legislation in the form of the NHS and Community Care Act in 1990.

The change strategies

In British Airways a coherent strategy was developed for implementing the vision. This identified the management style required to bring about the desired level of customer service, the reinforcement of that by training, performance appraisal and performance related pay. On the functional side, considerable sums were invested in a major re-fit of aircraft, new uniforms, corporate image, colours and so on, to symbolise the change, as well as to gear up the company for competition.

It was very noticeable that the early stages of the change process were much easier and that as customer service improved, the real challenge became how to sustain the improvement. Reinforcement of changed behaviour had to be more and more sophisticated.

In the NHS, the strategy consisted of a number of strands. In particular, they were all aimed at increasing efficiency and accountability by introducing market and private sector concepts. The main elements were: the creation of a split between the providers of care and the purchasers; the development of General Practitioner Doctor (GP) Fundholding and the enhancement of management capability. Purchasers were expected to develop an arm's length relationship with their providers in order to purchase, on behalf of their populations, the best service at the best price possible. The intention was to develop a market with providers competing for contracts from purchasers and through the competitive climate to be forced to increase efficiency and improve quality. The indirect effect was expected to be a diminution in the power of the consultant and an increase in the power of the purchaser or patient – through the auspices of GP Fundholders. The providers were allowed to bid for Trust status if they could prove that they were financially and managerially sound. The intention was that the creation of Trusts would engender greater local accountability through enhanced management capability, the introduction of boards with non-executive directors and chair to ensure sound governance and the creation of clinical directorates complete with business managers.

Another strand to the policies of the 1980s was to increase the accountability of GPs. This commenced originally by the introduction of new Service Contracts in 1990 which were negotiated over three or more years. Subsequently, GP Fundholding was introduced. A late addition to the strategy, GP Fundholding was intended to develop the, until then, rather independent role of GPs into a route for patients to exert influence over decisions to do with their own health care.

The human resource strategy

In British Airways, there was an HR strategy developed in support of the corporate strategy for developing and implementing the vision. It was identified early on that the culture shift would require a change in management style in order to elicit different performance from staff. The early thinking was based upon the concept of 'emotional labour' developed by Hochschild (1983) who, interestingly, used examples of cabin crew and nurses in her book. The thesis was that staff engaged in emotional labour require a particular kind of facilitative and support management, if they are to be able to continue to give a personal service which is believable, and demonstrates real commitment to the customer.

The systematic approach to achieving the culture change involved training managers in this style, inculcating all staff with the idea that they all have a responsibility to the customer, and then reinforcing the behaviour change by performance appraisal and performance related pay: 'the three-legged stool' as the strategy was called.

The concept was very elegant, the theory being that, in a customer service business, how work is carried out is as important as the achievement of an objective itself. The customer is sensitive both to the 'functional' aspects of the service he or she receives, that the plane needs to be on time and safe and clean and the seats need to work; and to the 'expressive' aspects of the service – in other words, how he or she is made to feel.

It was judged sensible to appraise people's performance on these two elements separately in order to reinforce the notion that it is not simply necessary to achieve a given objective, but to do so in a particular way. The achievement of objectives was measured by reference to the delivery of key result areas and the measurement of how they had been achieved was assessed against a number of behaviours which had been defined as being prerequisites for effective managers of customer service staff.

After several years of using the appraisal scheme, it was realised that the neat theory that one could persuade managers to distinguish between an individual's achievement of an objective and his or her behaviour in its achievement, was not happening in practice. The hope had been that it would be possible for a manager to recognise the fact that a subordinate had behaved very well even if he or she had not succeeded in fulfilling his or her objective or, even more controversially, that someone who had achieved their objectives but had behaved badly in the process would be penalised accordingly. In practice, it transpired that managers would allow the halo effect of good performance against objectives to cloud their overall marking.

Another basic belief was that the way the internal customer (namely the staff) is treated will determine how they treat the ultimate customer (namely the passenger), so the notion of internal customers was born. One of the later initiatives to try to sustain customer service was to conduct a staff input survey. In this, staff were invited to rank in order of importance such things as the different aspects of how they were rewarded or managed or communicated with, and then the staff were asked to identify how well the airline was performing. In this way it was possible to discover what mattered most to staff, and what the company was worst at. The results showed this very clearly to be seeing staff as customers so this gave a clear direction for the next stages of the culture change process.

The third element of the three-legged stool was based on the premise that rewarding particular behaviours would make them more likely to occur. However, after several years of performance related pay it became apparent that there were several disadvantages to this process. One problem was that team work was obstructed as people tried to earn more by not helping their colleagues. In addition the potential to demotivate seems higher than the potential to motivate. If people receive more money than expected, the delight lasts a few months, if less, the disappointment rankles for a year.

The one group still largely unaffected by most of these initiatives was that of the pilots. Many special workshops were run to engage the flight crew in the whole area of customer service and to convince them that they had a part to play.

By contrast, although the introduction of General Management into the NHS was combined with individual performance review and performance related pay for top and senior managers, there was no evidence of a coherent strategy involving professionals. The contracts of doctors changed to some degree and they saw some diminution in their autonomy, but in most cases, it was extremely difficult to deal with poor performance. However, the professionalisation of management proceeded increasingly. There was a steady shift away from administrators to managers. In particular, managers were developed by the use of management trainee schemes, and through the creation of business managers to advise clinicians on the management of their budgets for example.

Part of the Resource Management Initiative, pioneered initially at Guy's Hospital, was the development of Clinical Directorates headed by Clinical Directors. These key individuals were appointed to try to bridge the gulf between clinicians and managers. The main constraints on their effectiveness were that they had to continue to carry out a heavy clinical role – most only giving up two clinical sessions per week to carry out their managerial duties. This led to their having huge workloads, but it was essential for them to retain their clinical expertise both for their own credibility with their colleagues, and because most appointments were only for three years. The other constraint was that most of them were elected by their medical colleagues! (There are interesting parallels here with the situation faced by flight crew managers who still tried to fit in flying duties while fulfilling management posts.)

There was real evidence that, in some places, the role of clinical director was beginning to take effect and many consultants now sought training to try to understand the challenges of management and to develop the required skills. The role of the medical director on the boards of Trusts had also been an important development as it brought the issues of clinical freedom versus financial judgements right to the fore. (Again there are parallels with the balance between safety and commercial decisions in the airline.) The 1990 GP Contract encouraged most practices to introduce management and good administrative systems. The practice of GP Fundholding began to change the balance of power between GPs and consultants and led to consultants recognising that they had to be responsive to the GPs' requests on behalf of their patients or they could go out of business.

New structures have been introduced in British Airways and the NHS, both with the same purpose but very different in shape. In British Airways, before the changes began, the directors of flight crew and engineering departments effectively ran the airline. During the first few years of the culture change, their positions in the airline were so far eroded that they were not even members of the operational board. Although they are now part of the executive team of the company, they do occupy offices in a separate building from that occupied by all the other directors. For some time, the power balance between these two operational directors and the customer service directors shifted too far in favour of the customer-oriented directors, but this may have been a tactic to demonstrate the culture shift away from the dominance by the professionals. However, later stages of the changes have stripped out layers of management so there has been an overall reduction in the number of managers.

In the NHS, the structure recognised the shift in emphasis towards management by the appointment of chief executives with medical directors as advisors to them. As part of this shift there had, at least temporarily, been a large increase in the numbers of managers. This was thought very necessary in order to bring in some of the management processes for finding out what work was being done, whether there was a contract for it, for example, and who will pay. There was also an attempt to introduce information systems that would provide hospitals with mechanisms for an assessment to be made of the value of tests performed on patients and whether certain operations had any beneficial effect.

In both organisations the role of the finance function had changed to reflect the culture shift. The presence of a finance director was mandatory on the boards of Trusts and in most cases there were non-executive directors with a financial background. One of the duties of the board was to have a financial audit committee. All this had served to raise the profile of the finance function and the presence of contracting departments engaged in the debates with purchasers had further underlined the importance of income and finance in the life of NHS organisations.

The training of finance trainees entering the NHS reflected the move from bookkeeping and accountancy to management accountancy aimed at helping managers to manage their part of the business more effectively. Exactly the same transition could be observed in British Airways, who found themselves having to recruit externally for what were, effectively, in-house financial advisors to managers.

Lessons for the management of human resources

The human resource strategy for the NHS evolved as the changes were taking place. As the desire to devolve accountability to Trusts continued, the requirement to abandon national wage bargaining mechanisms led to the need to develop local pay systems. This was complicated by the fact that doctors and nurses tended to have careers which required them to move across the whole service, so differences of pay rates had potentially quite problematic results.

The new managers in British Airways were confronted with a much simpler task than their NHS colleagues in that their only priority was to achieve customer satisfaction and satisfy the shareholders and staff. By contrast the general managers in the NHS also had to consider issues of equity, access and relevance to need.

Both organisations have, over time, demonstrated the same ambivalence between control and delegation. Both began with a strategy of decentralisation and empowerment and delegating accountability. However, in British Airways empowerment came to be seen as a dirty word implying anarchy. There is also a long history of the government and NHS infrastructure giving freedom with one hand and taking it back with the other. Both organisations looked to the development of shared values as a way of achieving an appropriate level of freedom with discipline.

In particular, the creation of the purchaser-provider split in the NHS was intended to bring about greater accountability and greater awareness of the requirement to be responsive to the needs of the population. There was always an element of coercion and threat in the principle behind the split and the emphasis on the influence of the market. This made it more difficult to win the hearts and minds of the employees of the NHS, perhaps because of the very values of public service/personal care that people carried with them into the NHS.

Many managers were excited by the idea of the formation of Trusts as provider units, hoping for greater freedoms from central control. Doctors viewed the concomitant increase in the numbers of managers required to run these new organisations with mistrust and dismay. The concept of the purchaser buying health care on behalf of the population and the provider being required to offer the most cost-effective ways of meeting these requirements drove a coach and horses through the individual clinician's prerogative to decide what was best for his or her particular patient in the light of his or her clinical judgement. The attack on clinical freedom was acutely felt and fiercely resisted.

It has to be admitted that the pilots in British Airways similarly fought for their position to be protected and their system of bidding for routes according to seniority was still preserved. However, it is markedly apparent that they came to see themselves as being part of customer service, that they were not just employed to enjoy flying the planes safely.

The role of the HR function was central to the change programme in British Airways with the original strategy being developed by the then HR director. For several years British Airways did not have an HR director and gave the role to other directors with no professional knowledge but during the crucial early phases of the changes, did have an extremely powerful change agent as Human Resources director. The personnel function as it then was, changed to an in-house organisation development resource and changed its name to Human Resources to mark the change.

The role of the personnel function in the NHS was more limited although there were attempts to develop people into a more strategic resource. National Health Service Trusts were not required to have an HR director on their boards and many did not. In many cases the personnel department, as it was frequently still called, was regarded as an administrative function and had, if anything, lost its power base as it no longer was needed to rescue managers from difficult industrial relations problems. There was an attempt to develop HR directors in the NHS as strategic thinkers.

Looking at the development of purchaser-provider relationships, there are again interesting parallels between the two experiences. In the early 1980s British Airways had a very large number of suppliers and was eager to see competition between them as a way of reducing their power and negotiating harsher terms that were seen as more favourable to the airline. Over the period of the early 1990s there was a significant shift to fewer suppliers with longer-term relationships and the development of partnerships. The notion was that fewer and better relationships led to better deals in the long run.

At the time of writing the NHS was still in the immature phase where competition is seen as a good thing and purchases and providers are keeping their distance and sometimes even have adversarial relationships. This even led to arbitration being necessary between purchasers and providers who could not agree their contracts. There was a political imperative reinforcing this state of affairs, but despite this, some purchasers and providers were trying to develop sensible relationships and the concept of strategic commissioning, rather than short-term purchasing, was developing.

It is interesting to note that in 1989 the *British Medical Journal* (BMJ) published a booklet 'The NHS Review and What It Means' which demonstrated its continuing antipathy to the reforms. By 1995, it was still very apparent that the hearts and minds of the major professional groups in the NHS, namely the doctors and nurses, had still not been captured by the leadership of the organisation. In 1995, there were examples of doctors ousting chief executives and chairs in a last ditch attempt to demonstrate their power. However, the increase in GP Fundholders continued to erode the power of the consultants and many feared a future where all the interesting, caring work is done by GPs and nurses and some doctors become technicians.

By contrast, recently travelling on a British Airways flight, the captain asked passengers to fill in customer survey forms personally issued from him. He clearly saw himself as part of creating customer service. Even the engineering division sees itself as being in the customer service business. How is it that this change has been achieved in British Airways but much less successfully in the NHS? One suspects this is fundamentally because the values and mission of the NHS are much less comfortable for staff than those of British Airways to its employees.

In the case of British Airways, it has been possible eventually to persuade even the operational professionals that their role in life is ultimately to serve the customer as that is the way to ensure profitability and consequently the survival of the business. This understanding of the business imperative even enabled British Airways to reduce by 4500 employees during the Gulf War period without loss of morale.

For the NHS, by contrast, the fundamental missions and values are much more complex. The conflict between the individual doctor wanting to do the best as he or she sees it for an individual patient, versus the requirement to provide in the most cost-effective way for the total health needs of the population served by the organisation, is a problem that has not been resolved. The ambivalence between service and efficiency remains an area of values conflict across the NHS.

The real challenge and the battle that was not won was for the hearts and minds of the doctors. If they had felt that the things they held dear, such as status, personal freedom and their clinical integrity, could have been safeguarded and even promoted by the change, it might have been possible to move the reforms much faster. As it is, the reforms look like a rough-grained mallet brought down upon the NHS, leaving the consultants like pins – slightly bent over at the top, but still unbowed – but flattening all the rest.

The signs that some aspects of successful change have occurred lie in the fact that there were new sources of leadership emerging: there were some doctors and nurses driving forward changes that were leaving the medical dissidents rather isolated. Some senior figures of the medical establishment began to espouse the virtues of GP Fundholding.

When consultants were permitted to join in contracting discussions with their clinical colleagues from Public Health departments of purchasers, attitudes really began to change, and more creative ways of utilising limited resources were being devised.

The overall learning is that it is simplistic to apply private sector solutions to public sector issues because, by their very nature, the values and motivations that underpin any public sector service organisation will be fundamentally more complex than those of their private sector counterparts. There are many useful lessons that can be learned, however, from the comparison, in particular, the enormous value of harnessing the energy and ability of the most professional groups, by exciting them about the role they can play in the new order of things. If pilots can get involved in generating ideas for customer service initiatives linked to 'red nose day' it must be possible to persuade doctors that they too have a crucial part to pay in the total 'business' of health care.

From the comparisons of the two cases we can see that the overall significance of context, the history and specific circumstances, caution us against blanket change management solutions. The two cases also emphasise the overall significance of people management practices in orchestrating successful change. The priorities of the different stakeholder groups were critical to the change in management strategies. In both British Airways and the NHS, professional groups played an important role. Any group which is tied to the purpose of the organisation could be in this position, for example the doctors and nurses in the NHS, the pilots and engineers in British Airways. One criterion for a successful change strategy is the support of such groups. It is also clear that organ-isation structure changes, combined with appropriate culture change programmes, bring about new management approaches, and symbolise the new reality to employees. Both these cases also illustrate the importance of customer service improvements which had to be achieved alongside efficiency gains. How to achieve both these objectives, while retaining staff commitment and enthusiasm, is a concern to managers often engaged in handling downsizing, as part of their new profit and cost conscious roles.

REFERENCES

Best, G. (1987) 'The Future of NHS General Management', King's Fund Project Paper No. 75.

Hochschild, A.R. (1983) *The Managed Heart*, University of California Press.

'The NHS Review and What It Means', *British Medical Journal*, 1989.

CHAPTER 3

DOWNSIZING

Noeleen Doherty

It is not news that organisational downsizing is becoming the norm rather than an unusual practice experienced by a few companies in trouble. (Cameron, 1994a, p. 183)

Downsizing has become a euphemistic term of the 1990s and Cameron's observation reflected a growing trend in the use of downsizing tactics throughout the 1980s and early 1990s. The term originated in the USA where it was coined in reference to the scaling down of car sizes by automobile manufacturers. Subsequently, it was used to describe situations where companies went on 'crash diets' to reduce in size, in their search for greater efficiency, necessitated by recessionary pressures (Appelbaum et al., 1987). Now the word has assumed intrinsic meaning in the vocabulary of management and has become synonymous with other terms used to describe organisational change such as rightsizing, reorganisation, restructuring and rationalisation.

Although originally attributed to recession, in this continued era of constant change, many factors may contribute to the need for downsizing. These include international competition, the pace of economic growth, changing markets, mergers and acquisitions, and technological innovations many of which are designed to improve productivity with less personnel. It has been argued that downsizing does not equate automatically with redundancy and layoffs (Vollmann and Brazas, 1993). They suggested that downsizing need not be sudden, drastic or disruptive but is just one management method that can be used to help the company to survive. However, Cameron (1994b) distinguished downsizing from other organisational changes. Downsizing is explicitly associated with the strategic impetus to improve organisational productivity, effectiveness and efficiency through an intentional set of activities which result in a reduction in employee numbers which also affects work processes. Therefore, in essence downsizing aims to cut costs by reducing head count.

The press has been full of announcements of downsizing, throughout the UK, bearing testimony to the scale of change being experienced by British business and industry. Many organisations have succumbed to this type of event and downsizing has been legitimised as a strategy for organisational survival and posed as a 'necessary evil'

Curtis (1989) observed that although the language of cutback may be recent there have always been cycles of commercial and demographic reductions within business. However, most research and literature has been characterised by a focus on the management of organisational change which results in growth, while the dynamics of change in declining organisations have been largely ignored. Many of the changes now being experienced result in redundancy, and often repeated episodes of redundancy.

Organisations are no longer just stripping out a layer of management but are shedding large numbers of employees, in successive tranches. Companies now face the need to manage repeated episodes of transition which are resulting in the reduction as opposed to an increase in the labour force. The current scale and pace of change is therefore both quantitatively and qualitatively different from any experienced before and the best practice principles of the past may no longer be sufficient to address the contextual variables currently at play.

An era of insecurity

Not only is change endemic to organisations but the advent of the widespread practice of downsizing with the resulting reduction in labour force requirements has had many macro and micro repercussions. Even industries which have traditionally espoused a patriarchical attitude towards employees, offering security of employment and a life-long career, have not gone unscathed. The multifaceted nature of such change has posed a new challenge to organisations as they now need to navigate many transitions in order to achieve a successful outcome. This has led to the rhetoric of *change as a constant* and *insecurity* as the doctrine of the decade.

Downsizing is one practice which has posed the threat of insecurity for individuals, organisations and society (Feldman and Leana, 1994). At a societal level, downsizing has resulted in unemployment for larger numbers of people and unemployment which is becoming characteristically long-term. Redundancy and lay-offs of the scale now experienced have changed the rules of the game – that is the redundancy practices which have traditionally been adhered to by organisations and employees alike. The apparent demise of organisational commitment to providing security of employment also leads to individual insecurity and individual suffering both for those losing jobs and for those who remain in the organisation. Hartley et al. (1991) argue that this fuels job insecurity which has become pervasive in nature and extent. An exploration of the potential impact of downsizing exposes some of the underlying causes of this insecurity.

The impact of downsizing

Cameron (1994b) outlined the impact of organisational decline which is pre-empted by downsizing. The negative outcomes of a downsizing situation can include the centralisation of decision making, a short-term planning horizon, the loss of innovation, resistance to change, decreased morale, the politicising of the organisational climate, across the board cutbacks, loss of trust and confidence among employees, increasing internal conflict for diminished resources, lack of communication, an increase in individualism and lack of leadership. The organisational responses to changes imposed by downsizing tend to focus on tried and tested solutions to manage the change situation and not on innovative behaviour. Such reactions from both organisations and individuals indicate that downsizing, in a worst case scenario, can invoke a cut-throat environment which breeds vulnerability and insecurity resulting in a 'backs to the wall' mentality. Downsizing can therefore create turbulence of considerable proportions (Fisher, 1988; Froiland et al., 1993; Overman, 1991; Rice and Dreilinger, 1991).

The HRM challenge

The fundamental need for organisations to remain effective and efficient in order to survive, drives business strategy. Downsizing is now a commonly used strategy to achieve a reduced workforce in order to meet business objectives, therefore the management of the HR issues is a recurrent challenge for the HR function (Fisher, 1989). Hendry and Pettigrew (1992) argued that HRM should link operational and strategic activity through policies which proactively address conditions of continuous change. The contextual and continuous nature of change suggests the need for companies to develop policies and practices to address their unique circumstances. However, the management of HR issues and in particular the continued development of people becomes a universal requirement, fundamental to success throughout a downsizing event.

There is an emerging consensus that HRM strategies should match the business strategies designed to maintain organisational success. Tyson (1995) suggested that companies use different routes to achieve such integration. Because of the current nature of change corporate strategies appear to have become more short-term and this is reflected in the increasing prominence of HRM policies and practices which are used to manage change. The strategic HR influences currently in operation include employee relations policies which are designed to reinforce working relationships which meet the business objectives, organisation development programmes which increase responsiveness to external pressures, and management development policies to ensure competitive advantage through the development of the right skills and abilities of people in the organisation. Achieving the integration of the policies and practices which address the downsizing situation highlights the role of HR in driving and sustaining the change efforts at a behavioural level and accords with Tyson's (1995) view of the role of human resource management as 'an interpretative, representative and determining force for management intentions at work' (p. i). This provides one of the most exciting opportunities to consolidate the role of the HRM function for the next century.

Managing exits

It has been argued that job loss is an integral part of a downsizing strategy. In many cases downsizing signals the tragic reality of redundancy for employees and a potentially traumatic transition for the individual. Work is a social activity which not only provides the means for economic existence but is a source of social identity and status. Because of the various functions of work, redundancy can provoke a range of responses from individuals. These include a loss of dignity, a loss of confidence, anxiety, despair and even relief and excitement. It is now well documented that the way in which the redundancy situation is managed can help to overcome some of the adverse effects for people made redundant (for example Doherty and Tyson, 1993; Latack, 1984; Latack and Dozier, 1986; Nicholson and West, 1988; Swinburne, 1981).

The humane management of redundant employees has been on the agenda for some time, and, within personnel management and HRM paradigms, is a central concern of the personnel/HR function. The recession of the 1990s which resulted in large-scale redundancies had encouraged the development of new policies and practices to deal with the redundancy transition. The HR function played a key role in the development and implementation of such policies. The provision of support in the event of redundancy forms the basis of best practice models of managing the situation, and includes the use of structured programmes of help (The Institute of Personnel Management Redundancy Code, Hogg, 1988).

Outplacement

One intervention which has been used in the management of redundancies is outplacement. This concept permeated from the US and enjoyed prolific growth throughout the 1980s in the UK. Those being exited receive help in the form of structured programmes which include advice on preparing job search strategies, practical assistance with secretarial support, skills training and counselling through the change process. By providing a tool-kit of techniques and skills, individuals can be facilitated through the redundancy transition and helped to re-enter the job market. The benefits of such programmes included easing the redundancy transition for both the individual and the organisation and helping the redundant person to manage their own personal transition issues (e.g., Crofts, 1992; Doherty and Tyson, 1993; Eggert, 1991; Hyde, 1988).

Considerable financial resource is often allocated to ensure the smooth passage of redundant employees out of the organisation. Outplacement policies have assumed a near normative stance in the UK and are now often an integral part of redundancy packages for all levels of employees. Along with other mechanisms for managing major change, outplacement represents one element in the portfolio of policies designed to ease the transition process for individuals. In addition to helping redundant employees, organisations are also increasingly recognising the value of such programmes as a damage limitation exercise for those who remain (Boynton and Thomas, 1991; Doherty, Tyson and Viney, 1993). Organisations which are seen to be behaving humanely towards redundant employees, through the use of outplacement, are communicating an ideology that they value people. Within this ideology, the rationalisation for redundancy is that the sacrifice of some jobs will improve performance and allow the remaining employees to survive in an increasingly competitive environment.

Survivors of change

Although considerable attention has focussed on the impact of the redundancy situation on those leaving the organisation, there can be casualties of the change among those who stay: the so-called survivors. In the aftermath of downsizing those who stay in an organisation can be as much victims of change as those who leave. The term 'survivors' syndrome' gained popularity in the mid 1980s following research which simulated the impact of a lay-off situation. This research indicated that co-worker layoffs can have a dramatic effect on the people who retain their jobs (Brockner, 1986), therefore after the actual downsizing event the 'survivors' may be as adversely affected as those who leave.

The impact of redundancy on remaining employees

Survivors' syndrome is a concept now common in academic and anecdotal literature and can pose a very real problem due to its potentially negative manifestations. The reactions of the survivors, like those experiencing redundancy, can vary considerably between individuals and even within organisations (Armstrong-Stassen, 1993). The emotions and responses can range from shock, anger, anxiety, animosity towards management, concern about their colleagues who have left, to guilt and relief that they still have a job, to fear about future security.

Survivors' syndrome is characterised by behavioural outcomes such as decreased motivation, decreased morale and increased stress due to the remaining employees having to work harder, over longer hours, to fulfil the tasks of departed colleagues, decreased confidence and commitment and a lack of trust and loyalty to the organisation. Survivors also face the dismay of losing the peers who have formed the social fabric of their work life and the threat to their own jobs of further redundancy. Not surprisingly these many factors can leave the people who keep their jobs feeling shell shocked, cynical and less than positive towards the organisation (Brockner et al., 1986, Covin, 1993; Doherty and Horsted, 1995).

Ultimately, the reactions of the survivors may have a detrimental impact on organisational performance and adverse effects on bottom-line results. Since it is the actions and reactions of the employees who remain that dictate the organisation's effectiveness, survivors' syndrome has become an increasingly legitimate concern for management when a downsizing event occurs. Often the very reason that the organisation institutes downsizing and redundancies in the first place is to increase output and consolidate competitive advantage but the detrimental effect of survivors' syndrome if not managed satisfactorily may severely undermine this.

The complexity of survivors' syndrome reactions

There are many complex interactions among the emotions and behaviours displayed in survivors' syndrome. The extent to which remaining employees exhibit the 'symptoms' is mediated by a variety of factors. These include organisational and individual variables. The way in which the company decides which people will be made redundant has been found to be important to survivors' reactions, as have factors such as the person's position in the organisation, their attitudes towards work and personality factors. Self-esteem, the individual's personal coping mechanisms, the perceived fairness of the lay-offs and the perceived threat of further redundancies all influence how individuals react when work colleagues leave (Brockner et al., 1986, 1988, 1992a, 1992b, 1993).

One of the most fundamental factors which can exacerbate survivors' reactions is the perceived fairness of the redundancies. Survivors' perceptions of the fairness of how the situation was handled are determined by beliefs about why it occurred and the justification for redundancies, therefore it is important that the corporate culture is consistent with a redundancy strategy. For example, until recently IBM had espoused a no redundancy policy and used other means of reducing the workforce including early retirement and voluntary resignation. When such an organisation then resorts to layoffs this runs contrary to employee beliefs about the corporate culture and may therefore be more likely to be perceived as unfair.

The handling of the redundancies is also an important factor in determining survivors' reactions. Survivors appear to be concerned with what might be considered the detail of the lay-off procedure, for example how the notice is communicated, what decision rule was used to decide redundancies, whether good services were provided to soften the blow for those leaving, including severance pay, counselling and the continuation of benefits. The policies and practices which are applied to the people leaving the organisation, therefore, can determine the reactions of the survivors.

After redundancies working conditions in the organisation often change. Workload may increase in the first instance since remaining employees may be required to fulfil the jobs and tasks of departed colleagues. The nature of the work can also vary. New working practices may result from technological changes and business process re-engineering which means that people have to cope with different ways of working together. Job security often decreases after lay-offs as employees may perceive the threat of additional cuts in the workforce. For many survivors this involves different threats and opportunities and this type of change can create a lack of clarity and mission, feeding insecurity and uncertainty about future prospects within the company.

Clearly the survivors of organisational change such as downsizing are sensitive to a number of issues which are interlinked and are impacted by the policies and practices used to manage the situation. Brockner (1992) suggested that many of the factors that contribute to survivors' syndrome *can* be influenced by management, therefore it is argued management should plan any downsizing exercise with special consideration for the survivors. This requires strategies which are consistent, integrated and compatible since it is important to remember that all actions have significant symbolic meaning to both those leaving and those staying and may be interpreted as an exposition of the covert philosophy of the organisation by both groups.

Employee involvement

Employee involvement strategies have been used to address the many HR issues which result from downsizing. British Aerospace embraced a downsizing situation through the institution of a programme which used a high employee involvement strategy (Guest and Peccei, 1992). The closure of a site was achieved through a programme of redeployment and redundancy which included carefully planned communication, generous severance terms and a package of 'special measures' such as job search, counselling, training and retirement advice. This approach was designed to fulfil four major objectives. The programme aimed to minimise the risk of collective union disruption, guarantee no compulsory redundancies, provide special help to those remaining employees such as counselling, training, job search and retirement advice and to retain skilled employees by offering the opportunity to transfer to another site.

Analysis of the outcomes indicated that management objectives were met. The programme successfully disarmed collective action and enabled the transfer and retention of over a third of employees including professional and skilled workers. However, from the employees' perspective the outcomes seemed less successful. Although the involvement strategy was extensively used and highly valued by a large proportion of the workforce, a substantial minority of employees felt worse off after the plant closure. Forty-two per cent of those who had been redeployed believed they were definitely *not* better off as a result of the closure and 59 per cent still found the exercise a stressful event. This case is a potent indicator of the difficulty in attempting to address the whole range of issues which arise due to the redundancy situation and shows how survivors' syndrome issues can persist despite a concerted effort to implement a strategically planned intervention.

Downsizing and employee involvement

Buch (1992) outlined the effects of downsizing on employee involvement activities and attitudes in a sample of US organisations. The types of employee involvement activities reported in the downsizing organisations included employee involvement teams, quality circles, total quality management, suggestion schemes and survey feedback. Over half of the organisations surveyed reported that downsizing had an overall negative impact on employee involvement. This was apparent in decreased motivation and morale among employee involvement participants, cynicism towards employee involvement efforts and a decline in the quality and quantity of employee involvement activities leading to the conclusion that downsizing can threaten the health and survival of employee involvement. However, some organisations considered the downsizing as a challenge. Such companies were characterised by a corporate culture which embraced employee involvement as an integral part of their overall strategy and these organisations were more likely to allocate dedicated resources to employee involvement initiatives.

These studies indicate that employee involvement strategies are only part of the solution to managing the downsizing situation. Guest and Peccei (1992) suggest that any employee involvement strategy should be integrated into a coherent company-wide personnel strategy in order for it to succeed. The integration of interventions is clearly key in addressing the HR issues associated with downsizing.

Current interventions for survivors

Recent research on the extent to which changes in the financial services sector in the UK have impacted on remaining employees reflected the continuing very real impact of survivors' syndrome (Doherty and Horsted, 1995). Human resource managers reported many of the symptoms of survivors' syndrome such as decreased motivation, morale and loyalty to the company in tandem with increased stress and scepticism, similar to findings in organisations in the USA (Pinola, 1994; Richey, 1992; Skopp, 1993; Tombaugh and White, 1990).

However, this survey showed that, while 79 per cent of respondents indicated that outplacement was provided for those leaving, fewer than half (45 per cent) reported that structured help was provided for survivors. Redundant employees were being given assistance to leave the organisation and help in finding a new job or career, but the survivors were receiving much less attention. The structured help which was provided for remaining employees focussed mainly on the immediate needs for job and task training.

Formal strategies were reported for the retention and motivation of remaining employees. These were mainly reward strategies (84 per cent of respondents), and training strategies (83 per cent of respondents). Fewer respondents reported strategies focussing on the individual, for example, succession planning (43 per cent), career management (44 per cent) and cultural change (38 per cent) strategies were much less prevalent. Survivors appeared to be receiving little help to redress their personal change issues or to re-orient themselves to the new organisation and few actual or symbolic messages about their long-term security.

Short-term tactics

These findings may reflect a firefighting approach which is driven by the current pressures for change and has concentrated organisational interventions on short-term requirements. This has put job and task issues at the top of the agenda. There is often an immediate need to address new skills requirements, hence a need for job and task skills training to maintain if not increase productivity. However, individuals can experience a short-term organisational focus in personal insecurity and anxiety. Many employees work harder or are seen to be working harder, through fear and insecurity about their position in the company. This may result in short-term gains for the organisation but at the expense of individual well being.

The impact of short-term tactics on individuals is apparent in the attitudes and behaviours exhibited by remaining employees. There appears to be a move away from corporate allegiance to more close identification with peers and the immediate work group. This may be a factor of the changing working practices that many companies are attempting to institute in the form of team working and semi-autonomous work groups which focus attention on an immediate group of colleagues. These often naturally follow changes associated with technological innovation and business process re-engineering. In tandem there also appears to be a changing emphasis from the current concept of employment to the idea of employability, with the focus now being on the relevance, flexibility and transferability of work skills. As a consequence there appears to have been a shift in loyalty from the corporate body to loyalty to colleagues and a re-orientation from organisational to personal goals. These changes are indicative of a different working relationship between the organisation and the employee. However, individuals are struggling to accommodate such a change without the security of a job for life philosophy and, it would appear, little assistance in developing the skills required to assume personal responsibility for coping with major change or for managing their own transitions and future career.

After the downsizing

When downsizing is over managers should be allowed to direct their energy towards recovery (Bunning, 1990). This recovery requires a re-orientation of attitudes and behaviours. However, there appears to be a lack of programmes that are designed to encourage a renewed relationship with the downsized organisation (Boroson and Burgess, 1992; Doherty and Horsted, 1995). The practical implications of downsizing require a radical rethinking of organisational dynamics. Not only does downsizing impact on organisation size but structural issues, working practices and working relationships are also highlighted. Therefore organisations need to find alternative ways to accommodate the changes imposed by downsizing (Leana and Feldman, 1989; Loucheim, 1991/2).

Addressing downsizing as major organisational change

It has been suggested that an organisation development strategy which matches organisation development interventions to downsizing challenges can meet this need (Buch and Aldridge, 1990). They propose that an approach which consists of strategic interventions, technostructural interventions, HRM interventions and human process interventions can be used. Strategic interventions enable the creation of a new corporate culture which is compatible with the new business strategy and structure of the down-sized organisation. These would help to create a clear vision of the future and facilitate employees to become active agents in supporting and achieving the new vision. The change programme at British Airways described in the previous chapter fits into this category.

Technostructural interventions, it is suggested, are needed to help employees to respond to the structural changes which often accompany downsizing. Structural changes often imply different co-ordination and control systems which emphasise authoritarian and rigid management. Participation, communication, problem solving and employee involvement programmes are recommended to redress the powerlessness that remaining employees often feel. It is well documented that communication through a period of change is very important. Positive messages about the organisations' future security are good press in times of chaos. However, in the current context such messages do not necessarily assuage the concerns that individuals have about their own future. Therefore, it is not just the quantity and quality, but also the focus of communication which can have a fundamental impact on how survivors feel. Survivors need information about their future role and position within the company and enabling mechanisms to help them achieve this.

Human process interventions include team-building activities to facilitate open communication, which helps to instil the new vision and culture of the organisation and rebuild trust, morale and commitment. These should be complimentary to the HRM interventions which are necessary to re-establish the psychological contract. The psychological contract encompasses the expectations of the individual and the organisation in the employment relationship, like a glue that binds the two together (Herriot, 1992). Major change upsets the balance and currently appears to have changed the rules of the game completely. Employees can no longer expect security of employment in return for loyalty and commitment to the organisation. Individuals' concerns, therefore, include the changing nature of work, personal development and career issues.

Counselling and support for the survivors could be used to facilitate the personal change required by the 'new deal'. Such programmes need not only address the issue of surviving the immediate change but also facilitate discussion of the individual's aspirations and longer-term needs. The interventions available include stress management to manage feelings of job insecurity, role and career confusion. Career development would also help retained employees to achieve clarity about the different career opportunities within the new organisation and to develop compatible career goals.

Practice in pursuit of theory

Buch and Aldridge (1990) suggested that an integrated and compatible series of programmes can be compiled from this menu of interventions to redress the imbalances created by the downsizing event. Such interventions can meet both the organisational and the individual objectives by equipping survivors to cope with personal change, providing the skills for future survival and also facilitating more flexible and responsive change for the organisation. Despite a sound theoretical basis for the use of a combined and integrated approach to the problems of downsizing, in practice the organisational responses seem to be lagging behind. The HR interventions that are currently being applied need to become much broader, with more innovative investment in survivors to accommodate the evolving new relationship between individuals and organisations. Organisational survival strategies are abundant, but strategies for individual survival should be an integral part of the change management process as the successful transformation of attitudes and behaviours are essential to organisational success. If the implications of survivors' syndrome are not adequately addressed at the personal level the impact could be quite detrimental to the company. A demotivated, demoralised, cynical, sceptical and insecure workforce with little organisational commitment is not an ideal on which to drive industry ahead into the twenty-first century.

Redressing the balance

Undoubtedly there is little that the HR function can do to prevent the external circumstances which impose change on the organisation. However, the reality of the transitions imposed by organisational change of the magnitude and pace currently being experienced has led to both organisations and individuals being put in a situation where they are not just addressing a learning situation, but in many circumstances are being expected to unlearn old responses and relearn a new way of responding to the pressures being put upon them (Stuart, 1995). This has created a new era of survival values where prescriptive approaches to the management of downsizing may no longer be satisfactory in managing the highly complex and interactive process between the organisation and its employees. Balancing the needs of the organisation and the individual requires consideration of two sides of the psychological contract. Both are experiencing the stresses of surviving in an ever-changing environment with the immediate demands of coping with the present change and the unknowns of the future. Models for organisational change need to more fully encompass the variety of issues that are now on the agenda at the organisation and individual level, in order to be able to implement *downsizing without capsizing* (Feldman and Leana, 1994, p. 258).

The role of HRM

The successful management of a downsizing programme requires long-term commitment and adaptability. Human resources can usefully contribute in the design and delivery of policies and practices that are symbolic of the organisation's commitment to the individual in times of crisis by facilitating positive messages and complementary actions. Specialists in HR need to be instrumental in the management of the new workforce and its requirements by driving change at the strategic level (Tyson, 1995) and fulfilling a new role as consultants, counsellors and brokers of the psychological contract (Herriot and Pemberton, 1995). The ability of HR to play an active role in managing change at these levels may be critical to the survival of the function itself.

Conclusions

British industry has yielded to many unprecedented changes recently. Although downsizing may not remain the major impetus for change in the future, organisations will undoubtedly continue to experience metamorphoses through expansion, contraction and reconfiguration in response to the external pressures of market changes, technological innovation and the global economy. Such external factors generate the strategic impetus to be flexible and adaptable, driving organisations to deploy their labour forces in increasingly diverse ways. Strategies, policies and practices are needed which afford the organisation the freedom to shed labour and reorganise the workforce in order to achieve this flexibility and adaptability.

However, although there are many prescriptions on the management of downsizing and other pervasive major changes, organisational practices seem to be lagging behind. In particular, the way in which organisations deal with the human issues needs to be reconsidered and management rhetoric about people as the most valuable asset must be tempered by the reality of an insecure, unstable environment which seems to offer little to the individual. Many organisations have addressed the challenge of exiting people from the organisation humanely through the use of outplacement interventions. The outplacement industry itself has developed a variety of programmes which now include provision for all levels of employees and interventions designed to help employees through change within the organisation, such as inplacement. These developments are testimony to the continued evolution of the industry to meet the diverse needs of organisations and individuals in coping with change. No doubt the industry will continue to develop programmes and interventions, since organisations and individuals now face a constant barrage of change.

The strategies, policies and practices which organisations adopt in the management of change such as downsizing have many strategic implications. They are fundamental to the speed at which the organisation can react to and manage the change situation and they also determine the capital and human costs. These strategies, policies and practices need to be designed to facilitate responsive and cost-effective change and also to assist individuals through the change process. They are the chief mechanism through which organisations and their employees can reach a sustainable equilibrium.

REFERENCES

Appelbaum, S.H., Simpson, R. and Shapiro, B.T. (1987) 'The Tough Test of Downsizing', *Organizational Dynamics*, 15 (2), pp. 68–79.

Armstrong-Stassen, M. (1993) 'Survivors' Reactions to a Workforce Reduction: A Comparison of Blue-Collar Workers and their Supervisors', *Canadian Journal of Administrative Sciences*, 10 (4), pp. 334–43.

Boroson, W. and Burgess, L. (1992) 'Survivors' Syndrome', *Across the Board*, 29 (1), pp. 41–5.

Boynton, J.W. and Thomas, R. (1991) *The UK Outplacement Report*, London, Kingsland James Ltd (BMSL).

Brockner, J. (1986) 'The Impact of Layoffs on Survivors', *Supervisory Management*, 31 (6), pp. 2–7.

Brockner, J. (1992) 'Managing the Effects of Layoffs on Survivors', *California Management Review*, Winter, pp. 9–28.

Brockner, J., Greenberg, J., Brockner, A., Bortz, J., Davy, J. and Carter, C. (1986) 'Layoffs, Equity Theory, and Work Performance: Further Evidence of the Impact of Survivor Guilt', *Academy of Management Journal* 29 (2), pp. 373–84.

Brockner, J., Grover, S.L. and Blonder, M.D. (1988) 'Predictions of Survivors' Job Involvement Following Layoffs: A Field Study', *Journal of Applied Psychology*, 73 (3), pp. 436–42.

Brockner, J., Grover, S., O'Malley, M., Reed, T.F. and Glynn, M.A. (1993) 'Threat of Future Layoffs, Self-Esteem, and Survivors' Reactions: Evidence from the Laboratory and the Field', *Strategic Management Journal*, Vol. 14, pp. 153–66.

Brockner, J., Tyler, T. and Cooper-Schneider, R. (1992b) 'The Influence of Prior Commitment to an Institution on Reactions to Perceived Unfairness: The Higher They Are, The Harder They Fall', *Administrative Science Quarterly*, 37, pp. 241–61.

Brockner, J., Grover, S., Reed, T.F. and Dewitt, R.L. (1992a) 'Layoffs, Job Insecurity, and Survivors' Work Effort: Evidence of an Inverted U Relationship', *Academy of Management Journal*, 35 (7), pp. 413–25.

Buch, K. (1992) 'How Does Downsizing Affect Employee Involvement?', *Journal for Quality and Participation*, 15 (1), pp. 74–9.

Buch, K. and Aldridge, J. (1990) 'Downsizing Challenges and OD Interventions: A Matching Strategy', *Journal of Managerial Psychology*, 5 (4), pp. 32–7.

Bunning, R.L. (1990) 'The Dynamics of Downsizing', *Personnel Journal*, September, pp. 69–75.

Cameron, K. (1994a) 'Guest Editor's Note: Investigating Organisational Downsizing – Fundamental Issues', *Human Resource Management Special Issue on Downsizing*, 33 (2), pp. 183–8.

Cameron, K. (1994b) 'Strategies for Successful Organisational Downsizing', *Human Resource Management Special Issue on Downsizing*, 33 (2), pp. 189–212.

Covin, T.J. (1993) 'Managing Workforce Reduction: A Survey of Employee Reactions and Implications for Management Consultants', *Organisation Development Journal*, 11 (1), pp. 67–76.

Crofts, P. (1992) 'Outplacement: A Way of Never Having to Say You're Sorry?', *Personnel Management*, 24 May, pp. 46–50.

Curtis, R.L. Jr. (1989) 'Cutbacks, Management and Human Relations: Meanings for Organisational Theory and Research', *Human Relations*, 42 (8), pp. 671–89.

Doherty, N. and Horsted, J. (1995) 'Helping Survivors to Stay on Board', *People Management*, 12 January, pp. 26–31.

Doherty, N. and Tyson, S. (1993) *Executive Redundancy and Outplacement*, London, Kogan Page.

Doherty, N., Tyson, S. and Viney, C. (1993) 'A Positive Policy? Corporate Perspectives on Redundancy and Outplacement', *Personnel Review*, 22 (7), pp. 45–53.

Eggert, M. (1991) *Outplacement. A Guide to Management and Delivery*, London, IBM.

Feldman, D. and Leana, R.C. (1994) 'Better Practices in Managing Layoffs', *Human Resource Management Special Issue on Downsizing*, 33 (2), pp. 239–60.

Fisher, A.B. (1988) 'The Downside of Downsizing', *Fortune*, May 23, pp. 28–35.

Fisher, C.D. (1989) 'Current and Recurrent Challenges in HRM', *Journal of Management*, 15 (2), pp. 157–80.

Froiland, P., Geber, B., Gordon, J. and Pickard, M. (1993) 'Fear and Trembling after the Downsizing', *Training*, 30 (8), pp. 13–14.

Guest, D. and Peccei, R. (1992) 'Employee Involvement: Redundancy as a Critical Case', *Human Resource Management Journal*, 2 (3), pp. 34–59.

Hartley, J., Jacobson, D., Klandermans, B. and Van Vuuren, T. with Greenhalgh, L. and Sutton, R. (1991) *Job Insecurity: Coping with Jobs at Risk*, London, Sage.

Hendry, C. and Pettigrew, A. (1992) 'Patterns of Strategic Change in the Development of Human Resource Management', *British Journal of Management*, 3 (3), pp. 137–56.

Herriot, P. (1992) *The Career Management Challenge: Balancing Individual and Organisational Needs*, London, Sage.

Herriot, P. and Pemberton, C. (1995) 'A New Deal for Middle Managers', *People Management*, June 15, pp. 32–4.

Hogg, C. (1998) 'Outplacement Fact Sheet 4', *Personnel Management*, April.

Hyde, P. (1988) 'Offering a Helping Handshake', *The Times*, 14 December, p. 21.

Kiechel III, W. (1985) 'Managing a Downsized Operation', *Fortune*, July 22, pp. 103–4.

Latack, J.C. (1984) Pilot Study of Job Loss among Managers and Professionals, Columbus Ohio State University, College of Administrative Sciences.

Latack, J.C. and Dozier, J.B. (1986) 'After the Axe Falls: Job Loss as a Career Transition', *Academy of Management Review*, 11 (2), pp. 375–92.

Leana, C. and Feldman, D. (1989) 'When Mergers Force Layoffs: Some Lessons about Managing the Human Resource Problems', *Human Resource Planning*, 12 (2), pp. 123–40.

Loucheim, F.P. (1991/2) 'Four Lessons from Downsizing to Build Future Productivity', *Employment Relations Today*, 18 (4), pp. 467–75.

Noer, D.M. (1993) *Healing the Wounds: Overcoming the Trauma of Layoffs and Revitalizing Downsized Organisations*, San Francisco, Jossey Bass.

Nicholson, N. and West, M. (1988) *Managerial Job Change: Men and Women in Transition*, Cambridge University Press.

Overman, S. (1991) 'The Layoff Legacy', *HR Magazine*, 36 (8), pp. 29–33.

Pinola, R. (1994) 'Building a Winning Team after a Downsizing', *Compensation & Benefits Management*, 10 (1), pp. 54–9.

Rice, D. and Dreilinger, C. (1991) 'After the Downsizing', *Training and Development*, 45 (5), pp. 41–4.

Richey, M.W. (1992) 'The Impact of Corporate Downsizing on Employees', *Business Forum*, 17 (3), pp. 9–13.

Skopp, J. (1993) 'HR Paints a Bleak Portrait of Downsizing Survivors', *HR Focus*, 70 (3), p. 24.

Stuart, R. (1995) 'Experiencing Organisational Change: Triggers, Processes and Outcomes of Change Journeys', *Personnel Review*, 24 (2).

Swinburne, P. (1981) 'The Psychological Impact of Unemployment on Managers and Professional Staff', *Journal of Occupational Psychology*, 54, pp. 97–8.

Tombaugh, J. and White, L. (1990) 'Downsizing: An Empirical Assessment of Survivors' Perceptions in a Post Layoff Environment', *Organisation Development Journal*, 8 (2), pp. 32–43.

Tyson, S. (1995) *Human Resource Strategy: Towards a General Theory of Human Resource Management*, London, Pitman.

Vollmann, T. and Brazas, M. (1993) 'Downsizing', *European Management Journal*, 11 (1), pp. 18–29.

EMPLOYMENT POLICY – THE CASE OF THE BURTON GROUP

Keith Cameron

'Change is not made without inconvenience, even from worse to better', quoted Dr Johnson in the preface to his Dictionary.

Consistent with change being a preoccupying feature of twentieth-century organisational life, the management of the process of change and its consequences have become a dominating feature of HR departments. Samuel Johnson's epigram is a wry understatement of the scale and intensity of industrial and commercial change processes.

The unfolding example of the Burton Group's organisation changes of 1993 will provide a clear example of the significance of change at speed and on a large scale. This chapter demonstrates how business and human resources strategy are integrated. The case we discuss will also demonstrate the benefits of clear, underpinning HR goals which enabled the function to achieve its change objectives. The HR goals were yardsticks which provided the necessary reference points for managing the process of change through uncharted territory. This story needs to be set in a context as the sector of industry in which the organisation operates shapes many of the conditions and factors which affect the change process in the Group.

This study, therefore, takes the following route. It provides a thumbnail history of the Burton Group, a summary of the characteristics of the retail industry in the 1990s, an explanation of the key business issues and the HR developments and, finally, a review of the inter-relationship between the business strategy, the HR goals and the HR activities in managing a large-scale change process.

The Burton Group and its development

Montague Burton opened his first shop in Chesterfield in 1901. The First World War provided an opportunity for growth and success as Montague Burton produced Army uniforms. By 1929 there were 300 shops in addition to the suit-making factories. Throughout the 1930s, 1940s and 1950s Burton flourished and was the leader in made-to-measure suits but by the end of the 1960s demand for formal clothing had declined and Montague Burton had reached a difficult commercial position. For the first time, outsiders were brought in to top management positions but tradition and inflexibility were subsequent hurdles which prevented newcomers from achieving senior jobs. By the 1970s the company was ailing. The rapid decline in sales of made-to-measure clothing, unsuccessful attempts to sell more fashionable merchandise, inadequate stock control and distribution systems and unwise diversification pushed the company closer and closer to complete failure.

At the end of 1976 another generation of senior management took the reins and the rate of decline decreased. In 1981, Ralph Halpern (who had been running the retail chain Top Shop and Top Man successfully during Burton's lossmaking period) became Chairman and Chief Executive.

He instigated decisive action. Closure of the manufacturing sites was accomplished speedily, shops were refurbished and revitalised with a concentration on attractive products and displays which made it easy for the customers to see and buy. Burton became a retail business rather than a manufacturing company. Success through market orientated strategies enabled the Burton Group to expand by purchase and new retail business development, so that during the 1980s the Dorothy Perkins, Evans and Principles businesses were added to the portfolio of Burton Group names.

Following several very successful years trading out of high street shops, the Burton Group bought Debenhams in 1985 with the aim of revitalising a tired department store group consisting of 65 department stores, a shoe retailer and an account/credit card operation.

However, by the end of the 1980s The Burton Group had over-reached itself, buoyed by the inflationary encouragement of the decade. Diversification into property development proved to be an expensive mistake which was compounded by the unexpected amount of management energy soaked up by Debenhams' renewal and the difficult economics of the late 1980s. High retail rents and increasing high street competition turned the Burton Group into a lossmaker.

Following an interregnum after the inevitable departure of Ralph Halpern, John Hoerner, then Chairman of Debenhams, took the Chief Executive's role at The Burton Group. At that time there were eight retail divisions operating relatively autonomously and frequently suffering the consequence of independence. The lack of cohesive direction meant that very few synergies were achieved and the trading policies of one division could punish the operations of another. In the 90 years since its inception, the Burton Group had experienced a roller coaster of a ride through the decades. Significant periods of success as the market leader had been outweighed by periods of failure resulting from the inability to enact the changes perceived as necessary in the direction of the business and the Group's tendency to over-reach itself. In 1992 the Group was trading poorly, handling a large write-off of shareholders' funds from unwise property development, and was poorly regarded by investors and customers.

Characteristics of retail in the 1990s

This short historical description of the Burton Group embodies several structural and behavioural elements which are common to most retail businesses. Given the characteristics of (i) significant geographical fragmentation and (ii) a competitive marketplace with restricted scope for product and service differentiation, it is not surprising that speed is one of the important forces in retailing. Most medium to large retailers operate nationwide and therefore have shops and stores spread throughout the UK. This makes communication more complicated and good communication even more difficult. Retailers within the same product category, for example food supermarkets, frequently have little to differentiate between themselves. Branded products are available from all the competitors so to steal a march on the competition, each retailer places emphasis on customer service and the physical location of stores, for example. In the retail clothing sector there is, of course, difference in the product ranges from one company to another but where those products are similar and appeal to the same audience, the speed of translation from idea through production to the high street can be a point of critical differentiation between retailers. Additionally, in response to changes in competitors' pricing, organisations have to respond quickly to initiatives taken by others. Urgency, therefore, is a prized quality.

Other volatile industries sharing comparable circumstances (e.g. highly competitive sectors with only minor variations in product/service offering between companies) exhibit this characteristic: the airline industry and the package holiday market come to mind. As most of the retail industry is selling products which are not highly technical in nature, product knowledge is low and the commercial skill lies with the successful practical operation of a geographically diverse organisation. Application and operation are two dominating qualities. As a result the industry is highly practical and pragmatic and can be thought by some to be almost anti-intellectual. Associated with the need for urgency is the virtue of flexibility which is an understandable consequence of handling change at speed and the acceptance of frequent alterations or adjustments of direction. The behavioural extension of these features is the characteristic of compliance. Rather like the military forces on the battle-front, the combined demands for speed and flexibility can be best met by conformity. Challenge (or dispute) inevitably takes up valuable time: the mental state is one of acceptance unlike, for example, the academics' frame of reference which is one of questioning.

Key business issues

With the general background of urgency, pragmatism, flexibility and compliance combined with the particular circumstances of the Burton Group there were some significant changes necessary in 1992. Prior to these changes taking place, the Group had suffered from marketing drift resulting in some of the retail divisions overlapping into each other's territory so that members of the family 'stole' from each other. There were some limited economies of scale – the obvious pooling of warehouse facilities and transport arrangements existed, but there were few examples of these communal gains. Costs were far too high.

For example, there was an Information Systems function designed to provide a service for the Multiple shops divisions, but each of the five divisions had their own Information Systems Department which meant duplication. Purchasing and Commercial Services were provided as a central resource but divisions were free – and frequently chose – to buy direct themselves from elsewhere. The Buying and Merchandising functions had different methods of operation. Several divisions used the same suppliers and, although it would have been inappropriate to have the buyer purchasing from a supplier for several divisions (as products need to be bought in the context of their product range), the standardisation of commercial and accounting terms and procedures would have saved a substantial workload.

The Group set about tackling these issues by establishing a programme of review which was christened the 'Best Practice' programme. This comprised eight project teams, each of which looked at a particular subject area, for example, Buying and Merchandising, Finance, Marketing, and so on. The teams were led by members of the 16 strong Management Board of the Group but individuals were assigned to subject areas for which they had no operational responsibilities (although the most senior manager for the particular function was a member of the team). They were assisted by highly rated senior managers who were seconded to the project. The conclusions were brought back to the Management Board for discussion and agreement before they were agreed and implemented. Syndication was a critical consideration. Each aspect of each Project Team's recommendations was discussed thoroughly by the Management Board and brought to a conclusion. Some decisions were unanimous, some were the result of the majority view succeeding. The critical aspect of the process was that all issues were brought to this forum and all members were able to contribute and influence. In the circumstances where a member of the Management Board did not personally agree with a decision, the rules of collective decision making required that all members actively supported the Management Board decision.

Although the results were different for different functions (and the implications for divisions varied as there had been little similarity in organisational structures and operational matters) there were some common features within each element of the Best Practice programme. They included shortening the lines of communication, eliminating unnecessary administrative practices, standardising working methods to gain economies of scale and using a customer focus to all operations.

Achieving the business strategy through HR management

On 7 January 1993 the Burton Group announced changes following the Best Practice review which were designed to meet the criteria listed above and, as is so often the case, the major changes were in the area covered by the HR function.

For the purpose of this case study it is sensible to split the HR activity into two categories. The first category contains all the normal or standard objectives and processes which are tackled by HR functions at a time of change. The second category encompasses the elements of HR work which make this case study different and it is this second category which is more significant and interesting.

Without demeaning the effort and the complexities involved, the first category of HR involvement can be dealt with fairly briskly. As a result of subject/functionally based analysis by an informed (internal) group who were relatively impartial, major functions were reorganised. Either the most effective of (by then) six divisional ways of operating was selected as the organisational template or a new process was derived.

Conventional merging of duplicate activities and the reorganisation of responsibilities and management of consequential redundancies occurred, for example, in the Commercial Services function where there was one Printing Department with about 50 staff in the south-west and another Printing Department with another 50 staff in the north of England. In quantitative terms, the merging of activities and reorganisation resulted in nearly 1000 job losses from a base of 5000 within Head Office departments. (In the shops and stores there was an outflow of almost 3000 full-time jobs but there was a planned inflow of 7000 people. This aspect will be fully covered when dealing with the less conventional changes and the role of HR.) The Buying and Merchandising function in each trading division, for example, underwent significant change. Without exception, each division lost staff and needed to alter its organisation structure to adopt a common organisational template. The amount of change varied for each business, but the degree was somewhere between significant and very significant!

To enact the organisational changes in the non-retail functions, the HR function played a pivotal, albeit orthodox role, in design and implementation. 'Orthodox' because many of the tools and methods necessary to manage change were part of the standard battery of HR skills and responsibilities.

The role of the central and divisional HR departments concentrated on goal definition, determination of job objectives, the assessment of individual capabilities and potential, together with strengthening the internal communication system.

Clearly, there were many areas for the HR department to focus. Training for new roles and morale building programmes were also needed for example. These other aspects are placed separately in this narrative because they were necessarily second in practice. The speed at which these changes were being made, coupled with the work demands resulting from the shops' changes, separated one set of changes from the other.

The Head Office changes in Buying and Merchandising, and many other functions, were so substantial that they needed to be introduced with immediate effect. Gradual handovers were not possible with a transition to the new organisation template. Before the new organisation was introduced, the Buying and Merchandising departments were organised differently by division although there were some common points. For example, several teams of buyers and several teams of merchandisers would report to a Buying and Merchandising Controller. Several Buying and Merchandising Controllers would then report to the Buying and Merchandising Director who reported to the Managing Director. The Merchandising function was responsible for planning the sales levels and sales mix, the allocation of stock and the produce pricing to achieve profitability.

The Best Practice programme established an organisational template which removed the Buying and Merchandising Director and Buying and Merchandising Controller levels, removed the stock allocation process from the Merchandising function and established three senior specialist functional posts reporting to the Managing Director – Head of Buying, Head of Merchandising and Head of Distribution (with new positions as Distributors recruited from the ranks of the Merchandising teams).

Handling this amount of individual and organisational change over a large part of each division over a few days meant that the urgent and fundamental aspects of the change took the attention. The amount of HR work which could be undertaken in advance of the announcement of changes was limited as the pressure was to inform as soon as possible rather than to prepare a finished package.

Other than the factor of time, the HR department's activity was relatively conventional for this part of the Best Practice programme. Reorganisation of major central functions (at Group and divisional level) was designed to gain economies of scale and save costs through streamlined operation. The HR departments managed, advised and participated in the processes of defining goals and objectives, establishing roles and responsibilities in flatter structures and devising and managing the timetable of implementation. Overall, the annual savings resulting from organisational savings were over £20 million.

Out in the operational retail end of the business there was a less conventional series of issues and subsequent challenges for the HR function. One of the conclusions of Best Practice for the shops and stores was that the operating costs of the divisions were too high. In retail operations, the three big costs are rent, rates and staff. Rent and rates are, effectively, fixed costs. The variable, and therefore reducible, cost is labour. But there was another important criterion from the Best Practice analysis and recommendations which, at first sight, ran counter to any cutting of labour costs. This second consideration was customer service.

The Group's level of customer service was below its competitors and, more importantly, below that which the customers expected. A reduction in staffing levels to save money would adversely affect customer service. Based on previous work undertaken in one division and a short study of both the distribution of hours of employment through the week and the hourly level of sales measured through the electronic tills, there was an opportunity.

The opportunity was to reduce the number of staff employed when there were few customers and to boost the number of staff during periods with plenty of customers and high sales. The imponderable was the amount of sales being lost currently through the inability to serve prospective customers. If sales staff are unable to give customers advice or service because they are already busy or the queue at the cash till is substantial, customers will often go elsewhere. If the right judgement is made, what might appear on a planning schedule to be over-staffing quickly becomes a time of high productivity as those previously lost customers become purchasers.

The rebalancing of the sales force to provide a better match between demand and supply needed injections of commercial judgement as well as statistical analyses. But wherever the line was drawn, there were important unknown elements surrounding staff issues. Undoubtedly a great number of staff would need to change their working hours and in most cases this would entail a reduction in hours as they would be geared to the core trading hours. For many shops the (customer) demand/(service) supply equation would only be achieved by the loss of some jobs. At the outset, it was estimated that at least 2000 full-time jobs would disappear to be 'replaced' by approximately 5000 part-time posts. The changed requirements for working hours were expected to affect over half of the 36 000 retail staff. For most of them it would mean some reduction in the number of hours worked each week rather than a simple rearrangement.

Each division had a different way of operating. It was clear that a more customer service orientated, standard way of functioning would be needed. This led to the use of the competency approach as will be explained later. Also, the contracts and conditions would need to be common. Standardised job content across the divisions would require a standard approach to terms and conditions of employment and contracts.

But who should be selected for redundancy amongst those full-time sales staff? As the improvement in customer service was a goal, the Group was keen not to lose staff whose service skills were of a high order just because some other staff had several months more tenure in the organisation. And there was an additional point in relation to the future. If the divisions were able to nominate existing staff with good customer service skills, would management be able to retain them and would the terms and conditions be competitive enough to attract other high quality staff in the future? Based on rates of pay, the answer to this question varied by division. Although there were six operating divisions, there were nine sets of pay ranges (and benefits arrangements, and so on) and some divisions paid towards the top of the market while others were around the lower quartile.

The essential problems were judging the right staffing levels, determining who to select for redundancy or changed hours and how much to pay. The commercial managers adopted a series of commercial formulae for each branch manager to gauge the appropriate staffing level for each shop. At the centre, the HR function produced two critical inter-related proposals. In the absence of any formal or established appraisal system, there needed to be a legitimate method of recognising individual performance and capability (for customer service, if nothing else). Additionally the Group had a powerful pay-for-performance culture with variable bonus as the main element for retail staff. 'Merit rating determines pay' type appraisal systems operated in Head Office but the difficult mechanics of establishing and managing a legitimate appraisal system for 36 000 dispersed staff had resulted in shop staff not being included. The HR function wanted a way to assess staff, provide a pay for performance relationship and ensure the retention and attraction of high quality staff.

The two proposals were that the Group adopt competencies as the base for staff assessment (and for training) and that the nine pay structures (and benefits and other terms and conditions) were replaced by one structure. The new structure would include competency based pay levels which, by providing greater reward to those with higher competencies, would incorporate pay for individual performance.

Cost and timing were two other factors in managing change. There would be no advantage in basing a new, single structure on the lowest of the nine pay ranges as that would ensure the voluntary departure of the better staff inhabiting the other eight structures. So although there was pressure to cut costs, a significant portion of the savings predicted by balancing demand and supply was reinvested in a new pay structure positioned at the upper quartile.

The second factor was timing. These options were being discussed confidentially at the end of November, with 7 January 1993 as the predetermined date for the announcement of the consequences of the Best Practice programme. In the weeks before the announcement, a series of competencies were agreed for key retail staff jobs with line management from the six trading divisions. Work started on the sub-competencies with the requisite training elements being agreed and syndicated throughout the divisions.

The new pay and benefits structure was designed and costed based on working assumptions about the numbers of staff of each competency level. Transitional payments would be necessary for those reducing their hours of work or moving from a higher pay rate in the old structure. Fig 4.1 and Tables 4.1 and 4.2 demonstrate how one branch in a division, using its current pay scales A, B, C (which had no specific rationale), could convert to the new system of Bronze, Silver, Gold levels (these were working titles only) which were based on competencies and then incorporate the number of scheduled hours for the branch. The branch managers reviewed individuals currently paid at B and C levels in the table and allocated them to Bronze, Silver or Gold according to their assessment.

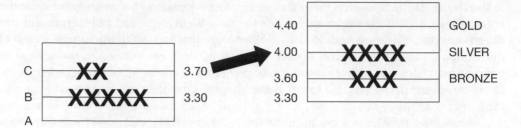

Fig 4.1   Assessing the staff (£ per hour)

Table 4.1   Cost comparison

	Old					New			
Level	*Rate*	*Staff*	*Hours*		*Level*	*Rate*	*Staff*	*Hours*	
'C'	3.70	× 2	× 39	= 288.60	**Silver**	4.00	× 2	× 36½	
						4.00	× 2	× 21	508.00
						4.00	× 1	× 12	
'B'	3.30	× 5	× 39	= 643.50	**Bronze**	3.60	× 1	× 36½	
						3.60	× 1	× 24	304.20
						3.60	× 2	× 12	
					Entry	3.30	× 2	× 12	=79.20
				932.10					**891.40**

As can be seen from Table 4.1, the rates of pay are higher in the new system but the total hours worked in the branch are fewer. This individual example was confirmed in practice. Of the retail staff, 75 per cent received an increase in their rate of pay.

Table 4.2 summarises the position – more people employed with higher rates of pay but lower overall costs for the branch which would, therefore, have meant that some existing staff would have lower earnings as a result of working fewer hours albeit at a higher rate of pay.

But throughout the Group nobody could predict the cost of transitional payments because nobody could identify the individuals. This could only occur after each of 1800 branch managers had been told of the new way of operating, worked out the distribution of staff into the necessary hours, assessed the quality of the individuals and then selected the appropriate staff for the revised working arrangements.

Table 4.2   Summary of the new system

	Old	New
Hours	255.5	223.5
Staff	7	11
Pay	£932.10	£891.40

From the point of announcement on 7 January 1993, the shop managers were briefed to calculate the labour needed in 'numbers per hour' based on their forecast of sales revenue potential (using prior year sales figures and area manager assessments of sales potential); staff were evaluated by them (and checking line managers) according to the new competencies; decisions on redundancies and revised working arrangements were made for each individual and back at Head Office, central HR departments repositioned staff on the new competency based pay and benefits system, organised their individual pay arrangements and transitional compensation and processed those who were being made redundant or who had chosen to leave rather than take compensation for change.

All this activity, which resulted in 3000 redundancies and the issue of 36 000 new contracts of employment (incorporating the new terms and conditions), had to be completed by 20 February – seven weeks from the date of the original announcement.

Two other major activities were started at the beginning of February although there was no prospect of them being completed by the end of that month. The first was the recruitment of 7000 shop and store staff to work the core hours where customers needed services but the shops were understaffed. These staff had to be recruited locally by branch managers and the role of the HR function was to provide these line managers with the props and techniques to enable them to recruit quickly and correctly. The revised pay structure was designed to make the positions financially attractive but the HR function had to make these jobs psychologically attractive. Part-time jobs were, for example, renamed as key-time jobs; much emphasis was placed on the fact that all entitlements were the same for all staff. The only difference between the full-time and part-time staff pay and conditions was pro-rating for the number of hours worked.

The second activity was the production of training material and the operation of training courses to take staff from one competency to another. Such moves generated higher salaries and, from the outset, employees were eager to move through the competency levels. During the first year of the new approach, 29 000 staff went through the one-day training course which was a part of the first level competency training. The training was run at 39 selected centres by a pool of 400 trained retail shop managers with all divisions sending staff to each course.

Following the frenetic six weeks of immediate change, the pace of change continued at an energetic level for the following year. The evaluation at the end of that year, in commercial terms, was that the HR based changes had been critical to business success. Quantitatively it was demonstrated that the selling costs had been reduced, that productivity per person had improved along with customer service (using anonymous test shoppers and customer surveys) and that higher quality staff had been attracted.

As managers grappled with the new system, staff turnover (always high in the retail industry) was too high and progress through to the higher levels of competency was slow. Another year on and both turnover and competency progress were in line with expectations. Staff turnover came down from 45 per cent per annum to 35 per cent per annum. This is still high by the standard of many industries but ranks reasonably in the service sector.

Two other advantages have been brought out of the changes described. The competency approach has been adopted throughout the other functions and, for example, is used enthusiastically to drive the training and development of Buying and Merchandising staff with competencies common to all divisions and common training and development activities. More than 25 per cent of promoted staff take up their new jobs in another division.

Also the standardisation of nine retail pay and benefit systems into one structure which incorporates all terms and conditions of employment has enabled the Group to move staff from one division to another. This has happened to hundreds of staff who may have worked in a town where the branch of one division closed as a lease expired and who transferred to take up positions in other divisions in the same town.

It can be seen that the HR measures adopted in the Best Practice programme were commercially successful but these measures succeeded not only because they were appropriate solutions but also because of the manner of their introduction. The HR function was able to manage the implementation as well as the design of the measures. Some, although not all, of the HR departments were fully integrated into the higher level business planning and decision-making processes. Using the Tyson and Fell models these HR functions were 'Architects' rather than 'Clerks of Works' (Tyson and Fell, 1986). The HR contribution to business performance is predicated upon this integration. The case here also shows how policies were integrated (competencies, rewards and employment contracts) and demonstrates how, as with the British Airways case, improvements to customer service are a consequence of organisation development and change. This still leaves the question of how far is HR's major contribution through implementation, or in conceiving strategies; or through being part of second- or third-order strategies, downstream from the main strategy development process (Purcell, 1989). In this case HR was intimately involved in key issues, influencing before decisions were taken rather than dealing with the consequences of decisions.

The opportunity for HR departments to operate in this mode was earned, in part, by technical merit and, in fact, from the HR function's ability to relate to the important characteristics of retail business as described earlier. The emphasis on speed of operation and practicality by the HR function fitted the needs of the company and the standards of line management.

Clearly, slavish adherence to industry conventions and standards can be compromising and counter-productive but in the 'wartime' conditions of Best Practice implementation, the circumstances made such singularity of approach a virtue. The HR function also had authorship and direction of the technical solutions which ensured a reasonable control of the balance and the process.

In summary, the HR function was able to contribute to the achievement of the commercial goals by managing the process of change appropriately. The appropriateness centred on the production of sound technical solutions but this needed to be coupled to the function's ability to recognise the behavioural characteristics of the organisation, drawn from its industry, and share and drive these behaviours for successful implementation.

REFERENCES

Purcell, J. (1989) 'The Impact of Corporate Strategy on Human Resource Management', in Storey, J. (ed.) *New Perspectives on Human Resource Management*, London and New York, Routledge.

Tyson, S. and Fell, A. (1986) *Evaluating the Personnel Function*, London, Hutchinson.

5

INDUSTRIAL RELATIONS IN BRITAIN

John Lloyd

Human resource strategy starts with one central choice. To what extent will the organisation decide on the terms and conditions of its workforce through negotiating with representative bodies like trade unions or staff associations? Since 1979, the component issues which affect that strategic choice have altered beyond all recognition. The power and resources available to trade unions have all been reduced, and their role has changed: as human resource managers look at their employee relations strategies and the industrial relations structures that give everyday expression to those strategies, they immediately recognise they are operating in a different world.

The change strategies discussed so far have been an examination of managerial actions in pursuit of strategic objectives. In some cases, employers have been able to follow employee relations strategies without engaging in collective bargaining. The integration of communication and performance management policies in a coherent package with rewards, management development and restructuring, for example, have been powerful levers for change. Such strategies appear to be directed to achieve an individual rather than a collective response from workpeople, and within the normative vision of HRM there seems to be a strong belief in individualism which trades upon a unitary perspective. How has this come about, what are the factors within the field of industrial relations in the UK which condition future development?

This chapter will seek to examine the issues which have irreversibly changed the employee relations landscape. Each issue examined is important: what is even more important is the way that each influence has interacted with all the others to intensify the unfriendly environment for trade unions as institutions (Metcalf, 1991). Latterly, unions in Britain have set in train a series of initiatives that seek to face up to this new environment. This chapter looks at those initiatives, and seeks to speculate whether the strategic options open to human resource managers will be altered by the unions' responses.

Organisations in both private industry and the public services have always sought to maximise consumer satisfaction by energising their workforce with a motivated commitment to the management's goals. Personnel managers before 1979 were often only too ready to say that they were unable to foster and encourage that high-performing, committed workforce because of the obstructive activities of trade unions. Unions were too 'political', they were constantly protecting irrational demarcations to protect their own institutions, they went on strike too rapidly and they resisted change in methods of work out of sheer habit. This respect, bordering on fear, seemed to accept the situation as a permanent feature of key aspects of the industrial landscape. Such a stereotypical response also insisted that if only ordinary workers were not prisoners of unrepresentative union leaders (both local and national), the ordinary workers would see the company's need to change to meet the challenge of increasing global competition.

Competitiveness was, therefore, the key: the demands of rapid change could not wait for trade union custom and practice to reach the twentieth century. Work done before the 1979 election by Keith Joseph and the Centre for Policy Studies identified the removal of the trade union veto as an important part in the process of reinvigorating British industry. Historian Hugh Thomas quoted Mrs Thatcher's phrase in her Airey Neave Lecture on 3 May 1980 as an 'exhilarating mission' that would destroy the 'ideologyless syndicalism [that] sustains unplanned statism'. Mrs Thatcher's first Secretary of State for Employment, Jim Prior, saw his attempts to reform the unions as central to the attempt to improve British industrial performance. In his 1980 Granada Lecture on the Future of Trade Unions he said, 'The real threat to jobs in Britain comes not from the use of microchips in Britain, but from their use in countries which compete with us.' Most personnel specialists who were also aware of the intensification of competitive pressures on their businesses looked wistfully to a union-free workplace or a great reduction in the unions' capacity to hold up change.

Political and economic developments since 1979 have given managers a choice of strategy that perhaps they felt was not open to them before. In this context, we ought to bear in mind the inter-related issues that have since affected the unions, and look at what human resource managers have done to increase their organisations' competitiveness under each heading.

Pressures on the unions – the impact of 'public policy'

First and foremost, public policy has changed dramatically. Every initiative of government employment policy since 1979 has pointed companies and public service organisations towards increasing their competitiveness by minimising the degree to which they order their affairs through collective intermediaries. The Conservative government announced in its 1991 Green Paper 'Industrial Relations in the 1990s' that it is of the view that there is 'every reason to expect the continuation of the decline of collective bargaining and the growth of individual pay negotiations' and that 'the most important challenge for employers in the 1990s ... is to deal with employees as individuals'. During the 1980s, 'People at work began to assert themselves as individuals ... the tide of collectivism – the drift towards a world where the workforce was treated as an undifferentiated mass with identical interests ... was turned back'.

Second, developments in the labour market have reflected, influenced and been reinforced by public policy emphasis on the atomised individual at work. More work is now done on short-term contract, part-time, at home, on the edge. For around 60 per cent of the workforce, there is no such thing as a 'steady job' any more.

Third, the national structures by which terms and conditions of employment were set for union and non-union employees alike throughout whole industries have largely gone forever. Such negotiations that remain – usually at company level – have been devolved to local factories and offices. In the public services, the contracting-out of work has had the same effect. Great set piece national negotiations for whole industries with journalists door-stepping the participants for the nine o'clock news have largely disappeared.

Fourth, unemployment has persisted through the two recessions since 1979 at a level that was believed impossible for society to sustain without producing grotesque social dislocation. Common sense dictates that this influence lies behind individual caution and union hesitation alike in contradicting the decisions of change managers every-where. The fear of sinking into unemployment – particularly long-term unemployment – is the source of insecurity of work. (Throughout the 1980s and the 1990s, over one mil-lion people were unemployed for over a year.) Two other influences are at work on peo-ple in jobs that add to their insecurity:

1. The development of personal contracts and individualised pay systems such as per-formance related pay; and
2. the acceptance of flexible working practices, which have left individuals feeling more vulnerable to the demands of the employer.

Throughout industry and commerce, in private and public sectors, the priority of meet-ing the demands of customers rather than the convenience of workpeople is tri-umphant. In particular, public service employers have set aside a certain traditional smugness in their attitude to being 'good employers'. In order to serve customers better, they too will reduce costs as an imperative, whatever the industrial relations consequences.

Fifth, the structure of industry itself has changed: shipyards are shut, leisure indus-tries are growing. Towns like Birkenhead that contained traditional heavy industry and traditional high levels of union density have not been replicated in places like Bracknell, where light industry and white-collar employment, often in smaller workplaces, have not been so quick to provide trade unions with equivalent high densities.

All these themes have presented HR managers with opportunities to develop strate-gies and introduce workplace change unencumbered by the trade union veto. Each suc-cess in implementing innovation has built managerial confidence ahead of introducing the next change. Few managers today hesitate and say that change is impossible because 'the unions won't wear it'.

The role of public policy in minimising union influence

Since 1945, all governments saw a legitimate role for trade unions in representing work people, and, by implication, having sufficient power to prevent unilateral imposition of change of work. During the 1960s and 1970s, however, this government sponsorship of some sort of notional balance between employers and unions broke down. The story is well-known. Government began to identify Britain's comparative economic decline with 'the British disease'. The unions could not control their plant-level negotiators. Spontaneous strikes that were local, inflationary, 'outside procedures', only served to show the inability of union leaders to deliver the wage policy that government needed. Matters got worse: not only did unions do nothing to prevent the casual disruption of unofficial strikes, they also seemed willing to confront the state itself in the set piece national battles in the coalfields of 1972 and 1974 and the 'Winter of Discontent' of 1978–9.

From 1979, the new Conservative government's assault on union influence can be seen to have been divided into three phases.

1. From 1979 to 1982, the Thatcher government grew steadily more confident in attacking union 'abuses' associated with the popular perception of the closed shop and picketing.
2. From 1982 to 1988, the main focus of legal change fell on the unions' capacity to organise industrial action.
3. From 1988 to 1993, the essence of union organisation itself was targeted – irrespective of its record, politics or contribution to the industry or the service in which the individual union might operate.

For HR managers, these three phases of legal reform have been vital in reducing the confidence of union activists, enlisting the support of union members in disassociating themselves from militant action, and diluting the influence of the Trades Union Congress (TUC) and union general secretaries in the wider councils of industrial and commercial Britain.

The first legislative phase, 1979–82, dealt with 'abuses'. Jim Prior's legislation was modest in ambition, seeming to imply that it is the government's role in industrial relations to hold the ring and not get into it. He made it easier to leave a closed shop (which covered five million workers in 1979), made it more difficult to establish new ones, restricted picketing to strikers' places of work and prevented shop stewards greeting sub-contractors at the factory or building-site gate with impertinent questions as to the trade union position, comparable wages, and other requirements that were on the steward's 'fair list' of employment practices. What was important, however, was that if secondary pickets appeared or sub-contractors were interfered with, the businesses that suffered could at last sue for the damages caused to their business. Trade unions were no longer completely immune from financial penalties associated with disputes. (Sometimes the police did not pursue this issue as hard as the legislation entitled them to do. During the 1982 nurses' dispute, EETPU and ASTMS shop stewards from the night shift at Mullards in Durham joined the handful of nurses picketing for the day outside the city's main hospital. At 6 a.m., a passing constable asked the stewards if they were secondary pickets: one of the stewards replied, 'No! We got here first!' The policeman smiled and moved on.)

The second phase of the legislation built on this beginning. What the unions called 'Tebbitt's Law' in 1982–3 stormed through Jim Prior's first breach in the 'immunities'. Since 1906, unions could not be sued for the losses their disputes caused for customers and suppliers alike, so long as the dispute was 'in contemplation or furtherance of a trade dispute'. Crucially, from the employers' point of view, Tebbitt's law set out to penalise the offending unions financially at national level, not to make martyrs of local activists with whom an embarrassed employer might have to deal long after the dispute had ended. The main changes amounted to a few pen-strokes which narrowed the definition of a trade dispute that could be pursued legally. Inter-union disputes – the classic demarcation rows – were now illegal. Disputes were only permissible between an employer and his employees – largely outlawing most types of sympathetic action. Disputes had to be 'wholly or mainly connected' with a tight range of industrial issues, thus outlawing 'political' strikes where sympathetic action was taken with British or international trade union causes. Telling the National Communications Union that its strike against Mercury was political, and nothing to do with protecting jobs in BT, gave all unions the message in 1983.

The 1982 Act clearly identified the illegality of industrial action outside the new definition of a trade dispute. Not only could employers deal with illegal action at their own workplaces (perhaps with sympathetic secondary pickets), but those employers who were customers or suppliers to strike-affected locations could also move quickly against the unions concerned. If employers took out injunctions to put a stop to *prima facie* illegal action, they would achieve a rapid end to action: if the unions refused to obey the terms of injunctions taken out on the strength of apparent breaches of the Employment Acts, the courts could then invoke the full draconian majesty of contempt of court hearings. The possibility of being exposed to fines of up to £250 000 by each aggrieved party suing a union of over 100 000 members under the Employment Acts concentrated the collective minds of trade union executive councils wonderfully well. Even more damaging were contempt proceedings. The National Graphical Association's dispute with Eddie Shah's Messenger Group in 1983 cost the union over £2 million in fines and the sequestration costs associated with its contempt activities (Goodhart and Wintour, 1986). On 9 December 1982, at one single hearing, they were fined £375 000 for contempt. Despite the opposition rhetoric emanating from the 1982 TUC Special Congress, the TUC general council was not going to imperil the TUC's funds in support of 'illegal' action, and the NGA was left to pay the fines: the other unions learnt the lesson. There was not going to be a heroic rerun of the opposition to Ted Heath's Industrial Relations Act. This legislation was going to stick, not least because sufficient numbers of individual employers were willing to take high-profile legal action. This early legal experience successfully undermined the typical 'sympathy' dispute, the high-profile public support by travelling pickets and the existence of the institutionalised closed shop (once policed effectively by personnel officers, but now probably covering less than 300 000 workers). It also largely curtailed the interference by shop stewards with relationships with sub-contractors, and in that way removed a very practical obstacle to the outsourcing of all sorts of functions within organisations.

Curing 'the British disease'?

Recent strike figures have shown that 'the British disease' is apparently cured. Figures from the Office for National Statistics show that the annual number of strikes in the 1990s barely struggle over the 200 mark, compared to the 1974–94 average of 1234 strikes per year. In 1980, the first full year of Mrs Thatcher's government, 11 964 000 days were lost in strikes. In 1995, only 415 000 days were lost in just 235 disputes of any sort, anywhere in Britain. The Conservative government understandably repeated these figures with great enthusiasm – the second best after 1994, since records began in 1891. Sceptics quickly pointed out that disputes were falling in both number and longevity all over Europe: Britain remains about halfway down – or up – the Organisation for Economic Cooperation and Development (OECD) strike league table. It is also true that British figures have been helped by the slump into insignificance of the mining, docks and vehicle-building industries as sources of routine industrial conflict. Public service disputes in the Post Office, higher education and transport are the most recent centres of strike activity. The great set piece strike is in abeyance, with 72 per cent of 1995's disputes lasting no more than two days. Nevertheless, the government is entitled to draw support for its views from the conclusive piece of evidence that only Denmark among the OECD countries experienced a greater reduction than Britain in days lost through strikes from 1988 to 1992.

There has been considerable speculation both as to the impact of legislation on these declining strike statistics and the wider economic impact of the legislation. Work published in Cambridge (Brown and Wadhwani, 1990) and the LSE (Dunn and Metcalf, 1994) both found it difficult totally to isolate the effects of the law. Structural change in industry, unemployment, new technology, the growth of HRM techniques, and the declining membership of unions have all affected the falling strike figures.

Whether conflict in British industry has entirely disappeared along with strikes is an entirely separate question. Applications to Industrial Tribunals will exceed 100 000 per annum in 1995 for the first time. Citizens Advice Bureaux – in some cases replacing unions by working for individuals in factories and offices that might in other times have become unionised – report overwhelming numbers of work-based enquiries. The CAB report on Job Security, published in 1993, showed a 30 per cent rise in employment-related inquiries between 1987–8 and 1992–3; 11.5 per cent of approaches made to the CAB in that year were work related.

Academic opinion is always frustrated when it proves impossible to isolate, measure and exemplify the behaviours which are being studied: senior trade union officials just *know* that the cautioning impact of the industrial legislation has given them pause time after time. The government's willingness to face down the great set piece disputes in the 1980s relied on their own intention to emphasise what an unnamed minister described to Hugo Young, political correspondent of the *Guardian*, as the 'Demonstration Effect' (Young, 1993). The government's willingness to see through the steel strike in 1980, the civil service and health service disputes in 1982 and the miners' strike in 1984–5 gave full rein to the 'Demonstration Effect', entirely separate from the impact of the employment legislation. However, on top of the perceptions of government determination that sprung out of that experience, the Employment Acts did have a background effect in the *Stockport Messenger* dispute in 1983, Wapping in 1986–7, the P & O dispute at Dover in 1988 and the Tilbury Docks dispute in 1989. Dunn and Metcalfe's conclusion is that 'as the 1990s arrived, unions were far less likely to approach legal problems like a bull at a gate'. There is not an executive council in any trade union in Britain today that does not employ expert legal advice from specialist industrial law firms like Lawfords, Rowley Ashworth and Thompsons, whose expertise long outgrew the routine grind of individual industrial compensation cases. No union executive meeting now endorses or repudiates local disputes without considering the possible costs involved.

These obstacles placed in front of industrial action by the second phase of the government's changes in employment law have been reinforced by the post-1984 laws aimed at the unions themselves. No strike is now legal without a 'proper' ballot before it takes place. The ballot process is engulfed in legal restriction: it has to be secret, and held again after four weeks if no strike has been called in that period. The ballots have to be postal, and no union can discipline non-strikers who cross picket lines, even if a legal majority exists for the dispute. All unofficial, spontaneous disputes have had to be 'repudiated' by the official union, or they would be held responsible for the actions of their local members. Strikers can be dismissed selectively, and unions banned from organising disputes that support selectively dismissed strikers taking part in unofficial strikes. Every legal dispute has to give the employer seven days' notice of the strike date and the names and addresses of those members who were being called out. Finally, in this context, it is now legal for employers to pay non-unionists more than trade unionists and to pay lump-sum inducements to individual workers to leave their unions. The decline in individual rights to protection from dismissal is well known. This extra element of ballot complexity isolates individuals and atomises any workforce with a collective grievance by undermining the union's capacity to organise effective action.

On top of this frustration, the unions as *organisations* have been thrown back on their heels by what they see as intrusion into their own governing structures. They were bemused when the 1993 Employment Act insisted that the automatic deduction of trade union contributions by an employer from a worker's wages had to be resanctioned every three years. No other voluntary contribution made via the employer or in any other way is so subject; it looked to the unions like casual vindictiveness. The employers largely resisted the invitation to take advantage of the situation, although some certainly asked for negotiating benefits when promising their bureaucratic assistance in sustaining these 'check-off' arrangements. For some unions, it turned out to be a beneficial imposition, now integrated into their 1996 organisation campaigns. Most returned percentage figures in the high 90s of check-off authorisations. Every workplace was visited and groups of members and non-members alike contacted for the first time in years. UNISON, the huge newly merged public service union, found the 'sign-up' campaign an enormously successful period in introducing the three old unions [NALGO (National and Local Government Officers' Association), NUPE (National Union of Public Employees), and COHSE (Confederation of Health Service Employees)] to each other in common activity. It helped enormously in their awareness of the need to modernise a common membership system. The National Union of Teachers (NUT) used the check-off campaign period to revolutionise their subscription collections by introducing direct debit – a system of collecting contributions that frees the union from the administrative assistance of the employers. The NUT direct debit membership now amounts to over 90 per cent of the total.

Despite evidence of the professionalising of trade union financial systems, further public policy impositions have made their position less tenable (Willman and Morris, 1993 and 1995). In February 1993, having insisted on ballots for disputes and elections, the government abandoned its own schemes (along with support for trade union education courses) for using public funds to pay for these activities. Between 1 April 1993 and 1 April 1996, the postal cost refunds were reduced in stages from 100 per cent of qualifying claims to nothing. The Certification Officer paid out £3.9 million for 380 ballots in 1993 and £3 million for 1469 ballots in 1994. In 1995, the last complete year in which reduced payments were due to be made saw 1644 ballots attract funding of only £1.1 million. Trade union finance is usually precariously balanced; membership decline sees to that. In 1993, the gross income of all the trade unions reporting to the Certification Officer was £724.35 million. Gross expenditure was £711.74 million. The loss of the ballot money support will be keenly felt and largely replaced by a fall in other union activities. Alternatively, there will be fewer elections or fewer dispute ballots.

Further intrusions – of somewhat modest practical impact in the early years – are provided by the Commissioner for the Rights of Trade Union Members to take up individual member complaints concerning union elections, admission procedures and accounts. Effectively, the legal changes ensured the close supervision of postal ballots in union mergers or elections and the political fund ballot authorisations every five years. Individual members of the public can proceed against unions they think are about to act illegally. Breaches of each and every provision, collective or individual, can be punished in the same way – injunctions and contempt proceedings in the immediate crisis and then suing the union for damages for actions now no longer protected by the immunities.

Each and every change is placed one on top of another: powerful obstacles stand in the way of spontaneous, furious eruptions of trade union outrage – legitimate or otherwise. No HR manager will miss the chance to point out to local activists that they risk legal action. This is particularly important in demonstrating the legal imperative to ballot properly. In itself, the enforced delays this process brings often redress the power balance in the employer's favour. No trade union office will miss the financial imperative of disowning local activists, however reluctantly. No local activist can fail to feel more exposed or vulnerable. Some sink back into acquiescence; more resign and pursue their careers in the company. Discreet anecdotal evidence from every substantial British union bemoans the decline in the number of members prepared to be a shop steward or staff representative. The deregulation and contracting-out of public services has undoubtedly intensified this problem.

This is of course due to many influences: but the feeling that for individual activists 'it is just not worth it' is an obvious common-sense deduction from the decline in shop steward numbers. No one should underestimate the extent to which managements everywhere have taken encouragement from the fall in self-confidence among lay trade union activists, the almost complete extinction of their capacity to organise 'rapid response' industrial action and the comparative ease with which reckless activists can be got rid of. The icing on the cake, of course, in the control of local trade union activity, is that national trade union leaderships, fearful of massive fines, are usually ready to repudiate the activities of local activists in the wider interests of the union's overall stability. Even then, unions are still vulnerable to the consequences of unofficial action. In February 1995, the postal side of the Communication Workers Union was fined £7500 for contempt of court, despite their energetic repudiation of local industrial action. They also had to find £100 000 in legal costs. The presiding judge, Judge Drake, was quoted in the *Financial Times* as saying 'the breach of the court order was by local officials [shop stewards] against the instructions of the full-time officials. I must, however, have regard to the policies of parliament that the union is to be held responsible for actions of *all* its officials.' There remains a certain piquancy in postal disputes that the government was not aware of as it framed the legislation. How can postal workers be balloted on industrial action issues if the Post Office is closed due to unofficial disputes?

The extent of the change in public policy has not been restricted to the liberation of innovative managers through the removal of the trade union veto as expressed through strikes and the threat of disputes in general. Trade union confidence has been most undermined by the emergence of a sense of irrelevance in trade union membership. When potential members are now approached to join a union, they may well say no and suffer no consequence from exercising that choice. The closed shop has disappeared in its formal sense. Trade union membership levels in both the public services and traditional private industries are no longer policed by personnel managers. Trade union officials are no longer seen to be influencing government policy. Negotiating rights are withdrawn from teachers. Membership of trade unions at GCHQ (Government Communications Headquarters) is banned outright. The only body that has improved the living standards of people at work in Britain in the public policy area is the European Commission. Legal improvements in the rights of pregnant women, in hours of work and in equal opportunity issues have been applied to all individuals at work – not just trade unionists. The Commission has little direct interest in encouraging the strength of trade unions as institutions, however much it may be interested in developing the 'social' side of the single market for individuals across Europe. Trade unions in Britain were given no role in setting minimum wage standards after the virtual abolition of Wages Councils (with the significant exception of the Agricultural Wages Board). There were formal committees and appeal bodies to present evidence of low pay to in order to raise earnings to a 'fair' level or an average level for the industry, although this is part of the new approach now in the Labour government. The same public policy that has immobilised much of union activity at local level has almost totally obscured it at the level of impacting on national consciousness. No managers needed to recognise, negotiate or defer to a trade union unless they wanted to. Increasingly, potential union members saw little point in union membership, as their influence appeared minimal at every level of the company.

Developments in the labour market – the way we go to work in the 1990s

The sense of freedom from veto has accelerated managerial initiative in transforming the way people are employed. Here again, the 'Demonstration Effect' is crucially important. Innovations like the outsourcing of professional and manual support operations in both public and private industry have become routine. Each significant change is widely reported in the professional press and is rapidly the subject of public seminars and consultants' expertise. These developments in the labour market that uniformly accentuate the fragility of the modern employment relationship are well known. Will Hutton's (1995) description of these forces is but the latest analysis of powerful forces that have altered the relationship between unions and HR managers forever. Hutton describes the '30-30-40' society. The first 30 per cent – the 'disadvantaged' in our society are the unemployed and the economically inactive within the potential adult working population. The second 30 per cent – the 'marginalised and insecure' – include the part-time, self-employed, temporary, short-term contract workers and the irreducibly poor. Part-time work has doubled since 1979. Five million work it; 80 per cent of part-time workers are women. Two million people work less than 16 hours a week, and 70 per cent of all new jobs being created in the mid-1990s are part-time jobs offering work for less than 16 hours a week. With 11.6 per cent of the workforce now 'self-employed', this category of workpeople has also doubled since 1979. Seven and a half per cent are 'temporary' workers – usually reflecting traditional seasonal employment patterns. Hutton also accentuates the growth of insecurity in temporary contract holding jobs, such as printing, university lecturing and the production of every sort of media. One million people in full-time jobs face the insecurity of poverty, earning less than 50 per cent of average wages.

Care must be taken within these categories – not all part-time work is 'insecure' – 15 per cent of part-time workers have held their jobs for more than five years. A tantalising, if unquantified, amount of part-time work may well represent second or third earners in a prosperous family. Half the self-employed say they work part-time, so they must not be counted twice, although the self-employed who have only been working for themselves for under two years should be viewed as 'insecure'. The net result is that 3.5 million people have been employed less than two years and have virtually no employment protection: add to them the one million 'poor', and there's Hutton's second '30' of 'marginalised and insecure people'.

That leaves 40 per cent of the 'privileged' in the workforce – full-time workers, part-timers with the same employer after five years, and the self-employed who have worked for themselves for over two years. It is hard to resist the power of Hutton's imagery that lies behind the simple statistic that between 1975 and 1993, the full-time, tenured work on offer to British workers fell from 55 per cent to 35 per cent of the workforce. He writes that 'the shadow of the new labour market is lengthening over the privileged'. For HR managers, the implications of these developments are immense. There are now vast swathes of all types of workpeople – from catering assistants to architects – who are not only available for short-term engagement (where they pay all the 'extra' employment costs associated with national insurance, holidays and pensions) but who also expect to work that way. This acceptance of new ways of work and the individual's own responsibility to meet his or her employment costs associated with pension, holiday and training costs have given the HR manager great freedom of action in building – *and* disassembling – work teams on a flexible basis.

Deregulation, devolution and disintegration of national collective bargaining

The third influence in the inter-related forces that greatly assists local HR managers in taking control of their responsibilities has been the devolution of negotiating responsibility to the local level – often simultaneously asking line managers to deal with the issues arising and continuing with just a skeletal, specialist, personnel service. The work of Marginson et al., 1993, showed that pay is now negotiated locally in over half of Britain's largest companies employing over 1000 people. Hill and Pickering, in 1986, suggested that over 80 per cent of the largest 200 companies have broken up their companies into semi-autonomous 'divisions', where line managers have assumed greater responsibilities than before. Marginson et al. published further evidence of this trend in their 1988 study *Beyond the Workplace: Managing Industrial Relations in Multi-Establishment Enterprises*. Brown and Walsh (1991) showed that 16 major national bargaining groups covering one million workers were abandoned between 1986 and 1991.

The picture varies in the deregulated public services. National bargaining of sorts is retained in Gas and British Telecom (BT). Electricity has replaced the elegant minuet at the Millbank Tower between the Electricity Council and the unions represented on the three different national negotiating bodies with devolved bargaining to the National Grid, the generators and the Regional Electric Companies. Further divisional bargaining within those new organisations completes a picture that is wholly different from the post-war Lord Citrine inspired model, in which the national agreements, including consultation and negotiation guarantees, were enshrined by statute. Again, the Civil Aviation Authority remains in the public sector, but has divisionalised its negotiating form into five separate divisions. (As with every other company or public service, it would be naive to think that the Authority's head office or sponsoring ministry is indifferent to the results of these modern negotiations. Senior civil servants are always speaking to public service managers in every public service behind the scenes – as became apparent in the 1994 signalmen's dispute). All this decentralisation mirrors private sector activity. For example, Securicor has made product groups into separate companies and set up different negotiating arrangements in each along an industrial relations axis that ranges from derecognition to business as usual with the union (GMB).

Multi-employer bargaining with multi-union federations is in steep decline. Professor Willy Brown at Cambridge has estimated that multi-employer bargaining may now cover less than 10 per cent of the total workforce, down from 46 per cent in 1979. More generally, the number of establishments employing over 25 people that set terms and conditions through collective bargaining fell from 71 per cent in 1984 to 54 per cent in 1990, according to the Workplace Industrial Relations Survey (WIRS) published in 1992. In 1984, 62 per cent of all workers owed their terms and conditions to collective bargaining, whether they were union members or not. By 1990, the figure had fallen to 48 per cent. The figures are more stark in private industry and services. By 1990, only 51 per cent of private manufacturing and 33 per cent of private services used collective bargaining. The figure in public services has fallen from 95 per cent to 78 per cent, largely due to the decline in the coverage of collective bargaining in the teaching and health service professions.

More damaging for perceptions of union effectiveness among potential members, the New Earnings Survey (1994) shows that the 'union dividend' produced by collective bargaining is under stress. In 1983, collectively bargained average earnings were £148.90, compared to £146 for workers whose pay was set individually. By 1991, however, non-collective gross pay had risen to £279.10, £8.50 ahead of the equivalent areas where collective bargaining reigned supreme.

However, no one should forget that collective bargaining still exists. The 'demonstration' effect of the Ford negotiations – national talks that are well-reported every Autumn – set the tone for any private or corporate concepts of 'the going rate' at the back of HR managers' minds. Printing and construction still have national agreements, as do textiles and key companies in the chemicals sector. Collective bargaining has not disappeared. We shall see later how unions take some real comfort from the fact that they are more likely to be recognised in both the most economically successful companies and those who most often use progressive HRM methodologies.

Changing structures of rewards and work content

The wage negotiations of the 1970s were usually advanced on the unions' side by some reference to productivity and ability to pay. If the company had made good profits, unions expected higher rises than the 'fodder' basis of negotiating (where the cost of living rise dictated the entitlement to wage rises, and nothing else). Today, that link between expectation of higher wages and the growth of productivity has been broken.

Company after company refers to the need to cut costs, to reduce unit labour costs, to remain 'competitive'. In their need to do this, they welcome the ability to break out of the annual wage increase for all, which is the usual claim by unions. Workforces are divided into 'core' (people paid at a level to retain their services) and various forms of 'periphery' (where people are paid on a range of short-term formulae at the lowest cost).

The parameters of this flexibility debate are well-known, both in Britain and in Europe (Brewster et al., 1996). The pressures of competitiveness in the international market economy and the deregulated, devolved public services are intense. Each cost-cutting triumph reinforces the need for competitors to equal it: each seminar on cost-cutting flexibility transfers ideas from company to company. Each senior management team asks its HR manager whether he or she, too, has thought about annualised hours, outsourced ever more functions and planned to retain and motivate key staff through the development of individual competences.

For traditional industrial relations, 'flexibility' has been at the heart of the marginal-ising process for collective bargaining: it has intensified the focus on the preferred employment relationship that seems to concentrate on the individual and the company. None of the tendencies in the 'flexible firm' debate have increased a sense of security. No group of workpeople expelled to the 'periphery' from the 'core' of the company can avoid a rising sense of insecurity. The inability of the trade unions to do much about these developments has reinforced the sense that far too often the unions are paper tigers. Potential trade union members draw the inevitable conclusions.

One of the best examples of the relationship between HRM, flexible work practices, the growing focus on the individual at work and the impotence of unions was provided in October 1994 by the Cadbury company. There was a special poignancy associated with this case study, given Cadbury's long-time reputation as a liberal, 'progressive' company with long-term relations with organised labour. Indeed, a *Management Today/Loughborough Business School* industry survey in November 1994 found Cadbury to be the seventh most admired company in the UK.

All this was undermined for the unions when Brian Revell, National Secretary of the Transport & General Workers Union (T & G) received an internal management dis-cussion document entitled 'Manufacturing Human Resource Strategy', dated 29 September 1994. The document was a 'Summary of Personal Values agreed by Factory Managers', signed by six managers. This summary of personal values called for indi-vidual factory HR plans to be integrated within the broad company manufacturing strategy which itself would be a 'key component' of the overall business strategy. All this would be achieved through 'communication and best practice' sharing rather than through a large central bureaucracy. The paper urged on all Cadbury managers a man-agement style that involved employees and was 'conducive to high employee morale'. They were to recognise that 'good ideas are not the preserve of the factory management teams but come from all employees and all functions'. The Quality Improvement Teams, Team Briefings and Communication meetings that encourage feedback were to be the hallmark of employee involvement. External benchmarking and visiting other companies should continue the search for best practice.

The third priority in the paper revolves round a style of manpower planning that should not be 'preoccupied with headcount' and only think of reducing numbers in the short term if [product] volume growth is not achieved or plant efficiency growth allows it. Finally, the HR strategy should be characterised by career development and training for enhanced skills. This ought to make it possible for the company to develop a 'performance focussed culture' in which the balance between the basic pay, skill-based pay supplements and gainsharing elements in pay get rebalanced closer to performance variables. It should also reflect more closely the local labour markets in which the company operated.

The significance of this summary of the Cadbury paper so far is its wholly conventional approach to the modern, developmental approach to HR in which management attitudes can clearly be seen to be achieving business improvement through motivating a more committed, skilled workforce. And then they added four paragraphs on the union's role:

> Consultative structures exist in all factories at present, and it is recognised that there is a need for consultative structures with all personal involvement of the Factory Managers.
>
> However, consultation needs to shift so that employees are consulted directly, rather than via Trade Unions. Mechanisms such as Quality Improvement Teams, Briefing Groups and 'morning meetings' go some way towards this.
>
> The role of the trade unions needs to be marginalised by greater focus on direct communication and consultation, but without an overt statement to this effect. Employee support for the TU should therefore decrease over time. However, it is not likely that the TU would be de-recognised, given the likelihood of downsizing. A re-defined role for the TU is therefore required.
>
> For those groups where the TU has already been de-recognised in recent years, it is important that they are not exploited by the company as this would lead to pressure for renewed TU involvement.

The union response to this was predictable. In a leaflet distributed round the factories, T & G National Secretary Brian Revell wrote

> HRM is all about management control and if the trade union is successfully undermined and weakened, people will be exploited more through increased work and lower wage costs. The proposed Cadbury application of HRM is basically dishonest and manipulative and seeks to persuade workers not to take account of their own interest ... it is one-sided and a disgrace ... .

Neil Makin, Personnel Director of Cadbury, moved quickly to downgrade the status of the document to one of discussion paper, emphasising in press interviews how much he did not like the idea of 'marginalising' the unions: he was much more interested in building on the use of union convenors as National Vocational Qualification (NVQ) verifiers, making a reality of his vision of the union role converting to one of facilitator of industrial change, not regulator of pay and conditions.

It is a fine irony that the TUC have identified the fact that 47 out of Britain's top 50 companies negotiate with unions, and the WIRS researchers found that the more comprehensive the use of recognisable HRM techniques, the more likely the company was to recognise unions. The Cadbury case study does seem to alert unions to the possibility of that link being undermined. It certainly adds to the pressures on new recruits in new workplaces and old alike to resist the invitation from union representatives to join.

The Institute of Personnel and Development (IPD) (writing for the House of Commons Employment Committee in February 1994, when they were still the Institute of Personnel Management) accepts this: they believe it reflects wider societal influences beyond the stern imperative of cutting costs. 'These changes may indeed reflect a more profound move away from collective representation, security and action within society; a move which for good or ill throws more responsibility on individuals and their families for their own welfare'. For the IPD, the advance of flexible working, short-term contracts and performance-related pay all reflect this understanding by workers that their individual lives are now closely bound up with the employers' goals.

> The more that employees appreciate that both the benefits and insecurities of employment relate in a tangible way to the results of mutual efforts to improve performance and less to the adversarial relationship enshrined in the collective bargaining process, the less important trade union membership will appear to be. This will hold true until collective bargaining has something substantial to offer to the improvement of performance.

Whether such personnel and HR managers are armed with the protective shield of moral righteousness, adapting to the tenor of the times, or simply taking advantage of a shift in power relations at the workplace, there can be no doubt that the majority of modern workpeople have their terms and conditions of employment dictated largely by the employer's award of some element of individual pay. However, it remains unclear as to the efficacy of individualising pay rewards in terms of motivating workers to increase their commitment to the company's goals. The Institute of Manpower Studies' (1992) research concludes that despite 75 per cent of employing organisations using performance related pay systems, 'recent studies of the effects of merit pay on employee motivation in the public sector have concluded that for all but a minority of employees, the link between performance and reward has no motivational effect, indeed, for many, the link serves to demotivate'.

Whether individual pay sits easily alongside the rhetoric of team working is also a moot point. Nothing destabilises and demotivates 'colleagues' more than the suspicion that workmates are being paid differently for doing the same work. At least traditional work study methods could be presented as attempting objectively to measure different workers' contributions. Unions and staff associations were usually partners in setting up such schemes, administering them and negotiating changes to them as products and processes altered. There is little evidence of workers' enthusiasm for individual appraisal schemes, however much sincere effort is put into their design by sincere HR managers. If the basis of reward is not trusted by workpeople, their motivation and commitment will usually suffer.

The changing industrial structure

The fifth main theme that has contributed to the decline of trade union influence has been the structural change in the economy which has closely affected the narrow basis of trade union institutional interest. Manufacturing enterprises, traditionally associated with high levels of trade union membership, have closed, and the small office blocks, hotel chains, and much of the new industry associated with new technology have not proved successful recruiting and negotiating ground for unions. We have already discussed the impact of Will Hutton's '30-30-40' society: the insecure, part-time, female workforce he describes do not instinctively join unions. The 1994 Labour Forces Survey showed that trade union membership was only of interest to 31 per cent of women workers, 21 per cent of part-timers and only 8 per cent of the self-employed. These figures were not replicated in mines, shipyards, engineering works and textile mills in years gone by.

The Department of Employment thought it could put its finger on the main issue in this equation between trade union membership and industrial structure when it told the House of Commons Employment Committee at the end of 1993,

> The causes of union decline are many. One stands out above all others – the inability of unions to recruit members in companies from the expanding areas of the economy. Unions have apparently failed to adjust to the restructuring of the economy over the last fifteen years. They have lost members in declining sectors – often heavily unionised – but failed to compensate elsewhere. As analysis of the WIRS surveys has shown, only 30% of newer workplaces in the late 80s recognised unions. Yet such establishments were being created at a faster rate in this period than before – a reflection, in part, of the dynamic growth of the small firms sector. Many of these newer workplaces were in private services, employing high proportions of female and part-time labour.

Many employers when opening greenfield sites chose to ignore unions, even when the same employers had traditional union arrangements in their older factories.

Every assessment of where this leaves HR managers as they ponder that central strategic choice of whether they work with unions or avoid them, points in the same direction. They are the Masters now, should they choose to be. Neil Milward's frequently quoted conclusion to his book *The New Industrial Relations?* (1994) is satisfied that

> British industry and commerce appear to be moving towards the situation in which non-managerial employees are treated as a 'factor of production'. Britain is approaching the position where few employees have any mechanism through which they can contribute to the operation of their workplace in a broader context than that of their own job ... there has been no spontaneous emergence of an alternative model of employee representation that could channel and attenuate conflicts between employer and employees ... the recent growth in inequality in wages and earnings ... is being matched by a widening in the inequalities of influence, and access to key decisions about work and employment.'

HR managers' reality is dominated by the ever-increasing pace of change. They must wonder if this current sclerosis in trade union relevance, standing and influence is likely to be permanent.

The trade union response

The response of trade unions to the scale of the crisis facing them will influence the development of HR strategy into the next century. Such responses are best examined by looking at the scale and nature of the unions' reforms of their own institutions, the growing impact of all things European on trade union policy and effectiveness, and the related issue of the extent to which concepts of 'social partnership' take root in Britain.

First, though, the scale of the crisis. The decline in trade union membership since 1979 has serious implications for union finance and, therefore, the nature and scale of union service provision. Membership has declined from around a half of the workforce to less than a third between 1979 and 1995. The latest figures for all unions – TUC affiliated or not – submitted to the Certification Officer in 1995 for the year 1994 show that 1994's overall figure of 8.23 million had fallen from a record figure of 13.29 million in 1979 – a decline of 38 per cent. Trades Union Congress figures have fallen from 1980's record affiliation for 107 unions of 12.2 million to 1995's figure of 6.9 million in 67 unions, a decline of 43 per cent. It may be that TUC affiliation figures of 6.9 million in 1995 are much more accurate than they have ever been. Most unions now see that affiliating phantom members in order to cut a dash at the TUC is now an expensive gesture. Affiliation fees that amount to one week's contribution do not encourage general secretaries to over-affiliate. This aspect of trade union decline has never been properly researched. It may be that union penetration in Britain was never as intense as unions claimed, and that the decline in real membership has not been so disastrous either.

Decline is real, however. The figures do not immediately reveal the extent of cultural change that in some ways may have been more disorientating for trade union activists. The 'movement' has indeed moved. The 1995 TUC Annual Report shows that the National Union of Mineworkers now has just 11 000 members while British actors' Equity has 40 000. In 1979, the figures for the NUM were 253 000 and for Equity, 27 000. The National Union of Rail, Maritime and Transport Workers (RMT), another union whose long traditions, iconography and contribution to the wider trade union world are central to trade union culture, has fallen from 222 000 (including the pre-merger figures for the Seamen's Union) in 1979 to 68 000 for RMT in 1995. More than 60 per cent of TUC members are now white-collar workers, augmented recently by the affiliation of new unions from the education and finance sectors. The unions that grew in the mid 1990s include professional workers in the health industry, probation service, education and the airlines. However, the specialist union for construction workers, UCATT, steadily approached oblivion on the building sites of Britain.

Union strategy to turn the tide

Union strategy to deal with decline (Taylor, 1994) can be analysed here under two broad headings during the 1979–95 period: the political dependence strategy, and the search for a British version of 'social partnership'. The political dependence strategy has probably been linked to the belief that the return of a Labour government would totally abolish the restrictive legal framework, re-establish the institutional place in the sun for unions and their officials – particularly in the public services – and rebuild traditional manufacturing industry. Throughout the 1980s, cruel experience and political defeat at three general elections ended any hopes that waiting for a Labour government was all that unions needed to do. This is not the place for discussing what the unions want from the Labour Party – in or out of government. It is worth remembering, however, that unions now recognise it may be preferable to have a degree of influence over a Labour government, rather than total control over a Labour opposition. Opinion polls show that the public are vaguely fearful of union influence over Labour. It may be to the unions' advantage, therefore, to constantly demonstrate that the Labour Party is *not* in the unions' pocket. The Civil and Public Services Association went as far in its evidence to the 1994 House of Commons inquiry into the future of trade unions to say,

> in future, too close an identification with any of the major political parties by the trade union movement as a whole may actually be damaging to the interests of our members. The often emotional and nostalgic retelling, on an increasingly regular basis these days, of the part played by a small number of trade unions in the early part of this century, in helping to form a political party, is also not particularly helpful in any future debate about the way forward for the trade union movement into the next. (p. 54 para. 21)

However much they appreciate the possible general benefits of a Labour government, immediate industrial priorities have dictated that unions turn their attention to attempting to organise within the devolved, individual-based, deregulated, cost-cutting obsessions of the modern workplace – irrespective of any assistance they might expect from a more sympathetic government tinkering with the legislative backdrop to their affairs.

Trade union mergers and the Trades Union Congress

First, a series of trade union mergers in the early 1990s has shifted the *strategic* picture irrevocably. The rise of 'super unions' – or, at any rate, big unions – has persuaded some observers that the union landscape of the next century will be dominated by one public service union built out of the current UNISON set-up; one general workers' union based on a merged TGWU and GMB; and one skilled craft, technical and professional union revolving round the Amalgamated Engineering and Electrical Union (AEEU). All the other unions will feel the lure of the big unions for both bargaining strength and financial defence within their own smaller industries. This view of the future is not greeted with equanimity by smaller unions. They feel that they offer a specialist, close-to-the-members service that large unions cannot deliver. They value their history, independence and culture. Their officials enjoy whatever position they hold in the union and the industrial world that merger might take away from them. Nevertheless, some models of merger offer such distinctive professional unions some measure of protection from derecognition procedures in organisations that may accept unwillingly trade union presence among manual workers while undermining its presence in professional areas of work.

The 'super unions' also pose problems for the Trades Union Congress. If individual, giant unions can resource their specialist support services for themselves (legal, education, safety, training), what remains for the TUC? This sense of futility at Congress House has been underlined by the virtual exclusion of the TUC from the tripartite institutions that the government has swept away during the 1980s. The TUC took action to relaunch itself in 1994, largely by redefining what it does and how it does it. The TUC is clear that it ought not to compete with the individual unions – particularly the large ones. It sets out under general secretary, John Monks, to concentrate on issues and activities that 'add value' to individual unions' inputs. They are concentrating on strategic long-term issues like defining through the NVQ structures the professional standards expected of trade union officers, Europe, campaigning on universal issues like low pay and the national minimum wage, equal opportunities and legal rights for

THE PRACTICE OF HUMAN RESOURCE STRATEGY

all workers, irrespective of their union position. They have commissioned research, published reports, organised public seminars. Conservative ministers have spoken to TUC conferences. The General Secretary has spoken at Conservative and Liberal Democrat conference fringe meetings. The new methods of TUC working have reflected their new role. They have abandoned the endless industrial standing committees and concentrate now on project teams reporting to the General Council which now meets quarterly. There is a small executive committee for implementing policy and keeping task groups on schedule. The significance of this internal reform spreads far beyond the Congress headquarters building. These dramatic new ways of organising trade union work have been picked up in many different ways by the individual unions. It is no longer a trade union principle to avoid 'managing' the union's human and financial assets.

'Social partnership' and Europe's part in redefining the British trade union role

Active trade unionists have been marginalised at both national and local level since 1979. They have not disappeared and total derecognition remains rare. However, as HR techniques and government policy alike appear to indicate to the average British trade union activist that they were 'not wanted on voyage', the reality of social partnership relationships between unions and companies, and unions and governments in Europe appealed to the bruised egos of British trade unionists. President of the EU Commission, Jacques Delors, spoke warmly of the union role in the EU at the 1988 TUC. It must 'guarantee that social dialogue and collective bargaining are essential pillars of our democratic society and social progress'. Mrs Thatcher elevated the EU's social partnership credibility with the unions by emphasising that the government had not cleared the unions out of British industrial and political life at home, just to let them reappear at supranational level in Europe. It is in that context that unions now look at union organisation, the union political role and union representation models in Europe with a new interest that would appal the anti-European union activists of the mid 1970s. Tony Dubbins, general secretary of the printworkers' union, illustrated this sea-change when he said in September 1993, 'There are more doors open in Brussels to the trade unions than there are in the United Kingdom.' As unions grew more familiar with European trade union activity at the European Trade Union Confederation, the various trade secretariats and their equivalents in different countries, they began seriously to examine what was expected of unions as social partners in terms of their relationships with companies and government.

This approach was much more congenial for the wider union movement than following the 'new realism' path apparently favoured by both the electrical and engineering unions who merged in 1992 to form the Amalgamated Engineering and Electrical Union (AEEU). The analysis of the impact of single union deals and 'no-strike deals' (often in Japanese inward investors) is familiar (Bassett, 1986; Wickens, 1987). The enduring inheritance of those agreements in the mid 1980s may lie in the way they introduced the option of partnership between employer and union, currently taking on a new lease of life in the form of European Works Councils.

Adding value to employers and employees alike

Most trade unionists know that recruitment and organisation are greatly assisted by employer co-operation. If individuals feel that their career will not suffer if they join the union, they are more likely to join. If the employer has a reason for actively encouraging membership, the whole process from the union's point of view is made that much easier. The opposite is a cruel truth. If the employer does not want to deal with unions, it is much easier these days to avoid them. There is no legal recognition procedure yet, and strikes to enforce recognition and what the Americans call 'good faith' bargaining are, frankly, unrealistic in today's climate. (The WIRS figures reveal that even unionised employers do not go looking for union recognition in all greenfield sites that they open today.) All this shows unions that they must have one eye on what the employer wants from them as well as what is required to tempt the potential member into membership. This point was well taken at the special TUC general council seminar in 1996 when group report backs at the seminar emphasised that unions 'have to show how we can add value to the employer'. There is much interest in persuading employers to take a benign attitude to 'stakeholding', which the same seminar tellingly referred to as being 'about the rights of union members, not the unions as a corporate body'. The 'key message' during these deliberations was that the unions have to get across the fact that 'unions are in the business to improve industrial relations, not stand in the way of change – our role is to facilitate, not obstruct'.

Union services that have appeal to employers and employees

The prime reason for unions' existence is to represent employees. Philip Bassett and Alan Cave's Fabian pamphlet *All for One: The Future of the Unions*, published in August 1993, was an important statement of the case that individual union members would no longer put up with being treated as an undifferentiated slab of humanity – they are individuals. The pamphlet underlined the instrumental, personal approach. 'The significance of instrumentalism ... lies crucially in the type of benefit identified: individual assistance and individual support on the issues of advice and representation on disciplinary matters, on grievances and on accidents at work – all of them individual concerns rather than collective problems.' Unions may not like the trend towards individual pay systems, but some have made sure they can provide a customised service to individuals – particularly through expert contract advice – rather than refuse to represent their members and destroy their very reason for existence in the process. One union, for example, the Association of First Division Civil Servants (FDA), has come to terms with these developments, as have other professional unions like MSF and IPMS. The FDA keeps a database of individual members' contracts and can offer specialist comparative advice as members move round government departments and agencies. They do not need recognition for collective bargaining to retain membership in these circumstances. Although each contract is supposedly different, trained union officials know what they are looking for. Collective bargaining may appear the easy way to help members: this individual approach may be the best way of showing members directly where the union does its work for them most effectively.

For unions in modern 'social partnerships', the issue of representation is also one they seek to turn to their advantage with employers. At one level, employers recognise that their employees are occasionally subject to petty disciplinary tyranny, and independent, competent, structured representation of individual disputes is useful to the company. At another level, most employers, particularly large ones, understand the utility of borrowing the union's credibility with their employees. If the union pronounces itself satisfied with the methods used to change, say, payment systems, discipline procedures or detailed issues like the allocation of overtime, the company knows its path will be smoothed for it by the union's acquiescence. The union will be the advocate for individuals otherwise embarrassed to put forward a case. Most of all, the union will provide a representational structure to add to the company's consultation processes on everything from European Works Councils to the 'licence to dissent' at early morning team briefings. One articulate company version of this argument was provided to the House of Commons Employment Committee inquiry into the future of trade unions at the end of 1993 by Guinness plc. They wrote,

> A good employer is not afraid of legitimate and robust challenge to business plans. Indeed, such a challenge will improve the quality and implementability of such plans by ensuring that the company adheres to its values and commitments and listens to the employees' views and contributions. To be effective, this challenge must be a coherent and unified view from the employee group as well as from employees directly through the normal communication methods. (p. 684, appendix 34, para. 1)

The unions that look to Europe have been struck by how social partnership is underpinned by unions offering the members and employers alike the union's expertise on carefully selected issues – an expertise that employers cannot easily find for themselves. Here again it is to the employer's advantage to enlist the union's expert support in underlining the employers' statements about the company's safety, or pensions or training policies. Safety issues are particularly well suited to this approach. The union network is ideal for gathering expertise on the subject and communicating it widely. So good can this service be that the AEEU's Safety Officer, Adrian Cunningham, was awarded the MBE in the Queen's Honours list for services to workplace safety! Pensions advice is a crucial collective service in negotiating changes in occupational schemes and the union's support for the integrity of pension schemes, post-Maxwell, is deeply reassuring to employers and individual workers alike. The National Union of Teachers takes this expertise further than most by having advisory services available to help members rectify the situation in which they may have taken out unsuitable personal pension schemes. Training is another issue where union activists' everyday experience both helps the development of individual's 'competences' and facilitates the employers' capacity to introduce change.

Unions are examining ways to deploy their political skills beyond the traditional interest in the affairs of local Labour Parties. The Communication Workers Union and UNISON have both understood that their vision of defending their members' jobs in public services cannot be sustained without public support. This means that their propaganda and campaigns in defence of public services such as the NHS or the Post Office cannot be presented simply in terms of members' job prospects. They have to present the issues as part of an appeal to the consumers of these services. They have to enter what are called by UNISON 'community coalitions'.

The area of expertise that is finding most resonance with both the 'instrumental' ordinary member and employer alike is the legal dimension. Unions have always pursued personal injury cases for members with great diligence. The National Union of Teachers has a regional solicitor in each of their ten regional offices who are steadily offering individual members legal advice in employment matters beyond their original personal injury remit. Increasingly, the world of work is becoming more hedged round with legal stricture that is equally confusing to the members and the local HR manager. Much of this is due to the European Union granting individuals legal rights at work in stark preference and contrast to granting unions organisational preferences for them to deal with workplace rights exclusively through collective bargaining. The whole process of monitoring legal entitlements at work will provide another area of expertise for unions to offer to both employer and employee as proof of their capacity to make a reality of social partnership.

For some union activists, perhaps none of this quite matches the thrill of anticipating the collapse of the whole economic and political system. For the rest, and for the employers and for the potential members of the next century, it may be the basis for the reinvention of a modern style of trade unionism that will make a wholly honourable contribution to the successful development of industrial life in the next millennium.

REFERENCES

Bassett, P. (1986) *Strike Free: New Industrial Relations in Britain*, London, Macmillan.

Bassett, P. and Cave, A. (1993) *All for One: The Future of the Unions*, London, Fabian Society.

Brewster, C. et al. (1996) *Working Time and Contract Flexibility in the EU*, Cranfield School of Management/DG-V of the European Commission.

Brown, W. and Wadhwani, S. (1990) 'The Economic Effects of Industrial Relations Legislation since 1979', *National Institute Economic Review*, February.

Brown, W. and Walsh, J. (1991) 'Pay Determination in Britain in the 1980s: the Anatomy of Decentralisation', *Oxford Review of Economic Policy*, Vol. 7, No. 1, February.

Certification Officer (1996) *Annual Report 1995*, London, HMSO.

Dunn, S. and Metcalf, D. (1994) *Trade Union Law since 1979: Ideology, Intent, Impact*, London, London School of Economics, p. 16.

Employment Committee of the House of Commons (1994) 3rd Report, *The Future of Trade Unions*, London, HMSO HC 676 I:II:III.

Goodhart, D., and Wintour, P. (1986) *Eddie Shah and the Newspaper Revolution*, London, Coronet Books.

Hill, C.W.L. and Pickering, J.F. (1986) 'Divisionalisation, Decentralisation and Performance of Large UK Companies', *Journal of Management Studies*, 23, January, pp. 26–50.

Hutton, W. (1995) *The State We're In*, London, Jonathan Cape.

Institute of Manpower Studies (1992) Report No. 232.

Marginson, P., Edwards, P.K., Martin, R., Sisson, K. and Purcell, J. (1988) *Beyond the Workplace: Managing Industrial Relations in Multi-Establishment Enterprises*, Oxford, Basil Blackwell.

Marginson, P., Armstrong, P., Edwards, P.K. and Purcell, J. (1993) 'Second Company Level Industrial Relations Survey: Executive Summary of Findings', MIMEO, Coventry Industrial Relations Research Unit.

Metcalf, D. (1991) 'British Unions: Dissolution or Resurgence?', *Oxford Review of Economic Policy*, Vol. 17, No. 1, February.

Milward, N. (1994) *The New Industrial Relations?*, London, Policy Studies Institute.

Prior, J., Rt Hon. (1980) *The Role of the Trade Unions*, St Albans, Granada Guildhall Lecture.

Taylor, R. (1994) *The Future of Trade Unions*, London, André Deutsch.

Thatcher, M., Rt Hon. (1980) Airey Neave Lecture, London, 3 May 1980.

Trades Union Congress (1995) *Annual Report of Proceedings*, London.

Wickens, P. (1987) *The Road to Nissan*, London, Macmillan.

Willman, P. and Morris, T. (1993) *Trade Union Finance*, Cambridge, Cambridge University Press.

Willman, P. and Morris, T. (1995) 'Financial Management and Financial Performance in British Unions', *British Journal of Industrial Relations*, Vol. 33, No. 2, June.

Workplace Industrial Relations Surveys (1980/1984/1990) Department of Employment (now Department of Trade and Industry), Advisory, Conciliation and Arbitration Service, and Institute of Policy Studies.

Young, H. (1993) *One of Us – the Final Edition*, London, Macmillan.

CHAPTER 6

MANAGING REWARD STRATEGY

Don McClune

The strategic importance of managing human resources is exemplified by reward strategy, which brings together the significant questions of employee motivation, management ideology, new occupation structures and new employee relationships. At the centre of these questions is the apparently prosaic issue of compensation and benefits, or 'pay'.

The whole subject of pay has become increasingly complex. Nowadays it incorporates an impressive and sometimes confusing range of aspects. In this chapter each aspect in turn is considered and the links between them that make up what has come to be called the 'remuneration package'. The journey will not be exhaustive, not merely because of space limitation but also because the subject of pay is dynamic – what is appropriate this year may well be out-of-date next.

An organisation's payroll can involve enormous sums of money. This investment in pay and benefits, combined with the effect that well-thought-through and appropriate pay policies have on a business, arguably promotes the subject to the realms of business strategy. In this chapter, therefore, the subject is considered under a number of different headings, each of which has an influence on current thinking on the subject. In summary these headings are as follows:

The pay debate – it is difficult to read a newspaper or business journal today without some aspect of pay being analysed, dissected and conclusions being drawn, be it excessive executive pay accusation at one end of the spectrum or motivation of blue-collar workpeople at the other. But this is an important debate and worthy of more serious consideration than granted by journalists.

The people interface – pay is not merely a numbers game. It affects individual people, with their baggage of attitudes, perceptions and willingness to co-operate or conform. If we forget this aspect we can easily end up with a pay policy which has all the right numbers but which is not cost-effective.

Corporate responsibility – corporate responsibility has reached the position, associated with issues of corporate governance, whereby shareholders, the general public and governments no longer allow companies to conduct their affairs, particularly in the realms of pay, simply in any way they see fit. This stewardship varies between censure, specific Stock Exchange rules for listed companies and voluntary codes of practice, and so the recent and rapid growth of this pay topic is discussed.

The pay package – having discussed the more 'macro' aspects of pay, the reader's attention is turned to the elements which make up the package to see how they link together and their importance, relative to each other. These elements are first, base pay – the foundation of the package sometimes referred to as 'come to work' money. Second, variable pay – an increasingly important part of the package and paid on top of base pay. The amount of variable pay to base pay 'gearing' is determined either by a discretionary reward based on some performance criteria over the preceding performance period or as a reward for performance achievement against pre-set performance targets. Variable pay is an increasingly important part of the pay package and we shall look in some detail at how performance plans are constructed. Third, longer-term incentives – depending upon the level of influence individuals have on the performance of the organisation, companies are shifting part of the emphasis away from annual (short-term) performance criteria to longer-term, more distant, performance targets. Long-term benefits – under this element lies the whole complex world of pension entitlement and benefits – of little or only passing interest to young employees but vitally important to their older colleagues. For a long time pensions were seen to be quite separate from pay but today, influenced no doubt by the rarity of 'one company' careers, pensions are viewed as an integral part of the package.

There are also other benefits – which includes a variety of items, sometimes hopelessly undervalued by the recipients. They include medical insurance, company cars, holidays and so on. It is interesting to note that a paid holiday is a post-1940s phenomenon.

Finally, flexible compensation is considered. The fairly recent innovation in corporate pay policies of introducing choice, an idea having taken off in the USA, is gaining increasing popularity in the UK and mainland Europe.

A brief illustrative case study is presented, which is intended to bring together some of the issues, to show how a consultancy intervention is used to resolve a 'reward problem'.

The pay debate

We live in a time when there is intense public interest in pay, and particularly the pay of senior people who run our large organisations. Certainly pay is a subject about which everyone feels they have inside knowledge because, except for the very few, most of us are paid salaries, pay or fees in some form or other. Hence there is an in-built barometer in each of us that gives us a view of what everyone else is paid relative to how much we are paid ourselves, loosely connected to the perceived size of the job and value of our own job. Hence someone on £30 000 per year may have difficulty in understanding how anyone can be paid, or can justify being paid £300 000 per year. The easy option is to say it is an obscene amount. Yet, companies are not charities. Most business people are 'hard-nosed' about costs, including payroll costs, so how does anyone come to earn this amount of money each year for doing a job? It is precisely this argument with which this chapter is concerned, because, unless all the factors of this increasingly complex subject are taken into account, the debate has little more relevance than buying a ticket in the national lottery, which is a non-strategic investment.

Many years ago there was an article that compared the pay of a vicar, a young accountant and a renowned barrister at the Commercial Bar. The story goes that the young accountant felt aggrieved that the barrister, whom he regarded as merely providing a social service, earned ten times as much as he earned. The accountant felt he did a real job of work but, compared to the barrister, he was seriously underpaid. The barrister's 'defence' was that he would not be able to earn his large fees unless someone was prepared to pay them. Both of them were at a loss as to where to place the vicar whose 'stipend' was a fraction of the accountant's salary. Eventually the vicar was categorised as a middle-level person, earning a working-class salary but living in upper-level accommodation.

This anecdote, in a way, encapsulates the pay policy dilemma which includes the market rate for the job, the contribution of the job to the organisation, relativities, perks and benefits, job security, the pay market, ability to pay and so on. Obviously we need to look at this subject much more closely to try to understand what pay policy is all about, and what place it has in the strategies of the business.

The pay debate is a most important subject since most businesses spend a very large proportion of their gross income on paying the people who work for them, and a high proportion of this is related to the senior people who direct the business.

The argument here is not one of emotion but rather a more business led situation whereby the company needs to spend a sum of money in order to pay those who work for it, hence it must set out to spend this money wisely, appropriately and in a businesslike manner.

To return to the example, the barrister may be appropriately paid for his High Court cases, which are very exposed, but he could run short of work if he went to a regional chambers and demanded the same level of fees. This is not to say that he is less skilled in country practice, it is just that the salary (operating fixed costs) may not meet the fees (gross revenues) for the work he can attract in a small country practice. Now it has long been argued that people do not work only for money. This is true but it is also true that there needs to be a balance between career opportunity, job security, locality, working conditions, social interaction and money. Fig 6.1 describes the 'perceived' balance.

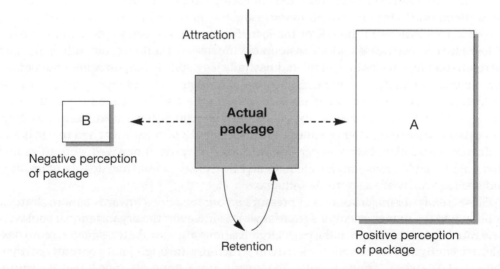

Fig 6.1   The perceived package

The requirement is to structure a salary package which will attract someone to the job in the first place. The salary package needs to be large enough to attract and indeed retain that person because, if they are good, everyone else in the marketplace is trying to employ them as well (often through the offer of an attractive salary). Once in the job then the object is to provide all the supportive people-related things like good communications, good working conditions, the opportunity to develop and progress. The salary together with the above supportive facilities will lead the person to have a perception of the package which may be larger than reality.

The opposite effect is that, in the absence of a supporting human resource policy, individuals can develop a perception of their salary package which is smaller than reality and there is a good excuse for them to leave. It is important therefore to establish the balance between the right package and the right supportive HR policy.

In this chapter, the changes to the working environment which have occurred over the last ten or so years will be examined. These pressures have caused major changes to managing people in general and pay policies in particular.

The people interface

At this juncture we perhaps need to step back a little and consider the social and business society in which we now find ourselves. The inference is that the workplace is just as socially complex as the non-working place. But society generally feels remote while the workplace is something which can be changed and, what is more, we pay people to manage that change. Pay and pay policies are interwoven in this society.

The argument can be made, that the pressure for change in HR policies and practices stems from economic, societal and technical change. Globalisation of business through new technology and capital mobility means virtually all businesses have to think in terms of international markets, suppliers and potential customers. Economic turbulence can spread from stock market fluctuations, and interest rate changes across the globe and the local economic conditions in each country combine with internationally determined trends to affect labour markets and the rate of price and wage inflation. The two major recessions in the UK of the last 15 years (in the early 1980s and the early 1990s) have in each case had a considerable impact on trading competitiveness, and therefore on HR policies in general and pay policies in particular, on trade union membership and militancy, on pay rates, and a more fundamental influence on organisation structure and the nature of occupations. Parallel to these wider economic pressures for change are new social trends. Expectations and values have also been changing, towards a climate of greater openness, towards an individual approach to rewards and a clearer association between performance and rewards. Improved education and changing lifestyle, demographic changes and the consequential debates about taxation and social security are also strong influences.

These trends are major sources of pressure on organisations towards a more strategic approach to the management of people at work. However, the organisational context is now much less secure than in the past. Organisations are now flatter, smaller, more flexible, are configured increasingly as federal structures, through joint ventures, partnerships and franchise arrangements. The steady trend towards developed structures following a differentiated business strategy has accelerated as companies seek to be close to their markets. Occupations are also changing: managerial work has become like other occupations, performance is measured, short-term contracts and casual work are common (for example interim managers and temporary executives), and managers work frequently in teams. 'Empowerment' implies a re-alignment in managerial roles and changes to management style. Many of these features are to be found in other occupations. For example teams working through semi-autonomous work groups, sub-contracting and the increase in part-time work are found in all occupations. The career concept has collapsed, with consequences for the psychological contract between employer and employee.

Gone are the days when the employer could offer a job for life. In those days even the term reward would not have been used. 'You are lucky to work for us laddy so don't do anything silly, obey the rules and one day if you do a good job you will be doing my job and ensuring that I continue to get a good pension', was the order of the day. But all that has changed, we now have a change to the psychological contract, which has an immense effect on employment practices.

The psychological contract is defined as an implied bargain between employer and employee, an understanding of the relationship in terms of what will be granted from the organisation (including reward in its widest sense, and status, power and influence, a sense of achievement, social relationships and job satisfaction), in return for physical and mental effort, commitment, co-operation, flexibility, enthusiasm, creativity and willingness on the part of the employee.

The end to any long-term career prospects, and the end of job security, mean most organisations have been re-examining the psychological contract, substituting 'employ-ability' for career. By playing on the other HR policies, such as development, job enlargement, and job enrichment, organisations try to offer employees sufficient interest and development opportunity in their current roles to enhance their employability in the labour market as a whole. This implies a broad coherence between the policies.

The importance of an integrated 'bundle' of HR policies was discussed at the start of this book when it was suggested there is also a need for integration of HR policies, so that they present a coherent management philosophy to employees, and that corporate values such as customer care and total quality management are embedded into the way work and people are managed. In the design of reward policies coherence and business strategy integration must be matched with the social acceptability of the policies, and their value as instruments to guide and to shape behaviours. The need for flexibility at a personal level and for an individual package supports the concept of cafeteria-based schemes for example.

Corporate responsibilities

So far social and internal changes to the subject of reward have been discussed, but over the last few years, under the banner of good 'corporate governance', a number of external changes of a more regulatory nature have taken place which have particularly focused on directors' pay.

One of the first of these initiatives was the Cadbury Committee, or to give it its full title The Committee on the Financial Aspects of Corporate Governance, which was set up under the Chairmanship of Sir Adrian Cadbury in May 1991. It was instigated by the accountancy bodies and the London Stock Exchange following a series of corporate scandals including a number of companies which, shortly prior to their collapse, had registered audited reports from which there was absolutely no indication that they were anything other than in a healthy trading condition. Membership of the Committee was made up of representatives from industry, shareholder groups and members of the accounting profession. The Committee's Report (Report on the Financial Aspects of Corporate Governance, 24 May 1995), which received a very mixed press, was based upon two major premises:

- self-regulation, rather than statutory enforcement, is the best way to improve the way companies are run; and
- it is the financial markets, rather than the regulators, that are likely to provide the most effective control over those companies that fail to reach acceptable standards of corporate governance.

The Report proposed a Voluntary Code of Best Practice aimed at all listed companies (but which others are encouraged to follow). This code covered:

- *Regular meetings* – that boards should meet regularly and retain full and effective control over the company.
- *Division of responsibility* – there should be a clearly accepted division of responsibilities at the head of a company. The combining of the roles of chairman and chief executive is to be tolerated only where there is a strong and independent element on the board.
- *Calibre of non-executive directors* – The board should include non-executive directors of sufficient calibre and number for their views to carry significant weight in the board's decisions.
- *Formal decision schedule* – The board should have a formal schedule of matters specifically reserved to it for decision.
- *Procedure for independent professional advice* – there should be an agreed procedure for directors in the furtherance of their duties to take independent professional advice if necessary, at the company's expense.
- *Access to the company secretary* – all directors should have access to the advice and services of the company secretary, a role which is critical to ensure that proper board procedures are followed.
- *Independent judgement vs non-executive directors* – non-executive directors should bring an independent judgement to bear on all issues and should be free from any business or other relationship which could materially interfere with the exercise of their independent judgement, apart from their fees and shareholding.
- *Selection of non-executive directors* – non-executive directors should be selected through a formal process and both this process and their appointment should be a matter for the board as a whole.
- *Directors' service contracts* – directors' service contracts should not exceed three years without shareholders' approval.
- *Disclosure of total emoluments* – there should be full and clear disclosure of directors' total emoluments.
- *Directors' pay* – executive directors' pay should be subject to the recommendations of a remuneration committee made up wholly or mainly of non-executive directors.

The Committee also made a number of further recommendations which were contained in the full Report rather than in the Code of Best Practice: in particular these referred to the disclosure of directors' total emoluments and those of the chairman and highest paid UK directors, where it was recommended that separate figures should be given for their salary and performance-related elements and the criteria on which performance is measured should be explained. In addition it was suggested that relevant information about stock options, stock appreciation rights and pension contributions should also be given.

The Committee stated that future service contracts should not exceed three years without shareholders' approval and the Companies Act 1985 should be amended in line with this recommendation. This would strengthen shareholders' control over levels of compensation for loss of office. It felt that boards should appoint remunerations committees, consisting wholly or mainly of non-executive directors, to recommend to the board the remuneration for the executive directors in all its forms, drawing on outside advice as necessary. Executive directors should play no part in the decisions on their own remuneration. The Cadbury Committee found it difficult to devise procedures which would allow a dialogue between shareholders and the remuneration committee on individual directors' packages because, as they see it, 'a director's remuneration is not a matter which can sensibly be reduced to a vote for or against'. The Committee also found that extending the rules for disclosure – such as increasing the list of directors who would be individually identified, along with the make-up of their remuneration (such as was happening in the United States) – would need to be further investigated before being put forward.

Many commentators consider the Cadbury Committee 'ducked' one of the most pressing remuneration issues at senior Director level. Commentators believe the Committee should have suggested that the accountability of the remuneration committee be exercised through the route of shareholder debate, if not at the annual general meeting (AGM) of shareholders, then by some other process.

The corporate governance issue has also been hot news in the USA for the last few years. Unlike our voluntary approach, the Securities and Exchange Commission (SEC) published rules that extensively modified existing regulation governing executive compensation disclosure and communications among shareholders. These new rules resulted in unprecedented debate. The rules on compensation disclosure became effective from 1 January 1993.

The requirement to produce Summary Compensation Tables is regarded as the linchpin of executive compensation disclosure and has replaced the former narrative. The new rules required that the tables be completed for each 'named' executive. A named executive is the CEO and the four other most highly compensated executives with salary and bonuses over $100 000. The table has seven columns and requires that these columns be completed for the last three fiscal years. It is broken down into annual and long-term compensation and includes:

1. Annual compensation for the last three years in terms of salary, bonus and other annual compensation.
2. Long-term compensation for the last three years in regard to restricted stock awards, options and pay-outs.

The other compensation column encompassed all annual compensation not properly categorised as salary or bonus (such as amounts reimbursed during the fiscal year for the payment of taxes). The amount in this column must include perquisites and personal benefits (such as a company car for non-business use) unless they are less than $50 000 or 10 per cent of reported annual salary and bonus.

The disclosure requires other details in the summary table such as individual stock options (including stock appreciation rights) granted to named officers and the values of grants, aggregate exercises and year-end holding values and long-term incentive plan awards during the last fiscal year.

The registrant may elect to disclose option values based upon the present day value at the date of grant under any option pricing model, or based upon potential realisable values of the option, assuming both 5 and 10 per cent annual stock price appreciation. Any option pricing model relied upon must be described. In addition, any other non-standard arrangements with directors (including consulting arrangements) must be described and the full amounts described during the completed fiscal year declared.

A Compensation Committee Report must be produced in addition to the summary compensation table: the compensation committee or, in its absence, the entire board must report the compensation offered to named executives and its relationship to company performance. The description must include the factors and criteria upon which compensation was based and each qualitative and quantitative measure of performance such as sales, earnings, return on assets, return on equity and market share.

There are also rules about performance presentation. As a complement to the compensation committee report, the registrant must report company performance in the form of a line graph. The graph must compare shareholders' return with a performance indicator of the overall market and a peer comparison. For performance indicators Standard and Poor's 50 index, or another broad equity market index including companies in the same exchange and comparable market capitalisation group, may be used. For peer comparison, either a published index or a self-determined comparison may be used.

The expanded compensation disclosure through charts and graphs will be likely to focus shareholders' attention on disparities between executive compensation and corporate results. During times of poor share performance, this focus may increase the likelihood of shareholder litigation citing excessive executive compensation. Under state law, excessive compensation may be considered 'a waste of corporate assets' by directors.

In the past, lawsuits of this nature have been infrequent in the USA; but commentators put this down to the inability of shareholders to furnish 'comparable' evidence. Under these new rules, the focus is clearly on comparability so, in the future, comparable evidence will be much easier to obtain.

One of the concerns that companies have in the USA is that, given the heavy reporting responsibilities of remuneration committees, and the emotive nature of the subject, involving shareholder and executive alike, it is sometimes difficult to persuade non-executive directors to serve on American compensation committees.

The continuing public interest and the fundamental questions about equity in reward policy have continued the debate in the UK. Following increasing pressure from the media and other sources on very large increases to directors, particularly those in the newly privatised utilities, the John Major government appointed a committee to make recommendations on the regulation of directors' pay. This committee was set up under the chairmanship of Sir Richard Greenbury and it made its report on 17 July 1995.

The Report and the Greenbury Code of Best Practice hit the headlines from the day they were published due to the limitation recommended upon the tax favoured discretionary option share schemes (which was immediately adopted by the government). In particular, one of the large food retailers, Asda, which granted these options to all its staff, complained bitterly that, rather than limiting the advantages to directors, the new regulations were actually more severe on lower level employees.

Greenbury's terms of reference were to identify good practice in determining directors' remuneration and to prepare a code of such practice. The resulting recommendations were generally welcomed, despite the fact that certain aspects were criticised.

The Code focusses on three issues, namely:

1. accountability – remuneration committees of non-executive directors should make an annual report for shareholders, with their chairmen being present at AGMs;
2. transparency – companies' approach to remuneration must be explained and full disclosure provided on all elements of the remuneration package; and
3. performance – linking rewards for executive directors to results, thereby aligning the interests of executive directors and shareholders.

For the future, remuneration committees will need to ensure that they have in place a process which begins each year with obtaining the pay data and other information needed to determine directors' remuneration and culminates with the AGM. Whereas in the past it was not essential for remuneration committees to formulate and pursue a written policy on directors' remuneration, this is no longer the case. At the very least, this will focus the minds of remuneration committees on developing policies which are fully capable of being justified and explained to shareholders in due course. It may also encourage explicit reward policies further down the organisation, covering all employees.

A key part of the process is for remuneration committees to seek objective external advice – particularly on comparative pay levels and how best to link rewards to the company's performance as measured against its sector peers or an appropriate index. This in turn begs the question of which performance measure(s) should be selected and, indeed, how the chosen performance measure(s) should be applied in practice in a way which ensures that executive directors are paid in line with performance and that the total rewards potentially available to executive directors are not excessive.

The goal must be for chairmen of remuneration committees to be able to attend AGMs in the knowledge that all reasonable steps have been taken to ensure that the remuneration policies adopted are not just defensible but are also manifestly in the interests of shareholders.

The Greenbury Code of Practice has yet to be evaluated and as yet it is difficult to see how it will all work. There are however some interesting questions to be answered which would enable us to see the contribution of the Code of Practice. For example, will all remuneration committees in future consist entirely of non-executive directors (as opposed to the Cadbury recommendation that at least a majority should be non-executive directors)? Some companies have already indicated to the Stock Exchange that they consider it essential to include their chief executive on the remuneration committee. How frequently will remuneration committees seek shareholders' approval for the remuneration policy set out in their annual report? This question is particularly relevant where there is no specific remuneration issue, such as the introduction of a new long-term incentive scheme, to seek shareholders' approval of.

What type of comparator information will be required? How should it be presented to shareholders? Should the report of the remuneration committee set out the comparative figures for remuneration and employment conditions in respect of other employees of the company concerned? Or is it enough for the remuneration committee simply to obtain these figures and bear them in mind when determining directors' remuneration? How best is the disclosure of pension entitlements to be explained to shareholders? This is likely to be an issue in cases where the figures disclosed are volatile from year to year or increase substantially year on year. Does obtaining shareholders' approval for long-term incentive schemes require a company to set out precisely what the performance measures and targets will be on a year-by-year basis, or just for the first year of a scheme's operation? When replacing share option schemes with restricted or incentive share schemes, how best should the initial value (expressed as a percentage of annual basic salary) of restricted share awards be determined? How practical is it for companies to pay termination payments in instalments? Could doing so encourage departing directors not to seek new employment while negotiations for compensation are continuing or, more generally, until the staged payments have ceased?

The answers to these questions will have a considerable bearing on the future of governance on pay. If you are one of those who believes that what happens in the USA eventually, in some form, finds its way to Europe via the UK, then we could be in for a period of fairly heavy legislation on executive pay which has a knock-on effect. But Europe, and Europeans, are in general much more secretive about pay than the Americans. For example, we still, after many years, feel uncomfortable about telling anyone who wants know how much we are paid; as a generalisation, we can say the Americans have no such reservations.

Total compensation

With increasing regulation on pay, the social move towards greater individual bargaining on pay and conditions outlined in Chapter 5 and the greater awareness about all reports of what and how we get paid, it is not surprising that the concept of total remuneration (or total compensation to use the American term) has rapidly developed. This entails the consideration of all elements of the package which are best broken down as follows:

- *Base pay* – The regular part of the pay package, reviewed usually on an annual basis.
- *Variable pay* – Includes annual bonuses which are dependent upon actual or discretionary rewards for the achievement of levels of performance of the company, or individuals or both.
- *Longer-term incentives* – Usually long-term bonuses or reward plans on usually three years, or longer targets.
- *Long-term or deferred pay* – Usually in the form of pensions.
- *Perquisites* – Sometimes called other benefits which includes status-related items like company cars, or social items like health insurance plans.

Let us therefore look at the strategic information on each of these elements in turn.

Base pay

There is still an ongoing requirement to know whether or not the base salary is 'appropriate'. This requirement leads on to a need to devise a pay policy that places the base pay of an employee on a relative footing for similar jobs in a particular marketplace and having parity within the internal corporate structure.

However where organisations can make mistakes is when they try to use comparative pay data (from surveys, salary clubs or published information) too simplistically.

In setting a pay policy, be it at the median, between the median and upper quartile, and so on, two considerations must be paramount:

1. Are you comparing like with like as far as the jobs are concerned? This takes one into the whole realm of 'job matching'. Most good professional surveys spend a great deal of time and effort to ensure that the jobs are reasonably matched before comparing salary information.

For example a general job such as company secretary can be modestly paid in a small firm where the duties are more administrative than legal. In a large conglomerate, this job may command a very high salary due to the expertise and experience required of the person fulfilling the role. Merely to select the median salary between these two extremes clearly is nonsense. Even if the sales turnover or market capitalisation of the participants is taken into account, care has to be taken that one is comparing the job in question with individuals who carry out the full range of duties and responsibilities expected of the job.

For this reason the survey material needs to be used with discretion and, wherever possible, some sort of job matching methodology needs to be applied.

2. Pay is often related to the business environment in which individuals work. Very often we are asked to compare pay in a defined comparator group of companies simply because they are in the same business sector or sub-sector as the enquiring company. However often when one runs some fairly simple business analysis ratios over the selected companies, one can see that there may be some companies whose performance is inappropriate. The simple question is 'do you want to hitch your wagon to companies which are either going out of business or contracting so much that they no longer enjoy the status they once had in your business sector?'

Figures 6.2–6.4 show examples of such analysis carried out with a selection of companies in the electrical retail and distribution sector to demonstrate the point.

Best practice

What companies are actually asking of pay research is what is best practice on pay in any sector, or among similar companies or jobs so that a solid foundation for the remuneration policy can be established. In undertaking best practice research, it is often helpful to look beyond the obvious, and to try to glean the best practices in as wide an area as possible. This takes time and effort but it is usually worthwhile because so many other human resource processes and policies can be built upon a good, coherent pay policy.

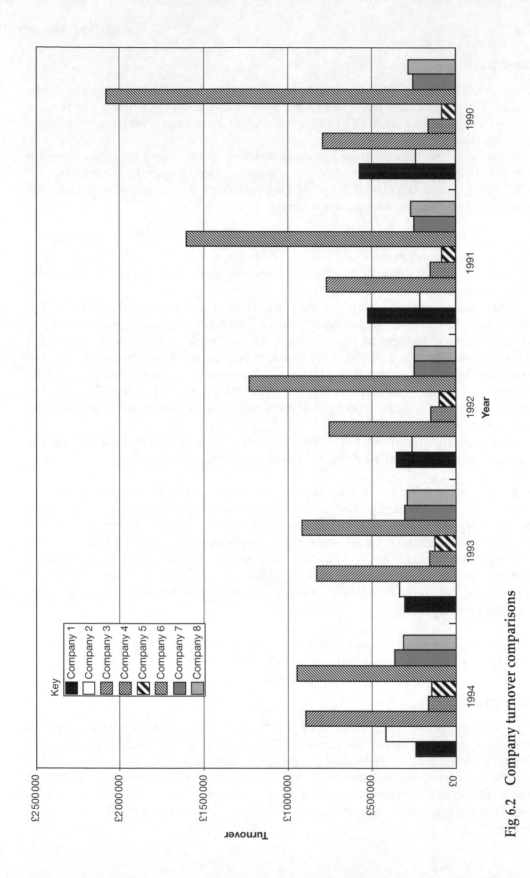

Fig 6.2 Company turnover comparisons

84

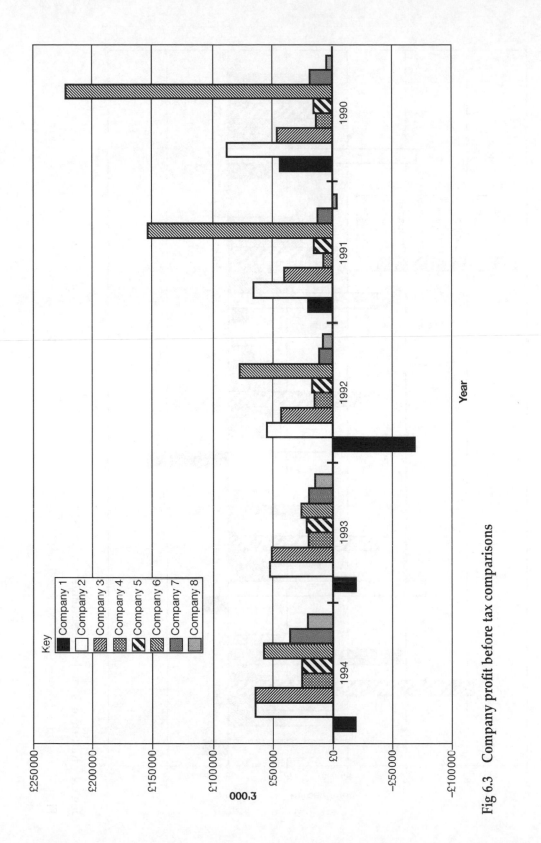

Fig 6.3   Company profit before tax comparisons

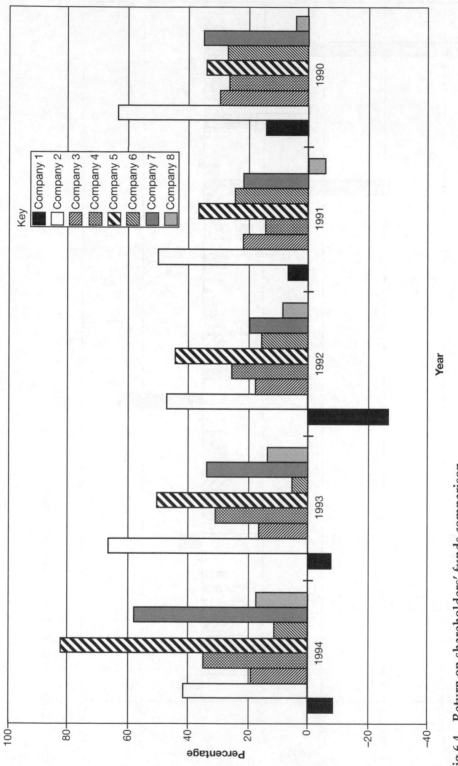

Fig 6.4 Return on shareholders' funds comparison

Variable pay

In the whole area of pay management and theory, it is probably the variable pay element of the package where the most change has occurred. The ratio between base pay and variable or bonus pay is steadily increasing. Ten years ago the average bonus paid was around 3 per cent to 4 per cent for staff and 5 per cent to 6 per cent for management. Of these bonuses, 80 per cent were at the discretion of the management and often come in some form of Christmas or summer bonus. As such they were really an enforced form of saving. All this has changed. Management bonuses, particularly in the very large organisations, can be as high as 30 per cent to 40 per cent of base salary. In other words, they are 'performance' bonuses, based on measurable criteria, and vary widely in accordance to the performance of the company. Sometimes they are share related, sometimes cash and it is these cash related bonuses which we consider first.

Probably the most important issue in business today is how to manage the organisation more effectively. Organisations can use their financial resources to purchase the best equipment, the best market information, the best information technology and so on. Chief executives generally agree that the one thing that is not for sale in the open market is motivation and commitment. Hence they spend a great deal of time trying to achieve this vital ingredient to corporate success.

For this reason, we believe that the whole subject of managing performance must be approached, not from the standpoint of simply designing bonus schemes, but as a business-led initiative which results in business performance improvement. In our experience, the success of the final performance plan will be very dependent upon performance concepts that are easily understood. However, the plan design must be capable of incorporating a number of diverse factors, business targets and required behaviours which are seen to culminate in the desired or optimum results. In other words, the end result must be apparently simple – regardless of how complex the inputs are in reality.

One of the common mistakes which we come across is that, in striving to achieve a high level of comprehension among the performance plan participants, companies tend to over-simplify their performance target factors. In reality most jobs are just not that simple. Incentive plans that are linked to a single performance factor are generally inappropriate to the management of performance and hence the management of the business in all its aspects. Therefore, the introduction of performance incentive plans that do address the business needs are not simple in their design although, to be effective, they must still be relatively simple to communicate, to understand and to implement.

To achieve the above, a process for the introduction of multi-factor incentive plan design needs to be considered. This approach takes account of:

- corporate and individual performance levels;
- the interface between team and individual contributions;
- the impact on the bottom line, calculated through cost value analysis; and
- the ability to weight the reward for the achievement of hard measurable targets against the softer (developmental, organisational, expediency) targets.

The discipline in establishing such 'multi-factor' incentive plans is complementary to the corporate planning process and moreover, often has the advantage of communicating the relationship between individual achievement and the overall corporate grand design. The other advantage of such a disciplined approach means that corporate objectives and goals systematically cascade down the organisation.

In less formal approaches to performance, we often find there is pressure to search for individual objectives which may not necessarily be adding anything to the business, or indeed may not be complementary to the corporate direction required at that particular time. Certainly among the more senior employees in the organisation, individuals often regard the outcome of a well-designed and carefully implemented incentive plan, not so much in terms of monetary gain (although this is important), but more as a finite measure of their personal success within the organisation. In such plans, care needs to be taken to ensure that individuals do not alienate themselves from each other. Hence, sufficient regard needs to be given to team performance.

We hold the view that incentive planning should be more than merely devising a system that will give a monetary reward for the achievement of a set of targets. At best such off-the-shelf systems end up becoming a pay delivery mechanism, at worst a source of expected additional income, that soon takes on the appearance of an entitlement. A properly thought through and specifically tailored scheme should become the cornerstone of an organisation's performance management philosophy in which the incentive payment is the *recognition* of performance, not the *driver* of performance.

A well constructed plan should:

- increase motivation;
- reward achievement in a manner which is defensible in terms of business performance and shareholder return;
- enable the effective management of performance;
- have the ability to balance hard, measurable targets and objectives with those that are less easy to measure but which are important to the business strategy and to the individuals themselves;
- ensure that all members of the team, at whatever level, are working and performing against targets and goals which collectively make up the corporate objectives;
- assist with the management of bad performance as well as good performance; and
- recognise the competencies required of the various job roles.

The definition of job roles is critical to understanding the 'demand' the organisation places upon its employees. Such definitions set the context within which individuals' performance against these 'demands' can be assessed.

The measurement of performance using a more generic framework often results in the use of criteria that are so generic they become meaningless in terms of communicating contributions and expectations. Role analyses can provide a base language that is both organisationally and functionally specific and a vocabulary that can explain the different demands of levels across the organisation and within job families.

Performance bonuses have, in recent years, come under a great deal of criticism – which is often justified. When we look at such plans which are not working, they invariably not only suffer from being too simplistic in concept, as previously mentioned, but also they fail because they start somewhere in the middle of the organisation where targets may not be readily identified with corporate direction. The only justification for bonus plans must be to 'oil the wheels' in order to take the organisation forward.

Fig 6.5 demonstrates this point and also takes into account that the four basic requirements of business are finance, markets, a product or service and people which should

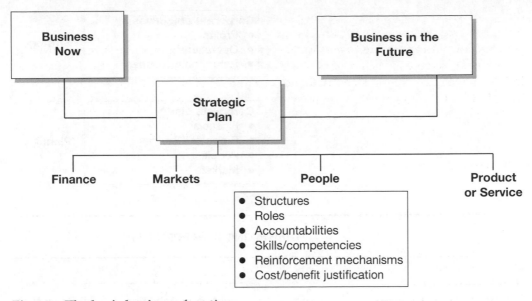

Fig 6.5   The basic business functions

all be considered in the original concept of the plan. Without any one of these basic requirements, the business will collapse. Hence it is essential to understand what the business must achieve, and how much it can afford to spend in order to get there. Turning the concept into a strategy which means turning corporate objectives into performance plans is the next step (Fig 6.6).

The 'making it happen gap' is most important. Many organisations spend a great deal of time creating their corporate plans and ignore the fact that, in order to realise those plans, a disciplined cascading of targets, buying-in of achievement levels and appropriate financial inducement need to be carefully considered. This latter stage is probably just as important and time consuming as the planning stage.

One of the important questions to be considered is whether the organisation is ready for the discipline of performance incentives. It is often assumed that every organisation is capable of taking on board a performance incentive programme and this is clearly not the case. If it were then life would be a great deal simpler – we would merely recommend that you triple all the salaries if a certain target level is achieved and then sit back and watch the business achieve success. Achieving strategic objectives requires more than merely throwing money at the problem.

One of the make or break factors that play a large part in the success of incentive plans is indeed the attitude of employees towards the organisation. Taking just two attitudinal aspects, those of 'clarity' and 'trust', we are given a great insight into the organisation. If employees demonstrate or are perceived to have a low level of trust in the top management, and they are also unclear of the corporate goals, this is not the environment in which to introduce an incentive plan. At the other end of the spectrum, a high level of trust by employees and a high clarity of corporate objectives is the ideal situation. Corporate approaches to top pay have a significant impact on trust and on the climate of relationships.

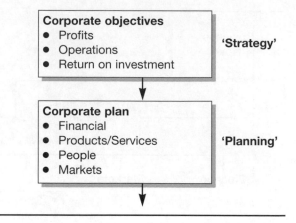

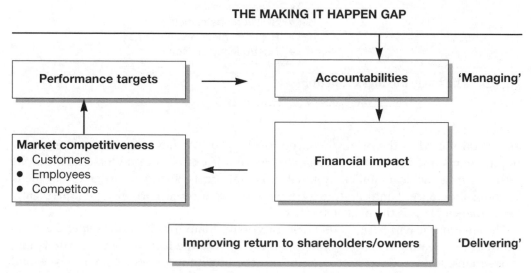

Fig 6.6   The business concept

The cost/benefit analysis is an important part of the incentive design and answers the question which every chief executive always asks, that is 'What is it going to cost me and, having spent the money what do I get back?' One ignores this question at one's peril because it often reduces performance incentive plans to personnel administration exercises thus excluding them from being an integral part of the strategic planning process.

Fig 6.7 shows what is required:

- a clear idea of the breakeven target at corporate, divisional, departmental and sector levels;
- a performance investment policy, that is how much will be paid out before the target is reached, known as the 'threshold';
- a projection beyond target which estimates the corporate gain and the individuals' gain. This line rises steeply because most of the overhead costs are actually catered for in the target; and
- a facility to shift the 'crossover' targets caters for the 'investment' in performance below target.

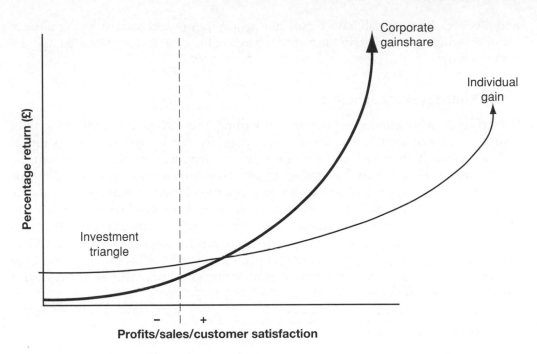

Fig 6.7   The cost/benefit concept

This exercise tends to answer the various questions that are posed when the plan is being introduced.

However one should not assume that the amount of incentive pay would be the same for each position in the organisation. For example, sales staff may best be paid on a highly geared total cash package with base salaries at or near market lower quartile and their total cash (after including bonuses) at the market upper quartile. Such a gearing may be totally inappropriate for senior management or other roles where the job should have a longer-term focus. Similarly the interval between the achievement of the performance target and the incentive payment may need to be considered in order to achieve the best financial impact. Hence an annual bonus pay-out, which many organisations automatically tend to opt for, may not be the most cost-effective way of gaining improved performance.

Longer-term tax-effective incentives

Over the years it has become more and more popular to make part of the employees' reward package in the form of shares. The reasons for this are twofold. First, it is assumed that employee company awareness will be enhanced if part of the remuneration is linked, in some way, to the company's share price. Second, the government has over the years provided tax relief for these kinds of payments, therefore there is a monetary advantage on the part of both the employee and the employer to consider these types of pay schemes. It should be noted however, that organisations such as the ABI (Association of British Insurers), NAPF (National Association of Pension Funds) and the Stock Exchange all have regulations which they expect companies to follow in order that their investment, in the form of shares in the company, is protected and not unduly diluted.

Profit sharing share schemes

Subject to certain conditions at the time of writing, these allow up to £8000 worth of shares to be allocated to employees each year, free of income tax and National Insurance contributions. All employees who meet a length of service requirement (no longer than five years) must be eligible to participate. Shares must be allocated to participants 'on similar terms' – for example in proportion to salary. Full tax relief is only available if the shares are left in a trust for three years. Combined with a 'single-company' personal equity plan, this can provide a very tax-effective method of capital accumulation. (It is worth noting that the value to which £8000 per annum accumulates over, say, 10 years is £105 654 at 5 per cent per annum and £140 249 at 10 per cent per annum. The potential for substantial capital formation through these plans over a career is obvious, if underexploited.)

Matching offer schemes

These are a specialised version of approved profit sharing schemes. Eligible employees purchase shares in the company (with after-tax funds) and the company allocates one or more 'free' shares for each one purchased. The tax position of the 'free' shares is the same as in the standard profit sharing schemes.

Savings-related share option schemes

Employees agree to save between £5 and £250 a month in a Save-As-You-Earn account with a bank or building society. When they start saving, they are granted options over the number of shares which can be bought with their total savings and tax-free terminal bonus. Assuming a 20 per cent discount and seven-year option term, options can be granted over shares worth up to £24 375 at the grant date. Again, all employees who meet the length of service requirement must be eligible.

The gain on exercise of these options is exempt from income tax. It is possible to avoid capital gains tax on disposal by transferring the shares to a 'single-company' personal equity plan soon after the option is exercised.

Inland Revenue approved schemes

At the end of September 1995 the Inland Revenue had approved the following number of schemes:

Scheme	Number approved
Discretionary (or executive) share option	6407
Profit sharing scheme (including the matching offer variation)	1175
Savings-related (SAYE) share option	1478

Longer-term incentives for senior executives

It is agreed that those who are the primary influence on the fortunes of an organisation are its senior executives and, because of this, longer-term incentives in the form of shares are most appropriate for this group.

Certainly the most frequently used long-term incentives for senior executives in the UK for many years have been what have come to be called discretionary share options – discretionary because it is the company who can choose who will be the recipients of these options. Some organisations give options only at senior director level, others provide them right down the organisation.

The concept of share options is fairly simple, that is the employee is given an 'option' over a certain number of shares and over a specific period, usually around three years. After this period the employee can take up his or her options. At this stage he or she pays back the company for the shares at the original price at which the shares were offered. So, if three years after the option was granted the share price has increased, the employee has increased the value of his or her investment in the company's shares. The idea originated in the US, and the original concept was to allow employees to accumulate capital in the company for which they work.

However, over the years, various limitations on such schemes have been realised on the grounds that they have tended not to encourage longer-term share ownership by executives, as many of them sell shares immediately after they have exercised options; when share prices fall, executives with 'underwater' options may have an incentive to leave to join a competitor who can offer options at current market prices. Although 'underwater' options continue to have a value, they are often seen as being worthless and/or demotivating by the option holder.

For these and other reasons, a number of leading companies have adopted other types of long-term incentive – either in place of or to supplement share options. This trend towards alternative types of incentive plan has been boosted by the Greenbury Report recommendations and by the lower limits on income tax relief for discretionary share options granted since 17 July 1995 (the maximum value of subsisting options which an individual may hold being £30 000). Companies are now more likely to consider a wider range of long-term incentive arrangements, including modified share options. These changes are to be welcomed, as the emphasis is shifting from largely tax-driven grants of options, to a more thoughtful and genuine attempt to link executive compensation to building shareholder value.

At the same time, it is felt that the communication, tax and financial merits of all-employee profit sharing schemes have been undervalued as executive compensation tools. It is expected that these plans, savings-related share options and single-company personal equity plans will attract renewed interest in the wake of Greenbury, the changes in the taxation of discretionary share options and the ABI's likely future approach. The ABI has welcomed the Greenbury recommendations but it held back from issuing further guidelines until the Stock Exchange had finalised its new listing requirements.

There are alternatives to traditional share options which have so emerged and these fall into the categories described below.

Modified share option plans

Some companies have come to the conclusion that share options are still the best way of achieving their objectives of attracting, retaining and motivating senior executives. They have decided to keep their share option plans but may change their performance criteria to comply with the Greenbury recommendations. Some companies are requiring executives to own a specified number of shares as a condition of being granted new share options. This trend mirrors the practice of many US companies. Other US techniques, such as performance acceleration of the exercise date under option plans and/or grants of options with progressively higher exercise prices, will also need to be considered.

Restricted/incentive share plans

These involve the award of shares to participants which do not vest until three to five years later. Vesting is generally conditional on continuing employment and on specified performance conditions having been met. No income tax is normally payable until the conditions are met and the shares vest.

Co-investment plans

Under these plans, a part of an executive's annual bonus is generally deferred and invested in the company's shares. In return, the company will make a matching investment. Neither category of shares can be disposed of for a period of three to five years. On cessation of employment, the matching investment is forfeited and, in some variations, the deferred bonus is also forfeited. Income tax is generally paid on the vesting date for the matching investment. The timing of the tax on the deferred bonus will depend on the terms of the plan.

Long-term cash bonus plans and performance unit plans

These are essentially deferred bonus plans which measure performance over more than one year and make a payment in the form of cash. This allows for maximum flexibility in the choice of performance measures and other design features. Income tax will generally be triggered at the time when any conditions of the award have been met, even if actual payment is deferred until a later date. If a payment is in cash, then there will also be a National Insurance contribution liability. The most appropriate plan will obviously depend on the company's precise circumstances and objectives.

Long-term benefits

Under long-term incentives the major element is that of the pension. Recent legislation and practice has made the whole subject of pensions very strategic particularly for the higher paid whose salary exceeds the so-called earnings cap.

Pension schemes can broadly be considered in the two categories (1) 'defined benefit' (including 'final salary') schemes, where the future benefits that emerge are driven by a formula based on pensionable service and future salary; and (2) 'money purchase' (or 'defined contribution') schemes where the future benefits emerging are the accumulated proceeds of the contributions paid by and in respect of each individual member.

1. Defined benefit schemes – the future benefits that will emerge from a defined benefit pension scheme for an employee will depend upon a range of factors, including the normal retirement age under the scheme, the accrual rate of pension, attaching spouses' and pension increase rights, and so on. Established actuarial valuation techniques involve projection of estimated future benefits in the various contingencies of future exit (early and normal retirement, death in service, early or ill-health retirement, and so on) discounting to 'present value'.
2. Money purchase – the company contributions to a money purchase scheme in respect of each employee's membership are the measure of the value of the arrangement.

Disclosure of pensions

Whereas the Cadbury Committee focussed on the disclosure of company pension contributions, Greenbury went a stage further in recommending that the value to directors of their pension entitlement should be disclosed. This entails disclosure each year of the assessed 'present value' of the further pension rights which have been earned during the year, less any contributions paid by the director concerned, that is an approach based on the yearly increase in entitlement. The logic behind this is that the contribution paid by a company in a particular year may bear little relationship to the value of the pension entitlement enjoyed by a director, for example if a contribution holiday has been taken or the overall contribution rate for a particular pension scheme has been used.

Greenbury recognised that there is a technical issue to be addressed as to how pension entitlements earned over the year under final salary schemes should be valued. The Faculty and Institute of Actuaries were asked to advise on how companies could adopt the recommended new form of disclosure.

They issued consultative papers in September 1995 and January 1996 and in due course, a concensus will be reached between the parties involved as to the precise form disclosure will take.

The earnings cap

The earnings cap (£78 600 from 6 April 1995) affects those joining an approved pension scheme after 31 May 1989 (13 March 1989, if the scheme was not then in existence). The earnings cap is still very much a topical issue. Whereas some companies are only now addressing the matter for the first time, perhaps because job mobility at senior levels was lower during the recent recession, others are reviewing the strategies they have used to date because they have been unsatisfactory or applied inconsistently.

A number of approaches are available, including:

1. *Positive 'inaction'* – That is allowing the earnings cap to bite – difficult to sustain in a competitive market.
2. *Cash allowances* – Recognising the lack of pension provision for earnings above the cap by increasing remuneration – this may not fit a company's culture.

3. *Unfunded promises* – Unfunded unapproved retirement benefit schemes (UURBS) – under which the company agrees to pay a top-up pension (or a lump sum equivalent) in retirement out of then current revenue – relatively simple to establish, but offers less security for executives than a funded arrangement.

4. *Fund arrangements* – Funded unapproved retirement benefit schemes (FURBS) – which may be on final salary basis but are far more commonly money purchase in nature.

5. *Personal pensions* – Possibly supplemented by one of the methods in (2) to (4) above; can be the most tax-effective option for older recruits with significant retained benefits from previous approved pension schemes.

Regardless of which approach they use for the top-up, companies may first augment the benefits from the approved occupational pension scheme to the maximum allowed by the Inland Revenue (normally two-thirds of final remuneration for 20 years' service) if their approved scheme provides a less generous accrual rate.

The early approach to the earnings cap in large companies which typically had final salary approved pension schemes was usually to provide an UURBS. This promised to make up the loss in benefits caused by the earnings cap – putting the executive in the same position as if he had not been capped, with the important proviso that the promise was not backed by a separate and protected trust fund.

Although relatively few companies have yet established FURBS, they are attracting increasing interest. The main reasons are because of the dislike of the growing balance sheet provision for unfunded liabilities and a wish to contain costs, or at least to be able to predict them accurately (by moving from an UURBS to a money purchase FURBS).

Companies have recognised the problems which can arise with UURBS where the senior employee leaves service before retirement – often neither the company nor the employee wishes to continue with an unfunded promise. Furthermore employees wish for greater security.

Cash allowances

Some companies favour a cash allowance approach to the problem. This approach is simple to explain and to administer. However, the adjustment can be fairly arbitrary because a strictly equivalent compensation tends to be unsatisfactory at an individual level, due to the uncertainties about an individual's career and personal circumstances which are involved. Despite this the main advantages of this approach are: simplicity; better security and less vulnerability to future adverse changes in tax legislation for the employee than under an unfunded arrangement; and the fact that the employee may be able to invest the allowance tax-effectively in PEPs and TESSAs.

On the other hand the main disadvantages are: higher National Insurance contributions; unwelcome effects on the disclosure of cash remuneration in the annual report and accounts; and a difficulty in fixing an equitable basis for the allowance, particularly for employees earning salaries close to the earnings cap and employees of different ages. Furthermore the adjustment may be 'lost' in future salary increases and/or cause upward pressure on salary levels if it becomes 'consolidated' into basic salary. If the allowance is fixed as a percentage of salary, it will tend to over-compensate in the early years and under-compensate in the later years – thus benefiting early leavers.

Other benefits

These include the whole series of company cars, medical insurance, subsidised meals, subsidised travel, and so on. Often these benefits are very undervalued and it is amazing to see newspaper recruitment advertisements dismissing their value by saying 'usual fringe benefits'.

Introducing choice

Pay systems that allow employees some choice in the type of payment they receive have come to be known as Flexible Plans or 'Flex'. Flexible compensation started in the US driven by health care programmes. The average company in the US today spends of the order of 15 per cent of its payroll on health care so the drive is to contain these very large costs through individual selection. With the introduction of flexibility in health care the flexible choices have evolved to include other benefits and compensation elements.

The advantages of flexible programmes in the US have been seen as the opportunity for the individual to choose the type of compensation and benefit programmes which suit his or her lifestyle best. There is also an opportunity for the organisation to contain employee costs and such schemes offer a system to manage employment costs more effectively.

Employment demographics

When looking at the introduction of flexible compensation programmes, it was discovered that the demographics of employment in the US was quite radically different to that which was presumed. Whereas most compensation policies are based upon the premise of single income families one finds in the US today, and indeed also in the UK, that they only represent some 10 per cent of those in employment. All the different family combinations of double income families, single parent families, single employees, widows, divorced, and so on, have different financial aspirations. A policy which responds to these aspirations without necessarily increasing the cost of employment is seen to be a further advantage of a flexible compensation policy.

Disincentives/opportunities in the UK

The attitude of the Inland Revenue and particularly the case of Heaton & Bell, the threat imposed by the Department of Customs & Excise on the application of VAT on a choice situation, and the perceived burden of administration all previously worked against companies enthusiastically taking up flexible compensation approaches to their remuneration policy. However now that the Inland Revenue attitude towards flexible payment systems has been clarified, the Chancellor stopped the VAT issue, much better administration systems and computer programmes are available, flexible compensation policies are a much more attractive and feasible proposition.

Types of flexible compensation policies

Originally in the US a 'cafeteria' system became known as 'à la carte' in that an employee could choose from any range of benefits or compensation elements provided that they did not add up to more than the total compensation figure for that individual. Most of these systems were seen to be too bureaucratic and indeed today in the US very few organisations operate à la carte systems. The next development was what is now know as the 'modular' system which means that the employee is able to choose from a number of set menus of pay and benefit items designed to cater for the different types of employee. For instance, Plan A may be geared to single people, Plan B geared to married couples without children, Plan C to double income families, and so on.

The most popular however, is a system now called 'core plus' in which the organisation offers a core of pay and benefits and there is then a flexible selection of items which the employee can either take as cash or as a benefit. For example, the organisation may offer single membership to a medical plan but from the flexible element the employee may choose to include his or her spouse or have family cover.

Total compensation

Whatever type of flexible plan is decided upon the concept of total compensation must be addressed. Total compensation is the sum of all the cash items and the annualised value of non-cash benefits provided to the employee. The elements of total compensation are:

- cash compensation
- basic salary
- deferred cash
- incentive cash.

Other direct compensation

- share options
- share ownership
- restricted shares.

Employee benefits

- retirement benefits
- death benefits
- disability benefits
- medical benefits.

Perquisites/fringe benefits

- cars
- holidays, loans
- other.

Some of the objectives the organisation might have for the introduction of flexibility are in the realm of matching employee needs, improving employee understanding/appreciation of the pay package, recruitment or retention issues, providing value for money, containing or indeed reducing costs.

The general principles of pricing benefit elements

The policy of whether the cost of the benefits or the value to the employee is going to be the basis upon which pricing will take place is of paramount importance. In addition, companies may wish to encourage the use of certain benefits and this will determine the policy towards it and the pricing. Policies need to be drawn up to decide on what will happen to group discounts, how frequently employees will be allowed to change the various benefits, what will be the ongoing costs, what happens with staff turnover situations and finally what perceived administration costs are likely to be incurred.

Underpinning all this is the need for a good robust communications system procedure in order that employees buy in the new policy otherwise they will perceive it as simply another method for the organisation to gain at their expense.

The introduction of a flexible compensation policy is not a simple administrative procedure but can involve many aspects of pay, benefit and the attitudes of the employees towards the organisation. The pay-off to the company can be very large. In real terms it can be cost containment or indeed a much more effective way of managing the cost side of the HR function. Now that many of the income tax, VAT and administrative hurdles have largely been removed, a flexible compensation policy does appear to make good business sense.

A brief case history from a consultancy intervention which was presented initially as a reward issue illustrates how payment systems are integrated with all other aspects of managing people at work, and how the process of determining rewards is as significant as the reward itself. The intent as well as the substance are important, but so too are the technical details within any reward strategy, especially in relating any reward solution to the particular context.

A case study

Background

The company was in the hotel and leisure industry operating world-wide. The compensation and benefits delivery system in place varied by region, by hotel and by type of employee. It was a complicated system and it did not support strategic decision making in the compensation and benefits area. In particular there was no position grading system.

From a performance management perspective, there was a formal Performance Development Review system, but this system had not worked well. It stopped at the general manager or division director level; appraisal forms were poorly filled out; only 60 per cent of incumbents actually completed the forms; and there had been no internal training on how to conduct the appraisal/review process.

Objectives

The principal objective was to develop a total compensation philosophy, performance management and pay/benefits delivery system that would:

- support the business mission, goals and objectives of the organisation;
- continue to attract and retain high calibre talent;
- facilitate executive transfers, career development, and succession planning; and
- provide the basis for decisions on compensation and benefits matters – such as annual merit reviews.

The philosophy had to address (specifically):

- short-term compensation: the competitive position, use of salary ranges, mix of base pay and bonus, position evaluation, and recruitment;
- long-term compensation: share plans, retirement plans and the retention of employees;
- performance management: annual reviews, objective setting, training, merit budgets; and
- the policy must be competitive within each marketplace, but maintain internal equity with respect to difficulty of individual hotel management and size of hotel (rooms, revenues).

The approach

The success of this project was seen to depend upon an in-depth understanding of the roles within the organisation. This was a key to the construction of an appropriate compensation policy, setting performance measures, and determining succession and man-power planning.

To achieve this the Project Requirements were divided into the following phases:

Phase 1

There were three parts to this phase:

- Part 1 was what was called the Role Challenge Process (RCP) which is a highly disciplined and vigorous method of looking at the nature of roles, their complexity and the demands and challenges placed upon them.
- Part 2 consisted of gathering appropriate compensation information about executive and management jobs in all locations and areas.
- Part 3 was the integration of these two disciplines which culminated in the construction of the Reward Scale. This formed the foundation to take the detail gathered in Phase 1 and turn it into a management process.

Phase 2 and beyond

In these phases the major processes were determined from the results of Phase 1, and included a performance management process, the development of competency management and a sophisticated career and succession planning process.

Discussion

From this case study it can be seen that it was necessary to resist the temptation of merely labelling the problems as pay policy issues, but rather to look at all aspects of the problems and progressively to address each of them in a logical sequence. In this way a viable and practical compensation policy was developed which provided management with the capability of effectively managing their human resources in both a pay and performance manner.

Conclusion

The chapter began with a description of the interface between people at work, their rewards and their performance, then proceeded by looking, in some depth, at the subjects, issues, restrictions, considerations and judgements which have to be made in order to formulate a business oriented pay policy.

This strategic approach to pay, in all its aspects, must remain one of the most fascinating and crucial aspects of running a modern and efficient business enterprise. One cannot help but to speculate, however, if one were to read this chapter in, say, 10 or 20 years' time what changes there would have been and what would remain unchanged.

Whatever changes occur in the future, the one thing which appears to be unaffected by time is that effective, well-motivated and appropriately rewarded people are pivotal to a successful business. It is in this sense therefore that reward strategy is one key level within HRM. The technical details of reward management systems are important because, for example, such issues as pay determination create the climate of trust, and the rationale for rewards if underpinned by role analysis or job evaluation can build a sense of fairness and equity. Without trust and a sense of equity, it is difficult to see how a performance management system could be maintained. Reward strategy both has a strategic, long-term purpose, and consists of a series of practical measures to sustain the psychological contract.

7

BUSINESS STRATEGY AND MANAGEMENT DEVELOPMENT – A SYMBIOTIC RELATIONSHIP?

Alan Fell with Tom Davies

This chapter discusses the results from research conducted on behalf of the British National Health Service (NHS) in order to establish the linkage between business strategy and management development in the NHS, and to assess the existence and nature of any linkage. Phase I of the research compared practices in the health sector and the private corporate sector, and Phase II extended the findings of Phase I to nine NHS Community Trusts.

Human resource strategy has as a central aim the support of the business strategy through people management policies and practices which, as part of the change objectives, inevitably require some form of management development response.

The work discussed in this chapter arose from a perception that management development professionals are marginal to strategy formulation and business planning. This in turn it is argued leads to vague, unfocussed management development performance targets. At one level, cash and time, there can be frustration at what management development is achieving for the resources that are being expended. In large enterprises, the resources can be very substantial, well into seven-figure sums. At another, management development can frequently be charged with helping a chief executive translate his or her *vision* into concrete realities, to altered ways of working and changed value systems in an organisation. Quite often a disproportionate importance is attached by the organisation to management development. Why is there, therefore, with such pivotal roles, an ambivalence about management development activity, and frequently HRM, more broadly? With notable exceptions, why typically does the HR function still follow in the train of reorganisation and not at the vanguard?

The perceived marginal status of management development could be for a number of reasons, for example:

- Business strategy formulation, leading to business planning, is not of the optimum quality (the problem lies in the planning process).
- The 'planners' (for example a board, management executive, planning officials, line

managers, and so on) regard people-development issues in a superficial way, despite strictures about the centrality of labour costs, the importance of management development, quality issues, and so on (the problem lies in professional attitudes).

- Human resource professionals are not thought of by the planners as other than marginal to the planning process, their input can be provided by others or can be added after core issues have been determined (the problem lies in the quality of the management developers).
- Lastly, the link between eventual strategies and planning is not sufficiently understood by all parties to be translated into quantifiable targets and performance measures in, for example, management development (the problem lies in the 'bridge' between business strategy and management development).

The rationale for the research additionally derived from a view that the marginal status of management development may be less, or the same but qualitatively different, in the private corporate sector from the public sector and a comparative analysis of both sectors (limited to two or three examples from each) would be constructive.

Though indeed constructive, there are weaknesses in the sectoral transfer approach from the private to the public sector. Pettigrew et al. (1992) commented that 'concepts derived from the private sector should not be mechanistically trundled across the sectoral divide (as significant differences remain between the two sectors, particularly in the degree of politicisation and the power and social position of the professionals)'. This is an important qualification in the light of the general belief of many policy makers that the private sector is the sole repository of 'good practice' from which the public sector must learn.

This notwithstanding, Phase I aimed to collect data and assess differences between the two sectors so that a general model could be developed for application in Phase II, and evolve practical strategies in HRM and especially in management development.

The areas of particular concentration were:

- perceptions about business strategy;
- purposes of business strategy;
- business strategy and management development; and
- approaches to human resource management.

It was recognised that there were broader developments within the NHS which were influencing the process of change. These include the encouragement of doctors into managerial roles, the separation of provider Trusts from purchasing organisations and the subsequent 'dislocation' of strategic planning from its traditional single-process role within health authorities and so on. In the period from the completion of the fieldwork until this date, many of these influences have gained a heightened importance.

The research base

For Phase I, four sites were selected. Two were large, acute hospital NHS Trusts and two private sector sites. As in the comparisons made earlier between the NHS and British Airways, we can learn about the contribution of management development by comparing two sectors. The four sites were characterised by:

- being driven by 'quality' whether in product terms or patient care;
- concern with *merger* and its impact on organisation;
- an openness and interest towards the issue of the relationship of management development to business strategy at all senior levels; and
- substantial investment whether in plant or people to maximise productivity.

The fieldwork included 118 interviews in total over the four sites. A core questionnaire of 15 questions was applied to all respondents. A further 6 questions were addressed to 'Chief Executive' respondents and those with strategic planning responsibilities. A further 9 questions were addressed to 'Personnel Director' respondents and those with human resource, management development/trainer responsibilities. A director of planning for example would therefore be asked 21 questions, a training manager 24 questions.

At the private sector companies, 55 of the 56 respondents were male, at the hospitals 25 were male and 37 female (that is 40.3 per cent and 59.7 per cent). There is no published data on whether men and women view HRM/management development differently, though gender views on 'management' is developing and is the subject of separate study. The possible impact of this is highlighted below.

Perceptions about business strategy and the importance of communication

At the heart of this research is the relationship between business strategy and management development. *Perceptions* about an organisation's strategy are as important as the existence of strategies, simple or sophisticated, or seemingly appropriate structural arrangements. There are very marked differences in perceptions between the hospital and private sectors (Fig 7.1).

There are noticeable differences too on the communication of those strategies (Fig 7.2). Of the hospitals' respondents, 43.6 per cent think that the corporate/strategic plan is not clearly communicated to them, compared to 23.2 per cent in the private sector

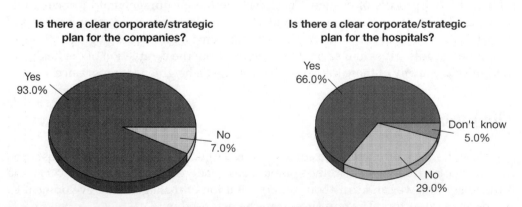

Fig 7.1   Corporate planning in hospitals and companies

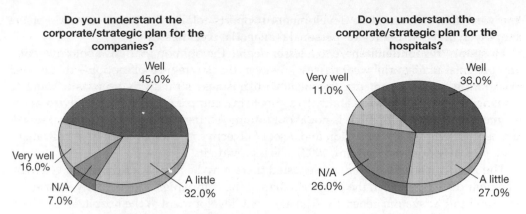

Fig 7.2   Understanding of corporate plans in hospitals and companies

companies. Of the companies' respondents, 55.3 per cent, compared to 45.2 per cent of the hospitals', think it is clearly communicated.

The bridge between business strategy and management development must in part turn on respondents' opinions as to the purpose of management development. Respondents were asked to rank in order the first three purposes of management development. Their responses are shown in Table 7.1.

An interpretation of this data is that respondents in both sectors virtually share the opinion that management development is about helping to structure and plan the business to meet strategic objectives. Companies' respondents underpin this opinion with

Table 7.1   Purpose of management development

	Hospitals %	Companies %
Nominate someone for a course off the job		
Action an appraisal recommendation		
Help structure/plan (the business) to meet strategic objectives	46.8	42.9
Help me become better at my job		
Help me 'get on', independent of employer's (business) requirements		
Help me with my career with this or any other employer		
Support totally business needs of my employer		26.8
Help overcome some weaknesses I have in being a manager	16.4	28.6
Keep me up to date in my management knowledge		
Keep me up to date with my management skills		
Give me a set of values about how we should relate to each other		
Help (the business) introduce new ideas about organisation/management practice	29.5	
	n = 186	n = 168

105

the view that management development supports totally the business needs of the employer, and is to overcome personal managerial weaknesses.

Hospitals' respondents share to a lesser degree the opinion that it is about overcoming personal managerial weaknesses; however, the 'strategic tool' notion – that is, that integrating management development with business strategy is seen as a route to enhancing an organisation's ability to compete in a complex and changing environment – management development is not about training courses, rather 'Management development is being given a mission and a set of objectives which position it as a strategic tool' (Osbaldeston and Barham, 1992) – is less evident.

The results from Phase I also suggested there may be a broader dimension to management development in the hospitals than at the companies, indeed between the private and public sectors generally. Management development at the hospitals may have *social policy* connotations which are understated at the companies. A current UK example could be Opportunity 2000. This particular example may be pertinent in the light of the 40:60 male/female divide in respondents at the hospitals. In other words, it may be quite legitimate at the hospitals to use processes of management development to introduce social/national initiatives which do not directly derive from a local business strategy, but from imperatives outside the business. This has important consequences for the evaluation of practical strategies in human resource management. To what extent is it necessary to derive and go on to implement strategies which have limited origin and focus in the business needs of the enterprise rather than the wider environmental or societal context? Is Business Ethics an example of an externally driven (that is, external to perceived business needs) strategic requirement? One of the topical issues the NHS faces in the 1990s is where is the locus of responsibility for raising such ethical imperatives? Is there a proxy to the private sector shareholder who increasingly fills the role outside the public sector?

Business strategy and management development

How, therefore, do respondents at the hospitals and the companies position management development in relation to business strategy, having disposed of the social policy dimension on the part of the hospitals and the 'strategic tool' notion on the part of the companies? The hospitals' respondents continue to attach marginally greater strategic centrality to management development than do the private sector companies (Table 7.2).

At the companies, more than twice as many respondents than at the hospitals do not know whether there is a relationship or not. Nearly three times as many respondents at the companies than at the hospitals put the relationship on a very important tactical footing but of no strategic concern: an apparent paradox.

What do the planners think?

At the hospitals, five respondents had directorial responsibility for corporate planning and eight respondents had senior managerial responsibility for planning. At the companies, five had directorial responsibility and four senior managerial responsibility.

Table 7.2   Strategic position of management development

'... in this organisation at the present time, management development policies are ...'	Hospitals %	Companies %
At the heart of strategic concerns	3.2	3.6
Very important to strategic concerns	46.8	41.1
They are tactically very important but of limited strategic concern	38.7	32.1
They are tactically important but of no strategic concern	3.2	8.9
They are of no tactical nor strategic concern, they are wholly peripheral	3.2	3.6
Don't know	4.8	10.7
	n = 62	n = 56

The respondents in both groups reported that the corporate/strategic plan documentation for the 'business' contained a section dealing specifically with HR strategy/planning. The fieldwork also elicited the fact that the personnel director is most frequently charged with writing that section of the plan.

There was however a spread in relative importance attached to that section of the corporate/strategic plan over other sections, though its importance was not minimised (Table 7.3).

Based on the hospital sites, it is clear that a sizeable majority of respondents understand the corporate/strategic plan well enough and attach significant importance to the business strategy and management development linkage. However, a sizeable minority, nearly one-third, do not think the strategy is clear, nor clearly communicated. What role do planners play in addressing this aspect and what contribution are HR functions expected to make? Are there policy issues for organisations in the clarity and communication of strategic intentions, and the ability of human resource functions to contribute to the formulation of strategy? Can human resource functions create in their clients' minds a clear distinction between the strategy role they are expected to perform and the operational 'firefighting' posture which is frequently the image of a busy personnel department? Is creating that distinction a key to the HR function playing a role

Table 7.3   Importance of HR in the corporate plan

'... what is the relative importance of the HR section of the corporate plan?'	Hospitals %	Companies %
It is the most important	0.0	0.0
It is one of the most important sections	66.0	66.0
It is not especially important	8.0	33.0
It is one of the lesser of the sections	25.0	0.0
It is the least important section	0.0	0.0
Don't know	0.0	0.0
	n = 12	n = 6

in the corporate structure which it is frequently said to covet? What strategies are necessary to bring it about? This is discussed below in respect of the NHS.

Approaches to human resource management

The taxonomy of human resource management practice divides into broad schools of thought associated for example with Drucker's (1955) 'hotch-potch' of activities (Drucker, 1955); the work of Legge (1978); the three models formulated by Tyson and Fell (1986). The common conclusion that can be drawn from all researchers is the view that there is no 'single best way'. The successful personnel/HRM adopted in a particular environment is best-fit for that organisation at that time.

Guest and Peccei (1992) in their research argued that 'there is no simple ideal measure of personnel management effectiveness'. Nevertheless, they go on tentatively to develop for the NHS an *Index of Personnel Management Effectiveness*. Guest and Peccei conclude (summary report November 1992) 'that effectiveness, as rated by personnel and line managers, is likely to be higher when personnel specialists and personnel policies are well integrated into the general management process'.

The ultimate integration can be viewed as occurring where personnel policies directly emanate from the business's strategic objectives, manifested through its plan, strategy documentation, and so on; where personnel specialists understand that their work is in support of corporate objectives and where the employee community in the organisation as a whole understands the corporate objectives and personnel/HRM contribution to realising those goals.

This implies a form of 'choice'. That is, personnel specialists have the conscious choice to create a function which integrates with a business plan. Strategies are then necessary to derive an appropriate personnel management model.

Respondents at the four sites were invited to consider which of the Tyson and Fell (1986) models of personnel management in their opinion overall most closely reflected the personnel function in their organisation at the present time. The three models from which they could choose were:

1. Clerk of Works

Characterised by: authority is vested in line managers; policies are not pre-set, nor an integral part of business policy; managers have complete control over people reporting to them; chief executives may take on the main personnel policy direction; tactics are formed to achieve short-term goals, not set out in policy documents; systems are ad hoc, mostly related to basic data collection; personnel department will administer basic routines often like 'paper machines'; personnel officers are likely not to have specialist qualifications and to be closely managed by a senior line manager.

2. Contract Manager

Characterised by: well established policies derived often from employer associations and industry norms industrial relations practices; typically found in bureaucracies where personnel systems are underwritten by industrial relations traditions and practices; trade unions have high density, line managers have grown up with the system and 'understand' it; relationships are very controlled with accent on procedures for the resolution of discipline problems, grievances and disputes; personnel staff are specialists with tightly controlled, defined roles; personnel's main achievement is seen as the pragmatic resolution of day-to-day problems; time horizons for planning are typically within one to five years; overall, the accent is on making the existing system work better.

3. The Architect

Characterised by: the corporate plan is prepared with people consequences in mind and explicit links are made between the plan and HR/manpower planning and so on; managers at senior level take business decisions in the light of the consequences for the management of people; a creative role is expected for personnel staff; they initiate policy changes and are expected to see how business policy changes impact on people issues; industrial relations strategy is explicit and seeks to create new relationships; there will be strong values held by the management team about managing people; the senior personnel specialists regard themselves as business managers first, as 'professional' personnel specialists second; they see themselves as diagnosticians with a range of interventions available to assist them; they will typically evaluate policy proposals in business items taking a medium- to long-term perspective; they seek out proposals that have pay-offs in terms of greater productivity, improved quality of work, cost effectiveness, empowerment, delayering, and so on.

The responses are shown in Table 7.4.

Table 7.4 Models of personnel management in evidence

	Hospitals %	Companies %
Clerk of Works	30.0	27.0
Contract Manager	43.0	25.0
Architect	27.0	48.0
	n = 62	n = 56

While it is not proven that the dominance of one model over another (especially as in large organisations models can co-exist) leads to a predisposition to relate HRM to business strategy, it is the case that the Architect is the 'business management model' of HR. At first reading, one could predict from those responses that HR professionals would have more difficulty at the hospitals in integrating HR and business strategy.

Guest and Peccei (op. cit.) in the construction of the *Index* distinguish between personnel management inputs (for example, size of department, board membership, personnel staff to employee ratios, and so on), personnel management processes (for example, policy priorities, formalisation and board support for policies, and so on) and personnel management outcomes (for example assessment of personnel management effectiveness). This study limited itself to comparing respondents' views in both sectors on a narrow range of possible personnel function activities. In other words, what do respondents think personnel functions do on a day-to-day basis? Table 7.5 shows the results.

Table 7.5 Main activities of the personnel function

'What do you think are the four current main activities of the personnel function?'	Hospitals %	Companies %
Fixing pay and benefits		
Personnel administration	43.5	46.4
Organise training		
Management development/training		
Welfare		
Recruitment	29.0	
Strategic personnel planning	25.8	23.2
Pensions		
Career management		
Sick pay administration		
Manpower planning		
Dealing with discipline and grievance matters	71.0	33.9
Other		
Don't know		
	n = 248	n = 224

The respondents' views at the hospitals are consistent with the preoccupations of a contracts manager mandate. The emphasis on recruitment no doubt reflects the fact that the NHS must be the largest recruiter active in the UK economy. The emphasis in discipline and grievance matters is on short-cycle tasks. They are the stuff of conventional personnel management. They compound the perception that HR departments are operational, service departments, especially as it is in such areas – industrial/employment relations and recruitment and selection – that Guest and Peccei found personnel management effectiveness was rated highest.

The contradiction is now evident. While the hospitals' respondents, for example, place management development policies in relation to business strategy at the point of being very important to strategic concerns/tactically very important (Table 7.2), the broader area of HRM is characterised by being 'contracts manager' and the day-to-day activities are a catalogue of a traditional personnel management department routine.

There would appear to be much work still to be done to establish the clear distinction between the strategy role and the operational 'firefighting' posture, a division Handy (1992/3) thinks increasingly necessary to support the management of the 'federal organisation', an organisation paradigm which may have particular appeal to the NHS, and one of the most significant lessons to be learnt in developing practical Human Resource Management Strategies.

Creating the general model

For the purposes of this research, we took as a working assumption that management development is an integrated, holistic approach to inculcating shared values and shaping organisation structure to best enable the organisation to meet competitive pressures. In the private sector, this conventionally is to secure competitive advantage and thereby greater revenues. In the health sector, this traditionally has been to secure a greater share of finite resources from the public exchequer. In the NHS of the 1990s, structured on the purchaser-provider model with the evolution of the internal market strategic environment, competition for revenues intrudes. We have not defined management development beyond that. In reality the activities of management development encompass a week down a pot-hole in Ross-on-Wye; a three-month Advanced Health Care Graduate Programme in the USA; the long-term planning of structures of the organisation to secure or penetrate new markets; subtle executive resourcing for future top leadership; and so on. Nothing is to be gained by seeking an encapsulating definition for this range of activity.

Research in the mid 1980s sponsored by the Foundation for Management Education and Ashridge Management College provided a convenient reference point for this project. The *Management for the Future* (Foundation for Management Education/Ashridge 1988) report consolidates research arising from the perception that 'as organisations approach the 1990s, they are looking with growing interest at the potential benefits of training and development as a means of facing highly competitive, complex and rapidly changing markets'.

The report of that project describes three phases in the role of training and development:

- the fragmented approach (activities which are peripheral rather than intrinsic to the organisation);
- the formalised approach (organisations adopt a more systematic approach to training and development); and
- the focussed approach (training and development becomes intrinsic to the organisation ... learning is linked to organisation strategy ...).

These three phases of training and development might be paraphrased:

1. *demand-led:* the fragmented approach;
2. *supply-led:* the formalised approach; and
3. *business-led:* the focussed approach.

An attempt was made in this project to develop frameworks to assess respondents' views as to which approach they thought the most prevalent to their Trust at that time.

Respondents were asked a series of 15 questions to ascertain their views as to the strategic position of management development in their organisation.

- Overall, there was a complimentary view for both groups as to whether or not training and development is *demand-led*.
- Overall, there was a stronger view held by the private sector respondents that training and development is *supply-led*.
- As to the *business-led* approach, there too was a broadly complimentary view.

This part of the research demonstrated that if it was possible to construct a series of highly structured questions reflective of each of the phases and if it was possible to discriminate between them, this could lead to an 'instrument', an audit of management development's evolution from a fragmented to a focussed approach. This could be of practical value in, for example, influencing chief executives of NHS Trusts regarding the strategic planning of management development and the assessment of the Trusts' HR contribution. In short, could an approach be developed which translates into functional targets for management development? This became a key objective for Phase II.

Evolving practical HR strategies at Community Trusts

Phase II of this research followed the same broad outline as Phase I but with some notable differences. First, the research base was not to be comparative, that is it was not to compare the private and public sectors but rather was to focus exclusively on the views of management at nine recently formed NHS Community Trusts. Second, not only were Trust employees to be interviewed, but the views of Trust collaborating agencies were to be gathered – that is, GP Fundholders, purchasing authorities (purchasing authorities are the bodies charged with 'commissioning' or 'buying' health care provision from Trusts to meet the authorities' statutory obligations), Social Service Departments and voluntary agencies.

This dimension was an important extension of the work and reflects a broader trend noticeable recently in the evaluation of HR functions: the weight being given to the views of the 'customers'. It is undeniable that the true 'customers' of Community Trusts are patients and their actual and perceived medical or care needs. This was not however a research project which focussed on patient needs for HRM strategies. Rather, it focussed on the inter-organisational relationship between a Trust and its corporate, if not patient, needs for HRM strategies.

Another dimension incorporated at Phase II was to glean the views of non-executive board members. Here, the comparison to the private sector is more apt. It is entirely possible and potentially valuable to gather information about non-executive directors' views of an enterprise's HR strategies. Issues which most frequently arise for example include executive remuneration, industrial unrest, senior management succession and at times an acquisition or business merger. These are among the most common examples of non-executive director interest in HRM strategies, but they are hardly definitive.

For Phase II (in the autumn and winter of 1993/94), 171 board members and management staff from nine NHS Community Trusts were interviewed along with 10 GP fundholders, 12 interviewees from the voluntary sector or Social Services and 10 interviewees from NHS purchasing authorities.

Separate and shorter questionnaires were used with purchasers (including GP Fundholders) and Social and Voluntary Services as not all questions on the detail of management development were relevant to them. Participating sites were asked to identify potential respondents on a 'vertical slice' basis, that is a range of people at different hierarchical levels; across a range of disciplines, functions, departments and so on. A selection criterion was that they had to be in the management structure/grade system.

At Phase I the dominant model of personnel management among hospital respondents was the Contract Manager (see Table 7.4). At the Community Trust sites in Phase II the situation is more complex. The respondents reported the preferences shown in Fig 7.3.

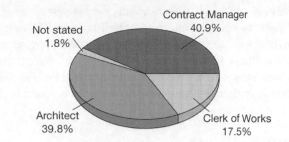

Fig 7.3   Model of personnel management at Community Trusts

The 'choices' referred to earlier were indeed consciously being made. Many Trusts were trying by deliberate intent to discriminate between a strategic function and an operational one. It was received wisdom that Trusts, as major employing organisations, faced a range of strategic HR issues which had to be actioned. However, at the same time, there was no avoiding the 'routine' of personnel management.

To sow more confusion, the strategic element was frequently titled 'Human Resources' and the operational element 'personnel management'. Time will tell if the separation is successfully achieved; in the short term there is confusion about each element of the 'personnel department' mandate.

Nevertheless, for those who view HRM in a strategic light, there are grounds for optimism: HR functions were moving towards the Architect model in the eyes of at least 40 per cent of the Trust respondents.

How do respondents at the sites position personnel/HRM policies – in relation to the strategic business concerns of the Trusts? (And are there differences between the Community Care Trusts of Phase II and the Acute Hospital respondents of Phase I?) See Fig 7.4.

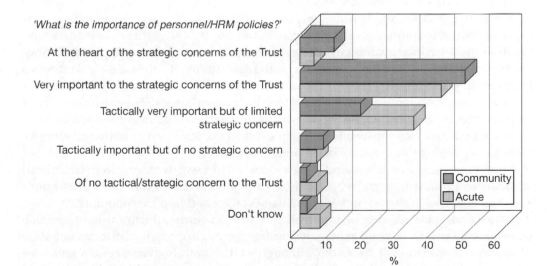

Fig 7.4   Comparison of community sector and acute hospitals

There was however a marked difference in responses as to *how well* respondents understood the Trusts' business strategy. Of the Phase I NHS respondents, 47 per cent answered they understood the strategy very well or well, compared to 41 per cent in the Community Trusts at Phase II.

Among the respondents, therefore, the centrality of HR policies in relation to their employers' strategic agenda would not appear to be in doubt.

A planned intervention

A key objective for Phase II, it will be recalled, was to attempt to create an instrument which might be applied to auditing management development policies' evolution from a fragmented to a focussed approach. The same battery of questions that had been asked at Phase I were now put to Phase II respondents.

The data indicated that respondents did not think that training and development was fragmented, that is, they were not being demand-led by the wishes or aspirations of managers pursuing personal development ambitions unrelated to business needs. Respondents were balanced in their views as to whether the Trusts were being systematic towards training and development. Many of the right attitudes prevailed, but the Trusts had still to adopt formalised approaches to the implementation of planned management development.

A pertinent example of a planned HR strategy is to be found in the creation of a business-led approach towards management development. The business-led approach is concerned to meet organisational and individual needs in a symbiotic way, with training and development becoming intrinsic to the organisation and individual development aspirations being realised. The notion of the 'learning organisation' – the focus of much current interest in creating HR strategies – is said to occur at this phase. In this situation, the organisation has developed a continuous feedback loop where learning relates to environment and a willingness to acquire and develop skills the employer has specified as necessary to the business future.

While firm views were held by respondents that training and development was intrinsic to the organisation, and this was borne out by the statistical evidence and much of the anecdotal evidence related to the interviewers, there were practical problems being faced by the Trusts, for example the availability of funds, residual attitudes towards staff development and so on. Nevertheless, there was a strongly held view that management development was focussed and linked to strategy. This had come about by planning and a realisation on the part of HR professionals, planners and senior management that such previously alien private sector concepts as 'competitive advantage' were to be derived through the Trusts' human resources.

It was very necessary to husband those resources, in a way removed from traditional approaches to 'staff training' with its historical connotations of training for training's sake and course-for-interest, rather than business focussed resource planning.

It was noticeable the degree to which this shift towards a business-led approach enjoyed wide support among managers. The fragmented approach with its lack of planning and co-ordination of resources, although to the cynical advantage of a few – for example, one respondent was happily engrossed in a sponsored MBA with his second employer – was held in wide contempt. Indeed, the apparent toleration by Trusts of such policies contributed to a lessening of credibility in HR policies. Managers knew, especially in an era of limited funds, that the traditional approach was untenable and undesirable.

It was still necessary to move further along the road of evolving an instrument of some kind which would help with assessing a current situation, thus enabling practical strategic interventions to be made. Lees (1992) has suggested that in recent years management development literature has concentrated on the activities which external consultants conduct on behalf of client organisations, and away from possible internal organisation perspectives on management development. His preliminary work considers internal perspectives and is therefore relevant to developing practical strategies.

Against the rhetorical question 'How do organisations justify their decision to commit resources to management development?' Lees argues that it is possible to construe management development 'as the intersection of three variables – individual career, organisational succession and organisational performance ... and ... in an idealised form all three variables can be integrated'. Lees goes on to identify ten very different reasons why organisations support management development. The first four have a function and performance emphasis and the remaining six are political, legitimatory, symbolic and defensive. The ten together, Lees asserts, represent a comprehensive set of rationales for the entire process of management development.

To test his argument and assess its utility as a diagnostic tool, Lees was invited to condense his ten rationales, or 'faces', into a model which would be helpful in understanding elements in the relationship between corporate strategy and management development in NHS Trusts. He adopted a strategic HRM perspective and derived a triangular model in which management development activity could be analysed in terms of the extent to which attitudes towards it were strategy-centred, organisation-centred or person-centred. This classification embraced the ten different rationales for management development already identified and simultaneously integrated into the strategic HRM frameworks of Fombrun et al. (1984) and Beer et al. (1985).

In summary, the Fombrun and Beer frameworks argue that for any HRM activity – including management development – to be strategic, four requirements have to be met:

- it must be fully integrated into corporate strategy and be central to its formulation, rather than simply following from it;
- it must attract full commitment from managers and staff at all levels of the organisation;
- there must be sufficient flexibility in organisational structure to allow line managers to take appropriate local HR action to improve performance and respond effectively to market requirements *as perceived at their levels*; and
- the organisational cultures must act to reinforce rather than constrain those activities.

In other words, if management development is to be a strategic HRM activity and make a significant contribution to organisational performance, there requires to be tight integration at the *strategic level*, high commitment at the *person level* and flexibility and cultural reinforcement at the *organisational level*.

To assess how closely current management development activity in the Trusts approximated to this HRM ideal and especially to identify obstacles to achieving it, Lees formulated for this assignment appropriate questions to diagnose internal attitudes to management development in terms of the extent to which they were person-centred, organisation-centred and strategy-centred. The expectation was that the more that these dimensions pulled in different directions, pursuit of one would most likely be at the expense of the other and, ultimately, to the detriment of strategic performance.

Strategy-centred

Questions were aimed at establishing perceptions of how far management development was integrated into strategy, and the extent to which line managers believed they should take responsibility for management development initiatives (see Fig 7.5).

Overall, there is a loose integration of management development with strategy. There is evidence of managers agreeing that HRM initiatives should pass 'back to the line', but also of the culture of dependency/professional bureaucracy where management development is a 'training department task'. Overall percentages however mask wide variations across Trusts, and even within each Trust.

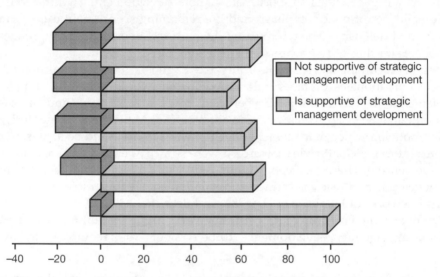

Fig 7.5   Strategy direction of management development

Organisation-centred

Questions were aimed at identifying perceptions of structural and cultural elements that could enable or obstruct management development as a strategic tool (see Fig 7.6).

This data illustrates the dual role of management development. Management development is also required to take on an organisation development emphasis. There are very powerful sentiments about the need to get the culture right and to break down traditional boundaries and help specialisms to 'gel' with one another. There is a fear of innovation on the job which is linked to the traditional NHS bureaucratic structure and culture, although some evidence of managers being proactive when the change process is legitimised first by management development activity.

Managers pursue strategic goals through the medium of the organisation (structure,

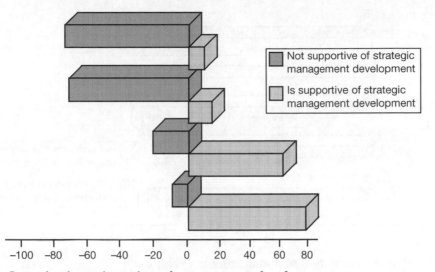

Fig 7.6 Organisation orientation of management development

systems, culture, and so on) and managers recognise that the organisation must evolve and change in line with strategy. Yet in times of major change and reorganisation an existing organisational format offers predictability and psychological security to managers which they may wish to cling to even though they know it is out of step with strategy. The balance between these two views needs to be in favour of the strategic objectives of the organisation, otherwise management development will tend to sustain an existing but inappropriate social order.

Person-centred

Questions were aimed at establishing the extent of managerial commitment to management development and beliefs about its possibilities (see Fig 7.7).

Overall, there is a high level of commitment to management development and strong belief in its potential efficacy as a strategic tool. However, alternative personal agendas for management development are clearly in evidence, but not to a point where they dominate over the needs of the business.

To realise the HRM ideal, managers at all levels must be committed to it and believe in its potential efficacy for improving performance and realising strategy. Given that management development is also a social and political activity, it is inevitable that it will continue to serve these other ends, although they must not take precedence over organisational performance.

The conclusion that can be drawn is that if organisational performance and business strategies are to be optimised, management development activities must be congruent with corporate strategy, earn the full commitment of managers, and allow for local workplace initiative, and that organisational cultures must all act to reinforce rather than polarise these variables.

The data suggests – with a wide variation between Trusts – that there is a loose but discernible integration of management development and strategy; management development is being broadly interpreted to include organisational development activities,

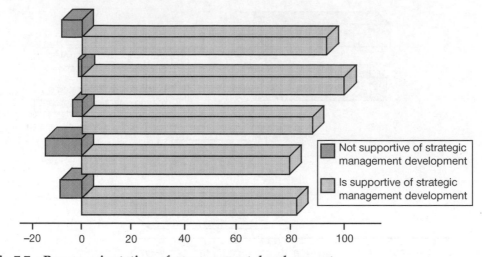

Fig 7.7   Person orientation of management development

with many of the anxieties present which typically surround organisational change. To individual employees, while there is an acknowledgement of the central importance of management development as a strategic weapon to the Trust, there is an equally firm declaration that they have a strong personal stake in management development and what it can do for them.

Conclusion

The work carried out in a number of NHS organisations confirmed the varying status and effectiveness of management development in supporting the strategic goals of the organisations. 'Management development' as perceived and described within organisations is covering a widening spectrum of activities and categorisation is increasingly unhelpful.

Much is claimed by HR specialists of management development as a proactive strategic lever to match behaviours (personal and organisational) to the changing needs of today's markets. However, managers of the function must be seen to dispose of the traditional roles which characterised many of the surveyed HR departments. A demand driven, 'advantage for the few' approach of traditional management development easily undermines HR aspirations to be business focussed and to add value. Instead it leads to low expectations of the HR contribution to strategic planning limited to reactive, last minute additions to a final draft plan.

The holy grail of management development as an efficient symbiosis of individual aspiration and organisational need requires changing links between management development and strategy formulation. Such changes can be seen as developing at varying speeds through a number of transitional phases; they are susceptible to identification through a survey instrument. This should allow both an audit of progress and targeting of subsequent resources. This approach supports the continuing internal (to HR) review of who *leads* in management development and the emerging shifts through badges of 'training', 'management development', 'organisational development', 'personal development' and other thematic variations.

The research carried out supports a more sophisticated blend of individual career expectations, organisational performance and organisation succession being at the core of a successful investment in any organisation's future through management development. Discrimination of current activities and perceptions can be achieved through inquiries which measure the extent to which they are people-centred, organisation-centred and strategy-centred.

Testing people's perceptions in NHS Trusts through the survey framework confirmed its value in discriminating perceptions and auditing the wide variation of management development activities and links to strategic planning.

Strategy itself is increasingly about perceptions – people do not 'do strategy' and thus it becomes a *perceived* framework within which people behave. Effective management development strategies are dependent on being perceived as characterised by tight integration at the strategic level, cultural reinforcement at the organisational level and high commitment at the individual level. Progress towards these attributes can be measured effectively through surveys which will inform decisions about internal organisational development and effective investments in managerial talent.

REFERENCES

Beer, M. et al. (1985) *Human Resource Management: A General Manager's Perspective*, New York, Free Press.

Bryson, J. (ed.) (1993) *Strategic Planning for Public Services and Non-Profit Organisations*, Pergamon Press.

Drucker, P.F. (1955) *The Practice of Management*, London, Mercury Books.

Fombrun, C.J., Tichy, N.M. and Devanna, M.A. (1984) *Strategic Human Resource Management*, New York, Wiley.

Grant, R.M. (1991) *Contemporary Strategy Analysis*, Blackwell.

Guest, D., and Peccei, R. (1992) *The Effectiveness of Personnel Management in the NHS*, NHSME.

Handy, C. (1992/3) 'Professor Handy's Master Class', *Human Resources*, Vol. 44, Winter.

Lees, S. (1992) 'Ten Faces of Management Development', *Management Education and Development*, Vol. 23, Part 2.

Legge, K. (1978) *Power Innovation and Problem Solving in Personnel Management*, London, McGraw-Hill.

Management for the Future (1988) Foundation for Management Education/Ashridge Management College.

Osbaldeston, M. and Barham, K. (1992) 'Using Management Development for Competitive Advantage', *Long Range Planning*, Vol. 25, No. 6, Pergamon Press Ltd.

Pettigrew, A. et al. (1992) *Shaping Strategic Change: Making Change in Large Organisations. The Case of the National Health Service*, Sage Publications.

Tyson, S. and Fell, A. (1986) *Evaluating the Personnel Function*, first edn Hutchison Press, 1986 and 1987. Second edn Stanley Thorne Publishers 1992.

BUSINESS EDUCATION AND BUSINESS STRATEGY

A case study of a financial services organisation

Zoe Gruhn

This chapter is a case study about a recent innovative approach to management development within and beyond a large multinational retail clearing bank. It illustrates how managers need to equip themselves with capabilities to initiate and manage change proactively. The approach taken demonstrates how management education is an integral part of the overall business strategy in a rapidly changing and demanding environment. A well thought through management development strategy is an important prop to the overall strategy of a business and it has a key role to play in the development of an organisation's managers and in the overall future performance of the business.

Technology alone will not help a business such as retail banking to be truly competitive. So, why not send your managers on an MBA course? This is a fairly typical response from some executives. Undoubtedly MBA qualifications are indeed useful. However, the effectiveness of such courses is somewhat impeded if they only produce well qualified managers who lack the necessary maturity to be adaptable to changing business environments and to be adept at demonstrating the appropriate political skills. What is required is for managers to acquire the essential strategies and competencies and a higher level of personal awareness and acceptance of the need for continuous improvement.

Background

This multinational retail clearing bank was founded in the mid nineteenth century, and currently employs about 45 000 employees based in both the UK and Europe. Its business comprises commercial banking, leasing, finance and factoring.

Its commercial banking activities are conducted through a branch banking network of over 1700 branches, consisting of an integrated management structure of five divisions within the UK. On the retail side, that is, personal banking, it has over five million customers and on the corporate side of business banking it has over 500 000 customers. Also, the bank has over two million credit card accounts as well as providing specialised financial services. In addition to the branch banking business it is also one of the largest financial institution groups within the UK and has a client base of large multinational corporates together with a highly profitable trade services operation. It is represented in more European countries than any other UK bank. Other financial activities include a rapidly growing personal financial services business, a 24-hour telephone banking service and the largest treasury trading and capital markets business in Europe which operates 24 hours a day, employing over 1000 dealers trading in London, New York and Tokyo. It also houses the most modern clearing banking operation with three national data centres and seven district services. Cheques and credits processed per month are valued at £60 million with a cash turnover of £3.2 billion. The strategy deployed for the operations and information technology aspects of the institution is based on a 'utility' concept, with all the processing work taking place in service centres which are the hidden engine room of the bank.

Over the last two decades the bank has undergone periods of volatility and organisational change. A long history of stability was severely disrupted during the mid 1980s following the ill-advised acquisition of an overseas bank with a troubled history of its own. The acquisition had huge debts and consequently devoured massive resources from its new parent. The British bank also had no experience of managing an operation of this kind let alone one which was suffering from serious internal difficulties. Within a relatively short time the bank took the only course open to it – to sell off its acquisition at a considerable loss. This episode severely dented the bank's reputation for financial probity both with the City of London and beyond. Its market position was consequently weakened and it rapidly became identified as an institution likely to be vulnerable to merger or takeover. In response to this weakened state, the bank underwent extensive internal restructuring and a considerable change in its strategy. It adopted a market segmentation strategy which was a deliberate policy to separate out the corporate side of the business from the retail side. This internal fracturing was another ill-advised move within the organisation as it resulted in customers becoming confused and irritated by the lack of cohesion and continuity when attempting to do business. The new structure was also poorly supported by IT systems which were intended to underpin the strategic change, but in practice only delivered in part.

The change in strategy was also prompted by the impact of deregulation, the need for innovative competitive products, changing technology and the extreme competitive pressures which were generated in the external marketplace at the time. All of this led to management instability. The constant turnover of chairmen and chief executives which took place within a short period was unheard of within the banking sector which normally prided itself on loyalty, stability and reliability. During the early 1990s came perhaps the inevitable loss of independence through the takeover by a multinational financial institution whose head office was then overseas but which subsequently based itself in London. This takeover was temporarily halted by another competitor perceived to be hostile whose widely publicised plans would have involved massive job losses. Although this never happened, as a consequence of the threat the original overseas bidder was able to complete the takeover with the image of a 'white knight'. The bank is therefore now part of a large profitable international banking and financial services organisation with assets of around £170 billion, generated by over 3000 offices in 66 countries.

The financial services sector of the economy has been subject to major internal and external pressures over the last decade. For years, banks felt arrogantly immune to any suggestion of competition. The political environment after 1979 and the impact of new technology, deregulation and product innovation all forced traditionally dominant players to review their business strategies. No longer did the club-like atmosphere which had previously cocooned British financial institutions from domestic and international competitive pressures prove sufficient to combat the major changes which were taking place within the sector, in particular internationally. London was managing, albeit with a struggle, to maintain its position as a global financial centre. Yet increasing competition was coming forward not just from London's traditional competitors but from emerging regional financial centres with their own stock markets serving some of the fastest developing economies in the world. The bank with its history of difficulties was inevitably going to come under pressure from those markets and institutions which were particularly strong in them. It was therefore perhaps not surprising that the bank's new owners drew their own strength from servicing those very markets which were likely to dominate the global economy in the twenty-first century.

The importance of HR strategies in a changing environment

In all sectors within the UK, the impact of short-term pressures is huge. For example, the fixation of the stock market to annual, half year and even quarterly results creates huge tensions and increased expectations. How can a human resource (HR) strategy of individual development be sustained if the chairman commits publicly to headcount savings? Thus short-term issues become short-term visions, people are perceived as a cost not an asset in the cost/income ratio. Development is viewed as a cost not an investment. This inevitably leads to organisational myopia – short-termism rules the day. The survival pressures have to be balanced with the long-term business goals. So often we see the chairman and/or chief executive quoted in a company's annual report as saying that 'people are our greatest asset'. Yet as soon as there is a sniff that times are hard, there is the usual knee-jerk reaction to remove heads, stop training, slash marketing, defer technology improvements and 'the time's not right' is usually the response to new people management strategies.

The reality is that this myopia leads to a lack of coherent vision about the future. So many companies learn by the mistake of failing to define and communicate clearly the strategic vision. The HR role is essential in helping to clarify and communicate the definition of such areas of strategic capability, reinforced with measurable behaviours. HR's value is in establishing the processes to ensure that there is a vision well communicated – not blurred and often confusing to employees. However, it is not necessarily a given: HR's credibility must initially revolve around short-term deliverables, identify the 'wants', add a touch of influence and satisfy the 'needs'. There is a requirement both to be flexible and to demonstrate professional integrity which will help to increase HR's profile and serve the organisation best by pragmatically creating a position of 'added value'.

HR – the marketeer

Clarity of purpose by the HR function is a vital ingredient together with an enduring style of internal customer relationship management. To influence the chief executive and his senior executives takes time, patience, sensitivity and a constant iteration with the business as well as a clear vision of what HR is about.

Management education traditionally had a small but useful role to play for developing senior managers which formed a part of the long-term investment of the business. To add value to the business it is important for HR to focus on relevance to the business. Management education is intended to keep senior managers fresh and alert to external competition as well as equipping them with the necessary skills.

The values of the bank had shifted from an environment which encouraged loyalty, focussed on income, drove status with an emphasis on bureaucracy and hierarchy towards an environment where the values of integrity, profitability, reliability, adaptability and quality applied to all stakeholders (that is, shareholders, customers and employees). The idea was to be able to measure and set performance standards in regard to organisation members' values, attitudes and behaviours.

The standards were set as follows:

- *Integrity* – open to staff and customers, earn trust – do what you say you will do, act honourably and ethically, promote enforcement of regulatory controls, equal treatment, personal commitment.
- *Profitability* – maximise opportunities, manage costs, increase income balanced with risk, delegation of profit accountability.
- *Reliability* – consistent decisions and actions, stable business relationships, dependable customer service systems and procedures.
- *Adaptability* – effectively manage change, creative problem solving, innovation and responsiveness.
- *Quality* – service orientation, getting it right the first time, act on customer needs, clear and accountable personal standards.

The strategic plan for the business included a stronger focus on customers aimed to provide a better quality service; to become a lean, commercially driven business where success will bring benefits to customers, staff and shareholders alike. Other objectives were to reduce the cost/income ratio from 60 per cent to 55 per cent over a period of three years; to empower line and business managers who would have increased responsibility and accountability; to reduce management layers and bureaucracy with a greater emphasis being placed on increased productivity and getting things right first time; and to continue to integrate and co-operate with the parent organisation to maximise business opportunities and promote the organisation's image.

The type of culture to strive for included one that would be flexible, responsive and streamlined with fast decision making. This involved the development of performance management, measurement and targeting, individual rewards and objective evaluation. There was to be a move from a hierarchical approach, managing upwards, with a supervisory, telling style towards skills which engendered power and influence, leadership and vision producing a management that was focussed and rigorous in its approach to setting high standards.

To support this new culture and operationalise the values, it was necessary to create a comprehensive management development strategy which fully supported the business strategy. As a consequence, a number of processes and products were initiated to support the culture change. One of the chief processes introduced was a competency based approach to career development. This entailed defining competencies and skills for managers, for example, leadership, management, customer focus, sales and sales management, risk management and operations and process management. In addition, a career management system was introduced which was modelled around a development review discussion in which individuals discussed career aspirations and development needs with their managers. The process was supported by skills and training matrices which facilitated discussions regarding career options available to individuals, considering both their skill base and personal aspirations. One of the most important policy aspects was a cohesive training and business education approach for all levels of management.

A strategy for business education

The need for a coherent business education strategy covering all management levels was essential due to the changing business environment, the need for greater competitiveness and to maximise the value of the bank's human resources. The bank had already established itself with a number of in-company management development programmes at specific business schools. They served a purpose in covering the foundations of business education largely within a closeted and fairly incestuous environment with little opportunity for comparisons with other organisations.

The creation of the strategy was sponsored by the then chief executive who initiated a review with the following objectives:

● to obtain a common understanding of the bank's executives' and senior managers' views on how business education might best be used to improve the bank's competitive performance;
● to establish the effectiveness of the current business education programmes used and the extent to which they met the bank's needs;
● to create a tracking system on business school graduates;
● to provide a framework for evaluating the effectiveness of the business schools as a way of assessing their 'added value' to the organisation; and
● to create and implement a cohesive business education strategy.

The information required to produce this strategy was gathered through three principal activities, namely, a review of the main business education in-company programmes the bank used; consultation with 30 executives and senior managers to elicit their understanding of the differences between business education and training; and the establishment of selection criteria for the most suitable business schools based on the needs of the bank.

The review had shown some of the limitations of the bank's approach to business education. The programmes were being provided in an ad hoc way and were not linked together. The in-company programme designs did not ensure that the learning process combined theory with practice, knowledge with skill and insight with action to enable the integration of learning to happen, which would in turn lead to different thinking and changed behaviours.

As a consequence of the review, a strategic management development plan was created for those managers who had been identified as having high potential. However, the high potential management population was not static, as managers could move in or move off the high potential track as a result of their performance and for other reasons. External hires could also be put into the fast track development process to supplement the existing cadre.

The strategic management development plan as illustrated in Fig 8.1 needed to include an individual career development plan that inter-related business education, training and development activities for individual and organisational careers relevant to their management grade. Arguably the combined impact of learning for the individual and the business would be far more empowering than just splitting each area of activities into isolated learning events.

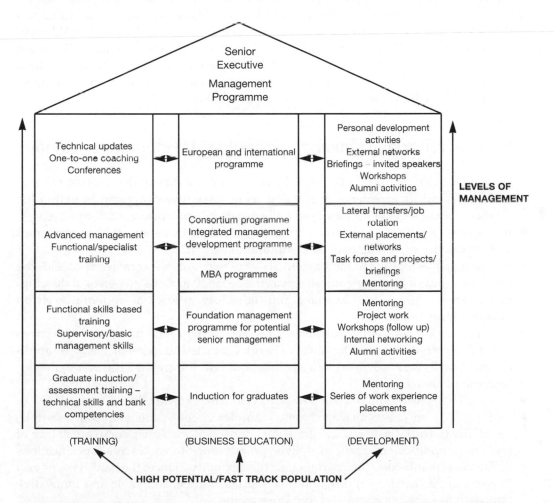

Fig 8.1   Strategic development plan (example of a range of managerial activities)

Consortium companies' needs

The view was that the development of insights and the acquisition of new knowledge and skills was best achieved through a variety of activities in business education programmes allowing maximum participation of participants, rather than the more traditional learning method of formal lectures. Another essential feature to this approach was the creation of a consortium programme with business partners from a range of different market sectors. It was important they did not all come from the financial services, but reflected a mix of market sectors which could potentially be competitors.

Consequently, to support and implement the strategic management plan, the structure of the programmes needed to include intensive group work, plenary discussions, and presentations to allow full expression to individual input and to facilitate the sharing and exchange of different experiences and views. A business school was an essential ingredient in supporting managers but the school had to be something special, something which could combine current thinking on management and strategy issues together with an expertise on interpersonal development. To ensure that total integration and the application of learning would happen, 'action learning' should form part of the programme in which executives and managers in teams work on real world problems to come up with real world solutions. In order to determine whether business schools were able to meet the bank's needs for business education, the following criteria were established. The intention was to focus on which would be the most suitable business school with whom to form working partnerships.

Selection criteria for business school as development provider

- *Centre of excellence* – the reputation and professional standing of the business school/ university and its experience in running senior executive programmes within the financial/retail services sectors. Preferably experience of working with consortia.
- *International reputation* – evidenced by international participation on its programmes and experience of dealing with cross-cultural issues.
- *Teaching staff* – the academic credentials and relevant research were considered important, but of greater significance was the capacity to focus on personal development issues, self-managed learning, and the ability to work at in-depth levels on personal transitions.
- *Learning process* – meeting existing senior level programme needs and objectives through appropriate use of top-level network contacts and external speakers, application of skills and experience of academic staff and the creative use of a variety of learning methods.
- *Pedagogical approach* – distinctive philosophy of management education.
- *Added value* – successful management of complex client relationships, for example, the ability to co-ordinate and integrate the inter-functional/inter-company nature of the programme commitment to deliver programmes to contractual specifications against acceptable cost/time parameters; the flexibility to meet the bank's needs and to work in partnership on programme design; a flexible, adaptable and innovative approach to a changing and evolving programme.

- *Location and facilities* – judged by the teaching environment, facilities and an accessible venue in acceptable surroundings.

Why a consortium?

The use of consortium-based management development programmes had been emerging as a means of educating and preparing individuals to take on broader or more senior jobs and to deal successfully with internal and external changes affecting large organisations. The most successful examples of consortium programmes involve companies with a similar employee development philosophy coming together and exposing carefully selected individuals to a broadening and benchmarking experience which enhances their ability to analyse situations and trends, and subsequently improve their decision-making capability. By working with a range of companies, it would provide managers with the opportunity to be exposed to different cultures, different managerial mindsets and values and an opportunity to challenge and confront their own personal issues and how they managed themselves and others. The identified target audience were managers who were in a functional specialist role, who had demonstrated their ability to progress to senior management positions in the future.

Aims of the programme

Broad parameters were set out in the form of a specification which was expected to be altered to accommodate the different companies' requirements. However the essence of the overall aims of the programme specification were:

- to present high-potential senior managers, primarily from across the UK operating companies and group departments, with the opportunity to broaden themselves beyond their existing functional areas to wider business issues;
- to increase the effectiveness of these managers within their existing role while being prepared to assume greater responsibility for their own development and career management;
- to develop the managers' capability to deal with issues at a more strategic level by increasing their knowledge, experience and networking contacts outside their current operating company environment; and
- also, to encourage the managers to assume greater responsibility for identifying their own learning and development requirements for the remainder of their career.

Choosing the consortium partners?

Consortium partners were initially sought on the basis of being existing corporate customers with the bank, so by tapping into the relationship management side of the business, this enabled warm leads to be pursued with external consortium partners. Other selection criteria adopted for the successful coalition of potential consortium partners included that each company should have identified development needs for their senior managers which would be met by this programme; partners should be used to dealing with large organisations which have a reputation for integrity in their dealings with all stakeholders; partners should be able to offer an active and visible contribution towards the development of the programme; and partners should have a clear strategy for managing the senior managers' transfer of learning and indicate their methods of assessing improved performance.

Consequently, four large blue-chip companies representing the financial, retail and manufacturing sector came together to form the consortium caucus. Each of the consortium partners already had extensive development and training programmes in place within their own organisations. In joint discussions however, it became clear that there was a common need which was not being met by existing development activities or external programmes. This concerned the needs of high-potential senior managers who are already successfully discharging functional or line responsibility and have developed a strong internal network within their function and/or across their organisation. In order for these managers to develop further, they needed to be exposed to a broader network of contacts and be given experience of how successful companies tackled similar problems and challenges to their own. This needed to be done in an environment which lifted their level of thinking and introduced them to a range of essential management techniques and concepts which would prepare them for taking on more substantial responsibilities.

Benefits of operating as a consortium

Quite apart from the significant benefits of having shared the development costs and offered more frequent programmes than were otherwise available to meet the then current needs of the organisation, there were other reasons for approaching this development need in a partnership arrangement which are summarised below:

- Many of the business schools approached responded extremely positively with far more interest in delivering a consortium programme rather than a single company, in-company or public company programme. Consequently, the calibre of the faculty and resources allocated to this venture were considerably higher in comparison with other types of programmes.
- The consortium concept brought together a strongly focussed group of business partners who had significant leverage over the relationship with the business school and provided ongoing opportunities to influence the nature and structure of the programme to ensure it met its business requirements.
- This innovative approach certainly helped to promote the image of the bank as one that was prepared to invest in such an extensive and collaborative arrangement with a number of large blue-chip companies. The consortium attracted a great deal of press coverage and attracted a degree of interest and publicity beyond the companies involved in the process. Thus the event helped to raise the image of the bank, both internally and externally.
- As a founder-partner in the consortium, the bank was able to influence the continuing development of the consortium project and also to vet the introduction of other potential partners into the arrangement as the programme matured.

To minimise the risks and the initial outlay involved in this venture, the commitment from each consortium partner was limited to sharing the development costs and the costs of running one pilot programme.

Having set out the parameters for the programme, eight top UK business schools were invited to tender to deliver the programme. Each education provider was interviewed in turn and four business schools presented proposals to a panel of executives and senior managers from each of the companies. A highly reputed business school was selected against the criteria previously described.

Programme content

In order to provide a suitable structure which could achieve the overall aims and objectives of the programme, it was necessary to produce a programme which spread over one month containing two one-week modules. As the programme design evolved, it became increasingly apparent for all the companies in the consortium that the organisations of the future need leadership, top team working, strategic, managerial, interpersonal, creative and conceptual skills. This also emphasised the importance of networking, benchmarking and best practice solutions. Consequently, the theme of the first module was the manager and the organisation; the second module was on the individual within the organisation. The programme was consciously designed to be demanding at all three levels, that is, intellectually, emotionally and physically, to ensure that the learning for the managers would be profound, intense and would enable the delegates to shift their thinking and their actions in a productive and positive way so that they are in a position to add real value to themselves and their organisation.

The thrust of the first module was on developing executive capability through examining the executive and strategic challenges of senior office, providing frameworks and approaches which could be employed to address these challenges. This programme encouraged self and peer assessment to identify each manager's executive capability; enabling managers to access the key ingredients of effective management by unblocking previously untapped energy and potential. It also included exploring the attributes of the discretionary leader: flexibility, creativity, vision, intellectual and physical fitness and it helped participants to develop an appropriate route map for operating successfully at a more senior level within their organisations. The first module also focussed on the challenge of managing diverse cultures coupled with strategic change and corporate culture. Specific executive skills were covered which concentrated on appreciating the visioning process, projecting a positive attitude and managing sensitive relationships.

The second module was underpinned with the bioenergetic approach which concentrated on body/mind psychology. Bioenergetic theory was used to help managers better understand the issues they faced at work within the context of positive human potential. The week involved extensive self and peer analysis which included one-to-one counselling, paired work and personal development groups which supported the creation and implementation of personal development plans. The module was linked to the previous one by reviewing visionary leadership and politics in the workplace. The programmes were started in 1995 and the programme has been well received. The design and structure were beyond most of the participants' education and development experience and the design enabled some powerful networks to be developed outside the participants' own organisations. The participants certainly felt they developed much greater confidence and resilience in being able to manage and work with significant change in their own organisations, and in some cases similar comments could be applied to the participants' personal lives.

Business education as a strategic intervention

Having traced the story of the programme in outline, we can learn much about management development interventions, by considering how the consortium was managed.

This section will discuss the key issues about this kind of intervention which arose from the establishment and implementation of the consortium. However, first of all, it will set the struggle to get the consortium going within the context of the organisation's culture and the extent to which that coloured its approach to business education.

Work to set up the consortium began before the bank's takeover. It was in its early stages when the takeover happened and the new owners could easily have cancelled the whole venture at little or no cost. That this did not happen probably owes more to luck than to design, not least because the new owners were, in principle, antipathetic to the whole concept of business education, in particular where it involved the use of external resources. This reflected, in large part, the organisation's historical socio-cultural background. It had originally developed on the basis of Calvinistic principles of self help and hard work. Its strengths came from inside rather than through reliance on others. Even in the second half of the twentieth century the new owners remained in many respects a colonial operation doing business in an increasingly post-colonial world. Compared with other multinationals, localisation of staff at management level remained modest. In a business environment in its home base where the MBA was king, the bank refused to waste time on such modish qualifications. What chance then for the survival of a proposal which involved a business school and co-operation with other British companies?

Thus the need for a strategic business education plan to support the bank's strategy was overridden by the takeover and deflected senior management's attention from implementing a fully fledged business education strategy. The original sponsor, that is the chief executive, was required to leave the bank which left many of the HR initiatives which he sponsored exposed and vulnerable to cuts. As Bowman (1990) stresses, 'day-to-day operational problems soak up the scarcest resource in any organisation: management time, talent, energy and commitment to change'. However, the focus of the business strategy had essentially not changed, that is to become a lean, commercially driven business where success would bring benefits to shareholders, customers and staff alike. The type of manager wanted within this new organisation was one who was more commercially driven and overtly operated the values of the acquiring organisation and not of the old bank. For the first time, managers were to understand the full extent of the term accountability.

So how did the programme manage to survive? What happened in practice was that initially the programme within the bank continued in spite of the new owners. This was in part because management was retained in the hands of employees drawn from the previous ownership and in part because the new owners were prepared simply to keep an eye on its development, not least because of its potential commercial value. Ultimately it became absorbed within the bank's own emergent strategy, the focus of which was primarily on internal training geared towards how to do business within the new culture of the bank's owners. As this strategy was still evolving, the consortium programme managed to retain a relevance to senior management and the organisation by offering teaching at both very personal and conceptual levels. Both levels were essential to the successful implementation of the programme and to the genuine achievement of its objectives.

The formation of the consortium took a considerable amount of time as the key to its success was the chemistry of the inter-relationships between each company's HR specialists. The consortium was established by each company's HR department with the support of their respective businesses and, in particular, senior management. However, it became clear that each company's approach to HRM was different, that is the HR function was either fully integrated within the business or was perceived as a separate entity. If the structure was such that it was integrated within the business, then this was reflected in the level of involvement from each of the consortium representatives: the more business backing there was, the greater the representatives' involvement.

Once the programme became established and received favourable national media coverage, considerable interest developed from those companies which had a more distant relationship with the consortium and this provided sufficient interest for the new recruits. Certain companies were initially approached on the basis of the customer relationship with the bank and the initial contacts were made at very senior levels in each organisation. Those companies which agreed to be involved then nominated someone as company representative on the consortium management committee.

Certain companies undoubtedly used involvement in the consortium to pursue their own agendas. For example, in the early stages, two large blue-chip organisations developed a bilateral dialogue without the wider involvement of other consortium partners which increasingly had the aim of undermining the consortium as a whole. It became clear that this was generated primarily because one of the two felt aggrieved that he was not leading the consortium and that the particular individual concerned could not secure any personal recognition for developing the initiative. A further complication was that these two organisations were in a customer-supplier relationship, with the customer clearly calling the shots in relationship to the supplier. Ultimately both organisations withdrew from the consortium, thereby affecting the initial constitution of consortium companies.

The evolving nature of the consortium blossomed in spite of that setback, due to a considerable amount of support from the two companies left to continue with the quest and the support from the business school which by then had been selected and was heavily involved in the negotiations; a mixed group, who were in a sense 'comrades in diversity'. If anything, that experience strengthened the resolve to make the consortium happen as those involved believed strongly in the concept and the huge value to the individual managers and each of the businesses involved.

A drive to find suitable partners was imperative and the two remaining company representatives, that is the bank and a large international insurance company, set out a plan of action to focus on certain sectors. Altogether over 70 companies were approached and of the ones which joined the consortium very few had a corporate relationship with the bank. Eventually the consortium was formed with over seven companies represented. It became a mixture of core and peripheral partners which reflected different levels of involvement and the number of participants nominated onto each programme. The programme was also designed to accommodate both core objectives, which were applicable to all members, and the differing strategic needs of individual consortium partners. The common denominator in all of this was the business school which provided the flexibility needed to satisfy the different needs of each company and yet maintain a common thread. As a consequence, as the programme matured, a tripartite relationship emerged between the consortium companies, the participants and the business school.

In addition a conscious decision had been taken at an early stage by the core consortium members that to ensure the success of the programme it would be necessary to establish a way of working together and thus ground rules were established. This reflected the importance of the chemistry of the relationships between individual members in maintaining the momentum and the energy required to secure the continued existence of the programme. These ground rules and the established working relationships which developed made it possible to accommodate a changing population of company representatives. Yet, ultimately, for all this to work an individual leader was required and who needed considerable interpersonal qualities and tenacity and stamina to keep the initiative going and together with a trusted deputy to drive it through to a successful conclusion. An atmosphere of shared creativity was encouraged at the steering group meetings – with a dolphin insignia to represent friendliness, and a kind of natural intelligence. Fig 8.2 shows a typical 'mind map' which was used to display the programme style and the ground rules for the consortium.

An important and increasingly significant aspect of the programme was the need for senior managers to manage change. This was particularly pertinent at the time as the bank's senior managers were experiencing the effects of the acquisition and the other consortium participants were subject to extensive restructuring within their own organisations. As the programme progressed, one of the core consortium companies underwent a merger and many of the participants commented on their increased ability to manage change positively in terms of greater confidence, better decision making, improved awareness of the needs of others during change and that their personal life had improved by giving some of the managers a broader outlook. One of the participants commented that 'the examples used on the course, the discussion with other delegates, the models and greater self-knowledge represent a major investment in my ability to manage change.'

There was a small element of risk to a programme which focusses at a personal level where the 'fallout' could not be predicted. It certainly helped to address many personal agendas, affecting both home and working life, but by delving deeply into an individual's motivations and levels of energy the programme could have had a disturbing impact on the individual as some managers were inevitably less self-aware than others. Nevertheless this personal development work was considered an essential part of all the programme and key to their own personal growth and the development of their own emotional maturity.

Implicit in the senior managers' development was an ability to diagnose the culture of their own organisations, that is, the prevailing patterns of values, attitudes, beliefs,

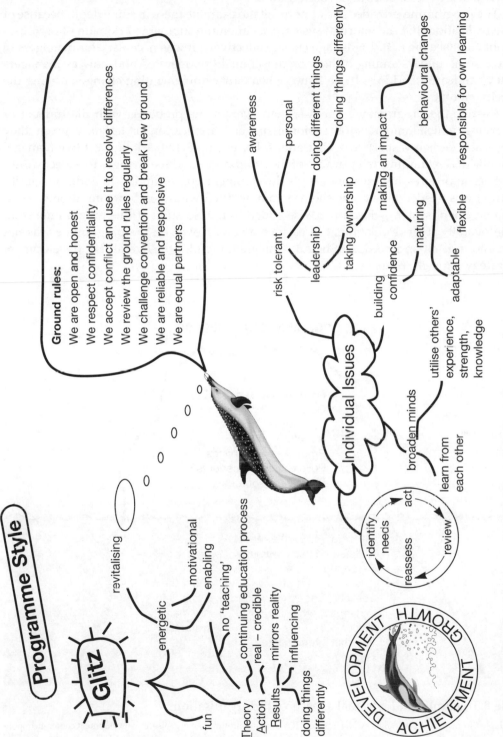

Programme Style

Glitz
- revitalising
- energetic
  - motivational
  - enabling
- no 'teaching'
- Theory
- Action — continuing education process
  - real – credible
- Results — mirrors reality
  - influencing
- doing things differently
- fun

Ground rules:
We are open and honest
We respect confidentiality
We accept conflict and use it to resolve differences
We review the ground rules regularly
We challenge convention and break new ground
We are reliable and responsive
We are equal partners

- awareness
- risk tolerant — personal
- leadership — doing different things
  - doing things differently
- taking ownership
- making an impact — behavioural changes
  - responsible for own learning
- building confidence
- maturing — adaptable
  - flexible

Individual Issues
- utilise others' experience, strength, knowledge
- broaden minds
- learn from each other

identify needs → act → review → reassess → (cycle)

GROWTH
DEVELOPMENT
ACHIEVEMENT

Fig 8.2   Ground rules for consortium liaison committee (for committee members' reference only)

assumptions, expectations, interactions, norms and feelings as embodied within the formal and overt aspects of the organisation.

The programme provided the opportunity to examine these in some depth because of the realisation that the informal system was often the submerged domain of organisational life (see Fig 8.3). To manage change effectively, it was necessary for managers to have some understanding of how organisational life operated and how as managers they can learn to address these issues when either implementing change or being the recipient of it.

Despite the programme's success, there were some problems with the transfer of learning which hindered the senior managers' application of learning when they returned to their respective organisations. For example, the lack of executive management's understanding and purpose of the programme and the changes to expect were a barrier to progressing each manager's development opportunities. In addition, clarification was needed about how the programme fitted within each organisation's career management system which otherwise added to the isolation of this programme from the overall career development in each company. However, the programme was not an end in itself and needed to be fully integrated within the overall HR development strategy for each company.

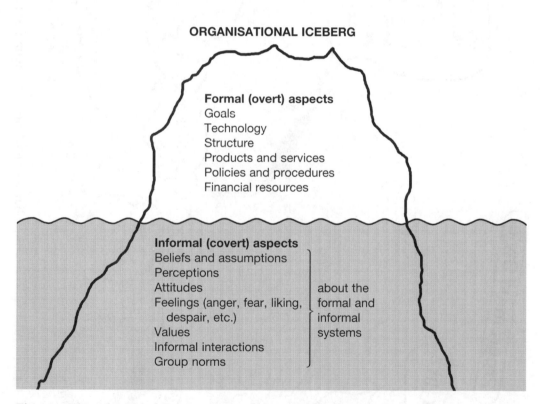

Fig 8.3   Formal and informal aspects of the organisation

Adapted from an address by Stanley N. Herman, TRW Systems Group, at an organisation development conference sponsored jointly by the Industrial Relations Management Association of British Columbia and the NTL Institute for Applied Behavioural Science, Vancouver, BC, Canada, 1970.

The consortium programme did succeed in providing a significant development experience for the managers and the benefits were seen in improving performance over time as well as from the immediate benefits to the business, derived from the managers' increasing ability to manage changes within their respective organisations.

REFERENCE

Bowman, C. (1990) *The Essence of Strategic Management*, Prentice Hall International (UK) Ltd, p. 6.

THE RELATIONSHIP BETWEEN MANAGEMENT DEVELOPMENT AND ORGANISATION DEVELOPMENT

Lessons from ethnographic research

Andrew Kakabadse, Andrew Myers, Siobhan Alderson and Lola Okazaki-Ward

Employee development through various kinds of learning is a well established process for changing organisations, and therefore for organisation development. From the previous two chapters the complexities of that process and the impact of organisational context have emerged. The questions of how to diagnose issues and how to intervene in the senior management process of top teams leads to using methodologies which are both diagnostic and developmental at a deep level. This chapter describes such an approach.

In a study of the behaviours and capabilities of senior level management, in medium- to large-sized corporations, the senior managers of 12 multinationals, mostly European but including five US organisations with substantial investments in Europe, were examined for a period of 35 months. The intent was to identify the key issues, role concerns, interfacing experiences and behaviours exhibited by senior managers who occupy roles of strategic responsibility. The learning from interview and extended participant observation substantially influenced the design of the Cranfield Executive Competencies questionnaire, initially validated through two pilot studies, later translated (and back translated) into five languages. The questionnaire was utilised as the vehicle for gathering data concerning senior manager performance and behaviour in over 2600 organisations in Europe.

However, the purpose of this chapter is not to outline the results of the European Executive Competencies Survey, but to present the experiences of the researchers in undertaking an ethnographic study of the senior managers of 12 multinationals over a three-year period. The researchers consider the ethnographic stage as fundamental to the progress of the overall study, as without it, the depth of understanding of the behaviours of senior management necessary to incorporate into the design of the main survey would, in their opinion, not have emerged.

Ethnography

Ethnography originated from the school of symbolic interaction and was promoted by the influential Chicago School of Sociology. It emerged as a fundamental alternative methodology of the 1920s and 1930s for the observation of the changing patterns of life and behaviour within urban communities (Malinowski, 1922; Park and Burgess, 1921; Thomas, 1961). In contrast to the analytical approach driven by multi-variate techniques (Pugh and Levy, 1969), ethnography involves the researcher attempting to understand the fundamental meanings which are assumed strongly to influence the behaviours and longer-term patterns of their subjects. Hence, in order to be appreciative of the diversity and plurality of interests within any circumstance, the researcher needs to become a part of the setting under scrutiny (Bott, 1955; Garfinkel, 1967). The imperative is to live among those under analysis, so that the interpretation of behaviours and meanings practised and relevant to those within that context is accurately represented to a broader audience (Berreman, 1968; Rosen, 1991). Ethnography has been applied to explore meanings and behaviours in different settings, such as developments within communities (Whyte, 1955), criminality (Mars, 1974; Patrick, 1973), quality of service provision in service organisations, such as hotels (Mars and Nicod, 1984), nightclubs (Analoui and Kakabadse, 1991), within industrial settings (Cavendish, 1982; Gouldner, 1954), leaders of organisations (Dalton, 1959) and the growth, development and demise of small businesses (Stockport, 1992).

Alternative terminologies, purporting to similar ideals and practice, have equally emerged. For some, participation and observation are not just modes of social inquiry, but more a deeper integration of purposes and interests in the interaction between the researcher and the subject(s) under investigation (Ackroyd and Hughes, 1981). Once that sense of integration is felt to be established, interpretations leading to hypotheses can be assumed as 'safe' to pursue. Further, the notion of Grounded Theory, namely a process of theory emerging from data as free as possible of preconceived values and models imposed by the researcher, is an alternative heading for the same fundamental rigours of ethnography (Glaser and Strauss, 1970; Smith, 1984).

The theme of 'theory from data' is strongly championed by Eden and Huxham (1993) who argue that access to data and maintaining credibility with the participants are crucial issues. Drawing on the work of Lewin (1946, 1947) and others (Rapaport, 1970; Susman and Evered, 1978) Eden and Huxham argue that promoting the mantle of consultant is an important consideration in order to negotiate in-depth penetration of any context. The authors argue that consultancy and any action perspective to inquiry are by no means mutually exclusive as long as a distinction can be drawn between what is relevant not only to the local context and implications but that can be drawn that have relevance across a number of contexts. In effect, consultancy and an action perspective to research merge if deductions made at any one site maintain relevance across a number of contexts and remain within the boundaries of the project.

Eden and Huxham locate their perspectives on action-orientated theory and practice within an action research setting. Frohman, Sashkin and Kavanaugh (1976) go further providing an action research perspective applied to organisation development. Under the action research banner, others in turn highlight the challenges, dilemmas and emerging practices for consideration (Foster, 1970; Heller, 1993; Rapaport, 1970; Susman and Evered, 1978).

Whether the distinction between the terms ethnography, grounded theory and action research is spurious in that they are simply different headings providing insight for similar processes, or not, certain common themes seem necessary to consider. These are:

- Interaction with the participants under scrutiny has to be sustained over time. Hence, issues of gaining entry, negotiating trust and maintaining credibility arise. How these issues are addressed may differ from one site to the next. However, the relationship building and maintaining skills of the researcher are of crucial consideration.
- The conditions of each locality of site is likely strongly to influence the mode of data gathering. A mix of approaches is likely to emerge including interviews, shadowing, attending meetings, running workshops and even casual meetings and conversations. Data is not invalidated because different models of approach are applied from one site to another. What counts more is the quality of data; less so how it was gathered.
- Data gathering and theory development are unlikely to be distinguished in terms of the different stages of a project. Data gathering and the emergence of broader generalisation which may or may not survive as concepts and theory are likely to considerably overlap and may be experienced as haphazard, and the drawing together of sound principles may only be done in retrospect. On this basis, validation is of prime concern and even then may be experienced as 'the best one can do at the time'.

Perspectives on senior managers

Studies of top managers have tended to fall into one of two categories. A popular area of inquiry is an exploration of attributes of individuals in terms of behavioural, attitudinal or deeper personality dimensions (Bennis and Nanus, 1985; Kotter, 1982; Margerison and Kakabadse, 1984; Margerison and Lewis, 1983). Related are the discussions on managerial performance (Boyatzis, 1982; Ghiselli, 1971; McCall and Lombardo, 1983). An interesting paper is that of Morse and Wagner (1978) who attempt to develop a questionnaire to evaluate which managerial behaviour(s) best succeeds. In contrast, Marshall and Cooper (1979) provide an easy-to-read analysis of how managers respond to stress and the impact of such experiences on work performance. Further, a recently emerging area which is likely substantially to influence thinking in the areas of managerial work and performance is that of values and personal beliefs. Boulgarides, Fisher and Gjelten (1984) and Watson and Simpson (1978) directly address this topic and conclude that the personal values and beliefs of the senior manager are an important influence on the work related performance of the individual.

An alternative field of study has focussed more on job, role and organisation related criteria. Mintzberg (1973) and Stewart (1976), in particular, have made a considerable impact with their studies highlighting the key elements of managerial work. Equally, attention has been given to the impact of managerial level and functional speciality on the work practices of managers. Parrett and Lau (1983), Paolillo (1981), and McCall and Segrist (1980) suggest that the nature of managerial work changes according to functional specialisation and position in the organisational hierarchy. Montanare (1978), in particular, emphasises that managerial work is strongly influenced by hierarchical position, in terms of the actual or potential discretion related to role. The discretionary elements of role refer to the choices that the role incumbent needs to make in order to provide shape and identity to their role and by implication to that part of the organisation for which they are accountable. For example, one interpretation of the role of director of HR is that the incumbent needs to form a view as to the shape and size of the organisation, the level of investment necessary for both production and R & D, the revenue potential of the distribution channels and/or channels to market, the measures of financial performance that are appropriate such as margin, profitability, revenue and from that total business understanding, only then form a view as to how the HR function should be developed in terms of its identity, shape and size in order to support the other line functions. In effect, the role incumbent may see their primary identity as business oriented, which in turn seriously influences the pursuit and practice of the functional components of the job.

The exercise of choice may be influenced by current issues of an operational or strategic nature or by future assumed concerns. Choice equally may be driven by more emotive experiences such as feelings of vulnerability, insecurity, anger or even 'difficult-to-justify' sentiments of not being able to cope. There is equally no reason to assume that those occupying discretionary roles of operational and strategic responsibility will respond in a comparable manner to the more so-called quantifiable 'objective' issues. Even if the emotive and mental capacity of the senior managers of the organisation is considerable, why should similar conclusions be reached as to the shape, size, direction and key qualities of the total organisation and thereby the configuration of each role incumbent's area of accountability?

Particularly evident is likely to be the potential disparity of choices during circumstances of more fundamental change. Argyris and Schön (1978) draw a distinction between change that takes place within existing frameworks and more fundamental alteration disrupting established boundaries, in coining the phrases single and double loop learning. Johnson and Scholes (1993), Daniels, de Chernatony and Johnson (1993) and Daniels and de Chernatony (1993) highlight that no meaningful change takes place unless core behaviours, and valued ways of interacting, are displaced and substituted with alternative behaviours at the group or organisational level. Argyris (1991, 1993) continues the theme by highlighting that the approaches to learning adopted by individuals substantially influence subsequent behaviours.

Pursuing the theme of utilisation of discretion, analysis of the leadership contribution to the effective management of the organisation, especially during phases of change, will require that attention be given to the quality of dialogue between the members of the senior management group. What happens to the senior executive grouping and the organisation, if two or more top managers form substantially, deeply held, different views as to the necessary current configuration and future organisational identity and shape? What if the experience of working within the senior management group is one of unworkable discomfort, whereby a restricted dialogue, debilitating tension at a personal level and minimal disclosure, become the norm? How do such experiences and processes impact on leadership practice and the future development of the organisation?

With a need to understand the intents of key managers, their processes of interaction and consequent behaviours, ethnography is considered as an appropriate lever for exploring potential multiple meanings within distinct circumstances. Rejected are the limited duration observation and interviews with just general managers (Kotter, 1982), revisiting individuals after limited periods of time (Mintzberg, 1973), the recording of relevant data through diaries (Stewart, 1976), sharing with the chief executive their work and social life habits (Bennis and Nanus, 1985) or even autobiographical accounts of leading change (Harvey-Jones, 1988) as such methods do not fully account for the impact of the interactive processes between the members of the senior management group(s) on the thinking, behaviour and leadership contribution of each of the senior managers of the organisation.

Ethnography with top management

Below are provided the experiences and emerging conclusions of the researchers in attempting effectively to apply ethnographic principles of observation in terms of open-ended interviews, more intensive private and confidential 'counselling' interviews, cross-comparison of views in group settings, participant observation, revisiting sites for further interviewing and observation and the sifting through of an accumulation of recorded materials or documents. As stated, the study was prolonged over three years, observing the behaviours and developmental experiences of over 500 senior managers in 12 multinationals. Relationships were formed with the majority of respondents by the study team. Often, numerous interviews were held with each individual. The researchers attended various management and staff meetings observing developments over time. The researchers equally attended workshops, other off-site training events and meetings, observing and later exploring the reasons for particular contributions and behaviours as exhibited by certain senior managers. Particular decisions or agree-ments to act were followed through in order to ascertain whether what was intended to happen occurred and how the individuals involved rationalised the outcomes. Throughout the study every attempt was made to maintain effective relationships, adjust to the conditions and locality and at the same time allow for broader principles to emerge, a process which the researchers labelled as theory development.

Fundamental to this study is the dimension of time and how with time, the role of the ethnographer evolved in order more fully to understand the nature and implications of the events and processes observed in the organisations under scrutiny.

1. Entry: needs driven intervention

The identity projected by the researchers seriously influenced the process of negotiating entry into the organisation, gaining access to the appropriate senior managers and the quality of subsequent interviews.

Projecting a more classical mantle of inquiry, that of academic researcher and/or functional expert, allowed for more limited access, both in terms of entry and scope and breadth of meetings and interviews. One common reaction from the participants was rejection and the most commonly quoted reason was lack of time. The reasons given were competitive pressures, restructuring or downsizing making the circumstances inappropriate for interview and conversation. The preoccupation of the respondents with their concerns, and the likely irritation they indicated they would experience in terms of making time for discussion and questioning, made it difficult to gain people's co-operation to attend meetings and interviews. In certain organisations, an added reason given was that people in the organisation were suffering from 'survey fatigue'. Internal questionnaire surveys, interviews and surveys organised by professional consultants and exposure to research initiatives from different organisations such as other academic institutions or professional associations (that is those representing the interests of personnel/marketing specialists or accountants) were quoted as additional reasons for people in the organisation to not be motivated to enter into further discourse with outsiders.

Even on having gained entry through projecting a more academic/researcher label, the researchers' experience was that similar time constraints and survey fatigue reasons were offered to limit the duration of the interactions to just one or two interviews. Certain appointments were cancelled outright. A considerable number of appointments were rearranged and/or shortened in terms of time for exploration in order to accommodate the circumstances of each respondent.

In contrast, adopting a more client needs driven image, in terms of being capable of providing support according to the needs of the respondents under the banner of consultancy, counselling or business expert, induced a more positive response. Less comment was made concerning pressing time constraints and hence the need to renegotiate commitments. More attention was focussed on how external assistance, or at least an 'unbiased' view, could provide for insights to help stimulate acceptable ways forward. The emerging psychological contract was that after full and meaningful examination of the respondents' circumstances (either individual, group or organisational) comment would be desired from the interviewer concerning the interviewee's circumstances and how best to proceed in that situation.

In order more fully to gain access, the profile of business expert rather than observer was projected. In order to continue with the project, living up to the expectations of being capable of appropriately responding to business and organisational dilemmas became a dynamic in its own right. The invitation to respond to the question, 'Well, what do you think?' required a display of understanding of strategic processes, as well as indicating a sensitivity to the experiences of those occupying senior managerial roles.

It was quickly learned that negotiating trust and credibility with the respondents was strongly desired in order to continue with the ethnographic survey.

2. Negotiating trust

As the pathway to gaining access to data concerning deeply held beliefs about appropriate and inappropriate conduct, attitudes and fundamental determinants of action (or inaction) required projecting an image alternative to that of researcher, the issue of gaining the trust of the participants became paramount. Taken for granted was confidentiality of disclosure, as was to exhibit being non-judgemental. The researcher/consultant was there to listen!

Negotiating the necessary trust so that the respondents would wish to invest their time for dialogue and inquiry was, however, strongly influenced by the researcher's sensitivity to executive exposure.

Executive exposure

All of the respondents in this sample were individuals who occupied roles predominantly discretionary and not prescriptive in nature. The respondents were general managers or directors (including chairmen, MDs and CEOs), either at subsidiary, divisional or corporate centre level. By the nature of the roles they held, they were required to exercise choice in order to provide identity to their role. Whether the choices made are conscious, in terms of clarity of detail and consistency of argument, or more emotive, in terms of current personal disposition, or more assumed, namely on a taken-for-granted basis, choice nevertheless is exercised in order for the leadership contribution to proceed. Clarity of thinking concerning options should not be assumed, because the role incumbent may not know, or not appreciate the full extent of the issues and concerns or the mechanisms for addressing such predicaments, may not be emotionally or intellectually capable of exercising choice, or may be faced with substantially conflicting evidence concerning options whereby choice may feel like guesswork. However, after a period of time, the quality (or lack of it) of the choices made become clear as events and processes unfold. Choices are made, agendas formed and particular avenues pursued and only after time has elapsed does the impact of those choices become visible. Hence, one feature of occupying roles where discretion predominates is the likelihood of being judged in retrospect. As one chief executive commented in interview, 'who was to know what was the right thing to do at the time with our particular problem, the ensuing shareholder neglect and the subsequent panic response, but it became very clear two years on.' The CEO was referring to the shared perception of most of the directorate of the organisation. At the time in question, their problems did not feel so urgent. However, some time later, their perceived muted response to so-called crisis was viewed as inadequate and incompetent by key internal and external stakeholders.

Coming to terms with one's own emotions of anxiety, sensitivity and defensiveness to potentially permanent exposure and critical comment, is necessary simply in order to function at senior level. Accommodating feelings of vulnerability while occupying a strategic role is a likely experience for such role incumbents. Particularly pertinent is the Analoui (1992) and Stockport (1992) viewpoint which emphasises the detrimental impact on the interview or even overall exercise of making premature and/or out-of-place judgemental comment or responses. Hence, in order to establish the necessary trust so as to access the more deeply held and meaningful viewpoints and attitudes of the respondents without introducing inappropriate comment by the researchers, it was recognised as pertinent to exhibit understanding of the experience of being potentially permanently exposed and vulnerable.

Such understanding is displayed, less by sensitivity of personal style but more through focussing on questions addressing issues of process. Crucial is to combine an examination of issues of strategy and policy with an exploration of the underlying processes concerning strategy formulation and implementation. The process questions highlight concerns over commitment, motivation and coping with differences and tensions. Appropriately timed, the 'how do (did) you feel' questions can unearth substantially rich data. For example,

> 'How do you feel about such views/developments/ideas being discussed/adopted within the senior management group?'

> 'How do you feel about working/interacting/co-operating with colleagues who seem to commit to a different point of view to you but talk as if they do not?'

> 'How do you feel about colleagues/bosses who say one thing but then seem to behave in a manner that is different/contradictory to what was said?'

Reading the interviewee so as to switch the line of questioning from examination of issues of substance to exploration of underlying processes can strongly suggest empathy with the person who is faced with the difficult-to-resolve tensions of high office. Exhibiting understanding of the experience of managing multiple demands through line of questioning emerged as a positive stimulus for the interviewee to wish to continue with the inquiry process.

3. Negotiating credibility

The appropriate combination of substance and process questions is likely to stimulate greater disclosure. Greater disclosure is likely to expose the researcher to more open and more intense dialogue with the respondents. Greater intensity of dialogue provides for the welcome opportunity to access valuable data. However, such a heightened level of intensity equally exposes the researcher, his or her values, inclinations and awareness to the respondents. Either during a conversation, at an interview or workshop etc., or some time after a data gathering event, the respondents indicated that they were judging the researcher in terms of 'what does this person know about business and organisation?' With more open and in-depth dialogue, the capacity of the researcher to enter into such conversation and exhibit understanding of the experience of attending to strategic and/or more operational challenges is highlighted. Ironically, the researcher is there to find out! Yet in order to find out, it became apparent that with senior managers, it is of considerable advantage to promote an image of 'knowing what it's all about' before finding out!

The researchers' experience is that increased disclosure often led into an exploration of two particular themes. The manner of analysis and examination of these themes has, in the experience of the study team, influenced the standing and credibility of the researcher in the eyes of the respondents. The themes in question are:

- uncovering the opportunity costs; and
- distinguishing between people problems and structure problems.

Opportunity costs

Senior managers may be exposed to balancing the demands and requirements of superiors, colleagues and subordinates as well as effectively discharging the primary duties they perceive as required of them in their role. In effect, any senior manager is likely to be exposed to multiple interfaces, with each, for good reason, requiring particular attention which the person may or may not experience as too demanding to service effectively. The degree to which managers respond to their key interfaces as well as addressing the task demands of their role is partly dependent on their commitment to act as well as their view of the costs likely to be incurred by not acting. By neglecting certain task requirements, particular problems may emerge, and as such are termed operational costs, in effect 'easier-to-see mistakes'. However, through lack of concern for nurturing certain key interfaces, difficulties arise but take time to crystallise, these being termed as opportunity costs, that is only after time has elapsed will particular potential concerns emerge as identifiable problems. At the time, opportunity costs can be experienced as 'maybe problems' – maybe there is a problem, maybe not, it is just not clear yet.

Within the context of opportunity costs, one issue that repeatedly emerged in the study and generated a broad range of opinion and considerable expression of anger, was that of sales and marketing. Especially at business unit level and occurring with surprising regularity was that within the same organisation, different senior managers displayed deeply held but divergent views concerning the shape, identity and philosophy of the sales and marketing processes and activities the organisations should pursue, such views often well supported by cogent argument and relevant evidence. The common experience in the 12 case studies was to have managers adopting quite different understandings as to the meaning and practice of sales and marketing to their colleagues, fully aware of the organisational implications of such behaviour and even able to describe accurately the different positions adopted by colleagues. The implications of such splits are potentially serious.

Colleagues may proffer commitment to each other, to the structure and the policies of the organisation, but in reality may not pursue and may even undermine agreements jointly reached at key executive meetings. By not being able to agree on the shape and identity of the sales and marketing contribution, the organisation's capacity to trade may be considerably reduced. One main board director commented,

> We are not getting the sales and marketing right. We just cannot agree what sales and marketing means for our business. Yet we all seem to appreciate what the hell is happening out there. The point is we keep going round and round in circles talking about the same thing with little or no progress. We have all become used to not solving our problems.

An additional feature of opportunity cost circumstances is the potential for acceptance of 'accommodating present circumstances', 'not quite' addressing key concerns and allowing issues which require resolution to linger. Most respondents displayed considerable understanding of the implications of not fully searching for resolution. Most equally expressed an awareness of how failing to reach resolution can all too easily become an organisational norm.

However, gaining access to such insights was no easy task. Naturally, the respondents were reluctant to enter into dialogue that would highlight fundamental tensions and by implication their (by their own admission) uncorporate-like behaviour. As one respondent stated, 'It is distressing to talk about one's Brutus-like behaviour with someone else, especially when one thinks of oneself as a supportive member of the corporate community, but you see I feel I have no choice.'

People versus structure problems

In attempting to understand current individual and organisational circumstances and the reasons as to the strategic and operational pathways being pursued, exploration as to what are viewed as problems, and how to address such concerns, may be required. In complex organisation structures, whereby senior managers commonly respond to multiple interfaces, differences of view may emerge as to whether the structure of the organisation is considered as working effectively. In so doing, it may be necessary to explore the distinction each person draws between structure problems and people problems. Portrayals of tensions and difficult to resolve concerns may be attributed to the outcomes of operationalising the current organisational configuration, namely the structure of the organisation encourages dysfunctional behaviour between the key managers in the organisation. Equally, others could attribute identical symptoms of problems to the low calibre and/or uncooperative attitude of the individuals occupying those senior and important interfacing roles. Hence, substantial differences of view can arise in attributing cause and effect to the same events and agreed areas of concern.

The way such data was 'teased out' was through sensitive examination of interfacing intent and behaviour. Discussion of the behaviour of particular individuals, their past declarations of commitment to key decisions, the reasons as to why certain interfaces were given greater attention than others and discussion of the likely opportunity costs to emerge from such behaviour, led to an understanding of the ways of working exhibited by senior managers.

Penetrating examination of the participants' circumstances emerges from pursuing themes which encourage the respondent to contribute to the inquiry process. Through exhibiting an understanding that opportunity cost and organisation structure concerns do not easily lend themselves to simple cause and effect attribution, the researchers recognised that it is more likely that deeper analysis of organisational circumstances will occur. The researcher is now seen to know something about business. The respondents in turn feel that through dialogue, they too are learning, satisfying a prime reason for continuing with the inquiry, namely, 'I am getting something out of this.'

4. Triangulation

Stockport (1992) emphasises the importance of triangulation as the concern of any ethnographic methodology is the validity of findings. Well documented is the requirement for cross-referencing in order accurately to record important events. Equal attention needs to be given to recognising and examining the inhibitors and stimuli to action. The degree to which there exists compatibility of views concerning the nature of key organisational and external issues, and of the processes underlying dialogue, decision making and commitment to implementation, seriously influences the value of the data gathered.

Concerning facts, figures and key events, substantial verification emerged from the senior managers in the 12 organisations. The key influences and events that contributed to present circumstances, the problems and challenges faced by the organisation and the requirements for appropriate action were compatibly relayed by the senior managers of the organisation concerned.

Far less compatibility was witnessed in the attempts by the participants to analyse and conclude on processes. Quality of dialogue among and between the senior managers of the organisation was identified as a primary influence that could enhance or inhibit the stimulus to act. Interestingly, quality of dialogue was perceived as an issue of substance – a fact. Most of those involved in any one circumstance would independently concur a poor quality or high level of dialogue. However, considerable divergence of view emerged in terms of people's behaviours and contribution during dialogue. Of interest is the nature of the attribution one person projects on to the other, especially in circumstances where inhibition has become a norm. Any one senior manager feeling uncomfortable may describe his or her inabilities to raise key issues as the result of interacting in a negative environment. Others may perceive the same individual as being deceptive or secretive, in that the person concerned could be viewed as selective towards promoting his or her advantage. In effect, one person feels uncomfortable to enter into dialogue, while others see the individual and his or her behaviour as 'political'. Such wide divergence of view, in terms of interpreting the behaviour of significant others and the impact of such interpretation within the organisation, needs to be accounted for in the interview or observation process.

In order to allow for involvement so that a more balanced range of opinion can emerge, it is necessary for consideration to be given to sample scope and consequent sample size. Whether the study is concerned more with finite issues, such as role, functionality or product or service analysis, or with broader concerns such as work and organisational processes, sample scope requires careful examination in terms of triangulation.

A fundamental question arose in the study as to who is in or is not in the Executive, drawing a distinction between being a member of the Senior Executive Committee (that is Policy Committee) and feeling that one's work and activities entitle one to be recognised as a member of the broader Executive of the organisation. Drawing such distinction has implications for any examination of strategic processes. According to the configuration and circumstances of the organisation, different combinations of individuals are likely to be involved in the processes of strategy generation and implementation, differentiated by role, functional responsibility, access to and influence over key external interfaces or even being recognised as an influential person (internally) irrespective of role title. Sensitivity towards triangulation may require negotiating to extend sample scope and size as the study proceeds, in order to encompass appropriate opinion that initially may not have been recognised as relevant.

Case example

In a study of strategic processes within the retail, branch banking business of an international bank, considerable frustration was repeatedly expressed by senior management at the organisation's inability to effectively implement certain product/customer service initiatives, seen by most as key mechanisms for increasing customer loyalty and market share and enhancing revenue streams. The emerging shared view at senior management levels highlighted one group, the area directors, as primarily responsible for not effectively promoting the initiatives generated by senior management. In terms of 'real' status, these managers were perceived by top management as senior/middle level managers, their principal contribution being that of co-ordination of key initiatives and activities between the branches of the bank. Confidential one-to-one interviews, feedback workshops and limited participant observation identified certain strongly held sentiments among area directors. Feelings of isolation from top management, which in turn strongly influenced both their will to implement initiatives from the Policy Committee and their understanding of the viability of new ventures, emerged as concerns. Fundamentally, the area directors felt themselves to be a part of the Executive of the organisation as they identified their role as a vital link between strategy and operations. Their strongly held view was that they, as individuals, were required to interpret the viability of corporate centre initiatives for their area. In so doing, they felt they needed to be attentive to the detail of operation of any one venture so as to draw a distinction between an initiative that was right for their area but required further auditing in terms of detailed application, or one that would not be appropriate for that area irrespective of attention to detail.

It was considered necessary by the study team to approach senior management to request to interview a sample of top managers in order to better understand the quality of interface between top management and area directors. Certain members of the Policy Committee expressed reluctance to be interviewed, while others displayed irritation that they were now 'under scrutiny'. Of the few that co-operated, it became clear that attention needed to be given to a more intensive examination of the interface between top management and area directors, rather than just focussing on the activities and attitudes of the area directors. With the assistance of one of the top managers, a meeting was arranged between the research team and the Group CEO in order to gain his backing to extend the scope of the sample. At the meeting, the CEO stated that it would be difficult to 'sell' to the other members of the Policy Committee that they should give up some of their time to discuss a 'bunch of pissed off area directors'. In turn, the research team emphasised that considerable attention had been given to the area directors, but the interface between the two levels of management remained unexplored and seemed to require examination.

After considerable discussion, the CEO agreed to support further study. The interviews and discussions highlighted that an expectation of blame existed between the two levels of management. Area directors expected to be blamed for 'things going wrong or at least not being right enough'. In turn, senior management expected critical comment concerning their style and attitude, from area directors. Such negative perceptions seemed to influence the manner in which work was allocated. Area directors were omitted from particular senior management meetings which addressed certain issues of strategy and market driven initiatives. Their presence had been viewed as disruptive, and hence they were no longer invited to attend. Certain of the top managers expressed frustration, lack of trust and dislike of their area directors. As far as the area directors were concerned, some focussed more on business circumstances and/or organisational constraints, while others outlined feelings of frustration, isolation and demotivation, which substantially influenced their work performance and non-work-related personal circumstances. Of the area directors who identified themselves as demotivated, a considerable number were viewed by top management as 'bolshy and over-critical'.

Only through the mechanisms of one-to-one confidential interviews, group discussions and participant observation did greater clarity of understanding emerge. The participants themselves were surprised to see how many shared feelings of frustration and/or poor morale for similar reasons. Such depth of data and emerging insight was unlikely to have occurred had not a conscious policy of triangulation been pursued.

In effect, triangulation is required not only for purposes of verification of activities or events, but as a lever for deeper penetration of understanding of processes within the organisation which in turn may require renegotiation of sample shape and size.

5. Prompting: being more than passive

The researcher's view as to the quality of data being generated is likely to influence strongly the ensuing strategy of the inquiry. Asking open-ended questions, observing and sharing experiences through living with the participants in question, is likely to highlight the degree to which passivity on the researcher's part is desired. Recollection, on the participant's part, of current and past events and processes may not achieve the quality and depth of data desired by the researcher. The researcher may consider that a more proactive attitude on his or her part is required. The researcher may consider it pertinent to prompt the participants to reflect more intensely on past or current circumstances and processes. Under such circumstances, the ensuing data is influenced by the presence of the researcher but such data should not be assumed to be of low value or undesired.

Prompting was experienced as constituting the two following elements:

Providing mental linkages

Questions are identified by the researcher, which may or may not be considered as immediately relevant by the participants but, at least, start a line of inquiry which would otherwise have been neglected. In effect, the questions being pursued by the researcher allow for linkages to be made between two or more areas of interest. One case example is that of a chairman/chief executive officer (dual accountability within one role) of a large multinational, whose preoccupation was with external market/competitor circumstances but little concern was expressed for addressing the internal interfaces except when perceived hindrances emerged to seemingly block effective strategy implementation. The researcher asked why a particular level of senior management seemingly had repeatedly been omitted from the strategic dialogue. In the researcher's opinion, the senior managers in question could strongly determine the effectiveness of strategy implementation. The chairman's response was to ask why the researcher had asked such a question. The response, in turn, led to a lengthy discourse as to the reasons for the current circumstances of the organisation and the nature of the perceived internal blockages. The chairman acceded that that conversation had brought new light to his thinking which influenced his analysis of subsequent organisational issues. From the researcher's point of view, attention was drawn to what seemed to have been an area of neglect.

Feeding from other respondents

In order to stimulate further discussion, relevant issues and/or perceptions gathered from other respondents can be fed into the discussion with any one participant. Where verification of events is not sufficiently forthcoming or differences of view emerge concerning processes, challenging respondents with data about events or processes that has been highlighted in other interviews, group meetings or observations with other participants allows for a more penetrating analysis. The danger is that by offering data that contrasts with the participant's contribution, this may lead the individual down an avenue of inquiry which he or she may initially not have pursued, and which could unnecessarily deflect the individual from his or her original line of thought. The researcher would need to be conscious that once a line of inquiry has been pursued, feeding in other data is not necessarily inappropriate, but attention should be given to helping the participant to return to his or her original line of thought.

Straddling research and consultancy

As the emphasis of this treatise is focussed on how the interaction and dialogue between the members of the Executive of the organisation can influence strategy, change processes and the pursuit of goals at an individual, group and organisational level, any third party, researcher or consultant, intervening in that situation, if accepted, is likely to stimulate considerable interest among the participant group. Irrespective of original agreements, if the involvement of the researcher has stimulated a dialogue which, at least, some feel has been a valuable learning experience, then the agendas of the organisation have, to some degree, been determined by the researcher/consultant's presence. Even more so if the sentiment expressed is that the issues that emerge from the inquiry should, in some way, be fed back to some or all of the respondents.

Feedback allows for further cross-comparison of perceptions. Feedback can be written or offered verbally to individuals or to groups. If the original data was gathered on a one-to-one basis, feedback on issues arising, channelled to different management groupings, can stimulate debate as to the private perceptions of the respondents, the significance of the findings or even whether there exists concurrence as to the relevance of the issues identified. Data gathered, through whichever mechanisms, but fed back to one individual, such as chairman or CEO, can generate further discourse concerning the implications for future initiatives or change programmes.

As far as the participants are concerned, an agenda has been determined, through both the content of the feedback and its manner of presentation, by the researcher. As a result of the initial feedback given, further feedback may be requested, possibly on points of detail but equally on the processes experienced in interview. Questions may be asked of the researcher, such as:

'How co-operative or resentful were the participants to open up on individual or organisational related issues?'

'Were more personal sentiments expressed which cannot easily be incorporated into any feedback exercise in order to maintain confidentiality? If so, is it possible to describe what is the nature of those sentiments and concerns?'

'You have interviewed our people, and they are aware that feedback is taking place, but what is their reaction to us hearing their views, and what do they expect to emerge from all this?'

Responding, even in a non-committal fashion, has placed the researcher in the role of developer of the organisation. The researcher has become a consultant, rather than just adopting the mantle of consultant. Addressing issues of process helps mould or alter the potentially fundamentally held views of others. The more the researcher/consultant responds to concerns of how managers feel, what they do and their attitudes to particular initiatives or even to top management, the more the organisation is being influenced to proceed in a particular direction.

If the researcher wishes to continue with the inquiry, the understanding (contract) the individual has with the organisation may need to be reviewed, so as to allow the person to promote data gathering more and downplay interventionist activities or vice versa.

However, whether the researcher attempts to remain a researcher or assume a third party interventionist identity, straddling between research and consultancy is the ensuing likely experience. The proposition being made is that in order to enhance understanding of organisational circumstances, continued interaction with senior management may require a proactive contribution from the researcher to the development of the organisation. Straddling between the two roles is not the problem. Recognising, accepting and respecting the value laden nature of the interventionist impact of ethnographic research with top management, is the point of debate.

Managing dependency

Mintzberg (1973), Bennis and Nanus (1985) and Kotter (1982) undertook an inquiry of senior managers that was of a limited time frame and examined only a limited number of roles. Particular roles such as CEO or general manager were scrutinised in terms of task content and comparability of application by the role incumbents. If however the intent is to examine the formation of policy and strategies and the impact of their implementation within different contexts, the time necessary for such study needs to be extensive. Where a 'snapshot-of-time' analysis is undertaken, the observer can adopt a more passive role. Where the time needed for inquiry is lengthy, such passivity is unlikely to be acceptable to the population being examined. The researcher has gathered data; data which is likely to be relevant to the senior managers in terms of their management of the organisation and its future. As the relationship between researcher and participants evolves, individuals are likely to disclose views, sentiments and facts to the researcher which they may not at all, or only partially disclose to colleagues and superiors. The question likely to be posed is how can all benefit from the researcher's data or emerging insights. The pressure on the researcher to become involved, especially if process issues are being explored, is likely to accentuate the longer the researcher is on site.

Involvement, even if that just encompasses feedback to stimulate further dialogue, can induce varying degrees of dependency by the participants on the researcher. Depending on the availability and empathetic inclinations of the researcher, the participants may identify the researcher as a counsellor or even consultant, irrespective of the original agreements and financial relationship between the two parties. The researcher is the person who is seen to 'know most' about the organisation. Line managers may refer to the researcher for guidance and facilitation in addressing particular concerns. From being asked to help, on occasions, the researcher may be invited to intervene in both the planning and execution of particular developments within the organisation. The role progressively is transformed from data gatherer to local 'guru'.

Mechanisms for reducing dependency on the researcher, through transference of ownership of the data to the participants, need to be examined. Are there one or more individuals within the organisation who may be required to continue with the data gathering/feedback process, and if so who and for what purpose? How effective has the data feedback process been and if the researcher were to exit from the organisation, would any further attention need to be given to the quality of dialogue between the respondents involved? If further interventionist activity is required, should insiders, outsiders or a combination of the two be tasked with providing such a service?

To leave the organisation under scrutiny simply when the researchers' needs are satisfied may be disruptive and damaging to those who co-operated with the inquiry activity. Reducing dependency, and if necessary helping to establish continuity of the data gathering and feedback processes, has been experienced by the research team as necessary within the corporate world, for not to do so would, in the long term, damage the credibility of the researchers, precluding future activity.

Conclusion

Pursuing an ethnographic inquiry in the world of senior managers is considered not only to be value laden, but a situation where potentially constantly negotiating credibility is the likely experience for researchers. The primary reason for consideration for both the projection and maintenance of a positive image is that the participants are likely to need to 'trust' the researcher. The need for trust emerges from the likely vulnerability experienced by senior managers from occupying roles where the discretionary content is high. Feeling overexposed, responding to and addressing foreseen and unforeseen contingencies and being held to account for activities and events for which the senior manager may even not feel responsible, can induce defensiveness and a reluctance to participate in any exploratory exercise. Hence, getting to know the researcher, feeling comfort that the person is reasonably understanding of the dilemmas of senior office and trustworthy over the custody of the data gathered, are likely sentiments of the participants which require a positive and supportive response for the researcher.

The senior manager world is observed as one where insight as to the nature of the challenges and concerns facing each person are reasonably well appreciated. The key managers involved in the strategic management of the organisation are more than likely to be well aware of the issues they and their colleagues face. The question is to what extent are such issues explored and discussed? The, at time, incompatible agendas, the different perspectives adopted by the managers involved and their style or even deeper personality characteristics influence the quality and manner of dialogue. Normality of experience for senior managers is likely to be one of strained executive relationships. A substantial number of conflicting demands can be made on each person which does little to ease the likely strain in addressing matters of importance to the organisation.

Particularly pertinent under such circumstances, therefore, is to concentrate on actively enhancing dialogue. Failure to do so, or senior managers being left to get on with it on their own, or argue from their corner, can lead to tensions which, in turn, may inhibit conversation. It takes familiarity with the senior managers and the manner in which they interact in groups to discern whether issues of substance or issues of style or both may be responsible for strained conversation and lack of examination of concerns facing the organisation. Hence, the emphasis on growing trusting relationships is paramount in conducting any intervention with top management.

Because of the likely multiple demands upon any senior manager, time is an additional consideration in terms of negotiating credibility. The researcher is likely to be treated similarly to others, in that only limited time will be devoted to exploration and inquiry as other needs equally demand attention. Hence, negotiating credibility in order to keep the attention of the respondent(s) is necessary, as otherwise they will turn to address the other demands made on them.

Within such a context, it is proposed that the practice of ethnography within the senior executive world involves a 'straddle process', straddling between inquiry and understanding and involvement and intervention. Addressing the boundary issues is likely to be ongoing due to the ever changing demands of different respondents in different contexts. To resist becoming immersed and responsive to the fuzzy nature of the straddle between data gathering and organisational development is either likely to mean 'marginalising' the researcher within that context, or that whatever data is gathered is of inconsequential value.

Ethnographic research conducted with senior managers is not just dependent on the accuracy of observation but equally on participating in the exploration of complex meanings, a process which requires the full acceptance of the researcher by the participants. Such acceptance is gained through active and perceived as 'valuable involvement' in the organisation in question.

REFERENCES

Achroyd, S. and Hughes, J.A. (1981) *Data Collection in Context*, London, Longman.

Analoui, F. and Kakabadse, A. (1991) *Sabotage: How to Recognise and Manage Employee Defiance*, London, Mercury.

Argyris, C. (1991) 'Teaching Smart People how to Learn', *Harvard Business Review*, May–June, pp. 99–109.

Argyris, C. (1993) 'Education for Leading Learning', *Organisational Dynamics*, Winter, pp. 5–10.

Argyris, C. and Schön, D. (1978) *Organisational Learning: A Theory of Action Perspective*, Reading, MA, Addison-Wesley.

Bennis, W. and Nanus, B. (1985) *Leaders: The Strategies for Taking Charge*, New York, Harper and Row.

Berreman, G.D. (1968) 'Ethnography: Method and Product', in Clifton, J.A. (ed.) *Introduction to Cultural Anthropology: Essays in the Scope and Methods of the Science of Man*, Boston, Houghton Mifflin.

Bott, E. (1955) 'Urban Families: Conjugal Roles and Social Networks', *Human Relations*, Vol. 8, pp. 345–84.

Boulgarides, J.D., Fisher, M.A. and Gjelten, J. (1984) *Are You in the Right Job?*, California, Monarch Press.

Boyatzis, R.E. (1982) *The Competent Manager*, New York, John Wiley.

Cavendish, R. (1982) *Women on the Line*, London, Routledge.

Dalton, M. (1959) 'Informal Factors in Career Achievement', *American Journal of Sociology*, Vol. 56.

Daniels, K. and de Chernatony, L. (1993) 'Differences in Cognitive Models of Buyers and Sellers', paper presented to the international Workshop on Managerial and Organisational Cognition, Brussels, Belgium, 1993.

Daniels, K., de Chernatony, L. and Johnson, G. (1993a). 'Validating a Method for Mapping Managers Mental Models of Competitive Industry Structures', unpublished internal Cranfield School of Management paper, ESRC Support Grant M036200E.

Daniels, K., de Chernatony, L. and Johnson, G. (1993b) 'Mental Models of Competitive Industry Structures. Issues in Mapping and Homogeneity', unpublished internal Cranfield School of Management paper, ESRC Support Grant M036200E.

Eden, C. and Huxham, C. (1993) 'Distinguishing Action Research: Theory, Method and Practice', Paper 93/18 September, paper presented to the British Academy of Management Conference, Milton Keynes.

Foster, M. (1970) 'An Introduction to the Theory and Practice of Action Research in Work Organisations', *Human Relations*, Vol. 23, No. 6, pp. 529–50.

Frohman, M.A., Sashkin, M. and Kavanaugh, M. (1976) 'Action Research as Applied to OD', *Organisation and Administrative Sciences*, Vol. 7, pp. 129–61.

Garfinkel, H. (1967) *Studies in Ethnomethodology*, Englewood Cliffs, Prentice Hall.

Ghiselli, E. (1971) *Explorations in Managerial Talent*, Glenview, Illinois, Goodyear.

Glaser, B.G. and Strauss, A.L. (1970) 'Discovery of Substantive Theory: A Basic Strategy underlying Qualitive Research', in Filstead, W.J. (ed.) (1970) *Qualitative Methodology: First Hand Involvement with the Social World*, Chicago, Markham Publishing Co.

Gouldner, A.W. (1954) *Patterns of Industrial Bureaucracy*, New York, Free Press.

Harvey-Jones, J. (1988) *Making It Happen: Reflections on Leadership*, London, Collins.

Heller, F. (1993) 'Another Look at Action Research', *Human Relations*, Vol. 46, No. 10, pp. 1235–42.

Johnson, G.J. and Scholes, K. (1993) *Exploring Corporate Strategy*, (third edn), London, Prentice Hall.

Kotter, J.P. (1982) *The General Managers*, New York, Free Press.

Lewin, K. (1946) 'Action Research and Minority Problems', *Journal of Social Issues*, Vol. 2, pp. 34–46.

Lewin, K. (1947) 'Frontiers in Group Dynamics: Channel of Group Life; Social Planning and Action Research', *Human Relations*, Vol. 1, pp. 143–53.

Malinowski, B. (1922) *Argonauts of the Western Pacific*, London, Routledge and Kegan Paul.

Margerison, C.J. and Kakabadse, A.P. (1984) *How American Chief Executives Succeed: Implications for Developing High Potential Employees*, An American Management Association Survey Report.

Margerison, C.J. and Lewis, R. (1983) 'Mapping Managerial Work Preferences', *Journal of Management Development*, Vol. 2, pp. 36–50.

Mars, G. (1974) 'Dock Pilferage', in Rock, P. and McIntosh, M. (eds) *Deviance and Control*, London, Tavistock.

Mars, G. and Nicod, M. (1984) *The World of Waiters*, London, Allen and Unwin.

Marshall, J. and Cooper, C.J. (1979) *Executives under Pressure*, New York, Macmillan.

McCall, M.W., Jr and Lombardo, M.M. (1983) 'What Makes a Top Executive?', *Psychology Today*, February, pp. 16–23.

McCall, M.W., Jr and Segrist, C.A. (1980) 'In Pursuit of the Manager's Job: Building on Mintzberg', *Technical Report No. 14*, Greensboro, North Carolina – Center for Creative Leadership.

Mintzberg, H. (1973) *The Nature of Managerial Work*, New York, Harper and Row.

Montanare, J.R. (1978) 'Managerial Discretion: An Expanded Model of Organisation Choice', *Academy of Management Review*, Vol. 3, No. 2, pp. 231–41.

Morse, J.J. and Wagner, F.R. (1978) 'Measuring the Process of Managerial Effectiveness', *Academy of Management Journal*, Vol. 21, No. 1, pp. 23–35.

Paolillo, J.G.K. (1981) 'Role Profiles for Managers at Different Hierarchical Levels', *Academy of Management Proceedings*, Vol. 24, pp. 91–4.

Park, R.E. and Burgess, E.W. (1921) *Introduction to the Science of Sociology*, Chicago University Press.

Parrett, C.M. and Lau, A.W. (1983) 'Managerial Work: The Influence of Hierarchical Level and Functional Specialities', *Academy of Management Journal*, Vol. 26, No. 1, pp. 170–7.

Patrick, J. (1973) *Glasgow Gang Observed*, Eyre Methuen.

Pugh, D.S. and Levy, P. (1969) 'Scaling and Multi-variate Analysis in the Study of Organisational Variables', *Sociology*, Vol. 3, pp. 193–212.

Rapaport, R.N. (1970) 'Three Dilemmas in Action Research', *Human Relations*, Vol. 23, pp. 499–513.

Rosen, M. (1991) 'Coming to Terms with the Field: Understanding and Doing Organisational Ethnography', *Journal of Management Studies*, Vol. 28, No. 1, January, pp. 1–24.

Smith, C. (1984) 'The Context of Doctoral Research', Vol. 1, No. 4, Summer.

Stewart, R. (1976) *Contrasts in Management: A Study of Different Types of Managers' Jobs, Their Demands and Choices*, New York, McGraw-Hill.

Stockport, G. (1992) 'Developing Interorganisational Networks within an Incubator on a Science Park – An Ethnographic Survey', Cranfield School of Management. Unpublished PhD thesis.

Susman, G.I. and Evered, R.D. (1978) 'An Assessment of the Scientific Methods of Action Research', *Administrative Science Quarterly*, Vol. 23, pp. 582–603.

Thomas, W.I. (1971) 'The Definition of the Situation', in Coser, L.A. and Rosenberg, B. (1971) *Sociological Theory*, (third edn), New York, Routledge and Kegan Paul.

Watson, J.G. and Simpson, L.R. (1978) 'A Comparative Study of Owner Manager Personal Values in Black and White Small Businesses', *Academy of Management Journal*, Vol. 21, No. 2, pp. 313–19.

Whyte, F.W. (1955) *Street Corner Society*, University Chicago Press.

10 RELATING HUMAN RESOURCE ACTIVITIES TO BUSINESS STRATEGY

Martyn Sloman

It is accepted that human resource activities and policies must be designed and delivered in ways that support an organisation's corporate objectives. To many human resource (HR) practitioners this may seem to be a self-evident truth. Personnel or HR (no distinction is intended at this stage) is a service function and as such must conduct its activities so as to meet the needs of the business.

It is easy to dispose of the converse of the proposition advanced in the opening sentence. No one would argue that HR activities and policies should be designed and delivered in a way that runs counter to the organisation's corporate objectives. Anyone who did adopt such a position could, for convenience, be labelled an advocate of the dissonance school. This school of HR management does not appear to have developed any literature; nor do they have public advocates of their position. Those who have worked in the profession will, however, have come across the occasional surreptitious underground practitioners in some organisations who have apparently adopted dissonance as their professional philosophy!

For most of us, however, it is easy to accept that what takes place in the HR department should be tied to the needs of the business. The sophisticated professional would want to analyse the statement that HR activities and policies must be designed and delivered in a way that supports an organisation's corporate objectives. There are a number of implicit assumptions that could be scrutinised: for example, that corporate objectives exist, and that they can be broken down into manageable functional objectives which can be pursued by the HR specialist. There are also some unanswered questions. Without embracing the 'dissonance' school it is reasonable to ask whether the HR department should consciously undertake activities which could be seen by some line managers as constraining corporate objectives: preventing, for example, inappropriate hires or stopping over-hasty dismissals.

These and other issues which follow from an analysis of the role of HR in business strategy demand serious consideration. It is one thing to accept that HR activities should reflect the business strategy; it is quite another to suggest that such a statement gives a sufficient description of the role of HR in the organisation.

The aim of this chapter, however, is not simply to consider the opening statement. The aim is the development of a set of guidelines or principles for linking human resource activities to business strategy; these will be based on the practical experience gained from activities in a corporate and investment bank. In practice, while the need to develop such a link is accepted, there is a dearth of practical advice. Little general guidance is available in the literature. Published discussions often move straight from a definition of the issues to descriptive case studies of how it is done in successful companies.

Inevitably much of the strategic activity undertaken by the HR professional will depend on the circumstances of the organisation. It is, however, possible to put forward general principles which offer a starting point in most cases. First, it is argued that the central importance of the devolution of responsibility for HR matters to line management must be recognised. Greater integration of HR activities with corporate strategy must be achieved in conjunction with the effective management of authority to the line – they are mutually dependent activities. As a general principle, line management ownership of HR activities is essential if strategic human resource management (HRM) is to take place.

Second, it is suggested that a practical approach should comprise two stages:

- mapping the existing organisation to assess the features which are of importance to the generation of an effective HR strategy; and
- developing and implementing a process which permits the appropriate involvement of HR in strategic business decisions, wherever they are taken.

Although logically separate, these two stages can take place in parallel, and need not be conducted sequentially.

It is hoped that, in the course of the ensuing discussion, the justification for the general principle and the rationale for a two-stage approach will become apparent. Both are rooted in a perception of the realities of HR practice in most organisations at the present time; both are drawn from the experiences encountered in attempting to deliver HR at a strategic level in a difficult, but not untypically difficult, environment.

Background

Although this chapter is not intended as a case study, illustrations will be drawn, where appropriate, from the corporate and investment bank. To assist in the understanding of the context in which these illustrative activities were undertaken, some features are described below.

NatWest Markets (NWM) is the corporate and investment banking arm of the National Westminster Bank Group, one of the largest and best capitalised banks in the world. NatWest Markets undertakes many of the City activities of the group: trading (of treasury, equity and capital markets products), corporate banking, asset management and specialist advice. Over 5000 staff are employed world-wide – 3500 of whom are based in the UK.

For the purposes of this chapter, a number of features of the specific NWM human resource culture are of importance. First, the overall environment is fast-moving, with some sophisticated knowledge workers among the employees. Although generalisation is dangerous, such people tend to regard any activity not immediately connected with bottom-line profitability as a distraction. Second, there is little tradition of proactive HRM – historically there has been limited value placed on training, for example, and a poor training culture has persisted. The 1988 report *Create or Abdicate*, commissioned by the London Human Resource Development Group, argued that in general the City had created jobs but not the necessary skills. The report concluded that 'The choice for the City is clear: create its own stock of skills in order to ensure global competitiveness into the nineties or abdicate its premier position to other global finance centres through benign neglect' (Rajan and Fryatt, 1988, p. 13).

The need for effective HRM is now recognised; its delivery remains difficult. Many of the staff of NWM are self-confident professionals who resist HR activities that they feel are inappropriate. HRM is not something that can be done to staff in NWM; the process must be developed with them and they must see the value of it.

The third significant feature of the context in which HRM must be delivered concerns the comparatively recent formation of NWM. The bank, in its present structure, was formed in January 1992 with the merger of three separate City-based arms of the NatWest Group. Two (County NatWest, and Group Treasury and Capital Markets) concentrated on investment banking, activities related to trading; the third (Corporate and Institutional Finance) concentrated mainly on corporate banking, that is activities related to lending. A new location for some staff gave an impetus to a fresh approach to aspects of management. Different management styles and cultures were brought together at the merger. In general, the acceptance of the role of HR was greater in the case of Corporate and Institutional Finance – in particular there was a tradition of far more active career and management development. Consolidation of HR activities therefore became a key element in the achievement of the central organisational theme of integration. Indeed the NWM vision was to become a leading integrated corporate and investment bank to our clients.

A strategic approach: mapping the existing organisation

Two organisational features therefore have shaped the implementation of strategic HRM in NWM: the reluctant acceptance of the value of HR by some line managers; the requirement to promote integration as a key corporate objective. The first feature will command a high degree of resonance in many different organisations. It, more than any other consideration, explains the emphasis on the general principle that strategic integration of HR activities must go hand in hand with the effective management of devolution to the line. A conceptual model of the relationship between these two dimensions will be introduced and developed later in this chapter.

Although this chapter is intended to offer some practitioner perspectives rather than serve as a textbook, some theoretical underpinning may be helpful at this stage.

Hendry and Pettigrew (1986) identified a strategic theme to HRM which comprised four elements:

1. the use of planning;
2. a coherent approach to the design and management of personnel systems based on an employment policy and manpower strategy, and often underpinned by a 'philosophy';
3. matching HRM activities and policies to some explicit business strategy; and
4. seeing the people of the organisation as a 'strategic resource' for achieving 'competitive advantage'.

This list of four elements will be used, for the remainder of this chapter, as the objective to which the practitioner of strategic HRM should aspire. The first of the four elements involves the acquisition of a set of tools or techniques; the last requires a new perspective – and not just from the HR department. It is the second and third elements, however, that have been used as the basis of the most general guidance offered to practitioners: the notion that all HR programmes should be internally consistent and matched to business strategy. Both are reasonable and sensible objectives – again their converse could only be advocated by the dissonance school.

If the search for a more strategic role for HR is accepted as a desirable objective, effective implementation of the four constituent elements of the strategic theme to HRM identified by Hendry and Pettigrew provides a good basis for proceeding. While one may accept that the aim is sensible, what is at stake is how to go about it in practice. As has already been emphasised, any practical steps must take account of the growing responsibility of line management for activities that fall within the domain of strategic HRM.

Against this background, the first part of the recommended approach involves mapping: assessing the main organisational features that determine the successful implementation of HRM. Although these vary between organisations, the list in Table 10.1, based on experience in the corporate and investment bank, is suggested as a starting point for the mapping exercise. These are discussed in turn below.

Table 10.1 Key organisational features for successful HRM

- The extent to which there is a clear business strategy which is communicated throughout the organisation.

- Whether there is a change management programme in existence, or another attempt to 'manage' the corporate culture.

- The degree of homogeneity that exists within the organisation.

- The attitude of line managers towards human resource activities.

The existence of a strategy

Any attempt to match HRM activities and policies to some explicit business strategy must presuppose the existence of such a strategy. If there is no articulated strategy, presumably strategic HRM is a lost cause and the HR professional is left to concentrate his or her energies on more prosaic activities.

In fact the position is not so black or white. In almost all organisations there is some gain in seeking out the existing corporate strategy or business plan. However, the simplistic model, where there is a clear, agreed strategy capable of immediate translation into HR terms, is far from universal. For most HR professionals, identifying and analysing the strategy or plan requires a high degree of proactivity.

At issue are the limitations of what has been called by Harry Taylor (1991) the strategic management paradigm whereby

> based on an examination of the current environmental circumstances in terms of problems, threats or opportunities for the organisation, top management sets the overall objectives which are then broken down into manageable functional objectives to be pursued by functional specialists working through their own sequence of stages. (p. 261).

For many practitioners, the strategic management paradigm does not apply, and corporate strategy is a more elusive phenomenon. The first operational step for those wishing to implement strategic HRM will be to gain a broad overview of the organisation's strategic management process – and to identify the key actors responsible for its delivery. Views on strategy are themselves changing as strategic planners (assuming there are such people in the organisation under consideration) develop their approach. Indeed, there seems to be no more clear agreement on how strategy should be formulated than there is on how HR should be matched with business objectives.

As is well documented, the concept of strategy was transferred from the military arena to the business arena in the 1960s. In the early applications the emphasis was placed on prescriptive linear strategy – a set of methodical, rational and sequential actions involved in planning from above, with formulation preceding implementation. This was a complex process based on detailed forecasts and it fell into disrepute as organisations realised that sudden changes (for example oil price rises) rendered voluminous plans, painstakingly achieved, obsolete overnight.

Subsequently planners have developed ideas and approaches which are less absolute and more practical. Encouragingly, each new perspective seems to make the place for HR more central to the organisation's strategy and make the management of human assets increasingly important in the achievement of strategic goals. For example, a new perspective was presented in a *Harvard Business Review* article in 1993 (Hamel and Prahalad, 1993) where strategy was seen in terms of stretch and leverage. Traditional frameworks in which companies effect a fit between their resources and the opportunities they pursue, and allocate resources strategically between investment opportunities are rejected – they are considered to be not wrong but unbalanced. The alternative is to replace the concept of 'fit' by 'stretch' and to seek to 'leverage' resources rather than merely allocate them. Goals are set which extend the company beyond what was previously thought feasible. Strategy becomes a rallying cry: 'an aspiration that creates by design a chasm between ambition and resources' (Hamel and Prahalad, 1993).

There is every possibility, given the nature of the current and future business environment, that the next generation of developments in strategic thinking will take strategy even closer to human resources. For the present, however, the best practical advice for those seeking to implement strategic HRM is to ascertain the methods used to determine strategy in their own organisation and to forge relationships with those responsible for this activity.

Fortunately NatWest Markets has benefited from a clear, well-defined business strategy and committed and co-operative business strategists. As is doubtless true of many organisations, however, HR elements did not feature strongly as a means of building competitive advantage. The initial task addressed in NWM, therefore, was mundane: to ensure that in revising and updating strategic plans, appropriate human resource considerations were introduced. In formulating their strategy, therefore, business units were invited to identify exceptional requirements for staff skills which could have developmental implications and also new activities which could have recruitment, remuneration, or other resourcing implications. This initiative should properly be regarded as an appropriate attempt to match HRM activities with business strategy – but one which, in itself, was limited in scope and ambition.

Change management or status quo

The second dimension to be mapped is the organisation's attitude towards change. Two distinct areas demand investigation:

1. the extent to which the organisation is positively seeking to change its beliefs, values, attitudes, workstyles and relationships (now commonly grouped together as 'organisational culture'); and
2. whether the organisation has embraced a specific change programme. The greater the commitment to change, the greater the scope for strategic HRM.

Few organisations would admit to an antipathy towards change, an unshakable commitment to the status quo. It is accepted as a management truism that transformation in organisations has intensified as a result of new markets caused by globalisation, increasing customer sophistication, easier access to technology and growing emphasis on quality. Managing the process of change is recognised as the precondition of organisational survival.

However, the commitment to change and the desired pace of change are much stronger in some organisations than others. At one extreme lie those organisations that need to readjust to a new organisational environment (ex-Government Departments now privatised for example) or are fighting for survival; at the other lie those organisations who think they have got things right. Operating in the latter case does not mean that HRM can be put on a care-and-maintenance basis: there could, for example, be a heavy ongoing investment in training and development taking place. It is in the former case that HRM programmes, and their appropriate link with business strategy, will receive greater prominence – and demand the attention of senior management and their commitment. Indeed, there is an argument that proactive strategic HRM would not be acceptable or implementable in the absence of a reason (or excuse) to rethink the HR role. Certainly a major corporate restructuring opens up all aspects of management to question and reinterpretation.

Within NatWest Markets, as will be demonstrated later, a particular opportunity was offered by the commitment to achieve an integrated organisation. This meant that the co-ordination, and arguably unification, of all HR systems was recognised as an essential underpinning of corporate progress.

The opportunity for the HRM professional to influence strategy is particularly strong where the organisation has embraced a specific, labelled change programme, but somewhat different considerations apply. Examples of such programmes are British

Telecom's Quality Programme, British Airways' Customer Care initiative and the BBC's Producer Choice. Such initiatives are under-researched, but it seems that the following generic features are present:

- they have significant implications on HR policies (for example, on the reward and appraisal systems);
- the authorship and ownership of such programmes lies primarily with the chief executive; and
- there is often a heavy involvement with external consultancies.

The combination of these three features is deliberately presented in a way that suggests a potential threat to effective strategic HRM. It is not simply a question of the HR manager losing influence where his or her professionalism, if it is of any use to the organisation, should be brought to bear. There seems to be a blurred area of professional responsibility for change management which could be filled by the strategic planner or the financial controller or the proactive HR professional. More important is the need to ensure that when change programmes take place the transformation is firmly embedded and retained in the organisation. If this does not occur there is a danger of implementing high-profile transient programmes, ephemeral in their impact; all staff will be taken through a sheep-dip – programmes will be seen as reinforcing policies that are imposed from above and cynicism will inevitably result.

One culture or many

The third dimension concerns the degree of homogeneity within the organisation – both the current reality and the desired state. Most of the recent discussions have addressed this dimension as part of a more general consideration of corporate culture. As has already been observed, the creation of NWM involved bringing together employees with some very different styles and approaches. This dimension, therefore, received much attention: movement towards greater integration was given the highest priority.

More generally, the extent of current and desired cohesion is of considerable importance in implementing effective strategic HRM. At the operational level it has profound implications on, for example, the management of recruitment (should this be left to business units or centralised?) and on the need for compatibility of payment systems. Two features of this part of the mapping exercise merit particular consideration: the extent to which the organisation as a whole is seeking cohesion; the extent to which it contains groups of employees who have distinct or special needs.

Not all organisations seek cohesion to the extent that NWM does. It should be recalled that NWM is a business subsidiary of the wider NatWest Group, which is far more heterogeneous. Many will at least tolerate, or positively encourage, diversity for sound business reasons. In these circumstances there may only be limited opportunity for instituting major strategic HRM programmes across the organisation as a whole. In the extreme case of some holding companies, no attempts are made to achieve any coherence of personnel practices across separate employing companies. Where the intention is to build an integrated organisation – often expressed in terms of desiring synergy – statements should not necessarily be taken at face value. The current situation should be investigated and the implications considered.

A particularly important aspect of this problem is the existence of groups of special-ist staff. Again, an extreme case can be posited. If an organisation is heavily dependent on the particular skills of a group of identifiable specialists – and these specialists are aware of their value, are marketable and have limited loyalty to an employer – there is a need to assess the situation very carefully before proceeding with any strategic pro-gramme. In the City, for example, key dealers and analysts are keen to protect their own position and are not immediately acquiescent to wider company programmes. The same could be said of groups as divergent as senior academics, hospital consultants and airline pilots, as discussed in Chapter 2.

Considerations of homogeneity apply at both the company level and the level of the individual employee. This is an important dimension to be mapped since many com-pany change programmes involve, either explicitly or implicitly, a unifying dimension. Such activity falls firmly under the heading of culture management and the underlying assumptions are:

- an organisation has a corporate culture which can be investigated and categorised;
- management can determine whether the existing corporate culture is appropriate to the organisation that they desire; in other words, a matching exercise is possible; and
- by a combination of well-identified organisational and personnel procedures such a structuring of corporate culture is possible; corporate culture can be manipulated by management.

These assumptions underpin many change programmes and, again, have achieved general acceptance. They should not go without challenge, however, especially in organisations which are heterogeneous in nature. In this case the implementation of strategic HRM is likely to be more difficult and a more cautious, pragmatic approach may be required.

Line managers and HR activities

The need to manage the devolution of HR activities to the line has been identified as a challenge facing the HR professional. The attitude of line managers towards HR activi-ties has therefore been suggested as the fourth dimension to be mapped in implement-ing strategic HRM. At the outset, the receptiveness of the line towards HR-driven policies must be assessed, since there will be a reliance on line managers to undertake activities and deliver policies. The following questions should be addressed:

- Will line managers undertake the tasks that the organisation demands of them?
- How strong is their commitment to HR activities?
- Have they the expertise to undertake their new HR responsibilities, or the willing-ness to gain such expertise?

Without wishing to be unfair, HR textbooks often seem implicitly to assume that line managers will do what they are told. Yet, modern management thinkers assure us that reliance on the command-control approach is no longer appropriate: Rosabeth Moss Kanter (1989), for example, emphasises the need to learn to operate without the hierar-chy crutch: the crutch of authority which must be replaced by personal relationships.

Certainly in practice line managers exercise a great deal of discretion over the extent to which they buy into HR systems. Such differing degrees of acceptance have been a significant feature of HR activity at NWM, as will be illustrated later. In general, HR managers are rarely faced by outright refusal to co-operate. It is, however, comparatively easy for line management to accept the need for HR policies in principle but to dismiss any particular manifestation (system or procedures) as 'imposed by human resources'. The above may appear unduly cynical to those readers who operate in more acquiescent cultures, but the capability of the organisation to deliver effective HR in a devolved structure is an important consideration – and one which is likely to grow in significance.

If the willingness of the line to embrace responsibility for human resources is one issue, their capability to do so is a second. Here the relevant questions concern the extent of their experience and sophistication in HR issues, something which can evidently be improved by training.

A strategic approach: managing devolved responsibility

The mapping exercise outlined above is a precursor to the second stage of developing and implementing a process, a stage which embraces the formulation, execution and monitoring of strategic HR activities. If detailed HR programmes are to be both internally consistent and supportive of the business strategy, they must be firmly based in operating reality. They must be robust and recognised by the non-HR line managers as legitimate. This demands a considered approach and a realistic awareness of the situation prevailing in the organisation. The suggestion that mapping is undertaken across four dimensions – the existence of a strategy, the commitment to change, the degree of homogeneity and line management attitudes – is not meant to be unduly prescriptive. Different organisational circumstances will demand different areas of attention. Some sort of serious investigation of the context in which strategic HRM is to take place is, however, essential.

The development and implementation of strategic HRM will be discussed in the next section of this chapter and illustrated by two related processes at NWM. First, however, it is helpful to return to the underlying principle introduced at the beginning of this chapter: greater strategic integration of HR activities must be achieved in conjunction with the effective management of authority to the line. The central importance of this principle can be illustrated both by considering empirical evidence and a theoretical model.

Empirical evidence can be drawn from the Price Waterhouse/Cranfield project (1990) on international strategic human resource management, which was based on a survey of 6000 employing organisations in five European countries. One of their central findings in 1990 was that 'personnel responsibility is increasingly being devolved to line managers – the trend is particularly marked in training and development' (p. 4). The tendency was emphasised in their 1991 report which found that the respective roles of line management and personnel specialist were changing, with more HR responsibility taken up by the line. Generally 'decentralisation in the level of decisions within the organisation and devolution to line managers continues apace' (p. 8).

It should be noted that the extent of devolved authority is uneven: it is pronounced in training and development but less so in industrial relations, which remains the most centralised activity. Training and development, however, are among the most strategic aspects of HRM. A recognition of the devolution of authority to the line, and the effective management of its consequences, must be taken into account when determining a strategic HR approach.

The Price Waterhouse/Cranfield project has given rise to a useful new model of the place of the HR department in the organisation. Since it has greatly influenced the approach used within NatWest Markets, it is described in the paragraphs below: the model proceeds from a recognition of the issues raised by the centralising and decentralising tendencies that emerge from the changing role of HR in organisations.

Brewster and Larsen, drawing on the Price Waterhouse/Cranfield research, suggest that HR practices in the different European countries surveyed can be categorised, inter alia, by the degree of integration of HRM with business strategy and the degree of devolvement to line managers (1992). Their article repays reading in the original, but their 2×2 matrix is reproduced as Fig 10.1. This matrix allows an analysis of both the role of the specialist HR department and the position of HRM as a general management activity; it offers a valuable insight on how the ambitious HR department may attain its strategic role – and what to avoid.

If the HR department operates at a low level of integration the scenario is that of the Professional Mechanic or the Wild West. These positions are of limited interest in the context. In neither case does the department play a strategic role. The Professional Mechanic emphasises 'the specialist, but limited skills and interests of the practitioners; the manager sees himself or herself as having "higher" imperatives above that of the organisation' (ibid, p. 414). The Wild West is a nightmare scenario with every line manager free to develop his or her own style of relationship with employees: the potential for incoherence, inconsistency and a strong employee reaction is obvious It is unlikely to exist in any organisation with an effective human resource department.

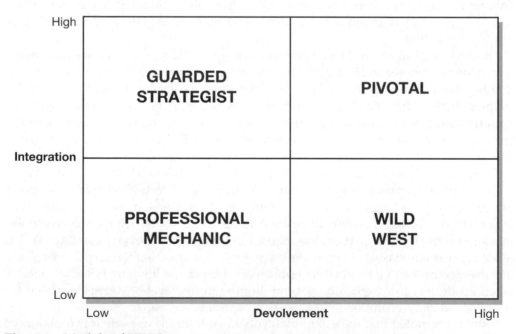

Fig 10.1   Models of HRM

It is in the two upper quadrants that the HR department is involved strategically, but in quite different ways. The top right-hand quadrant is where HRM is fully integrated and there is a high degree of devolved responsibility to the line: the senior personnel specialists operate as catalysts, facilitators and co-ordinators at the policy level of the organisation. This is styled a Pivotal position since 'small, highly respected personnel departments at the policy-making level can exert a powerful disproportionate influence' (ibid, p. 415). This offers a most attractive, if demanding, role for the department. The alternative position, the Guarded Strategist, occurs where devolvement is low. Although the HR specialists are powerful and have few problems (other than coping with an enormous workload) according to Brewster and Larsen this can be a situation of considerable inefficiency and frustration: 'the weaker managers will welcome the chance to slough off their responsibilities, while simultaneously having someone to blame for all failures; the better managers will be frustrated' (ibid, p. 415).

The inherent tensions involved in acting as a Guarded Strategist mean that such a position is likely to be untenable in practice, certainly for any sustained period. This underlines further the need to pay careful attention to the management of effective devolution of responsibility.

The task facing the department, therefore, is to move from the role of Professional Mechanic to the influential Pivotal position. The attraction of the Brewster-Larsen model is that inspection of the 2×2 matrix illustrates that this can only be achieved by moving diagonally – both the link with strategy and that with devolved authority must be promoted if progress is to be sustained. It is not enough simply to attempt to create a closer strategic matching of human resource activities. Indeed in NWM an intermediate position between the Professional Mechanic and the Pivotal role has been suggested. It has been called the Business Operative and defined on the following basis:

> The intermediate position between Professional Mechanic and Pivotal. It is characterised by a good relationship between the HR manager and the business area based on mutual trust and understanding. The main ambition of the HR manager is to give an effective service to the line – limited strategic ambitions are expressed beyond this.

Most members of the NWM human resource department would define their current practice as that of the business operative; furthermore, a number would question the legitimacy of seeking aspirations beyond this role. As a committed practitioner of HR development, however, the author of this chapter believes that the Pivotal role is where the attractive future for the profession lies.

A strategic approach: developing and implementing the process

It can be seen that what is put forward in this chapter is approaches to developing and implementing strategic HRM – not a prescriptive list of actions. Once mapping is complete, the HR department should seek to identify and formulate the policies, programmes and practices which are appropriate in supporting the business strategy; it should ensure that it is itself positioned to achieve this aim within the organisation. How all this is accomplished must depend on the circumstances of the organisation; given the many possible variations it is not necessarily sensible to attempt to produce a general checklist of activities. Essentially each HR department must be prepared to undertake its own journey: the process is as important as the product. However, the list reproduced as Table 10.2 is indicative of what could be involved. The list is drawn from experience of such activities at NatWest Markets.

Table 10.2 The likely needs of the HR department in developing and implementing a strategic approach for the organisation

- To access the existing corporate strategy, identify the evident HR components, and 'translate' the other components into HR terms.

- To input an HR element into any strategic planning process; ensuring that component business units address relevant HR issues in their business planning cycle (for example special activities with HR implications, particular recruitment or remuneration problems).

- To review existing HR programmes in the light of the above information and revise; where appropriate transmit the results back into the system.

- To formulate activities (including training programmes where necessary) to encourage greater awareness and commitment from line management.

- To specify strategic objectives for the HR department itself, using the same structure or format as those applied for business units.

- To devise and implement appropriate performance measures or monitoring arrangements to ensure the effectiveness of strategic HR activities.

The elements of Table 10.2 comprise a wide-ranging agenda and present ambitious targets for the HR department. They also underline one important assumption which has been present throughout: strategic HRM will not occur unless the human resource professional takes steps to make it happen. The activities of strategic HRM require positive volition from the practitioner. A key feature of the art of effective HRM involves seizing the initiative where appropriate, emphasising the need for strategic choice, while buying line management into the process.

Although every situation is different, certain HR activities are generally recognised as having more strategic importance – especially reward systems and appraisal systems. The remainder of this section of the chapter will concentrate on two brief descriptions of how the 'positive volition' referred to above was exercised at NWM. The first is concerned with the performance appraisal process, the second with improved selection methods. Underlying both is an approach to the analysis of competencies by business units. Some comments on the competency approach will follow at the end of the case study. At this stage, however, competencies can be simply described using the 1988 Training Agency definition: 'the ability to perform the activities within an occupational area to levels of performance expected in employment' (Training Commission (1988)).

At the time of the merger two separate and conflicting performance appraisal systems were present in NWM so the introduction of a new system presented an obvious opportunity for the exercise of strategic HRM. First, it was recognised by all parties (the Management Committee, line management, the HR department) that an appropriate and widely accepted system was essential for effective management. Second, there was a need for action if the central corporate objective of creating an integrated bank was to be achieved.

The original County NatWest and the Group Treasury and Capital Markets appraisal system centred on setting performance objectives and assessing subsequent out-turn against objectives. It made an overt link between performance and reward review. The competency element was almost incidental and there was no attempt to assess potential or to collect information on career ambitions.

Most other parts of the merged organisation (mainly Corporate and Institutional Finance) used a more paper-intensive system – six pages as opposed to the four-page County NatWest form.

This system was heavily based on competencies, requiring assessment against 15 competencies determined in advance and pre-printed on the form. Appraisal was not explicitly linked with bonus. The form did, however, require issues on progress and potential to be addressed specifically. Both systems considered training needs but otherwise had little commonality.

At the merger, a number of line managers inherited staff from different parts of the new organisation; this required them to conduct an annual appraisal round using two different systems – a practice which was likely to become more widespread as movement within the new organisation increased.

There was an evident case for introducing a new appraisal system. The new form eventually did not break new ground and, of itself, is of little interest in the context of this book; it is a four-page form, supported by a guidance manual, which must be completed after an interview between the line manager and the staff member concerned.

Two aspects of the introduction of the appraisal system are of interest since they illustrate the need to encourage greater ownership by the line of the HR activities. The first concerns certain choices on content; the second the process for embedding the new system in the organisation.

Three sections of the form are reproduced as Figs 10.2 and 10.3. Both are concerned with aspects of performance management and allow a number of important points to be emphasised.

First, there was general (near-universal) acceptance from Management Committee downwards of the need to introduce an appraisal form which could operate throughout the business units in NWM – a single form was essential if the integration was to be achieved. Second, there was a recognition that a single form would necessarily be a compromise: all parts of NWM would lose some appraisal information or be expected to undertake additional appraisal tasks.

This acceptance of the need for change created a particular opportunity to reinforce performance management as the prevailing management ethos. Performance management has been well defined in a recent publication from the Institute of Personnel Management (1992). Performance management systems are considered to be operating when the following conditions are met: a vision of objectives is communicated to employees; departmental and individual performance targets, related to wider objectives, are set; a formal review of progress towards targets is conducted; the whole process is evaluated to improve effectiveness. Such an approach to management could command acceptance throughout the NWM organisation; the need for the appraisal process to be used to identify reward training and development outcomes was therefore recognised. However, some different attitudes to implementing performance management had been evident in NWM, particularly in the use of objectives. The appraisal system had to be designed in a way that brought the organisation together in

SECTION 2.   PERFORMANCE AGAINST PREVIOUS OBJECTIVES

Enter below key business related objectives which were set for the individual in respect of the reporting period. Assess performance against these using the following key.

KEY: A   Achievement of objectives exceeded all expectations.
    B   Objectives achieved in full.
    C   Objectives achieved in part or not at all.
Comments to support assessment should be provided where appropriate.

Overall Performance Against Objectives	SCORES			Measures/Evidence
	A	B	C	

Performance Against Specific Objectives Set Last Year				

SECTION 3.   PERFORMANCE OBJECTIVES FOR NEXT YEAR

Please set, in consultation with the member of staff, **UP TO 5 key business related objectives** to be achieved during the coming year. (Further information on setting objectives is in the guidance manual.)

Objective	Measures/Comments

Fig 10.2   Performance against previous objectives

SECTION 4.   PERFORMANCE PROFILES
Below are 5 core or compulsory competencies against which the individual should be assessed. Most roles will require additional skills and these will differ across NWM. In the remaining rows add further competencies from the list provided in the guidance manual or elsewhere that most closely relate to the role of the individual. For example, for staff registered with a regulator such as SFA or engaged in investment business, 'Compliance' should be treated as a core competence.

Rate using the key below and provide evidence where appropriate.

KEY: A   More than fully meets or frequently exceeds required standards.
     B   Fully meets required standards.
     C   Does not always meet required standards.

Competency	RATINGS			Evidence
	A	B	C	
Team Skills				
Leadership				
Communication Skills				
Staff Development				
Need for Excellence				

Fig 10.3   Performance profiles

a consolidated approach to performance objectives – if necessary after a transitional stage.

This problem of transition was resolved in a number of inter-related ways. First, the form included both shaded and unshaded areas: completion of the shaded areas was essential; completion of the unshaded areas was encouraged but not mandatory. For example, it can be seen from Fig 10.2 that there was no absolute requirement to comment on specific objectives set in the previous year, since the previous use of objectives had been uneven.

Second, two separate approaches to performance management were included in the new appraisal system. Sections 2 and 3 placed the emphasis on performance management through the use of objectives. Section 4 (see Fig 10.3), however, placed the emphasis on performance against essential competencies displayed in the workplace. The inclusion of both approaches reflected a genuine debate within the organisation on the most appropriate mechanism for managers to signal the performance requirements to subordinates.

Section 4 of the form allowed business units to specify competencies appropriate for their circumstances. Five key competencies (team skills through to need for excellence) had been endorsed (by the NWM Management Committee) as essential for all staff. Each business unit was obliged to identify another two competencies and given the opportunity to add a further three. They received a menu of competencies to assist them in the task: the essential five competencies and another seventeen competencies were defined more fully, together with appropriate performance indicators. They also received guidance and assistance from the HR department. The choice, however, was firmly their responsibility.

It is recognised that the above paragraphs could offend purists among HR professionals. Some would argue that a painstaking approach based on functional analysis would be required to identify the 'true' underlying competencies needed for effective performance in business units. This point is important but must be rejected. There is a real danger that such functional analysis, which would necessarily be undertaken by the HR professional, would remain the property of the HR department. The list of competencies produced may never be regarded by the business units as their competencies.

In achieving change professional exactness is far less important than line management ownership. So far, within NWM, the need to choose competencies has been well addressed: equity research analysts are being appraised against the five compulsory competencies together with customer orientation, information gathering and technical knowledge; settlements staff against technical knowledge, problem solving, customer orientation, resilience and management control; and HR managers against energy, resilience and tolerance of stress!

The guidance and consultation process on competencies, as would be expected, is just one part of the wider ongoing process of selling the system into the organisation. Management Committee were involved in the initial design and advised of progress at each stage; some 26 members of staff participated in detailed interviews. Most importantly, once the system had been endorsed it was reinforced by introductory training sessions: over 650 members of staff attending 44 separate one-and-a-half-hour sessions held in a four-week period.

None of this may appear at all remarkable. It is, however, worth re-emphasising that parts of the NWM organisation were not favourably predisposed to HR systems. Although appraisal was accepted as a necessity, there was some degree of hostility to what was perceived as bureaucracy and form-filling. A major effort to devolve ownership was therefore essential.

Indeed, the discussion about the use of competencies in appraisal can be extended to illustrate a potential danger which threatens to undermine strategic HRM. This is the development of a vocabulary to describe HR activities which could serve as a barrier rather than a means of communication. The use of the term 'competencies' offers a useful example. Competencies have been the subject of extensive discussion in the literature and some commentators have argued that competency listings are little more than skills appearing under another name. Whether the identification of competencies represents a breakthrough or not, it is important that they are not seen as the exclusive property of the HR department. Line managers must not be excluded from the debate on the skills required by the organisation on the grounds that they do not possess sufficient knowledge to operate the new tool-kit.

The acceptance and ownership of competencies by business units and their line managers is also central to the second example of 'positive volition' undertaken within NWM. This concerns the move from straightforward interviewing to assessment centre techniques for selection and development.

There has been a general shift towards more sophisticated selection techniques in the organisation for some time. A sophisticated Graduate Assessment Centre has been in place for almost a decade, for example. No methodological breakthrough is claimed for any of the procedures currently in use in NWM: they are a combination of ability tests, individual and group exercises and interviews – sometimes using structured approaches where questions are predetermined against competencies. What does merit a mention in the context of this chapter, however, is deliberate and systematic intent to involve line management at all stages.

Assessment centres are increasingly being used for selection beyond the graduate stage. In these cases, the involvement of business units is ensured through three distinct mechanisms: they are asked at the outset to identify, in conjunction with HR, the appropriate competencies to be used for assessment purposes (these are based on competencies displayed by employees performing at high standards); they prepare the briefs or case studies for the individual or group exercises; as would be expected, they provide the assessors and interviewers.

A good example of this approach proving effective would be the selection system used in one of the traditional merchant banking units within NWM. There had always been a steady flow of recruitment of qualified accountants and MBAs. At the request of the business unit, this flow was consolidated into a series of assessment centres where the performance of six candidates was reviewed against eleven competencies chosen by the business unit (for example, personal impact and information gathering) demonstrated in the course of a boardroom exercise and a strategy exercise designed by the business unit.

Conclusions

The description of the approach used to introduce a new integrated performance appraisal system in NWM, and the brief discussion of the move towards assessment centres, are not presented as state-of-the-art human resource practice. Far more sophisticated procedures have been implemented elsewhere; the circumstances at NWM were particularly favourable for a more proactive approach to HRM. The case study is meant to illustrate the way in which the drive towards strategic HRM requires a recognition of both a general principle and a particular approach. The general principle is that progress towards a strategic role for human resources must proceed in tandem with a managed devolution of responsibility to the line. The approach is based on mapping followed by developing and implementing a process.

The drive for strategic HRM is an important challenge facing the function. There is a long conceptual and practical distance between the general acceptance of corporate statements that 'people are our most important assets' and effective strategic HRM, where HR implications of strategy are understood and implemented throughout the organisation.

It is questionable whether the need for such an approach has been generally accepted in the UK. To some the case for strategic HRM as stated above may appear to be unduly ambitious, a wish to assume a wider role that does not properly belong to the HR function. As has been noted, there are advocates of this view within NWM. Some critics would settle for the role of Business Operative if not the Professional Mechanic with HR seen as a support function. If this seems an unduly harsh aside, it should be noted that a recent national statement prepared with the support of leading practitioners suggested that the key purpose of the personnel function was to 'enable management to enhance the individual and collective contributions of people to the short and long term success of the enterprise' (p. 1). There is an underlying emphasis on a reactive rather than a proactive role in such a statement.

If the case for strategic HRM as stated here can be criticised for being over-assertive, it is equally open to the charge that it is limited in ambition. The mapping operation as described, for example, could be regarded as unduly bounded by the current organisation. The human resources function should, on this analysis, be part of the process whereby the business expands its horizons, going out into the environment to identify opportunities. This is a much more proactive view and is prevalent in current US thinking. There effective HR is seen as playing a more prominent role in building competitive advantage or, as one US textbook defines it, building organisational capability: 'a business ability to establish internal structures and processes that influence its members to create organisation-specific competencies and thus enable the business to adapt to changing customer and strategic needs' (Ulrich and Lake, 1990, p. 40).

Whether a maximalist or a minimalist view of the role of HR is taken, it is hoped that the propositions advanced in this chapter will receive consideration as part of the debate on strategic HRM.

First, it should be accepted that strategic HRM is not the property of the HR department, and certainly not the sole preserve of the HR professional. The matching of HRM activities and policies to the business strategy is a dispersed activity throughout the organisation; a whole series of managers, with differing status, take actions and decisions which fall within the domain of strategic HRM.

Positive steps, therefore, must be taken to encourage line managers to recognise and value the importance of a consistent approach to HR decisions which support corporate objectives. In short they must be encouraged to commit themselves to strategic HRM and to own the decisions themselves. This concept of line *management ownership* of strategic HRM – of matching HRM activities and policies to business strategy – is critical. Without that commitment, the implementation of strategic HRM is at best difficult and at worst impossible; the HR department will be formulating programmes and practices that are widely disregarded. Hence key tasks for the modern HR department are: the deliberate and careful nurturing of the organisation's acceptance of the importance of strategic HRM; positioning of the department itself so that it is equipped to identify and transmit the essential strategic programmes throughout the organisation.

If appropriate steps are not taken, there will only be limited matching of HRM activities and policies to business strategy – certainly there will be no attempt to use HR to drive the organisation towards the accomplishment of corporate objectives. Inevitably HR procedures will exist, but they are likely to be uncoordinated, and not seen as part of a holistic system of relevance to the business. Line managers will have less than full ownership of HR activities and could well regard any HR procedures as an imposition.

The HR department itself will retreat into the role described by Brewster and Larsen (1992) as the Professional Mechanic, a role with limited skills and interests.

The approach outlined in this chapter – mapping followed by developing and implementing a process – is presented as a way of seeking and articulating the HR options. Reward systems, grade structures and promotion policies are readily seen as strategic issues affecting the organisation; the approach to graduate (or other first-level) recruitment and other HR mechanisms are less likely to be recognised as lying in the strategic domain. The approach to training could easily be regarded as a subsidiary issue which can comfortably be left to the specialist. Effective strategic HRM, with its emphasis on line management ownership, involves convincing the organisation of the strategic implications of many activities that could otherwise have been seen as peripheral. In part, this involves demonstrating that there are choices to be made, and that the right choices, properly implemented, will support the attainment of corporate objectives.

The activities that must be undertaken by the HR professional to achieve these objectives are challenging. They involve seeking to develop new, wider relationships – operating without Rosabeth Moss Kanter's 'hierarchy crutch'. They will require new perspectives. A greater understanding of the strategic process will be needed and, on a practical level, influencing skills will become critically important. Above all it will require the HR professional to become far more adept at coping with uncertainty – strategic HRM is an exploratory rather than an absolute activity.

REFERENCES

Brewster, C. and Larsen, H.H. (1992) 'Human Resource Management in Europe: Evidence from Ten Countries', *International Journal of Human Resource Management*, 3 (3).

Hamel, G. and Prahalad, C.K. (1993) 'Strategy as Stretch and Leverage', *Harvard Business Review*, 71 (2).

Hendry, C. and Pettigrew, A.M. (1986) 'The Practice of Strategic Human Resource Management', *Personnel Review*, 15, (5), pp. 3–8.

Institute of Personnel Management (1992) *Performance Management in the UK: An Analysis of the Issues*, London, Institute of Personnel Management.

Kanter, R.M. (1989) *When Giants Learn to Dance*, New York, Simon & Schuster.

Personnel Standards Lead Body (1993) *A Perspective on Personnel*, London: Personnel Standards Lead Body, p. 18.

Personnel Standards Draft 3 (1994), Personnel Standards Lead Body, p. 1.

The Price Waterhouse/Cranfield Project (1990) *International Strategic Human Resource Management*, London, Price Waterhouse, p. 4.

The Price Waterhouse/Cranfield Project (1991) *International Strategic Human Resource Management*, London, Price Waterhouse, p. 8.

Rajan, A. with Fryatt, J. (1988) *Create or Abdicate: The City's Human Resource Choice for the 90s*, London, Institute of Manpower Studies, p. 13.

Taylor, H. (1991) 'The Systematic Training Model: Corn Circles in Search of a Spaceship?' *Management Education and Development*, 22 (4), p. 261.

Training Commission (1988) *Classifying the Components of Management Competencies*, Sheffield: Training Commission, p. 3.

Urlich, D. and Lake, D. (1990) *Organizational Capability: Competing from the Inside Out*, New York, John Wiley, p. 40.

HR STRATEGY IN THE UNITED STATES

Examples of Key Issues Identification and Execution

Randall Schuler and Mark Huselid

Key to the success of companies in the United States today and well into the twenty-first century is the effective utilisation of human resources:

> The best companies now know, without a doubt, where productivity – real and limitless productivity – comes from. It comes from challenged, empowered, excited, rewarded teams of people. It comes from engaging every single mind in the organisation, making everyone part of the action, and allowing everyone to have a voice – a role – in the success of the enterprise. Doing so raises productivity not incrementally, but by multiples. (Welch, 1994)
>
> Jack Welch, CEO, General Electric

> We're not anywhere near world class at a lot of these things [in the automobile industry]. The only way we can beat the competition is with people. That's the only thing anybody has. Your culture and how you motivate and empower and educate your people is what makes the difference. (Sherman, 1993)
>
> Robert Eaton, CEO, Chrysler Corporation

> If you take a look at the sources of sustainable, competitive advantage during the last decade, the only one that has endured has been the quality of the people who work for you. (Caudron, 1994)
>
> Jim Alef, Executive Vice President and Head of HR, First Chicago Corporation

Companies in the United States are attempting to become as globally competitive as possible, as rapidly as possible. A critical factor in this attempt is the effective management of human resources (HR). But how to be effective? Can companies manage their HR effectively in this new environment if they continue to manage them as they have in the past? An essential part of this process is the identification of major business objectives and issues and a careful examination of the HR implications of these factors. These implications become the key HR issues on which the competitiveness and survival of the company depend. While this process results in some unique HR management implications for each company, it also results in HR implications that are common across companies. Although both such factors are important components of a firm's HR strategy, in this chapter we address the HR strategy issues that tend to be common across firms. To highlight these factors, we also discuss what US companies are doing about these issues throughout the chapter.

Because people are important to short- and long-term competitiveness and survival, business analysts pay attention to whether companies are effective in the area of managing their human resources domestically and globally (Kanter, 1994; Pfeffer, 1994; Stewart, 1994). For example, the *Fortune* ratings of 'America's most admired corporations', published early each year, considers the *ability to attract, develop and keep talented people* as one of its primary performance dimensions, along with long-term investment value, financial soundness, use of corporate assets, quality of products and services, innovation, quality of management, and community and environmental responsibility (Farnham, 1994; Galen, Greising and Anderson, 1994). Why do *Fortune* and other business magazines include among their criteria of successful businesses the ability to attract, develop and keep talented people, in other words, great human resource management (HRM)?

Competitive necessity and organisational success

According to Massachusetts Institute of Technology (MIT) economist Lester Thurow, one reason is that human talent promises to be a major factor for competing in the twenty-first century:

> Consider what are commonly believed to be the seven key industries of the next few decades – microelectronics, biotechnology, the new materials industries, civilian aviation, telecommunications, robots plus machine tools and computers plus software. All are brain power industries. (Thurow, 1992)

If brain power drives the business, attracting and keeping great talent becomes a vital business necessity. But even for companies in industries other than the seven Thurow refers to, great HRM positively impacts the success of firms. While success can be defined in many ways, we use *success* here to mean effectively serving the interests of the organisation itself; stockholders and investors; customers; employees; society; and suppliers (Cascio, 1991; Nicholson and Brenner, 1994).

Gaining competitive advantage

Because competition is the name of the game, especially for firms in highly competitive environments such as Southwest Airlines, General Electric, Lincoln Electric and Weyerhaeuser, we find that firms seek ways to compete which can last for a long time and cannot be easily imitated by competitors. Harvard's Michael Porter refers to this as the desire of firms to gain competitive advantage (Porter, 1985, 1980). There are many ways firms seek to gain competitive advantage: for example, Wal-Mart uses rapid market intelligence so the right products are always available in the right amounts. McDonald's enters into agreements with shopping mall developers to secure prime locations in their malls. Au Bon Pain and Starbuck's negotiate special supplier arrangements to ensure that they receive some of the best coffee beans. Mrs Field's Cookies has developed a superior information system that enables the firm to monitor carefully and enhance the service of each store outlet on a daily basis!

Firms also gain competitive advantage through their wise and innovative use of HR. In fact, according to auto industry expert Maryann N. Keller, the 'enduring advantages will come from making better use of people' (Sherman, 1993). She nominates Saturn's dealers and Toyota's Georgetown, Kentucky, plant workers as examples of the kind of competitive advantage that will last: whole organisations of carefully picked, highly motivated people determined to make customers happy (Sherman, 1993).

The financial impact of HR management systems

The belief that human resources play an important role in a firm's efforts to gain competitive advantage is widely held among academics and practitioners. And in fact, scholars working in this area have found that firms adopting progressive or *High Performance* HR management systems have higher levels of profitability, higher annual sales per employee (productivity), higher market value and higher earnings-per-share growth than firms that do a less effective job managing their human resources. Such *High Performance Work Practices* (HPWP), including extensive employee involvement and training, compensation contingent on individual, workgroup, and overall firm performance, job-related and competency-based selection, and employee participation and involvement, help to produce a workforce with the competencies and flexibility necessary to compete in rapidly changing product markets. Moreover, these high performance work systems have a *strategic* impact and help to create sustainable competitive advantage, in part because they are difficult to imitate.

As an example of the magnitude of the impact of High Performance HR management systems, Huselid (1995) found in 968 firms that a one standard deviation (a measure of spread or variability) increase in the level of HPWP deployed by a firm was associated with 7.05 (relative) per cent lower turnover, and on a per-employee basis, £17 333 higher sales and £11 930 and £2444 higher market value and profits, respectively. These results were highly consistent and robust, even after statistical corrections for the propensity of higher performing firms to be more likely to invest in High Performance HR management systems, and the likelihood that higher performing firms, or perhaps firms with more effective HR management practices, are more likely to respond to survey questionnaires on this topic. Ichniowski, Shaw and Prennushi (1994) found the use of 'co-operative and innovative' HR management practices to positively effect employee productivity in the steel industry, while MacDuffie (1995) found the use of such practices to improve quality and productivity in the automotive industry. Huselid and Becker (1994) found in a longitudinal study of HR management systems and organisational performance that an increase in the use of HPWP from 1992 to 1994 was associated with a subsequent increase in market value in the range of £22 432 to £51 272 *per employee*, although at some cost in current levels of profitability. Finally, Huselid, Jackson and Schuler (1995) noted that the *presence* of HPWP does not necessarily mean that they have been *implemented* effectively, and in 310 firms they demonstrated that the implementation effectiveness of the firm's HR management system had a substantial impact on the performance of the firm. Huselid et al. (ibid.) found that each standard deviation increase in HR management implementation effectiveness increased sales £21 994, increased cash flow £12 298, and increased market value £7475 *per employee*. We summarise some of these results in Table 11.1.

Thus, managing HR well meets the needs of the organisation, stockholders and investors. Effective HRM can also meet the needs of the employees: as firms survive, expand, and increase their profitability, they provide more employment security, more job opportunities and higher wages. Successful HRM also serves the needs of society by elevating the standard of living, furthering the interests of society as reflected in legal regulations and ethical guidelines, and managing the impact of the firm on the surrounding community. That is, managing human resources effectively is consistent with contributing positively to society; this, in turn, supports a favourable corporate image in the minds of the public (Fryzell and Wang, 1994).

Table 11.1   The financial returns for investments in High Performance Work Practices (HPWP)

Huselid (1995)

In 968 firms, a one standard deviation increase in the deployment of organisational HPWP:

- decreased turnover 7.05 (relative) per cent;
- increased sales £17 333 *per employee per year*;
- increased firm market value £11 930 *per employee*; and
- increased profits £2444 *per employee per year*.

Huselid and Becker (1994)

Based on longitudinal analyses of 222 firms, a one standard deviation increase in the deployment of organisational HPWP (from 1992 to 1994):

- increased market value between £22 432 and £51 272 *per employee*; and
- reduced cash flow approximately £9613 *per employee per year*.*

Huselid, Jackson and Schuler (1994)

In 310 firms, a one standard deviation increase in HRM implementation effectiveness:

- increased sales £21 994 *per employee per year*;
- increased cash flow £12 298 *per employee per year*; and
- increased market value £7475 *per employee*.

* Presumably, this value reflects the costs associated with the adoption of more effective HRM practices, whose value is treated by accounting convention as an annual expense but is viewed by the market as an investment.

Identifying and executing the key HR strategy issues well

While the examples of companies just cited illustrate the importance of effective HRM, they also illustrate the variety of HR activities being done by successful companies in the US. What all these companies have in common is the ability to identify and execute the key HR strategy issues well (Schuler and Walker, 1990).

HR strategy issues are those identified as having critical value to the competitiveness and survival of the company that are associated with the managing of human resources. Without attending to these issues, the organisation will be less competitive in the short run and will eventually fail to exist in the longer run.

Of course it is one thing to identify the key HR strategy issues and it is often another thing to mobilise activities and resources to deal effectively with the issues identified. Without putting programmes in place to assist employees in changing or without developing effective cultural diversity programmes, the HR strategy issues identified remain just that: HR strategy issues identified. Without the successful development and execution of the programmes, companies will fail to achieve the necessary level of competitiveness for long-run survival. Thus, execution is a critical part of HR strategy.

HR strategy

Used here, HR strategy is concerned with:

(a) identifying the human resource implications of business issues vital to the success of the organisation; and
(b) implementing activities that can deal effectively with those implications.

Just as organisations such as GE and Chrysler have their own specific products, customers and competitors, they also have their own unique business issues vital to their success. Thus we would expect to find different HR strategy issues identified across organisations. On the one hand, a key strategy issue in the GE Appliance Division might be reducing the time inventory is held in the company's factories before being used. At Chrysler, on the other hand, a key strategy issue might be trying to improve product quality of their new Neon automobiles. While both of these have important HR implications, they are unique to each company.

But organisations also have common business issues vital to their success. These can include:

(a) pursuing total quality;
(b) having a greater capacity to change quickly;
(c) improving productivity; and
(d) meeting the needs of the customers for continually better products at lower prices.

As with key business issues unique to companies, these common key business issues also have HR implications. As examples, improving productivity may mean increasing the level of employee motivation and ability; having a greater capacity to change may mean having employees who have a greater understanding of and dedication to the goals and directions of the company. As we look across businesses in the US, we are finding that a substantial majority of them are concerned with many common business issues and common key HR strategy issues. Thus, in this chapter we describe five common key HR strategy issues associated with the effective implementation of the firm's HR strategy. Issues unique to specific companies are left for another time.

Common key HR strategy issues

The common key HR strategy issues we observe in US firms today include:

1. The need to align people with the business.
2. The need to link HR with the needs of the business.
3. The need to facilitate a global organisation operation.
4. The need to reconceptualise the delivery of the HR function: partnership.
5. The need to reposition the HR department.

Because of their importance, these five key HR strategy issues are reviewed in this chapter by way of examples of what some exemplary firms in the US are doing. These five issues, though different and distinct, are often addressed simultaneously by companies seeking to improve their chances for competitiveness and survival well into the twenty-first century. The reader will experience this in the description of these companies in each of the following key HR strategy issues.

1. The need to align people with the business

Global business communication at AT&T

Players in the highly competitive telecommunications systems and services industry often face formidable challenges, including razor-thin profit margins and shameless imitation from competitors. Such was the case when AT&T merged two business units in July 1992 to form its Global Business Communications Systems (GBCS) division. With the additional challenge of integrating two distinct cultures and business processes, GBCS entered the arena.

Now, after several years of declining revenue, the £1.93 billion, 26 000-person unit is on the verge of a dramatic transformation. The revenue growth since 1992 has translated into a success and added to AT&T's growing reputation as a dynamic competitor. Some of the success has come with the alignment of the people with the business. Essential in this alignment is the GBCS Pyramid (Plevel, Nellis, Lane and Schuler, 1994).

In July 1992, fuelled by the quest to transform GBCS into the global leader in its target markets in an industry that is experiencing accelerated financial growth, the GBCS senior leadership team, referred to as the Quality Council, developed the GBCS Pyramid. Coincident with the introduction of the GBCS Pyramid, the senior leadership team announced a fundamental change in the strategic focus of the unit. Previously, the strategic focus was to improve profitability by growing revenues in existing and new market segments while improving the basic cost structure of the unit.

The Pyramid established a new framework for aligning the people with the business. It consists of a new vision, mission, values, objectives, strategic plan, tactical business plan, business processes and management system (Fig 11.1). The Pyramid serves as a framework for action with a strategic long-term perspective. Its power is based on the employees (referred to as associates), who are the foundation for building all other elements of the Pyramid.

There are several important components to the pyramid. Each is integral in aligning people to the needs of the business (Schuler, 1992). The *vision* of GBCS represents the organisation's purpose: 'To be your partner of choice: Dedicated to Quality, Committed to Your Success.' The *mission* of GBCS represents a broad plan of action for what the organisation wants to do: 'To be the world-wide leader in providing the higher quality business communications products, services and solutions.' The *values* of GBCS are

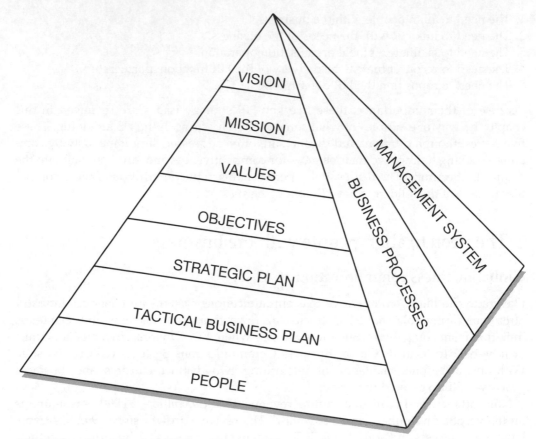

Adapted from Plevel, M. et al. (1994), p. 62.

Fig 11.1   The GBCS pyramid

used to guide decisions and behaviour. They represent how the organisation and its members treat customers, suppliers and other AT&T associates. The seven GBCS values are:

1. *Respect for individuals* – We treat each other with respect and dignity.
2. *Dedication to helping customers* – We truly care for each customer.
3. *Highest standards of integrity* – We are honest and ethical in all our business dealings, starting with how we treat each other.
4. *Innovation* – We believe innovation is the engine that will keep us vital and growing.
5. *Teamwork* – We encourage and reward both individual and team achievements.
6. *Accountability* – Each of us takes ownership for the success of GBCS.
7. *Excellence* – We will be satisfied with nothing less than being the best in everything we do.

GBCS objectives

GBCS objectives reflect the quantitative commitments for the business. Each objective addresses an element of the 'Value Equation' (Fig 11.2) which represents GBCS's

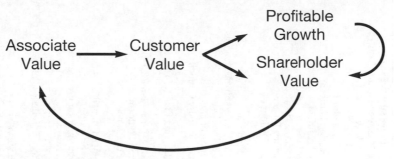

Adapted from Plevel, M. et al. (1994), p. 63.

Fig 11.2   The 'Value Equation'

underlying philosophy regarding the key drivers of success and their inter-relationships. The 'Value Equation' starts with Associate Value, the only sustainable competitive advantage (Schuler and MacMillan, 1985; Ulrich and Lake, 1990). Associate Value is achieved by ensuring that all associates are continuously provided with the knowledge and have the core competencies needed to do their jobs effectively, have the ability and accountability to satisfy customers, and are extremely satisfied. Customer Value is achieved by delivering value to GBCS customers. This is done by ensuring customers are provided with superior products, services and integrated solutions by all GBCS associates taking special care to delight customers and ensure that their needs are met. Together, Associate Value and Customer Value generate profitable growth for AT&T and increase value for its shareholders. Completing the cycle, Profitable Growth and Shareholder Value produce growth in Associate Value, which in turn enhances Customer Value, and so on. At first glance, the equation seems simple. However, these are a complex set of interdependent relationships that require continuous attention to balancing all elements of the equation. The paths to achieving these goals are identified by the GBCS strategic plan.

GBCS's strategic plan

The GBCS senior leadership team has defined six key strategic business principles that guide and shape the strategic plan. These principles reflect management's overall direction for *how* successfully to achieve the business objectives with plans and actions that support those strategies. All day-to-day actions, from handling a customer's inquiry to manufacturing a system, must be performed with this strategic direction and focus in mind.

The GBCS strategic business principles are:

- make people a key priority;
- win customers for life;
- utilise the Total Quality Management approach to run the business;
- profitably grow by being the leader in customer-led applications of technology;
- rapidly and profitably globalise the business; and
- be the best value supplier.

These strategic business principles serve as a guiding force to link the employees with the needs of the business by helping them understand the business direction. GBCS's

Table 11.2 HR strategy and planning model

GBCS Business Principles	GBCS HR Strategic Imperatives	Human Resources Mission	Focus Areas	HR Plan Initiatives
Make people a key priority.	I Associates actively take ownership for the business success at all levels, individually and as teams, by improving associate value.	To create an environment where the achievement of business goals is realised through an acceptance of individual accountability by each associate and by his/her commitment to performance excellence.	Cultural change	Learning forums, such as: – Change Management and You – GBCS Strategy Forum – PEP Workshop – Quality Curriculum Communication Platform – Ask the President – Answer Line – All Associate Broadcasts – Bureaucracy Busters – Associate Dialogues Diversity Platform – Pluralistic Leadership: Managing in a Global Society – Celebration of Diversity – National Diversity Council
Use the *Total Quality Management* approach to run our business.	II GBCS HR contributes to increased shareholder value by achieving process improvements that increase productivity and customer satisfaction.			
Rapidly and profitably globalise the business.	III Ensuring GBCS HR readiness to expand its business initiatives into global markets which requires a business partner that is sensitive to the unique needs of various cultures and people.			
Profitably grow by being the leader in customer-led applications of technology.	IV HR strategic plans and processes support and are integrated with GBCS's strategic and business planning processes so that the HR management system attracts, develops, rewards and retains associates who accept accountability for business success.		Rewards and recognition	Progress Sharing Plan (PSP) Special Long-Term Plan (SLTP) Recognition Platform – Partner of Choice – Trailblazers – President's Council – Achiever's Club – Local Recognition Programmes – Touch Award
Be the *best value supplier*.	V GBCS HR provides a level of service to internal and external customers that establishes the HR organisation as their value added business partner.		Ownership	Performance Excellence Partnership (PEP) Associate Surveys – ASI (Associate Satisfaction Index) – AOS (Associate Opinion Survey) Organisation Effectiveness – Work Teams – Process Teams
	VI The HR leader and team are competent to provide leadership and support to GBCS by championing HR initiatives that contribute to GBCS's success.			

Adapted from Plevel, M. et al. (1994), p. 66.

strategic business goals have been successfully linked to the strategic business principles by a collaborative effort of the business leaders and the HR leaders with their respective teams. A business strategy and planning model (Table 11.2) has been developed and serves as the driving force for the business and HR initiatives that are enabling GBCS to transform itself into a global leader in its target markets.

Business process and management system

There are two quality-related platforms that touch all parts of the pyramid – the GBCS Management System and the Business Processes. The Business Processes throughout GBCS are defined and continue to be re-evaluated for continuous improvement based upon Total Quality Management (TQM). The GBCS Management System is the blueprint for how the business is run. The Management System provides the framework within which teams of associates systematically apply TQM principles – using the Malcolm Baldrige National Quality Award criteria.

As stated at the start of this chapter, aligning people with the needs of the business is more general than actually linking HR with the needs of the business. This linkage with business strategy is described in detail below.

2. Linking HR with the needs of the business

Conveying to employees what behaviours are needed by the organisation and what behaviours are rewarded is a major objective of 'linking HR with the needs of the business'. A description of this activity followed by an example facilitates our discussion of this key issue. In our description of this activity we introduce the term 'strategic human resource management'. This term is introduced because it conveys the complex reality of what organisations and their HR departments are doing as they link HR with the needs of the business.

Strategic Human Resource Management

For Bill Reffett, former Senior Vice President of Personnel at the Grand Union, a 20 000-person supermarket operation on the East Coast, strategic human resource management is getting everybody from the top of the human organisation to the bottom doing things that make the business successful (Schuler, 1992).

The viewpoints of academics about strategic human resource management, stated in slightly different terms, echo the thoughts of the practitioners. For example, strategic human resource management is largely about integration and adaptation. Its concern is to ensure:

1. that human resource management is fully integrated with the strategy and the strategic needs of the firm;
2. that HR policies cohere both across policy areas and across hierarchies; and
3. that HR practices are adjusted, accepted and used by line managers and employees as part of their everyday work.

Extending this a bit, other academics have defined the field as existing to ensure that the culture, values, and structure of the organisation and the quality, motivation and commitment of its members contribute fully to the achievement of its objectives. Strategic human resource management should match, fit and follow from the thrust of the organisation.

Together, these viewpoints on what strategic human resource management is suggest that it has many different components (Baird and Meshoulam, 1988). These include human resource policies, culture and values and practices. They also suggest descriptions of what strategic human resource management does, that is, it links, it integrates and it coheres across levels in organisations. Implicitly or explicitly, the purpose of strategic human resource management is to utilise more effectively human resources *vis-à-vis* the strategic needs of the organisation. Based upon these viewpoints then, strategic human resource management is defined as *all those activities affecting the behaviour of individuals in their efforts to formulate and implement the strategic needs of the business.* This definition of strategic human resource management incorporates several important aspects. These include:

(a) the systematic linkage of human resource management and people with the strategic needs of the business;
(b) recognition of several strategic human resource management activities; and
(c) the existence of a consistency in the way these strategic human resource management activities are implemented.

Together these aspects constitute the 5-P Model of strategic human resource management.

The 5-P Model

The 5-P Model of strategic human resource management melds many human resource management activities to the strategic needs of the business (see Fig 11.3). Viewed this way, many human resource management activities can be strategic. Thus, categorising human resource management activities as strategic or not depends upon whether they are systematically linked to the strategic needs of the business, not upon whether they are done in the long term rather than short term, nor upon whether they are focussed on senior managers rather than non-managerial employees.

A benefit of the 5-P Model is in providing a way to link several human resource management activities that tend to be treated separately by practitioners and academics alike. For example, articles on strategic human resource management tend to focus on the relationship between strategic business needs and HR *practices*. While this more narrow focus is understandable given the demands of doing manageable research, it does understate the complexity of HR activities influencing the behaviour of individuals and groups in their efforts to formulate and implement the strategic needs of the business. Thus, by utilising the 5-P Model we may be able to obtain a greater understanding of employee behaviour in organisations as impacted by strategic human resource management activities.

There are several different types of strategic HRM activities affecting the behaviour of individuals that occur at different levels in the organisation. They are categorised according to the 5 Ps: HR Philosophy, HR Policies, HR Strategies and Programmes, HR Practices and HR Process. While these activities may be done regardless of the strategic needs of the business, when done with these needs in mind, they become the five sets of *strategic* HRM activities (Schuler, 1994).

Human resource philosophy

The HR philosophy is a statement of how the organisation regards its human resources, what role they play in the overall success of the business and how they are to be treated and managed. This statement is typically very general, thus allowing interpretation at more specific levels of action within an organisation. A firm's HR philosophy can be found in its statement of business values.

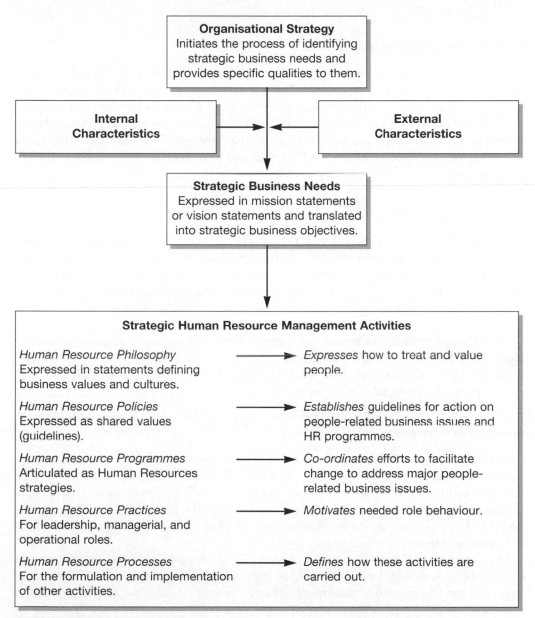

Adapted from Schuler, R.S. (1992), p. 20.

Fig 11.3   The 5-P Model: linking strategic business needs and strategic HR management activities

Human resource policies

These are statements that provide guidelines for action for the development of HR programmes and practices based upon the strategic needs of the business. This use of 'HR Policy' is to be distinguished from the term when used as 'HR Policy Manual'. While an HR Policy Manual may contain statements of general guidelines, they are more often perceived as a 'rule book' prescribing very specific actions permitted in very specific situations.

Human resource programmes

HR programmes can be initiated, disseminated and sustained for many types of strategic organisational change efforts. These efforts, however, have in common the fact that they are generated by the strategic intentions and directions the firm is taking and that they involve HRM issues, that is that they are major people-related business issues that require a major organisational change effort to address. They also share the reality of having strategic goals that are used to target and measure the effectiveness of the HR programme.

Human resource practices

The final component of the strategic HRM activities includes various human resource practices that are compatible with the needs of the business. These HR practices address all employees in the organisation, but somewhat differently, depending upon their organisational roles (traditionally correlated with level in the organisational hierarchy). There are three categories of roles in organisations: leadership, managerial and operational.

Once the behavioural content of these roles is identified, specific HR practices need to be selected that signal the appropriateness of these roles and reward those for performing them. How the content of these roles is identified and how the relevant HR practices are selected are questions of HR process.

Human resource processes

'How' all these other HR activities are identified, formulated and implemented is a significant strategic HRM activity. At the Forest Products Company (FPC), a Leadership Institute and the HR programmes were established to HR process issues. According to Horace Parker, 'the trump card in closing the deal (to establish the Leadership Institute and the HR programs) was to involve the executives at various levels of organisation in the planning stages' (Schuler, 1992).

This process of involvement at the FPC (a division of the Weyerhaeuser Corporation) was not done solely to get greater understanding (by both the executives and the HR people) of the organisational strategic change, but also to get greater buying-in to the programmes through involvement. This involvement, of course, is consistent with the aims of the programmes themselves and the strategic business needs. That is, the programmes aim to get the executives oriented to giving their employees more participation and involvement and the strategic business needs, for example, to improve quality, depend upon the suggestions and commitment of all employees. The willingness to get the executives to go along and the rest of the employees to offer suggestions and give commitment begins with how the strategic HRM activities are put in place and what the activities actually are. To the extent that suggestions, commitment and executive willingness to change are not necessary, the need for a participatory HR process diminishes. Increasing demands by employees at all levels for empowerment, ownership and participation, however, make these rare situations.

Linking HR with the needs of the business: the case of Grand Union

The Grand Union is a large retail grocery operation whose retail stores are primarily located in well-established neighbourhoods. In the mid 1980s, a new phenomenon appeared in the traditional retail grocery business: the advent of the super store, the smallest of which was about twice the size of Grand Union's largest store (Schuler, 1992).

The Grand Union had always defined itself as a grocery store, a traditional high-volume, low-margin, limited-selection, space-driven, discount-driven, 40 000 square foot grocery store. Five years ago the top team decided that competing with the new 100 000 square foot stores (for comparison, Wal-Mart's largest Hypermarket is 260 000 square feet) was not a viable merchandising strategy. Their competitors' volume and the size of their parking lots were so much greater. Competing with them would not be possible because it would mean moving from all the current, space-bound locations and uprooting relationships with all its current customers, suppliers and communities. Top management decided that it had to revise its strategy.

New strategic business needs

Strategic concerns addressed by top management resulted in the new definition of what it meant for Grand Union to be a grocery store. The mission of the firm was more clearly identified as serving the customer. The need for this clarification and re-examination of the strategy was caused by the environmental forces, especially new competition and the changing habits and preferences of customers. The strategy was basically changed from a commodity, undifferentiated business to a high quality, customer-driven business.

From an individual store perspective this meant the elimination of many of the current items to make room for more brand items and higher margin items. A major objective was ensuring the best quality products. The latter meant having a deli section, an expanded fresh fruit section, a variety of small, ethnic food booths and a pastry shop.

The culture of the firm changed to one of prizing the customer and doing everything possible in listening to and serving the customer. Store managers and top management started to provide the leadership Kotter (1990) talks about, that is articulating and providing excitement, giving vision and showing confidence in the firm's ability successfully to change in the new, more uncertain environment, and setting objectives that all relate to the new way of doing business.

Linking HR with the strategic business needs

Under the guidance of the Senior Vice President of Human Resources, Bill Reffett, the firm developed an HR philosophy that said the employee was a valuable, long-term source of competitive advantage, and that all efforts would be made to provide exciting jobs and promotion opportunities (promotion from within) and continuous retraining as needed. The firm described this philosophy as developmental. It was clearly recognised at this point that the role behaviours needed from all employees would change in order to match the needs of the new business.

While the physical size of the stores remained the same, employees were added because of the new sections and additional staff who were needed. The new business meant that it was important to keep employees longer so that they could get to know the customer and the store. Consistent with the new business, the traditional command and control relationship across all levels was modified to accommodate a more self-directed, self-managed approach. Similarly, an individual orientation was modified to be more team oriented to better serve the customer. The developmental HR philosophy was carried down to this level because this was the glue that kept all the employees together. Key issues were addressed by formalising all the activities that were occurring to support the new business. Success depended upon managing the business systematically, including human resources. While there was formality in the establishment of new HR practices, there was allowance for adapting to local conditions. Regardless of location, however, decision-making authority was pushed down in the organisation. Store managers and their staff could make more decisions in the interests of the customer and the needs of the business.

New HR practices

In the final stage, the employees identified the HR practices that had to be formulated to match the business, based upon the role behaviours needed from the employees, especially those in direct contact with the customers. The analysis and formulation resulted in several HR practices that represented significant change. Those practices most affected by change and how they changed are illustrated in Fig 11.4. While these changes in HR practices were necessitated by what the employees thought was necessary for the business, it was in large part driven by what they thought would enable them to perform as needed by the customer.

In summary

This Grand Union case highlights the several strategic HRM activities that were affected by the strategic business needs resulting from a change in organisational strategy. It also suggests the necessity for making changes in these HR activities in a rather consistent manner. Not content to assume that all the changes made were working, the company did employee opinion surveys for two years. This resulted in the fine tuning of some of the HR activities and further communication and clarification of others.

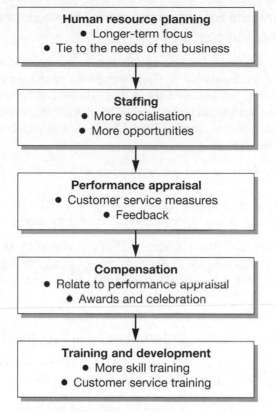

Adapted from Schuler, R.S. (1992), p. 20.

Fig 11.4 Human resource management practices affected by the change at Grand Union

3. The need to facilitate global organisation operation

As the area of HRM has expanded and become more linked with the strategic needs of the business, a similar phenomenon is occurring in the area of international HRM, namely, the linkage of international HRM with the strategic needs of the business and thus the development of strategic international HRM (Schuler et al., 1991). Reasons for this development include the recognition that HRM is critical to business strategy implementation (Hambrick and Snow, 1989; Lawler, 1984; Sherwood, 1988); that there are common HR demands that transcend national boundaries in managing HR, for example, those associated with advanced manufacturing systems and competitive strategies targeting quality improvement (Jelinek and Goldhar, 1983; Wickens, 1987); and that the significant sharing of business experience and education is creating a world-wide workforce with more commonality rather than less (Reich, 1990). This has resulted in two strategic business needs for multinational companies (MNCs): the need to link the separate units (interunit linkages) and the need to manage the local (internal) operations.

Interunit linkages: the role of performance management in business unit co-ordination and control

Interunit linkages have been a traditional focal point for the discussion of international HRM generally and performance measurement and management more specifically (Pucik and Katz, 1986). The focus of these discussions has typically been around the themes of control and variety, in particular, how to facilitate variety and how to control and co-ordinate that variety (Bartlett and Ghoshal, 1987; Doz and Prahalad, 1986). Discussions have focussed on:

(a) factors impacting MNC employee performance (particularly expatriate managerial performance);
(b) constraints on unit-level appraisal in MNCs (Pucik and Katz, 1986); and
(c) criteria used for measuring, appraising and managing performance of employees.

Basically these topics have been addressed within the context of MNCs exporting people to distant and different locations and/or exporting the entire HR function itself and specific practices such as performance appraisal *en masse* to other parts of the world (Fisher, 1989).

Internal operations: thinking globally and acting locally

The second major strategic business need of MNCs is concern for the HRM activities within each geographic location (unit), which becomes critical as MNCs strive to integrate an otherwise global set of diverse businesses. Headquarters wants to have some ability to co-ordinate operations, yet it recognises the reality of local cultural imperatives (Adler, 1991). In these efforts to deal with local cultural imperatives, MNCs quickly become involved with internal operations of foreign units. This overlap of the issues pertinent to both internal operations and interunit linkages reflects the complexity of MNCs seeking to operate in globally co-ordinated yet decentralised ways. This is certainly evident in the discussion of balancing imperatives. Further specific impact of this balancing act on internal operations is played out as performance measurement and management need to be aligned with other HR practices within the unit (Adler, 1991; Adler and Jelinek, 1986; Enz, 1986; Schneider, 1988).

Balancing business imperatives with cultural imperatives

The cultural imperative here addresses the local culture, economy, legal system, religious beliefs and education. The cultural imperative is important in strategic international HRM because of its impact on acceptable, legitimate, and feasible practices and behaviours (Adler, 1991; Schuler et al., 1993); acceptable in terms of: 'Can we appraise workers in the same way world-wide and thereby differentiate them, according to performance?', legitimate in terms of: 'Are there any legal statutes prohibiting us from formally appraising?'; feasible in terms of: 'While the society is hierarchical, authoritarian, and paternalistic, can we empower the workforce to appraise its own performance in order to facilitate our competitive strategy of quality improvement?'

All three components of the cultural imperative are important for MNCs to consider in decisions about:

(a) what behaviours to address;
(b) which performance measurement and management tools to use; and
(c) which tools can be used within the local units.

Because questions about which tools to use are also influenced by the MNC's need for world-wide co-ordination and control (the administrative imperative), it may be necessary to balance the needs of the cultural imperative with those of the administrative imperative (Doz and Prahalad, 1986).

The approach at Pepsi-Cola International

Pepsi-Cola International (PCI) is the international beverage division (outside of North America) of Pepsico, Inc.; its brands are sold in over 150 countries and it faces the challenge of matching the demand for high standards of individual performance with the needs of a globally diverse workforce in a highly decentralised organisation that can be most successful when its strategic activities are co-ordinated on a world-wide basis. Pepsi-Cola International is meeting this challenge by providing a foundation of HR practices that are modified to meet country-specific requirements. The design of HR practices starts with the basic assumption that the improvement of individual and organisation performance, along with a co-ordinated, yet decentralised approach to the business, are the desired outcomes (Fulkerson and Schuler, 1992).

In 1985, there was some confusion about what it took to be individually successful in Pepsi-Cola International. There was no shared value system or vocabulary for describing individual performance. For example, in the socialist countries the concept of individual performance was practically non-existent, whereas in Germany it carried meaning similar to its meaning in the US. The business was developing and growing at a rapid rate, and the pressures on individual managers were considerable. As a consequence, a 'Success Study' was launched.

With the full support of the division president, a study was initiated, in co-operation with the Center for Creative Leadership, to determine what factors might be associated with individual performance success across many markets and nationalities. Because the study was aimed at identifying the factors that contribute to the success of the business, it was clearly a study in strategic performance measurement and management. The study team looked at 100 successful and 100 not-so-successful managers from different functional specialties and from different nationalities. The factors that emerged from the study are shown in Fig 11.5.

The impact of the results of the study on building common values was remarkable. The greatest impact was to focus people for the first time on a common vocabulary for discussing individual performance and development. Prior to the study, it had been difficult to articulate dimensions of performance in a consistent, globally acceptable way.

Through the study, Pepsi-Cola International developed a multinational vocabulary that could be used to unite people from many different cultures and countries. For example, 'handling business complexity' might translate differently in China than it does in France. In China it might mean that you get a product produced and to the loading dock. By contrast, in France it might mean being concerned with marketing, distribution and merchandising, in addition to getting a product produced and to the

1. **Handling business complexity:** Figuring out what needs to be done and charting a course of action.
2. **Drives/results orientation:** Focussing on an outcome and driving for completion.
3. **Leads/manages people:** Directing the work of and motivating others.
4. **Executional excellence:** Putting ideas into action.
5. **Organisational savvy:** Knowing how the organisation works and how to maximise it.
6. **Composure under pressure:** Staying focussed in the international pressure cooker and still getting things done.
7. **Executive maturity:** Always acting with maturity and good judgement.
8. **Technical knowledge:** Understanding and applying technical knowledge.
9. **Positive people skills:** Knowing how to get along with people from all cultures.
10. **Effective communication:** Knowing how to communicate cross-culturally.
11. **Impact/influence:** Being able to get things done when faced with obstacles.

Adapted from Fulkerson and Schuler (1992), p. 258.

Fig 11.5   PCI success factors for performance measurement and management

loading dock. Though different in meaning, the outcome is the same: generating sales in the local environment.

Summary

As multinational firms seek to enhance their levels of competitiveness, they are attempting to maximise their use of human resources. A major component of this utilisation drive is the systematic linkage of HRM activities with the strategic needs of the business. For MNCs this amounts to the development of strategic international human resource management (SIHRM).

An essential activity in SIHRM is strategic performance measurement and management. As with the other activities, strategic performance measurement and management is relevant at two points for MNCs. The first is the interunit linkages. These linkages are those connecting the far-flung operations of the MNC into a cohesive whole that maximises diversity while facilitating co-ordination. The second is the internal operations of the international locations. The need is for balancing administrative imperatives and cultural imperatives and aligning all the HRM activities within the location.

4. The need to reconceptualise the delivery of the HR function: partnership

Clearly, managing Human Resources is not just something to be done by those in an HR department. Managers are the ones responsible for the management of people. No department alone can effectively manage a company's Human Resources. So, regardless of whether a line manager ever holds a formal position in HRM he or she will be accountable for the task of managing people. In the long run, every manager's portfolio of knowledge and skills must reflect this reality:

> **There is a saying at Merck that goes like this, 'human resources are too important to be left to the HR department.' Fully one-third of the performance evaluation of the managers is related to people management.** (Schuler and Walker, 1990)

The line manager has always been responsible

In small businesses, the *owner* must have this expertise because he or she will be building the company from the ground up. As the company grows even larger, more specialists may be hired – either as permanent staff or on a contract basis to work on special projects, such as designing a new pay system. But as with other business activities, the presence of a few specialists in the company does not mean that these specialists bear all responsibility for the activity. For example, many companies have a marketing department; nevertheless, they employ people outside that department to engage actively in marketing activities. Similarly, most companies have a few people with special expertise in accounting; nevertheless, employees throughout the company engage in activities related to the accounting function. The same is true for managing human resources.

What we see in companies linking people with the business is that managing Human Resources is a responsibility shared by everyone in the company – both line employees and HR professionals of the HR department and both top-level executives and entry-level new hires. Consistent with the stakeholder model (Savage et al., 1991), this partnership can even extend to HR working with managers in supplier firms, with customers, and even with members of community organisations. Yet for the most part, on a day-to-day basis, it's the firm's line managers who have responsibility for actually managing most people in an organisation. Those who recognise the importance of this responsibility work in partnership with HR professionals who have specialist knowledge and skills.

Partnership between line managers and HR professionals is the ideal situation, but it is not happening in all companies. The IBM/Towers Perrin world-wide survey referred to earlier found that both CEOs and Human Resource managers felt more partnering was needed by the year 2000. Figure 11.6 details the shifting HR responsibilities of line managers. While the indications are that line managers will be much more involved in the crafting of HR strategy, policy and programme development and the management of HR programmes, the level of involvement in the administrative details of HR is likely to remain low.

Employees are now sharing the responsibility

The responsibilities of line managers and HR professionals are especially great, but partnership involves even more sharing of responsibility. Each individual employee in an organisation, regardless of their particular job, also shares some of the responsibility. For example, it is common for employees to write their own job descriptions. Some even design their own jobs. Employees may also be asked to provide input for the

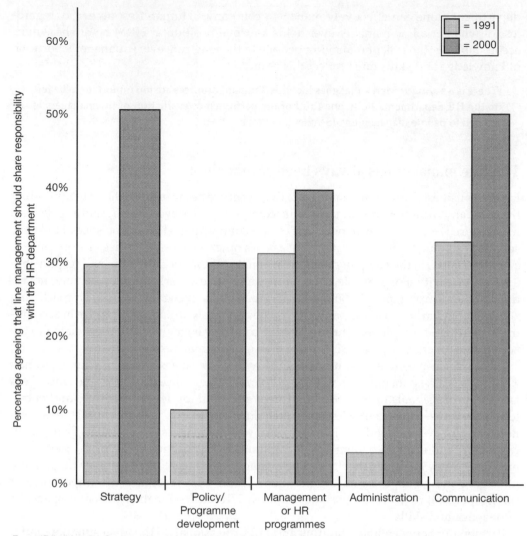

From 'Priorities for Competitive Advantage? A world-wide Human Resource Study' (IBM and Towers, Perrin, (1992)) p. 26.

Fig 11.6   An emerging role for line management

appraisal of their own performance and/or the performance of their colleagues and supervisors. Perhaps most significantly, employees assess their own needs and values and must manage their own careers in accordance with these. Doing so effectively involves understanding many aspects of their employer's HRM practices. As we move toward the twenty-first century, we all need to position ourselves for the future. For all of us, learning about how effective organisations are managing HR is an essential step for getting into position. This theme of partnership is shown in Fig 11.7.

HR professionals need to change in this partnership

Thus, while functional expertise is still important, HR professionals are now expected to work side by side with line management as partners in topics such as mergers and

Line managers	HR professionals	Employees
• Include HR professionals in the formulation and implementation of business strategy. • Work closely with HR professionals and employees to develop and implement HR activities. • Accept shared responsibility for managing the human resources of the company. • Set policy that is supportive of ethical behaviour.	• Work closely with line managers and employees to develop and implement HR activities. • Work with line managers to link HR activities to the business. • Work with employees to help them voice their concerns to management. • Develop policies and practices to support ethical conduct.	• Work closely with line managers and HR professionals to develop and implement HR activities. • Accept responsibility for managing their own behaviour and careers in organisations. • Recognise the need for flexibility and adaptability.

Source: Schuler and Jackson (1996), p. 31.

Fig 11.7 Partnership for managing human resources

acquisitions, productivity and quality enhancement efforts – activities not necessarily function specific (Schuler, 1994).

HR leaders

Being a member of the management team will mean that the HR leader assumes some new key roles (Walker, 1989). These roles include:

- being a business person;
- functioning as a business executive, not just a personnel specialist;
- understanding and communicating how HR programmes directly impact business objectives and bottom line;
- being a shaper and agent of change;
- anticipating and focussing on change management;
- helping articulate and build evolving company culture and value system;
- becoming a driving force in making change happen in attitudes, behaviour, skills;
- becoming a consultant to the organisation and acting as a partner to line managers;
- earning acceptance by being a creative problem solver;
- being a strategic planner-formulator and implementor;
- integrating specific business strategies into key people requirements and culture;
- translating specific business strategies into key people requirements and culture;
- identifying gaps, evaluating alternatives, developing programmes, pushing delivery;
- finding the best management talent;
- continually learning and changing;
- anticipating future HR needs;

- doing outstanding succession planning;
- being a proactive asset manager, cost controller and server of customers;
- extending workforce management into productivity improvement; and
- developing pay plans that are productivity related and cost-effective.

HR staff

Similar expectations are made for the HR staff as the HR leader. Firms, of course, may attach different degrees of importance to roles played by the leader versus the staff. What are the competencies required to play these roles?

Managers would like human resource staff to work closely with them to help solve their people-related problems as efficiently and promptly as possible, allowing them to give more attention to their concerns. While line managers may best understand their own people, they increasingly seek help in handling people problems. As HR staff become more capable and effective, managers seek to work with them as partners (Lawler, 1988).

Being at the top of the organisation reporting directly to the CEO and having business skills allows the HR leader to play a part in HRM policy formulation and to have the power necessary to ensure fair and consistent implementation. When the HR department has this much importance, it is likely to be performing effectively at the operational, managerial and strategic levels of HRM. Doing this well takes many important competencies including:

- financial knowledge;
- market/product knowledge;
- demonstrated ability to learn and keep up;
- ability to recognise management expectations and act on them;
- empowerment/political skills;
- influence in organisation;
- problem solving skills;
- business knowledge/organisation sensitivity;
- knowledge of stakeholders affected by change;
- proven project manager: be able to gather data, analyse situations, prescribe approach, make a workable plan, get agreement on contract specifying who will do what by when – and for how much, execute project on time to customer satisfaction within the budget, and evaluate;
- business person, shaper of change, consultant to organisation/partner to line;
- knows compensation techniques to reinforce business plans;
- has division and corporate experience; preferably line experience, too;
- has strategic conceptual skills, knows how to formulate plans and structure systems;
- knowledge of succession/career planning systems;
- has established relationships and acknowledged leadership skills – is an advocate;
- capable of analysing data and planning from it;
- computer literate;
- competent in HR functional areas;

- sees financial impacts in HR function as well as organisation, particularly in areas like pension costs, health care, compensation; and
- is talent manager and strategy/business planner.

While this list of qualities or competencies is rather extensive, these will be the ones that those in world class HR departments in firms in highly competitive environments in the twenty-first century will need (Schuler, 1994). Some firms are now adopting procedures to systematically identify required qualities for their HR staff:

> **At Weyerhaeuser each major division, led by its human resources director, is responsible for developing a list of specific, required competencies. Of course, overlaps occur among major divisions. The HR directors help generate a slate of competencies based on their interviews with the 'customers' – others in the organisation – and HR professionals, and on their own requirements. The corporation is also aiming to predict future HR issues as a basis for updating human resources strategies and developing future competency require-ments for HR staff.** (Walker, 1990, p. 39)

Now that the question of staffing the HR department is addressed, the next critical issue involves repositioning the HR department to the business.

5. The need to reposition the HR department

What has happened at the GBCS of AT&T

Implementing the preceding changes at the Global Business Communications Systems (GBCS) required new roles, new competencies, new relationships, additional resources, and new ways of operating – for both GBCS associates and the HR organisation. Prior to its reorganisation, GBCS Human Resources provided salary administration, HR information systems, staffing support, and other related administrative services. Human Resources had to transform itself from a 'provider of basic personnel services' to a strategic function, one that would be seen as adding value to the entire organisation (Fitz-Enz, 1991).

With support from Jerre Stead, the HR organisation was repositioned as a key mem-ber on the senior management team and assumed the role of providing leadership on strategic HR issues. Three areas were emphasised because of their linkage with the business strategy: diversity, labour, and HR strategic planning. The incumbents in these positions were charged with understanding how these areas could be enhanced to strengthen GBCS's ability to achieve its business goals.

In forming the new HR team from the former GBCS and BCSystems HR organisa-tions, the HR leadership team chose not to assign associates, by fiat, to new roles. Rather, the team asked each associate to state a job preference. The associates were told that the team would try to accommodate preferences, but that business needs would prevail in determining each person's ultimate assignment. It should be noted that 98 per cent of the preferences were honoured.

As a result, the senior team was able to place highly skilled HR professionals in key assignments that reflected their preferences. This enabled the organisation to proceed on a transformation path with an excited, challenged, and motivated HR staff.

The GBCS Human Resources organisation is now made up of six teams, as shown in

Fig 11.8. Individuals on these teams are accountable for a wide variety of activities that support GBCS associates.

The Associate Services Team comprises four sub-teams:

1. Resource management, which includes salary administration, compensation, and organisation design;
2. Associate enrichment, which concentrates on recognition and reward systems, quality, performance management, development, associate surveys, and work and family issues;
3. Associate support programmes, which provides expertise and support in the areas of staffing, relocation, HR information systems, and employment; and
4. Personnel services, which works closely with GBCS HR associates in the field to design support processes and optimise delivery, maintenance, evaluation, and continuous feedback for improvement of HR programmes in order to maximise their effectiveness.

GBCS has made substantial progress in developing and implementing its HR plan initiatives. Further, every effort is being made to ensure that the operational plans which support its strategies are integrated across all functions. As a result, planning is an integral part of the HR organisation. Three teams focus on HR planning.

The Labour Planning Team focusses on a partnership between the unions and GBCS management. The primary focus of this team is to jointly determine how to prepare associates for the workplace of the future, that is, to create a readiness to engage in the changing marketplace which is being driven by technological changes and new ways of working (for example, self-managed teams).

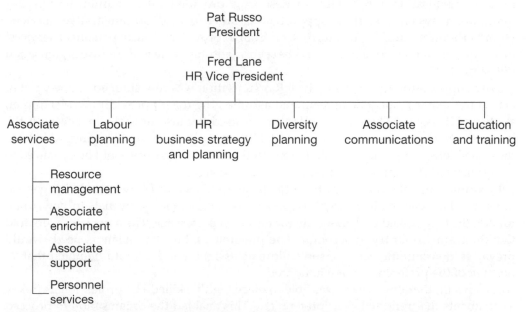

Internal company document provided by the Global Business Communications Systems business unit.

Fig 11.8   GBCS human resources organisation chart

The HR Business Strategy and Planning Team is responsible for ensuring that HR initiatives support the success of the business strategy. The HR strategy and planning model, discussed earlier, was developed by this team with significant support from Fred Lane, Vice President of Human Resources.

The Diversity Planning Team ensures GBCS's constant attention to full utilisation of the company's human talent. Efforts are directed at achieving awareness, understanding, and acceptance of all associates and ensuring a firm commitment to diversity throughout the organisation. As part of this team's efforts, a Global Diversity Council provides advice and counsel to associates and coaches on all issues, concerns, and opportunities related to equal opportunity and diversity. This team also develops and delivers programmes, seminars, and events on matters related to EEO policy/law and valuing diversity.

Of the two remaining teams, the Associate Communications Team focusses on ensuring involvement and participation from all associates by establishing multiple lines of communication with senior management. This supports one of the key themes in the new GBCS culture – that all associates have the power, protection, and permission to help GBCS improve the business.

The Education and Training Team focusses on developing and delivering leadership training as well as management and technical courseware and seminars for GBCS associates and customers. This team responds to the learning needs of their targeted audiences and delivers the educational experiences that will ensure their success.

Conclusion

It has widely been asserted that a firm's employees are among its most important organisational assets (Peters and Waterman, 1982; Pfeffer, 1994), capable of creating and sustaining competitive advantage. In this chapter we have briefly reviewed the research demonstrating the substantial and positive impact of progressive or High Performance Work Practices on the performance of the firm. In addition, we have also made the point that firms which manage their HR effectively make a positive contribution to society, through increased wages, job security, and promotion opportunities for employees.

Given the importance of HR management for a variety of organisational stakeholders, we next identified five key (and interdependent) areas related to the effective implementation of a firm's HR strategy. The first issue was the need to align people with the business. This process includes the provision of an integrated framework that involves and aligns the firm's employees at every level throughout the firm. The second issue was the need to forge an explicit link between the HR function and the needs of the business. We defined this process to include:

1. HRM systems that are fully integrated with the strategy and the strategic needs of the firm;
2. HR policies that cohere both across policy areas and across hierarchies; and
3. HR practices that are adjusted, accepted and used by line managers and employees as part of their everyday work.

The third issue was the need to facilitate a global organisational operation. Here we highlighted the importance of two strategic business needs for MNCs: the need to link the separate units (interunit linkages) and the need to manage the local (internal) operations. Issue four concerned the need to reconceptualise the delivery of the HR function through a partnership between line and HR managers in the development and implementation of the firm's HR management system. Finally, the fifth issue was the need to reorganise the HR department into a strategic function, where HR executives play an important role on the senior management team and provide leadership on strategic human resources issues.

The experience of strategic HR management in US firms contains some clear lessons for both academics and practitioners, we believe. In addition to the importance of the five key issues outlined above, practicing managers must focus not only on the specific HR management policies and practices they adopt but also on the *effectiveness* with which they have been implemented. One important way to do this is by gaining an understanding of how HR management systems can affect employee skills and motivation within their own firms. Human resource managers can help to gain such an understanding through a determination of how their HR management systems influence intermediate employment outcomes, such as absenteeism, turnover, and productivity, and thereafter how these factors influence the financial performance of the firm. Such skills, we believe, represent key core competencies for HR managers in the new competitive environment.

In closing, as domestic and international markets become increasingly competitive, the effective management of HR has become an important determinant of competitive advantage. Practising managers can enhance the value added contribution of their firm's HR management function through the practice of SHRM; integrating what we call High Performance Work Practices with the wider strategic needs of the business. The goal of such an enterprise should be the development of the mutual gains (Kochan and Osterman, 1994) associated with increased competitiveness for shareholders, employees, and other organisational stakeholders.

REFERENCES

Adler, N.J. (1991) *International Dimensions of Organizational Behaviour*, second edn, Boston, PWS-Kent Publishing Company.

Adler, N.J. and Jelinek, M. (1986) 'Is "Organizational Culture" Culture Bound?', *Human Resource Management*, 25 (1), pp. 73–90.

Baird, L. and Meshoulam, I. (1988) 'Managing Two Fits of Strategic Human Resource Management', *Academy of Management Review*, 13 (1), pp. 116–28.

Bartlett, C. and Ghoshal, S. (1987) 'Managing Across Borders: New Organizational Responses', *Sloan Management Review*, Fall, pp. 43–53.

Cascio, W.F. (1991) *Costing Human Resources: The Financial Impact of Behavior in Organizations*, third edn, Boston, PWS-Kent.

Caudron, S. (1994) 'HR Leaders Brainstorm', *Personnel Journal*, August, p. 54.

Doz, Y. and Prahalad, C.K. (1986) 'Controlled Variety: A Challenge for Human Resource Management in the MNC', *Human Resource Management*, 25 (1), pp. 55–72.

Enz, C.A. (1986) 'New Directions for Cross-Cultural Studies: Linking Organizational and Societal

Cultures', in Farmer, R.N. (ed.) *Advances in International Comparative Management, Vol. 2*, Greenwich, CT, JAI Press, pp. 173–89.

Farnham, A. (1994) 'America's Most Admired Company', *Fortune*, February 7, pp. 50–87.

Fisher, C.D. (1989) 'Current and Recurrent Challenges in HRM', *Journal of Management*, 15 (2), pp. 157–80.

Fitz-Enz, J. (1991), *Human Value Management*, San Francisco, Jossey-Bass.

Fryzell, G.E. and Wang, J. (1994) 'The Fortune Corporation "Reputation" Index: Reputation for What?' *Journal of Management*, pp. 1–14.

Fulkerson, J. and Schuler, R.S. (1992) 'Managing Worldwide Diversity at Pepsi-Cola International', in Jackson, S.E. (ed.) *Diversity in the Workplace: Human Resource Initiatives*, New York, Guilford Publications.

Galen, M., Greising, D. and Anderson, S. (1994) 'How Business is Linking Hands in the Inner Cities', *Business Week*, September 26, p. 81 and p. 83.

Hambrick, D.C. and Snow, C.C. (1989) 'Strategic Reward Systems', in Snow, C.C. (ed.) *Strategy, Organization Design and Human Resource Management*, Greenwich, CT, JAI Press.

Huselid, M.A. (1995) 'The Impact of Human Resource Management Practices on Turnover, Productivity, and Corporate Financial Performance', *Academy of Management Journal* 38, pp. 635–672.

Huselid, M.A. and Becker, B.E. (1996) *Methodical Issues in Cross-Sectional and Panel Estimates of the Human Resources in Firm Performance Link*, Industrial Relations, 35, pp. 400–422.

Huselid, M.A., Jackson, S.E. and Schuler, R.S. (1994) 'The Significance of Human Resource Management Practice Implementation for Corporate Financial Performance', working paper, School of Management and Labor Relations, Rutgers University.

Ichniowski, C., Shaw, K. and Prennushi, G. (1994) 'The Effects of Human Resource Management Practices on Productivity', working paper, Columbia University.

Jackson, S.E., & Schuler, R.S. (1995) 'Understanding Human Resource Management in the Context of Organizations and their Environments. In M.R. Rosenzurig & L.W. Porter (eds) *Annual Review of Psychology*, Vol. 46, pp. 237–264.

Jelinek, M. and Goldhar, J.H. (1983) 'The Strategic Implications of the Factory of the Future', *Sloan Management Review*, Summer, pp. 29–37.

Kochan, T.A. and Osterman, P. (1994) *The Mutual Gains Enterprise: Forging a Winning Partnership among Labor, Management, and Government*, Boston, Harvard Business School Press.

Kotter, J. (1990) *A Force for Change: How Leadership Differs from Management*, New York, The Free Press.

Lawler, E.E. (III) (1984) 'The Strategic Design of Reward Systems', in Schuler, R.S. and Youngblood, S.A. (eds) *Readings in Personnel and Human Resource Management*, second edn, St Paul, MN, West Publishing Company.

Lawler, E.E. (III) (1988) 'Human Resource Management: Meeting the Challenge', *Personnel*, January, pp. 24–7.

MacDuffie, J.P. (in press) 'Human Resource Bundles and Manufacturing Performance: Flexible Production Systems in the World Auto Industry', *Industrial and Labor Relations Review*.

Nicholson, N. and Brenner, S.O. (1994) 'Dimensions of Perceived Organizational Performance: Tests of a Model', *Applied Psychology: An International Review*, pp. 89–108.

Peters, T. and Waterman, R. (1982) *In Search of Excellence*, New York, Harper and Row.

Pfeffer, J. (1994) *Competitive Advantage through People: Unleashing the Power of the Work Force*, Boston, Harvard Business School Press.

Plevel, M., Nellis, S., Lane, F. and Schuler, R.S. (1994) 'How AT&T Global Business

Communications Systems is Linking HR with Business Strategy', *Organizational Dynamics*, Winter, pp. 59–71. Materials on the GBCS at AT&T are adapted from this article.

Porter, M.E. (1980) *Competitive Advantage*, New York, Free Press.

Porter, M.E. (1985) *Competitive Strategy*, New York, Free Press.

Pucik, V. and Katz, J.H. (1986) 'Information, Control and Human Resource Management in Multinational Firms', *Human Resource Management*, 25 (1), pp. 121–32.

Reich, R.B. (1990) 'Who Is Us?', *Harvard Business Review*, January–February, pp. 57–64.

Savage, G.T., Nix, T.W., Whitehead, C.J. and Blair, J.D. (1991) 'Strategies for Assessing and Managing Organisational Stakeholders', *Academy of Management Executive*, 2, pp. 61–75.

Schneider, S. (1988) 'National vs. Corporate Culture: Implications for Human Resource Management', *Human Resource Management*, 27, pp. 231–46.

Schuler, R.S. (1990) 'Repositioning the Human Resource Function: Transformation or Demise?' *Academy of Management Executive*, 4 (3), pp. 49–60.

Schuler, R.S. (1992) 'Strategic Human Resource Management: Linking the People with the Strategic Needs of the Business', *Organizational Dynamics*, Summer, pp. 18–32. Materials on Weyerhaeuser, Grand Union, and the 5-P Model are adapted from this article.

Schuler, R.S. (1994) 'World Class HR Departments: Six Critical Issues; What HR Departments in Effective Firms in Highly Competitive Global Environments in the 21st Century Need to Address', *Accounting and Business Review*, 1 (1), pp. 43–72.

Schuler, R.S. and Jackson, S.E. (1996) *Managing Human Resources for the 21st Century*, sixth edn, St Paul, West Publishing Company. Materials in the introduction section and Weyerhaeuser Company section are adapted from Chapter 1.

Schuler, R.S. and MacMillan, I.C. (1985) 'Gaining Competitive Advantage through Human Resource Management Practices', *Human Resource Management*, 23, pp. 241–56.

Schuler, R.S. and Walker, J.W. (1990) 'Human Resources Strategy: Focusing on Issues and Actions', *Organizational Dynamics*, Summer, pp. 5–19.

Schuler, R.S., Fulkerson, J.R. and Dowling, P.J. (1991) 'Strategic Performance Measurement and Management in Multinational Corporations', *Human Resource Management*, Fall, pp. 365–92.

Schuler, R.S., Dowling, P.J. and DeCieri, H. (1993) 'Strategic International Human Resource Management', *Journal of Management*, special yearly issue.

Sherman, S. (1993) 'Are You as Good as the Best in the World?' *Fortune*, December 13, pp. 95–6.

Sherwood, J.J. (1988) 'Creating Work Cultures with Competitive Advantage', *Organizational Dynamics*, Winter, pp. 5–27.

Stewart, T.A. (1994) 'Your Company's Most Valuable Asset: Intellectual Capital', *Fortune*, October 3, pp. 68–74.

Stonham, P. (1994) 'Change in the Global Economy: An Interview with Rosabeth Moss Kanter', *European Management Journal*, March, pp. 1–9.

Thurow, L.C. (1992) *Head to Head*, New York, William Morrow and Company, Inc., p. 45.

Ulrich, D. and Lake, D. (1990) *Organizational Capability*, New York, Wiley.

Walker, J.W. (1989) 'Human Resource Roles for the '90s', *Human Resource Planning*, 12, p. 55.

Walker, J.W. (1990) 'What's New in HR Development?', *Personnel*, July, pp. 38–41.

Welch, J.F. (1994) 'A Matter of Exchange Rates', *Wall Street Journal*, June 21, p. 23.

Wickens, P. (1987) *The Road to Nissan*, London, Macmillan.

12 KEY ISSUES IN HRM IN JAPAN

Toshitaka Yamanouchi and Lola Okazaki-Ward

There has been a continuing debate on the concept of 'lifetime employment' as a policy in Japan since it was first brought to the notice of academics by Abegglen in 1958 (Abegglen, 1958). A Report by the Organisation for Economic Cooperation and Development (OECD) drew the attention of western observers to it as one of the so-called three pillars of Japanese-style of management towards the end of the 1970s (Takanashi, 1994). The debate on the value of this concept has cropped up every time there has been a need for labour adjustment in Japan (Takanaski, 1993). In the recent period of deep recession following upon the bursting of the 'bubble' economy in 1990 in Japan, the collapse of this policy is being debated in the West again.

However, policies on 'lifetime' employment have not remained unchanged: in fact they have undergone substantial changes in their essentials in the 1970s when the first oil crisis of 1973 brought the period of fast growth in Japan to an end, and as a consequence sections of Japanese industry had to resort to massive labour redeployment measures. Japanese human resource managers at the time instituted programmes to outplace middle-aged and older workers for example, through the 'open window programme', the one-way transfer of employees to subsidiary companies and the fixed-age retirement scheme for managerial staff. These practices were clearly aimed at different objectives from those commonly associated with 'lifetime' employment. Nevertheless, the exercise has been accomplished with relatively minor disruption to the existing labour markets, and without harsh confrontation between capital and labour, which kept the unemployment level at a remarkably low rate of below 3 per cent. These factors were noted in the West where the effect of the first oil crisis on employment was much more severe and the recovery was much slower than in Japan. The subsequent OECD Report brought to the notice of the world the 'lifetime' employment, and seniority-based systems of pay and promotion as the characteristics of the Japanese style of Human Resource Management. The other element of Japanese-style management is seen in enterprise-based unionism.

After the first oil crisis, Japan entered a period of slower growth, and this necessitated the modification of employment practices which had become established in the period of fast growth in the 1960s. In fact, these practices have been undergoing continuous modification at the level of individual corporate HRM, to adjust to changes in the economy. What has brought this to the renewed attention of western observers is the effect of the recent recession in Japan which has forced Japanese companies to resort to severe restructuring. The ensuing debate also focussed the attention of Japanese scholars on the concept of 'lifetime' employment, which is now being re-examined.

> **If we took notice of the economic depressions, the debate would have concluded that lifetime employment was already over.** (Tsuda, 1994)

> **Lifetime employment does not represent the actual Japanese employment system and may lead people, especially foreign people, to misunderstand the actual Japanese employment system .... [so] the concept of stable employment should be used instead of 'lifetime employment'.** (Okuda, 1994)

> **Lifetime employment system has never existed in Japan. It certainly does not exist as a legal contractual term. The concept has grown up alongside the practice in the fast growing 1960s when a tacit mutual expectation for a stable employment has become established between the employer and the employed. It would be more appropriate to describe the employment practice in Japan as long-term stable employment, to avoid confusion.** (Shimada, 1994)

These quotations show that the actual issues in Japanese HRM cannot be understood through discussing 'lifetime employment' as a given fact of life. The term itself is not usually defined by scholars. Nor can the concept be used to include all types of employment in Japan, for such a system is only applicable largely to male, regular employees in large companies which comprise less than 1 per cent of the total number of firms in Japan and less than 30 per cent of the total workforce. These regular employees are also the main part of Japanese unionised labour. Because the influence of the large companies on the rest of the economy is powerful, the concept is used sometimes rather indiscriminately.

The debate has had some positive outcomes, however, as it has highlighted the need for Japanese HRM to be restructured. The most significant suggestion is that the basic framework in Japanese HRM has become unsatisfactory. First we should explain the basic framework now required. Shown in Fig 12.1 is the Ranking System of Workers

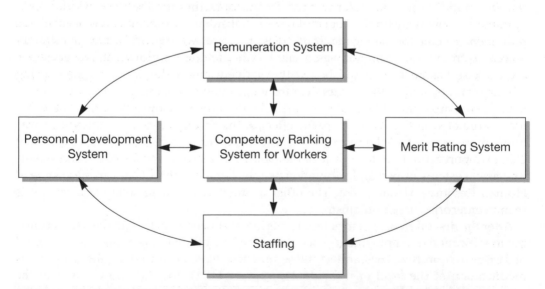

Fig 12.1   Japanese HRM system on the basis of Competency Ranking System

(*Shikaku-seido*) which foreign scholars have insufficiently understood, but which provides the underlying framework for HR policies. How to revise this ranking system of workers is the key strategic issue in Japan at present (Rômugyôsei Kenkyûjo, 1990, Tsuda, M. 1994).

It could be said that we are currently in the third period of HRM reconstruction after the Second World War. A brief history of how HRM developed in Japan will help to explain the current state of Japanese HRM.

A short history of Japanese HRM

The first period started in the 1950s. Because Japanese companies thought that the original Japanese management system was feudalistic and irrational, Japanese companies introduced the US management system based on job analysis and job classification as a modern, rational management system to rebuild Japanese management. The second period was between the 1960s and 1970s when Japanese companies reconsidered the Americanisation of Japanese management practices and revised them further. Under the job ranking system, an employee doing a higher job would refuse to do a lower level job, so a tight social order was developed within the company. Consequently, the job ranking system that was introduced at the first period prevented movements within the company and damaged the company's capacity to respond to technological progress. Japanese companies therefore altered the basic criterion on which an employee's remuneration was based and created a system for movements within the company through a new ranking system for workers instead of the job ranking system. This trend can be understood by reference to Table 12.1. The Japanese ranking system of workers can generally be classified into three types:

1. an occupational, ability-based ranking system of workers;
2. a competency ranking system (*Nôryokuteki-shikaku Seido* or *Shokunô-shikaku Seido*); and
3. a ranking system of workers based on the distinction between white-collar and blue-collar workers (*Shokukôteki-Mibun Seido*).

As Table 12.1 shows, the proportion of Japanese companies which introduced the job ranking type of scheme declined from 27.9 per cent in 1958 to 17.0 per cent in 1974, and the percentage of companies introducing the 'competency' ranking systems of workers increased from 30.0 per cent in 1963 to 64.0 per cent in 1974. One important consequence

Table 12.1   The trends of job ranking systems and ranking systems of workers

The basic framework of HRM	1958	1963	1968	1974
Job ranking system	27.9%	18.9%	16.7%	17.0%
Ranking system of workers	47.0%			
Competency ranking system		30.0%	45.1%	64.0%
Seniority-based ranking system		38.8%	33.1%	35.5%
Ranking system of workers based on the distinction between white and blue collar	34.2%	21.8%	13.5%	5.5%

Source: Nihon Keieisha Dantai Renmei (1975).

of this trend has been the discontinuance of the practice of distinguishing between white-collar and blue-collar groups found in the old ranking system of workers. This discriminating practice has been replaced by unified systems embracing all employees. The competency ranking system and the seniority-based system both have therefore narrowed the disparity in remuneration between such employee groups. The new ranking system for workers is not based on their jobs. This new system has encouraged flexibility in response to technological progress and changing economic conditions. Employees have become much more oriented towards the company than the job. [The ratio of companies introducing the competency ranking system of workers increased to 83.6 per cent in 1990 (Rômugyôsei Kenkyûgo, 1994, p. 59).]

The third reconstruction started in the middle of the 1980s. The competency ranking system as then existed had not been working effectively owing to the stronger yen, globalised business activities, deregulation, the mature economy, the ageing workforce, changes in young workers' social values and the shift from a mass production system to small lot production for many products. The ratio of companies reporting no problems on the competency ranking system compared to total companies replying was only 9 per cent in the late 1980s. The competency ranking system has been encountering several serious problems in its implementation (Rômugyôsei, 1990, pp. 126–7), which are listed below in the order of the magnitude of the rates of response they drew.

1. A gap existed between an employee's actual rank and his/her actual job. (43.2%)
2. The number of employees staying at one level has increased, possibly causing them to lose the will to work. (38.7%)
3. Occupational ability and the results of performance were not clear. (31.0%)
4. The concept of standard requirements of occupational competence is fuzzy. (29.7%)
5. With an increase in employees who are ranked high, their aspirations for higher posting have become keener. (28.4%)
6. An increase in labour cost resulted from the increase in the number of employees with higher rankings. (24.5%)
7. Employees have not understood the nature and the purpose of competency ranking system, and are not responding to the new system well. (24.5%)
8. No clear links have been established between the competency ranking system and the personnel development system. (23.9%)
9. The competency ranking system has largely been built on the existing seniority based promotion standards. (22.6%)

Clearly the system was unable to cope with the structural problems caused by the changes.

In addition, large Japanese companies have suffered a considerable overmanning problem among the workforce, particularly among the white-collar, 40-plus age group. This problem was caused by the Japanese applying traditional criteria for recruitment: Japanese companies generally fix volumes of recruitment according to a certain ratio of operating profits to labour costs each year. In a boom, Japanese companies therefore recruit large numbers of young people newly entering the labour market in the spring, but cut them back in a slump. In the boom period in the economy, Japanese managers failed to understand when the economic growth was reaching its zenith, and consequently recruited large numbers of new graduates and school leavers into the regular employment category, using the traditional recruitment criteria. This has happened in the late 1960s and early 1970s, and these employees, termed the 'bulge' generation of white-collar workers, are in their mid-40s; many of them were on the first rung of the middle management ladder by the end of the 1980s (Okazaki-Ward, 1993). And it is among this group where the so-called 'working unemployed' was estimated to have reached the one million mark by the end of 1992 (*Tokyo Business Today*, May 1993).

The recession of the 1990s forced many companies to reduce cost by trimming the number of employees, particularly in the 40-plus age groups who, by the definition of the seniority-based wage system, are more expensive to maintain than the younger employees. How much more expensive they are can be seen in the table of wage rates produced by Nihon Seisansei Honbu (Japan Productivity Centre, JPC) in 1989. According to this, if the average starting salary of graduates at the age of 22 in firms with 1000 or more employees in 1988 is taken to be 100, the salary of a 30-year-old was 161, increasing to 254 at the age of 40, to 353 at the age of 50, peaking to 377 at the age of 55 and then falling to 348 at the age of 60 when they retire. As an average for all companies, the ratio of salary for graduates at the age of 55 was 3.46 times that at the age of 22 (Nihon Seisansei Honbu, 1989). The situation was made worse by a recruitment spree by companies in the peak years of the 'bubble' economy. To deal with overmanning the companies have resorted to secondment and transfer of older employees to subsidiaries and affiliated companies, and offered enhanced early retirement packages to entice voluntary retirement, and even, as the last option, to the severance of named individuals where their policy failed to work, among the 40-plus age groups.

The need for a substantive restructuring of their organizational structure is forcing Japanese companies to revise their competency ranking system for workers. As Japanese companies each operate in their own particular context, and they naturally differ from one another in their management strategies, so there is no one best way to reconstruct HRM. Nevertheless, HRM is in the urgent process of being 'reconstructed' within all the different companies within Japan. As an example of these changes, we will examine the case of Yamatake-Honeywell.

A brief history of Yamatake-Honeywell

Yamatake-Honeywell (Yamatake from now on) is referred to as the most successful joint venture in Japan, because the relationship between Yamatake and Honeywell (US) has remained friendly. Yamatake's annual turnover reached one hundred million yen in 1988. Yamatake is a major producer of automation equipment. It employed 4630 people in 1993. It was capitalised at 4.2 billion yen in 1993. The joint venture was formed in 1952 by Yamatake Shoji (a trading company) founded in 1906 and Honeywell (US). They each owned 50 per cent of the shares in Yamatake, but Honeywell (US) then decided to sell half of its stock to Yamatake Shoji in 1989. Honeywell (US)'s shares had declined by 24.15 per cent but they reached an agreement that the business co-operation would continue as in the past. Honeywell (US) as a shareholder sent three directors to the board of directors and one of them was based in Tokyo. They provided support and acted as advisers to Yamatake. The original relationship between them was based on the transfer of technological know-how from Honeywell, but Yamatake has since collaborated with Honeywell in researching new technology, developing products, and Yamatake now shares production between Japan, the United States and Europe.

Yamatake has also learned management techniques and management tools from Honeywell. It actively brought these into its management and absorbed, then adapted them to meet its own needs. Yamatake has increasingly developed a management method that was created in the United States and has been evolving its own unique management method. Honeywell in turn has learned from Yamatake how to carry out strategic planning.

When we observe Yamatake's growth process we note that it has faced two crises – the impact of the dollar shock in 1971 and the second oil crisis in 1979–80. The rate of Yamatake's growth between 1972 and 1973 was zero. This shock made all of Yamatake's management and employees alter their attitudes towards their tasks. They recognised that the management style suited to the higher economic growth period would cause the company to fail, because the industrial instrument business had matured. Yamatake changed the management planning system and its implementation. It established the business philosophy 'Savemation' that Yamatake coined from 'Save' and 'Automation' in 1978. Savemation means that Yamatake contributes not only to human happiness through its operations but also to the development of society through saving energy, saving resources and the saving of labour. Savemation provides a Japanese guideline on how to run a business in industry and how to develop diversified management.

Yamatake's Trade Union and its Management published 'the joint declaration of productivity' in 1978. They each confirmed that they gave their co-operation and endeavour to make Yamatake an excellent company. The declaration at the same time fixed the bonus calculation method as 4.24 times an employee's monthly wage plus a percentage of operating profits. To carry out this joint declaration Yamatake re-examined its management planning system and amended it. Yamatake changed the previous management system by strengthening top management's role in carrying out strategic planning and co-operated with Honeywell in its globalisation strategy. Yamatake has been attempting to grow its business in a mature industry and a world economy which is dividing into trade blocs.

The ranking system of workers at Yamatake

Yamatake revised its original personnel and remuneration system in 1979, and in 1981, soon after the second oil crisis, a special committee was set up, composed of union and management, to clarify points at issue in the revised system. The committee highlighted some problems:

1. the old personnel and remuneration system did not help to develop employees' abilities;
2. the feedback of appraisal results relating to the development of employees' skills did not work well;
3. the old personnel and remuneration system was neither innovative nor creative; and
4. the nature of performance appraisal amounted to a point deduction scoring system.

Having identified the major problems mentioned above, the committee set up guidelines to address these problems and planned for another revision in 1989. When it was introduced, the second revision was an extensive modification of the then current system and included the following major points:

1. competency ranking system (*Shokunô-shikaku Seido*);
2. systematic performance appraisal;
3. a new remuneration system;
4. systematic development of employees' ability; and
5. a new policy on the relocation of personnel.

The competency ranking system (*Shokunô-shikaku Seido*)

The old personnel and remuneration system was based on the job classification system and a system called *Shikaku-Seido* by Yamatake. The job classification system determined wages and *Shikaku-Seido* determined the portion of the wage paid for the acquisition of specific skill. Although both systems had been used separately, job oriented thinking has been firmly established in Yamatake and employees have recognised that job and job ability are two sides of the same coin. Under the job classification system an intra-company movement sometimes caused wages to reduce, because the job classification system classified jobs into three types and there were three job wages tables. Where intra-company movements resulted in a loss of pay, this lowered the morale of employees and made employees less willing to move. In order to get round this problem, Yamatake integrated the two systems and set up a new personnel and remuneration system, namely the competency ranking system as shown in Table 12.2.

This consists of three levels – the Professional grade, the Principal grade and the Operating Grade – and ten ranks of competence within a type of job group (*Shokunô-Tôkyû*). Ranks I–VII are each divided into nine steps (*Gô*) that correspond to the degree of competency by type of job group. The relationship between the rank of competence, status of ranking (*Shikaku* in Yamatake) and position/post (*Shokui*) is shown in Table 12.3.

The status ranking system is the old system. If the rank of an employee in the new system is below that employee's status in the old system, then in order to guarantee the status in Yamatake the old status of ranking is retained in the new system. Consequently

Table 12.2 Competency ranking system

Grades	Status (*Shikaku*)	Rank of Competence	Steps	Standard requirements for occupational competence
Professional Grades	M3	X		
	M2	IX		
	M1	VIII		
Principal Grades	L3	VII	1–9	
	L2	VI	1–9	
	L1	V	1–9	
Operating Grades	G4	IV	1–9	
	G3	III	1–9	
	G2	II	1–9	
	G1	I	1–9	

Table 12.3 The relationship between competency ranking system and position

Rank of competence	Status (*Shikaku*)	Position (*Shokui*)		
		Line	Staff	Engineer
X	M3	Divisional director	Departmental manager	Chief engineer
IX	M2	Plant general manager		Chief researcher
VIII	M1	Branch general manager / General manager		
VII	L3	Head of section	Acting head of section	
VI	L2	Head of office	Head clerk of section	
V	L1		Deputy head clerk	
IV	G4			
III	G3			
II	G2			
I	G1			

Rank IV of competence is a port of entry for PhD.
Rank III of competence is a port of entry for Master of Arts.
Rank II of competence is a port of entry for graduate.
Rank I of competence is a port of entry for non-graduate.

the status of ranking is equal to rank of competence. The rank which an employee has in the competency ranking system shows the employee's other status in the status ranking system and determines that employee's particular position in Yamatake.

In the job classification system, in which each position was linked directly to a corresponding place on the status ranking, jobs in the company were fixed and the number of employees who could have higher ranking jobs was further restricted. If a higher job was not vacant, it was very difficult in this system correctly to reward an employee of ability. As the relationship between position and status in the new system is more flexible than in the old system, it is possible for Yamatake to promote and reward an employee of ability on a basis commensurate with his or her ability. By introducing the competency ranking system, Yamatake can have the right person in the right place.

This system is based on standard requirements of occupational competence (*Shokunô-Tôkyû-Kijun*) which is the only criterion for the evaluation of an employee's performance and ability, for the development of an employee's ability and for the remuneration system. There are two types of standard requirements of occupational competence. One is the standard requirement of occupational competence in the whole company (*Zensha-Shokunô-Tôkyû-Kijun*). The other is the standard requirement for occupational competence by occupational group (*Shokushubetsu-Shokunô-Tôkyû-Kijun*). Standard requirements of occupational competence in the whole company provide criteria for evaluating the level of job performance, knowledge and skill, the level of understanding, decision making, practical ability, ability to plan, the level of development, power of expression, ability in negotiation and leadership. On the basis of standard requirements of occupational competence in the whole company, the standard requirement of occupational competence by occupational group gives criteria for evaluating employees by occupational group. These criteria are the basis for evaluating job competence, the performance level and a target for the development of the employee's career within each of the occupational groups.

Under the ranking system of workers the minimum and the maximum length of service in each step is fixed. If the minimum length of service is relatively long and the maximum length of service is relatively short, the number of years required for promotion correlates more closely with the number of service years. This ranking system of workers is therefore ranking by seniority. On the other hand, if the minimum length of service is short and the maximum length of service is long, the number of service years does not necessarily correlate to the number of years of service required for the promotion as shown in Fig 12.2.

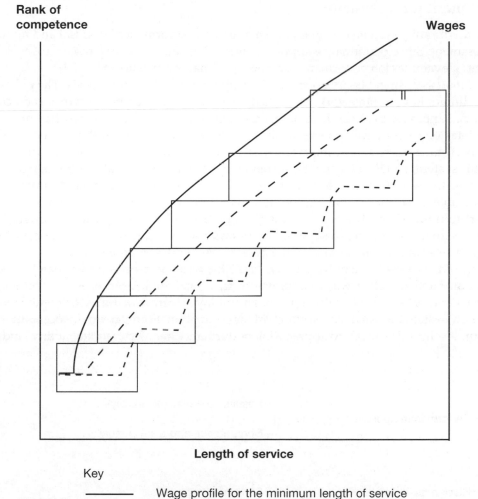

Key

——————— Wage profile for the minimum length of service

– – – II Wage profile for the maximum length of service

– – – – – I Wage profile for an average worker

Fig 12.2 Schematic representation of relationship between rank of competency, length of service and wages

This system is based on the merit system. To understand the nature of a ranking system of workers one must appreciate the importance of the minimum length and the maximum length of service in each step. In the case of Yamatake, the minimum length of service in each step has been reduced from three years to one year. Moreover, an employee can be promoted up a rank without having to go through all the nine steps if his or her skill level reaches a satisfactory level. Thus, theoretically, it is possible to promote a brilliant employee up one rank each year, while some employees will take nine years to move on to the next rank. In reality, the employees would be distributed somewhere between these two extremes, depending on their individual ability, as is indicated in Fig 12.6 (page 215). This system is based on the merit system and can open up opportunities for the talented.

The merit rating system

The merit rating system in Yamatake is made up of performance appraisal and human assessment. Since performance appraisal aims principally at human resource development, it evaluates job performance and occupational competence (Fig 12.3).

Human assessment backs up career development on a long-term basis. The old system did not have a framework that linked the evaluation of job performance and occupational appraisal to career development. In the new system the framework to provide feedback on career development consists of the personal career development card and the personnel development interview system. The line managers are heavily involved in this system, and they must not only obtain their own goals but also train their subordinates. In the old system there was no system which forced managers to train their subordinates, so managers concentrated mainly on their own goals and made little effort to train others. The new system gives priority to improving each subordinate's abilities. In the new system a superior interviews a subordinate in order to improve that employee's abilities on the basis of the personal career development card.

The old appraisal system had two criteria. One was the criterion to evaluate job performance and the other was to appraise occupational ability. Since these criteria differed, the results of these evaluations for an employee were sometimes different. Under the new system the standard requirement for occupational competence by occupational group is a useful criterion to appraise job performance and occupational ability, and to

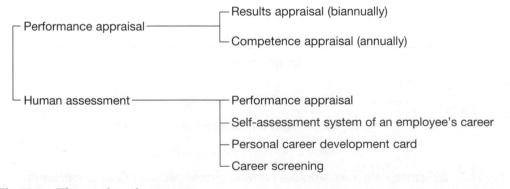

Fig 12.3   The merit rating system

evaluate human assessment, making the process of evaluation very clear. The old system directly linked the results of the evaluation to a wage increase and bonus so that the evaluation was calculated backwards from the intended wage increase and was therefore inexact. Under the new system, the bonus is mainly based on performance appraisal and the annual routine wage increase is based on performance appraisal and job ability. Valuation factors in the old system were uniform regardless of the job performed so that the results of appraisal tended to ignore the characteristics of each job group and did not appraise the specificity of each occupational group. Standard requirements for occupational competence in the new system fix the content of the valuation factors and weight them so that appraisal on the basis of them reflects a characteristic of each occupational group.

The new remuneration system

By introducing *Shokunô-Shikaku-Seido*, Yamatake changed its remuneration system from personal wages (*Honnin-kyû*) + job wages (*Shigoto-kyû*) + wages based on the ranking system of workers (*Nôryoku-kyû*) to personal wages + pay for job ability (*Shokunô-Kyû*) as shown in Fig 12.4. Pay for job ability is divided into two parts: one is basic job ability wages (*Shokunô-Kiso-Kyû*), the other job ability wages (*Shokunô-Hon-Kyû*), both based on the standard requirement for occupational competence appropriate to the employee's job ranking.

The personal wage is a seniority-based wage and continues from the old system and is based on the life cycle. Its ratio of total monthly earning in the old system was 46.6 per cent, but in the new system this declines to 45 per cent. Japanese people increasingly go

Old style

Personal wages 46.6%	(Based on life cycle) stability
Job wages 26.0%	(Based on job) stimulative fairness
Job ability wages 27.4%	(Based on job ability) stimulative fairness stability

New style

Personal wages 45.0%		(Based on life cycle) stability
Pay for job ability 55.0%	Job ability wages 27.5%	(Based on occupational competence) stimulative fairness stability
	Job wages 27.5%	(Based on occupational competence) stimulative fairness stability

The major differences are:
a 1.6 per cent reduction in the proportion of total remuneration in personal wages; and
b 1.6 per cent increase in job wages.

Fig 12.4   The ratio of wages to total remuneration

on to higher education and typically get married later in life today so the peak of personal wages in the new system extends from 49 years of age to 51 years of age. The new age-wage profile is flatter than the old one and narrows the range in remuneration on employees' age, motivating younger workers.

The job ability wages are fixed through the rank of competence and the step. A basis for raising the rank of competence is to improve occupational ability, and a basis for raising the step is to become more skilful. As raising of the step is based on the skill-ability profile that Yamatake has set up as shown in Fig 12.5, the rate of increase in job ability wages declines on each succeeding step as shown in Fig 12.6. Normally, to increase job ability wages an employee has to raise his or her status/rank. Consequently the job ability wage aims to motivate an employee to improve his or her occupational ability.

Job wages based on the standard requirement for occupational competence are fixed through demonstrating job ability and the results of performance. Yamatake established two wage schedules for the job wages each year: one for the annual routine wage increase and the other for the increase in the wage base. A rise in job wages is fixed through an employee's level in the rank of competence and the results of performance. In the old system, even if the employees' rank in the competency ranking system and the results of their performance are the same, older employees' wages were higher than younger employees'. Age had a large influence on the job wages based on the standard requirement for occupational competence. The new system removes age from the factors that fix job wages.

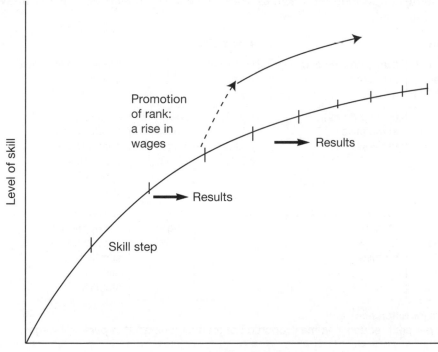

Fig 12.5   Occupational ability curve: Yamatake Images

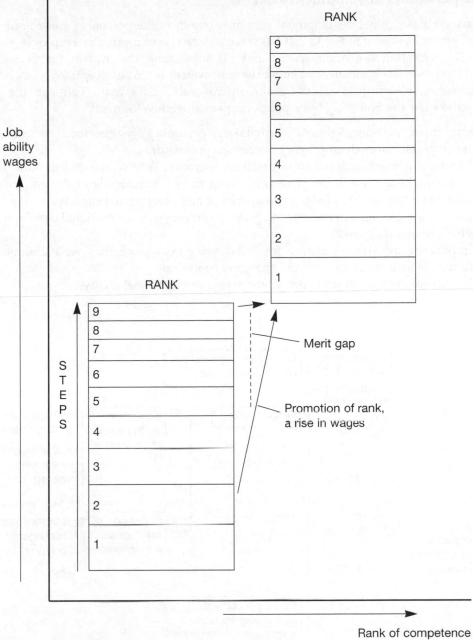

Fig 12.6   Job ability wages and rank of competence

The personnel development system

Yamatake's personnel development system is based on the personnel and remuneration system as shown in Fig 12.7. It has three pillars: (1) promoting an employee's ability; (2) activating the organisation; and (3) supporting the system for personnel development. The basic theory behind the new system is that each employee, as his or her leading role improves, enlarges, deepens and creates more value in the job. Yamatake has the following basic policy for personnel development:

1. Supporting self-development: Yamatake's personnel system focusses on self-development for each employee to become a professional.
2. Attaching greater importance to practical education than to theoretical education: Yamatake believes it is the process of doing the job that develops the employee's ability to integrate knowledge into experience and theory into practice.
3. Courses are arranged in order to integrate the employee's occupational development with Yamatake's growth.
4. Employees are given a chance for self-development since they well understand Yamatake's business mission and changing conditions.
5. Employees are treated fairly according to their occupational ability.

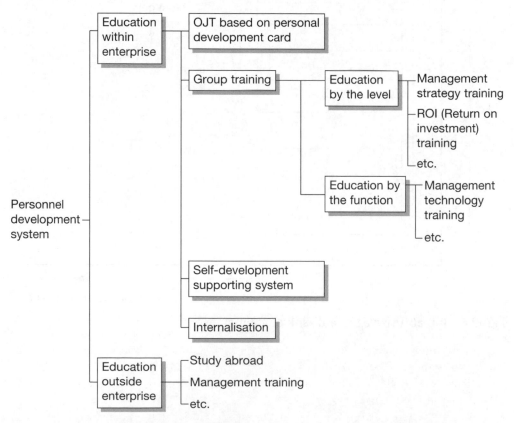

Fig 12.7   Personnel development system

Although the personnel development system is constructed as part of the training role of the personnel function, on-the-job-training (OJT) plays a key role in the occupational training based on the job classification. The supporting system for the personnel development system is shown in Fig 12.7.

In addition, Yamatake has a long-range development programme (LDP) which reviews the development of the employees' occupational ability from the time of joining as a new employee to the stage when the employee is about thirty years of age. Under LDP a superior interviews a subordinate to examine what training that employee has received and in what area he or she has ability. On the basis of the interview, the next stage of development for the employee is mapped out. LDP's aim is to develop personnel of high talent, to improve their ability and to put their occupational ability to practical use.

Summary on Yamatake

The success of Yamatake's competency ranking system is clearly due to the company's ability to address the key problems generally associated with the implementation of the system, and in particular, to creating an integrated personnel and remuneration system linking the competency ranking to the personnel development system and the merit rating system. This aimed to redress the imbalance between reward and the contribution the individuals made to overall company performance and was intended to stimulate motivation.

Also reflected in the new approach is the recognition of individual differences in ability and the capacity for development, which is a move away from the old, unitary, and group-oriented personnel system. It is also set in a broadly long-term, stable employment background.

Introduction of the competency grading system to Japanese HRM

Since the 1970s when there has been a considerable labour redeployment exercise after the first oil crisis, Japanese companies have tried to accommodate the seniority-related wages and promotion system in a period of slow growth that followed when the number of posts did not increase, by separating the existing system into status ladder (competency grading) and job appointments (posts). In this double track system, every employee was located on the status ladder where it was commensurate with the length of years he or she worked in the company, but only a limited number of people were given line posts. In this system, employees who had been with the company for roughly the same number of years were located on the same grade on the status ladder with roughly similar basic wages, with those who were in management posts having additional allowances. There was also a proliferation of meaningless job titles to placate the dissatisfaction of those whose aspirations for managerial posts were not fulfilled (Okazaki-Ward, 1993).

However, whereas the progress on the status ladder was more directly related to seniority during the 1970s, a merit element was progressively introduced by more companies in the 1980s reflecting the recognition that there are individual differences, but without jettisoning the seniority element entirely, partially because competency requires a certain amount of experience. See Table 12.4.

Table 12.4 Reason for changing to competency grading system

	No. of employees		
	300–999	1000–4999	5000+
	%	%	%
Organisations with competency grading system	70.1	82.2	91.4
Reason introduced:			
Merit based	70.9	84.2	90.3
Stimulates motivation	67.1	69.0	69.4
Copes with shortage of posts	26.5	28.0	25.5

Source: Ministry of Labour in Japan, 1990 (survey of 6000 firms).

The survey from which the data in Table 12.4 was drawn shows that although by this time the bulge generation graduates (born between 1947 and 1950), who had been employed in large numbers in the career streams in the expansionary years of 1969–72, had already arrived at the stage of their career when they could expect to be in the first level of middle management, and while the shortage of managerial posts was still an issue, the problem of the swollen ranks of high-earning senior employees without a job to do who were low in morale, had become a more important issue. The example in Table 12.5, of a major manufacturing firm with a total of about 12 700 employees, where the practice of 'lifetime' employment was firmly in place, indicates the relationship between the competency grading system and posts in numerical terms.

Table 12.5 Structure of the middle management

Competency grading		Post	
Riji	(25)		
Shukan	(723)	*Buchô* (head of major department or its equivalent)	(170)
Shuseki	(765)	*Jichô* (administrative head in a department or its equivalent)	(207)
Shusa	(446)	*Kachô* (head of a section or its equivalent)	(375)
Total	(1959)		(752)

Source: information obtained by L.I. Okazaki-Ward from the company in the course of research in 1990.

The alignment between the grading and post in Table 12.5 is slightly misleading because the relationship is not unitary as the table suggests. For example, a *buchô* could be appointed from among *Shukan* or *Shuseki*, *jichô* from all three lower grades, and *kachô* from the two lowest grades to give some flexibility. However, the fact that 1167 of those on the managerial status grades are without posts should be noted. Also those on the middle management competency grades accounted for 15.4 per cent of the total work-force. Additionally there were 2028 white-collar employees below these grades coming up through the competency grading system, and these two groups comprising the white-collar employees accounted for 31.4 per cent of the total workforce. Admittedly, this leading manufacturing company in the electric cable and fibre optic industry had a sizeable R&D staff with seven separate R&D establishments. But this example indicates the scale of the problem of overstaffing in the middle management grades and the cost implications for the company. In general, the so-called *madogiwa-zoku* (the tribe whose members sit by the window), those who had no subordinate to manage and often without specific jobs, was a phenomenon of the 1980s, and the predecessor of a larger, 'in-company unemployed' of the mid 1990s.

The same survey by the Ministry of Labour mentioned above, also indicated how the upgrading was determined. Sixty-five per cent of the firms in the survey had set criteria for upgrading at each of the competency grades. These clearly varied by size of the firms and also by contents as Table 12.6 shows.

Table 12.6 Criteria used for upgrading for middle management in the competency grading system

Size	Total	All	With test	No test	Years of service	Performance evaluation	Upgrading study course	Educational level	Personality
All firms	**65.3**	87.0	19.5	67.5	62.1	89.2	9.4	17.3	48.7
5000 & over	**95.2**	92.9	29.5	63.4	63.4	85.8	16.9	5.1	25.4
1000–4999	**91.5**	94.7	30.8	55.9	71.2	87.4	20.1	13.8	33.9
300–999	**94.1**	94.1	30.8	63.3	66.2	87.8	14.3	15.4	40.8

Source: Ministry of Labour, 1990, p. 83.

Although ability assessment is practised by the majority of the firms in the survey, a large proportion of these firms do not use objective testing. Also seniority is a factor to be considered in almost two-thirds of the total. Nearly half of the firms in the survey also use subjective criteria termed 'personality'. This all indicates that the use of these criteria varied among the firms.

Downsizing

The severe and prolonged recession in the early 1990s after the collapse of the 'bubble' economy, in which the rate of profit for all industries fell continuously for four consecutive years, has forced companies to undergo a drastic restructuring, and brought into the open some of the problems inherent in the so-called 'lifetime' employment practice which had lain largely dormant in the period when the economy had been expanding rapidly. The most serious of these was the cost factor, particularly the labour cost from overmanned white-collar employees whose productivity was low. A further appreciation of the yen, which rose 80 per cent between 1990 and 1995, put an added urgency to the problem. By 1993 the estimated figure for the in-company unemployed had been upwardly revised, and according to one such estimate, Japanese corporations held about four million excess employees who would have been the object of rationalisation if it were in the US (Takeuchi, 1994). However, in Japan there is a considerable cultural and social resistance to such a direct and brutal process. Nevertheless, the first explicit move to reduce the white collar employees was made by TDK in the summer of 1993 when the firm told a sizeable number of its *kachô* without subordinates who were over the age of 50 to take a permanent holiday with pay until their retirement age. It created a considerable criticism from commentators, and the scheme was later shelved by the company. This was followed early in 1994 when Pioneer, a largish, medium-sized manufacturer of audio equipment which had been very successful during the 1980s, picked 35 of its *kachô* who had not been performing well, by name, for 'voluntary' early retirement and when some of them did not comply, dismissed them. This news apparently shocked Japan and there were strong condemnations of the company. But the apparent absence of litigation following the enforced retirement and dismissal, set the course for many other and larger companies to embark on the road of actively reducing their older white-collar employees. As managers were not part of the company union, they were an easy target. Since then there has been an attempt at a formation of a union of such managers, and in particular those who had felt to have been forcibly and unfairly dismissed, to help them fight their cases where they were thought to have been illegal (Tokyo Kanrisha Union and Nihon Rôdô Bengoshidan, 1994).

Dismissal is a process which takes both time and effort, as companies must first show that they have exhausted all possible means to avoid it. These include reducing/scrapping overtime work, non-renewal of all short contract work, temporary lay-off with reduced pay, short working week, redeployment of employees to growing part of the business, reduction or a temporary discontinuation of recruitment, secondment to subsidiaries or group companies with a possibility of permanent transfer, soliciting for voluntary early retirement, and reduction of pay/bonuses or no bonus award across the company. Only then outright dismissal is allowed to proceed, and the company will normally ensure that all such personnel in this category are found an alternative employment. Apart from the cultural constraints mentioned earlier, Japanese corporations are also reluctant to shed all excess labour during a period of economic downturn because of the demographic trend, which predicts labour shortages by the early next century. In any case, they are also aware that when the economy picks up and they need to recruit vigorously again, the enterprise-specific skills and experience of personnel which the company had spent money and time to develop and nurture will not be easily replaced once they have been lost.

A combination of some or all of the means of labour adjustment is used in a period of labour rationalisation. Increasingly, many large firms are openly soliciting volunteers to opt for an early retirement with an offer of a generously enhanced severance allowance, and the age limit is becoming lower. For example, Shin Nippon Steel with 50 000 employees decided to reduce its white-collar staff by 7000 over three years from April 1994, and NTT, the biggest employer in Japan with over 200 000 employees, reduced by 14 000 employees in a six-month period from October 1993 (Tokyo CCI Research, 1995). Though a large amount of natural wastage is involved in both cases, the companies offered enhanced retirement lump sums to encourage others to take early retirement. Secondment with a possibility for complete transfer later has been a more traditional way of reducing the number of senior employees, though this has an obvious limitation to absorb large numbers.

But in large companies and mainly in the manufacturing sector where slimming down of organisations has been happening, attention came to be focussed on tackling the seniority wage system. Since most companies acknowledge in principle the advantages of stable employment – which allow the company a long-term planned development of the employees through in-company education and training system, an improvement in employee morale, stability of employees by guarantee of livelihood, engendering loyalty in the employees towards the company – they are not likely to scrap the system of stable employment. However, the high cost of older employees is the main concern, so that a re-examination of the wages system is inevitable. With the introduction of the merit principle, the proportion of wages which comes from seniority has been decreasing. Some companies are taking this a step further to introduce what is called the *nenpô seido* (the annual salary system) in which the seniority element as the criterion for promotion and pay is removed.

The case of Honda

The so-called annual salary system (*nenpô seido*) in Japan has been introduced before 1990 by a number of companies, such as Sony, Sanstar and Tokyo Gas, but the introduction of this system by Honda in June 1992 drew fresh attention from the media and other companies because this was probably the first full-scale changeover introduced by a large company. For Honda, however, it was not merely a change in the wages system to cut cost, but an integral part of a more fundamental restructuring of its management structure. This was necessitated by the changing external circumstances engendered by such factors as the recession and high yen, placing the car industry in a particularly difficult position, an increase in fierce competition in domestic market share which is further threatened by the inroads made by foreign cars, and globalisation of the company with manufacturing bases scattered in four major global regions.

Honda, which began as a small motor cycle manufacturer in a province in Japan in 1948, had gone into four-wheel vehicle production in the early 1960s against the guidance of the Ministry of International Trade and Industry. It was the first Japanese company to build a car plant in the US, and has remained something of an entrepreneur among the companies in the motor industry. Today it competes with Mitsubishi for the third position after Toyota and Nissan in the domestic market, with capital of 85.76 billion yen. Its sales in 1994 were 2.5 trillion yen, with 31 000 employees in Japan. The company has been known for its unique corporate culture of free-speaking, innovative and individualistic values with flat organisational structure in its earlier stage generating agility and vitality, and its growth was led by a vision of its founder, Soichiro Honda, to become a world class company. However, since Honda has become a world class company, with 80 000 employees world-wide, it also has developed the problems of large bureaucratic organisations: rigidity, ambiguity of responsibility and role, an excessive delegation of power downwards and delay in decision making. The restructuring of the company was triggered by the need to deal with these problems and led by a new philosophy which was symbolised by a slogan of 'three Ss; Simplicity, *shûchû* (concentration), and Speed'. One of the problems with which it had to deal was the reduction of the middle management which had grown to 4500 accounting for over 10 per cent of total domestic employees – far larger than either Toyota or Nissan – and it was with these 4500 middle managers that the new annual salary system began.

Before that the managers' total emolument, made up with two parts, the wages and bonuses, was closely related to seniority and included non-work personal elements. The wages were composed of four elements: basic pay determined by location on the seniority grading; managerial post allowance; housing allowance; and family allowance, while the bonus was calculated by the assessment of each individual's performance which was converted into the bonus amount on the basis of his or her seniority. So on both counts, seniority had a very large influence on the total amount of individual emolument. A younger *kachô* who achieved a high performance could never be rewarded for his or her result with a higher bonus than another *kachô* who was senior to him or her but had made only a token contribution. The resultant frustration, of course, ate into motivation. The revision was implemented initially with a bonus element, and while the new salary system more or less reflected the amount one had been getting under the old system initially, a major change to the competency grading system designed to do away with the seniority element got under way.

The old competency grade consisted of seven grades encompassing all white-collar employees, and of these grades V, VI and VII applied to the middle management. Each grade was further subdivided into a fairly large number of steps which roughly corresponded with the number of years one worked in the company. The new competency grading system for the middle management was disconnected from the lower levels, and comprised of five grades, starting with I at the top which dealt with the business division managers and directors, and II, III, IV and V grades in the descending order to *kachô* (section chief) level. Each of the grades was also subdivided into a smaller number of steps to take account of the differences in the skills and competencies and the degree of complexities of the job contents (Kodama, 1993). It is possible for an employee to take more, or even less years than the number of steps there are to get to the next grade thereby opening a chance for a bright employee to be promoted rapidly. Also a standard salary was set for each of the grades which took no account of seniority.

With the abolition of seniority as the sole yardstick for upgrading, there had to be a system of merit which functioned as a new criterion. What Honda established was a system of 'managerial competency recognition' for all new upgrading, which had a set of standard assessment criteria for each grade. Assessment is carried out by a team of superiors using various methods including human assessment. Thus it was clear for all to see what was required of one to be upgraded, and promoted. Total Quality Management (TQM) was also introduced to ensure the quality of one's management task performance. Some will not reach a high level of achievement, and the tenure for the post is not permanent because Honda introduced at the same time a limited tenure system in which all *buchô* (grade III level), for example, can remain in the post for eight consecutive years only, and this was twelve years for a *kachô*. After this length of time, a manager has to resign from the post and become a plain employee, though he or she will stay on the same grade.

The bonus payment is the reward system in which, under the new scheme, one's contribution to the company is fully reflected. A given basic amount for bonus is fixed for each competency grade (which now has no seniority element) and an individual performance reward is added in full amount on to the basic amount. How the performance is assessed and evaluated therefore becomes of crucial importance. Honda introduced a notion of Honda Job Concept (HJC), which is based on the principle of two-way communication between the employee and his or her superior to achieve an agreed target for the individual. Assessment is carried out twice a year, in October and April, on the result each employee has achieved in the previous six months, and the outcome will be reflected in the bonus given out in December and June. The April assessment also affects the incremental rise with the grade for the following year.

The procedure for assessment under the new annual salary system is as follows. At the beginning of each year, each manager will draw up his agreed target for the year in two six-month periods on a form, and at the end of each six-month period, write down in detail his own comments on the degree to which he has achieved the target, and the state of the progress of the tasks, as well as self-analysis. Then he sits down with his assessor, perhaps his immediate superior, and they discuss thoroughly about the level of performance he has achieved. When they both agree on the outcome, then the papers are sent higher up, and his case is further assessed by more than one superior in terms of the degree of difficulty of his target, and the level of his performance in relation to the grade he is on, and the final mark is given. The mark can be one of six classes: S, A, B+, B, C and D, with S the highest class. A new policy is to award many more Ss and Ds which had hitherto been largely and often undeservedly withheld.

For Honda the new annual system, which is made up of pay and bonuses, is more than just a superficial change in the method by which the total emolument is calculated. It was designed to stimulate individuals to bring out their best, and also to change their attitudes to jobs because as managers, they must be seen to meet the required professional standard. As it is no longer related to seniority, it gives the younger and brighter managers the opportunity to be promoted faster. Furthermore, it motivates them to work for their own benefit as for the company, because personal achievement is directly rewarded, creating a culture where individual differences and creative ideas flourish. But this does not mean that it is a jungle: the discipline of TQM ensures that tasks are progressed scientifically and rationally on the agreed and shared basis of facts and figures. Already, the beneficial effect has been evident in the development of the new recreational vehicle model, Odyssey, which hit the market with a remarkable speed and considerable impact in 1994, reviving Honda's then flagging fortune at a stroke. A promotion by two competency grades was awarded for the leader of the project team (Nihon Keizai Shinbun, 1996). The message, which Soichiro Honda, the founder of the company, used to give at the new entrants' welcome ceremony each year was 'work for your own self fulfilment, not so much for the company, and become an expert who is valued also outside Honda'. This message, born of his basic philosophy of 'respect for individual person', had fired the imagination and enthusiasm of generations of Honda people, but with the rapid growth of the company came to be buried under the weight of bureaucracy. The new move is to restore it to its rightful position, urging the managers to establish themselves as individuals and professionals. This is also important for their new role as managers and co-ordinators of operations located in the four regions of the globe (Works, 1995a).

While the majority of Japanese corporations who introduced the merit principle into their reward system, grafted it on to the existing seniority system, applying to either the pay system or more often to the bonus scheme, Honda took a bold step abolishing the seniority concept completely, and revising the total wages system. But the change in the wages system was not an isolated measure aimed simply to cut cost. It was a strategic move, and an integral part of the fundamental restructuring which the company consciously adopted to ensure that the company will be in a better shape to survive in the ever increasing competition both in the domestic and global market. In the changeover period, there are inevitable problems of morale for those who have to accept lower emolument and a more rigorous climate, but the company is fighting for its survival. Many companies are watching with interest Honda's progress in this experiment in the reward system totally linked to performance. If it works successfully, there will be many companies that will introduce it into their own systems.

Another example of revised competency grading system which is designed to link performance with reward and promotion in the service sector is given below.

Revision of the competency grading system – the case of Skylark

Skylark is a family restaurant chain established in 1962 with capital of 12 billion yen, and grew rapidly in the high-growth period. Today, it has 2847 regular employees with an additional 30 000 non-regular employees with a revenue of 133 billion yen. It has been known to be an innovative company which has managed to respond successfully to the changes in the economic situation, and expand. It has expanded to have a number of group chains of restaurants each of which operates in a slightly different market niche. But the recession also forced it to take a bold strategic move in its operational policy in 1993, and to introduce new personnel system in which performance and ability are the only criteria for promotion and reward. Since the company includes many employees who moved from other companies, the question of seniority does not appear to be a problem. Because the performance is most clearly seen in the profitability of each restaurant, the managers of one of the restaurant chains, Gust, who are at around the age 38 and numbering 61, were the first group to be brought into this scheme (Works, 1995b).

Named the 'System of High Performance Restaurant Manager', this scheme evaluates the performance of each manager purely on the basis of such numerical results as the number of customers his or her restaurant served and profit, and places each manager in a position of quasi-owner-manager. A change was also wrought to the competency grading system in 1994, as Fig 12.8 indicates. Of the 10 competency grades, the restaurant managers used to occupy grades 4 to 6, and these managerial posts were regarded as junior posts on the route to the senior middle management positions. The new system places these restaurant managers across grades 4 to 9, and divides these managers into two groups of general managers and high-performance managers. Grade 9 is equivalent to the *buchô* in the head office. All staff experience the job of general restaurant manager initially, but are given a choice before they are to progress to grade 5 whether they continue to pursue the course of restaurant management or opt for staff appointments in the head office. Since remaining a restaurant manager gives them just as good a promotion prospect as those in the head office, it holds great attraction for those who prefer restaurant management to staff functions. What is demanded of them, however, is a high level of professionalism and entrepreneurship as each restaurant is managed as an independent business. The reward system has also been completely overhauled so that high performance is directly reflected in the basic pay on the competency grading plus enhanced bonuses. It is possible for managers of excep-

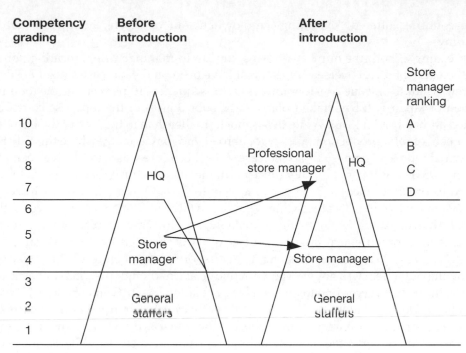

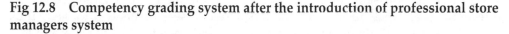

Fig 12.8 Competency grading system after the introduction of professional store managers system

tionally successful restaurants to earn much higher emoluments than those in the staff function. Already, the result of the first year has been translated in an enhanced bonus for 80 per cent of the restaurant managers, and is leading to the change of attitudes and awareness toward the job in managers themselves. A ranking of restaurant high-performing managers into A, B, C and D will also be introduced from 1996 to classify the management ability of each manager.

The company plans to bring all restaurant managers into the category of high-performance managers. Though there are still problems to iron out, the future of the scheme appears to be bright. The scheme enhanced both the status and the reward of the restaurant managers and increases the opportunity for a round peg to remain in a round hole without paying a penalty. This entirely performance-based system of evaluation and reward is expected to be extended to the rest of the organisation.

Hollowing out of the economy

The variation in the forms of employment has been increasing rapidly in the non-regular employment sector of the labour market as the result of the recent restructuring, replacing some of the tasks hitherto performed by regular employees (Nihon Keizai Shinbun, 1995). The rising yen has rendered the per capita earning in Japan the highest in the dollar terms among the G7 countries (Keizai Koho Santaa, 1995) causing Japanese firms to stream out into south-east Asia and to China to seek cost advantages which these countries offered, 'exporting' employment out of Japan, 'hollowing' out the economy.

For example, both the number of firms, mostly in manufacturing, locating abroad, and the value of direct overseas investment have been on the increase since 1993 when the yen began to revalue considerably. As a consequence, 10 per cent of the total production of Japan will have taken place in the subsidiaries of the Japanese companies located abroad (MITI, 1996). While this is much smaller than in the case of the US where 26 per cent of total production takes place abroad and for Germany where this rate is 15 per cent, it represents quite a rapid increase since this figure was said to have been 7 per cent in 1993 (Focus Japan, 1996). Of the firms in the manufacturing sector which located abroad to produce since 1993, 80 per cent went to Asia. Of these firms which went to Asia 60 per cent went to locate in China [per capita GDP in China was one-seventieth of Japan's (Keizai Koho Senta, 1995)]. Inevitably, the increase in offshore production increases local procurement taking the place of parts supplied by domestic suppliers, and exporting to Japan of products made in offshore plants. Before 1993 the so-called 'hollowing out' effect was not viewed with undue alarm though the total domestic production in 1992 fell, according to one reliable calculation (Asahi Seimei Hoken, 1995), by 4.1 billion yen, and employment by 135 000, as the result of reduction in exports and increase in import which were a direct effect of the overseas direct investment. This was because, it was thought, the increase in imports from Japanese subsidiaries located in Asia was more than offset by the increase in the export of high value capital goods with high technological capabilities which the Japanese overseas plants had to have, thus enabling the division of labour between the home-based operation of high value added, high-technology manufacturing and more labour intensive, medium technology production in the overseas subsidiaries. By fiscal 1995, the picture was a little more stark as the increase in overseas direct investment had resulted in a loss of further 110 000 jobs (MITI, 1996). According to one estimate, if the domestic economy remains sluggish with an annual growth rate of 1 per cent, and the hollowing out continues as a result of more firms going abroad to produce, in search of expanding markets and cheaper labour cost, causing a further structural change, the unemployment could rise to 12 million, or 17.1 per cent by 2010 (Rengo Sôgô Seikatsu Kaihatsu Kenkyûsho, 1995). Admittedly, this is the worst scenario, based on the most pessimistic figures, but it shows the scale of the potential problems that Japan could have if this trend continues.

A new employment paradigm

With HRM in a period of rapid and unprecedented change, there have been some attempts in recent times to formulate a new employment paradigm in order to map out the direction of the future of HRM in Japan, by some of the major economic organisations. Nihon Keieisha Dantai Renmei (Federation of Employers' Associations in Japan, Nikkeiren for short – one of the four major economic organisations in Japan, created in 1949 by employers as their counterpart to trade unions in industrial relations) has been in the forefront of such an attempt, but maintains a position where it sees the long-term continuous employment practices, being far from rigid, endowed with enough flexibility which in fact supported its continuation as a system. Another crucial element in it is its central philosophy of placing an importance on employees. The new employment paradigm should, while maintaining this philosophy, be capable of responding flexibly to the demands of the rapidly changing business environment by adjusting the internal structure of the existing employment practice.

According to the Nikkeiren's proposal for the future employment paradigm, the new type of employment system will be the result of the increasing diversity of employment types and change in the relations between the demand and supply of labour, and it sees the future formal employees in a typical company to comprise three distinct groups, as is indicated in Fig 12.9.

A. This long-term, stable employee group is oriented towards in-company accumulation of skills and experiences, and developed mainly through OJT (the on-the-job-training) but with an active OffJT and self-development input. A career group, they seek promotion to management.

B. This highly specialised professional employee group is not necessarily employed on a long-term basis is oriented towards solving specific problems the company faces, bringing their expertise and professional capabilities to tackle them. They have had experience of other companies, and development is mainly through OffJT with a strong company support for self-development in upgrading skills and expertise.

C. The flexible employee group encompasses many job categories from routine to near-specialist, whose development is on the need-to-have basis. They will not be on a career ladder.

Table 12.7 gives the detail of conditions of employment envisaged for each group.

Clearly, the first group reflects the current system of the core group of employees on the so-called 'lifetime' employment. But the innovative element is the existence of the

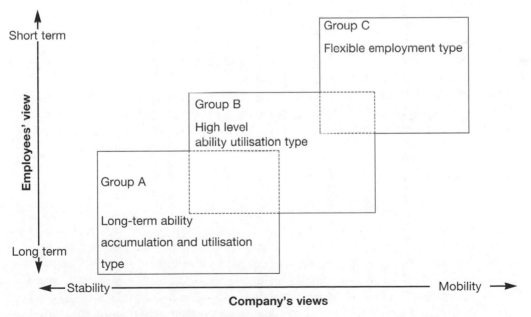

Source: Nihon Keieisha Dantai Renmei, May 1995.

Fig 12.9 Relationships of company and employee in terms of employment and length of continuous service

Table 12.7 Details of conditions of employment of the three groups

Group	Type of contract	Job category	Wages	Bonuses	Retirement lump sum/pension	Upgrading and promotion	Welfare provision
A.	No fixed term	Management career route	Monthly/annual total emolument job allowance and incremental rises	Fixed rate plus sliding scale performance-related amount	Point system	On the competency grading and to managerial posts	Lifelong total welfare and benefit system
B.	Fixed term	Specialist (Planning, Marketing, R&D, etc.)	Annual salary performance-related pay, no automatic rise	Proportional to achievement	None	Performance assessment	Living standard support measures
C.	Fixed term	General/routine skilled, sales	Hourly pay system, job-related, no automatic rise	Fixed rate	None	Conversion to high grades	Living standard support measures

Source: Nihon Keieisha Dantai Renmei (1995), p. 32.

second group of highly specialised employees who are probably hired mid-career and with a fixed term contract, though this can be renewed as is deemed desirable by both sides. Another innovative element is the overlap of employment status between the adjoining groups, as Figure 12.9 shows, allowing the flow of personnel across the boundaries. Apparently, the flexibility is provided by the groups B and C, and of necessity, group A will be smaller in size. This paradigm does not exclude the use of part-time and contractual labour. In terms of emolument, an annual salary system is envisaged for groups A and B.

Conclusion

Clearly, Japanese HRM is in a state of flux of a fundamental nature, and further changes are likely. However, it seems fairly clear that, while the long-term stable employment system will be retained albeit on a modified scale and form, the seniority system is likely to undergo a rapid decline to be replaced by the merit-based system. Increasingly, both compensation and promotion will be dependent on demonstration of personal capability, and this is not incompatible with the long-term employment pattern. Also an increase in interfirm mobility is acknowledged as the trend of the future, though to what extent this will spread is not as yet clear, and the important issue is how corporations will find a balance between the so-called 'stock' type and 'flow' type employees to maximise their operational efficiency.

REFERENCES

Abegglen, J.C. (1958) *Japanese Factory: Aspects of its Social Organisation*, Glencoe Free Press, USA.

Asahi Seimei Hoken (1993) *'Keizai Geppô'*, February, in Suzuki, N. 'The Middle Aged and Older Employees in Japanese Corporation – Their Plight during the Process of Major Historic Change', *The Journal of Management Development*, Vol. 15, No. 8, November.

Chuma, H. (1994) *Nihongata Koyôchôsei (The Japanese Type Employment Adjustment)*, Shûeisha, Tokyo.

Focus Japan (1996) 'Corporate Restructuring Sweeps Japan', *Focus Japan*, Vol. 23, No. 3, March, pp. 1–2.

Japan Labour Bulletin (1994) '60% of Managers are Content with Annual Pay Scheme', *Japan Labour Bulletin*, June, pp. 3–4.

Keizai Kôhô Centre (1995) 'Japan 1995 – An International Comparison, Table 1–9, GDP, GDP per Capita (1993); and Growth Rate of GDP (1989–1993), *Keizai Kôhô Centre*, p. 11.

Kodama, J. (1993) *'Honda Giken Kôgyô, nenpôsei no tekiyô han'i kakudai e* (Honda Motor Co. – Towards Expansion of the Annual Salary System)', Jinzai Kyôiku, October 1993, p. 37.

Ministry of Industry and International Trade (MITI) (1996) *'Kaigaijigyô Katsudôdôkô chôsa (Survey on the trend of business activities overseas)* MITI, March, p. 73.

Ministry of Labour (1990) *'Heisei-2 koyô kanri chôsa hôkoku* (Report on the 1990 Employment Management Survey)' in *Jinzai Kyôiku*, November, p. 83.

Nihon Keieisha Dantai Renmei (1975) *Wagakuni Jinji Rômukanri no Genjô (The Current State of Labour Management in Japan)* Nihon Keieisha Dantai Renmei, Tokyo.

Nihon Keieisha Dantai Renmei (1995) *'Shin-jidai no Nihonteki-keiei – chôsen subeki hôkô to sono shutaisaku* (Japanese Style Management for the New Era – The Direction on which It Is to Be

Focused and Concrete Measures for Its Implementation)', *Nihon Keieisha Dantai Renmei*, 17 May, p. 32.

Nihon Keizai Shinbun (1995) *'Kawaru nihonteki koyô – shinayakasa o motomete, jô, chû, ge* (Changing Japanese-Style Employment – in Search of Flexibility, Pts I, II and III)', *Nihon Keizai Shinbunsha*, 23, 24 and 25 May.

Nihon Keizai Shinbun (1996) *'Shoku o hiraku – Jitsuryoku takuwae chosen no bane ni* (Developing Job Opportunities – Nurturing One's Ability for the Challenge of the Future)', *Nihon Keizai Shinbun*, 29 April, p. 1.

Nihon Keizai Shinbunsha (ed.) (1994) *Shûshin koyô wa owatta (The Lifetime Employment System Has Come to Its End)*, Nihon Keizei Shinbunsha, Tokyo.

Nihon Seisansei Honbu (1989) *'Seisansei moderu sôgôchingin chôsa hôkokusho* (Report on the Survey of Model Productivity Wages)', *Nihon Seisansei Honbu*, pp. 2–7.

'OECD tainichi rôdôhôkokusho' (An OECD Report on Labour in Japan) in Takanashi, A. (1994) p. 35.

Okazaki-Ward, L.I. (1993) *Management Education and Training in Japan*, London: Graham and Trotman.

Okinobu, H. (1990) *Yamatake Haniweru no senryaku keiei (Yamatake-Honeywell's Strategic Management)*, Daiyamondosha, Tokyo.

Okuda, K. (1990) *'Sengo Jinjikanri no hensen to kongo no tenbô* (Changes in the Postwar Personnel Management in Japan Personnel Management in, and Its Future Outlook)', in *21seiki no paradaimu (A Paradigm for the 21st Century)*, *Rômugyôsei*, No. 3000, December.

Okuda, K. (1994) *'Antei-koyô no konseputo o teishoô – shûshin koyô wa gokai maneku* (Advocacy for the Concept of "Stable Employment" – "Lifetime" Employment Invites Misunderstanding)', *Rôseijihô*, No. 3157, 8 April, pp. 7–12.

Rengô Sôgô Seikatsu Kaihatsu Kenkyûsho, (1995), *'2010nen no sangyô to koyô* (Industry and Employment in 2010)', *Rengô Sôgô Seikatsu Kaihatsu Kenkyûsho*, in *Works*, Jan/Feb, 1996, p. 57.

Rômugyôsei (1990) *'Shokunô shikaku seido no genjô to kadai* (The Current State of the Japanese Competency Grading System and its Issues)' in *'21seiki no paradaimu (A paradigm for the Twenty-first Century)'*, No. 3000, December, Rômugyôsei.

Rômugyôsei Kenkyûjo, (ed) (1994) *'Nihonteki keiei no kenshô to sono mirai–ge (Examination of the Japanese-Style Management and its Future–Pt 3)'*, *Rôseijihô*, No. 3158, 15April, p. 59.

Shigeta, I. and Morita, Y. (1995) 'Hukiareru resutora (The Blowing Restructuring Gales)', *Yomiuri Shinbun*, 10 October, p.11.

Shimada, H. (1994) *Nihon no koyô – 21-seiki no saisekkei (Japanese Employment – A Redesign for the 21st Century)*, Chikuma Shobô, Tokyo.

Takanashi, A. (1993) *'Nihonteki-Koyô Kankô Kuzurezu (The Japanese-style Employment Practices Have Not Fallen Apart)*,' in Keiei Kyôshitsu (Management Series), *Nihon Keizai Shinbun*, 13 June.

Takanashi, A. (1994) *Kawaru Nihongata koyô (Changing Japanese-Type Employment)*, Nihon Keizai Shinbunsha, Tokyo.

Takeuchi, H. (1994) 'Reforming Management', *The Journal of Japanese Trade and Industry*, No. 2, pp. 13–14.

Tokyo Business Today (1993) 'On the Corporate Dole: Japan's One Million Working Unemployed', *Tokyo Business Today*, May 1993, pp. 10–11.

Tokyo CCI Research (1995), referred to in Shigeta, I. and Morita, Y. above.

Tokyo Kanrisha Union and Nihon Rôdô Bengoshidan (ed.) (1994) *Kaisha o yameru chichi kara Kaisha ni hairu musuko musume tachi e (From Fathers Who are Leaving the Company to Sons and Daughters Who Are About to Enter a Company)*, Kyôiku Shiryô Shuppankai, Tokyo.

Tsuda, M. (1994) *'Korekarano jinjikanri no kichô* (The Basic Trend of Japanese Personnel

Management in the Future)', in *21seiki jinkikanri no zahyôjiku* (*A Coordinate Axis of Personnel Management in the 21st Century*), *Rômugyôsei* Kenkyûsho, Tokyo.

Works (ed.), (1995a) '*Ichiritsu issei, oshikisekara dappi shi sekai ni tsûyôsuru ko no jiritsu o mezasu – Honda* (From Mass Conformity and Enforced Homogeneity Towards the Establishment of Autonomous Individuals of Global Standing – Honda's Case)', *Works*, No. 1, April/May, pp. 84–8.

Works (ed.), (1995b) '*Sukairâku: Seika shugi no puro-tenchô tanjô – shokunô tôkyû mo 3tôkyû hikiageru* (Skylark: The Birth of Professional Store Managers under the Performance-Oriented Approach – Three Grades Up in the Competency Grading System)', *Works*, No. 1, April/May, pp. 88–9.

13 KEY ISSUES IN HR STRATEGY IN GERMANY

Michel Domsch and Martina Harms

Defending a leading role in business perhaps has never been as difficult for Germany as it is today. While striving for economic growth in the former GDR, Germany still has to cope not only with enormous costs and the other consequences of the reunion but also with an ongoing recession. More than four million people are jobless, social peace is endangered. Facing high labour costs, more and more companies have started to produce in other countries where these costs are lower. In the global market Germany's companies are in danger of losing their supremacy, because they missed the connection to key technologies. 'Innovation' seems to be the only way out of the momentary crisis. In order to be innovative Germany's companies have to rediscover their most important resource: human resources.

This chapter takes first a brief look at the present basic conditions for HR strategy in Germany; then concentrates on key issues in HR strategy. In defiance of the fact that presumably parts of the responsibility for HR will shift from HR departments towards line management, we will include these aspects in our article, because HR departments will still be involved in such processes as facilitators – the HR department´s task will be to support line management (and of course also employees in general) and to set basic conditions for dealing with human resources.

Basic conditions for HR strategy in Germany

One major objective of all company divisions is to keep and increase the company´s competitiveness. But the (national and international) competitiveness of enterprises also depends on a variety of local conditions. Some of these, which are especially important for HR strategy in Germany, are described in this chapter; they are summarised in Fig 13.1.

Demographic development

The demographic development in Germany leads to a reduction of population (Heese, 1991, p. 29), but this does not necessarily mean a rapid reduction of the labour force

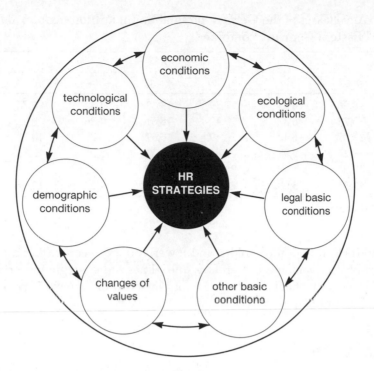

Fig 13.1   Basic conditions for HR strategies

(Franke, 1991, pp. 28–39). It can be assumed that there will be a growing number of working women and foreign workers (see Table 13.1). Nevertheless there will be a reduction of junior staff (see Table 13.2). This means, Germany´s working population will get older: from the turn of the century onwards we will have more 50-year-old than 30-year-old gainfully employed people, so that German companies will have to learn to

Table 13.1   Active labour force (data for Western Germany only, except where marked differently)

Year	Active labour force (1000)	percentage of men (German and foreign)	percentage of women (German and foreign)	percentage of foreign employees (male and female)
1970	26817	64.1 %	35.9 %	6.8 %
1975	27184	62.1 %	37.9 %	8.6 %
1980	27948	61.1 %	38.9 %	8.4 %
1985	28897	60.8 %	39.2 %	7.3 %
1990	30378	59.4 %	40.6 %	7.6 %
(East)	9028	52.9 %	47.1 %	data not available
(East+West)	39406	57.9 %	42.1 %	data not available
1994	32088	58.5 %	41.5 %	10.8 %
(East)	8148	52.3 %	47.7 %	2.1 %
(East+West)	40236	57.3 %	42.7 %	9.0 %

Source: own calculations, based on IW (1995), Table 13.11.

Table 13.2   Age classes of the German population (in million people), data for Western and Eastern Germany combined

Year	Age						
	0–15	15–21	21–40	40–60	60–65	65 and over	overall
1950	16,06	6,05	17,29	19,83	3,37	6,75	**69,35**
1960	15,74	6,37	19,49	18,81	4,26	8,47	**73,14**
1970	18,07	6,42	20,49	17,52	4,79	10,78	**78,07**
1980	14,27	7,98	20,64	20,33	3,01	12,16	**78,39**
1990	12,94	5,47	24,12	20,96	4,35	11,91	**79,75**
1993	13,31	5,08	24,66	21,68	4,23	12,37	**81,33**

Source: IW (1995), Table 13.6.

maintain production with more older and fewer younger people (Badura, 1993, p. 4). The demographic development therefore underlines the strategic importance of personnel marketing, personnel development and the creation of working conditions that are suitable also for older employees.

Change of values

Studies show that German employees are increasingly looking for a meaning within their jobs. Almost every second employee names 'meaningful work content' as a motivating factor (Opaschowski, 1993, p. 232); more than two-thirds of German working people aged up to 34 define 'career' as 'to have a job that is fun' (Pauwels, 1993, pp. 2–3). The following aspects describe some of the changed values (Stengel, 1995, p. 788):

- accentuation of self-fulfilment and enjoyment of life;
- people strive to keep their health;
- women fight for assimilation in same status as men;
- people are less willing to subordinate;
- work is less often seen as a duty;
- leisure time is valued higher; and
- the natural environment is valued higher.

The change of values can be recognised to a different extent in different segments of the population: it is carried mainly by young people with high qualifications, especially with academic education (Stengel, 1995, p. 789). These are the people companies recruit as their high potentials for management positions. Germany´s companies have to accommodate their working conditions to these new trends.

Ecological conditions

Studies conducted among German students (prospective managers) and managers show a consistent estimation of these groups that the most important *actual objectives* of companies are economic growth, increase in profit and technological progress, *but should be* environmental protection and job security (Rosenstiel, 1993, pp. 60–63). The preservation of natural necessities of life is one of the central objectives of society, and also for companies ecology is an issue to which they have to attach importance (Wunderer and Kuhn, 1993, p. 95).

- *Companies can open up new markets by developing ecological technologies and products* – In Germany there is an estimated market volume for environmental products of 40 billion German marks with an estimated rate of increase of 6–8 per cent per year (Hopfenbeck and Willig, 1995, p. 74). Germany holds a 21 per cent share of the world market for ecological technologies and products, that means an export volume of 35 billion German marks (K. Töpfer, 1995, p. 20). About 680 000 people are employed in about 8500 German companies that produce environmental products (Niejahr, 1995, p. 156).
- *Companies need to act increasingly according to environmental legislation* – Up to 1970 there were about 12 laws concerning environmental protection in Germany. In the 1970s their number grew up to 25 laws, during the 1980s about 80 new laws were added. And not only the number of laws increased, they also became stricter (Winter, 1995, p. 160).
- *Companies have to prove to a critical society (mass media, environmental groups, local pressure groups) that they act according to a high ecological sense of responsibility* – A study conducted among 621 companies shows (Antes et al., 1992, quoted from Hopfenbeck and Willig, 1995, p. 55):

    - 77.5% of all defensive measures against environmental risks are technical measures;
    - 14.5% are organisational measures; and
    - only 8% are personnel measures.

However, environmental protection means a change of behaviour of people as well as of organisations – so without human resources it will not be possible to reach ecological objectives. Therefore a key issue in HR strategy in Germany is to intensify the efforts to set basic conditions that enable and motivate employees to act in an environmentally conscious way.

Economic and technological conditions

Germany's economy is in a paradoxical situation: on the one hand there is a recognisable upswing, on the other hand there is a new record of more than four million unemployed people in February 1996. 'Jobless growth' is the word for this paradox.

If German companies not only want to keep but extend their international competitiveness, they have to cut production costs. High production costs in Germany are mainly due to high labour costs; they strangle productivity (Anon, 1995a, p. 79). In addition to this problem, costs for environmental protection, energy costs and of course the tax burden are often mentioned.

The reaction of German companies to these high costs in Germany were cost-cutting programmes such as lean production or re-engineering and the establishment of production sites in other countries where costs are lower. These programmes led to the upswing mentioned above. But still there is the unemployment crisis to overcome. Politicians, unions and employers are now discussing various ways. One way is to create *new* jobs – for example by developing the service industry in Germany and of course also by investing in key industries such as computer industries, mass media and the communication industry. Technological progress nowadays can be seen as a central parameter for industrial development and national prosperity (Kobel, 1991, p. 1).

In Germany the better than average growth sectors are nearly all parts of the tertiary sector, but also:

- important parts of the capital goods industry (manufacturing of office machines and EDP (Electronic Dataprocessing) equipment, aerospace industry, electrical engineering and vehicle building);
- the basic and manufacturing goods sector (for example chemical industry); and
- energy supply/gas supply/water supply companies (Schnelldienst 3/96, p. 5).

To be competitive in today's key industries, innovations are needed. Taking the number of international patent applications and the number of national patent applicants as indicators for innovative strength, the German dynamic of innovations is unsatisfactory (ifo Schnelldienst 3/96, p. 15). Furthermore, the composition of patent applications classified according to certain industries has not changed in the last few years; in such internationally dynamic sectors as electrical engineering or the chemical industry (telecommunications/ microelectronics, genetic engineering/pharmacy) the number of patent applications is relatively low, while the number is relatively high in sectors with an internationally lower dynamic, for example vehicle building (Schnelldienst 3/96, pp. 15–16). But German enterprises need to become competitive in today's key industries, otherwise they might not be able to survive. Therefore companies need qualified, creative and innovative staff.

HR's part is here to commit employees to quality, customer satisfaction, and so on, and to support innovative employees. But to be innovative, employees need an atmosphere of trust and relative safety – this can only be developed by supporting an open communication throughout all hierarchical levels in a company – and by offering relatively safe jobs. Jobs could become safer if the distribution of existing jobs changed: alternative time systems (part-time models, flexible working hours) can reduce unemployment. To develop such concepts is a key issue in HR strategies in Germany.

Legal basic conditions

In Germany a variety of laws sets a frame for personnel management, for example

- supranational laws (law of nations, human rights conventions and so on);
- the basic law for the Federal Republic of Germany (constitutional law); or
- parts of general German laws (German Civil Code, Trade Regulation Act, German Commercial Code).

Labour jurisdiction is based on the industrial law, which is a compilation of many single laws. The most important ones are (Domsch, 1993a, p. 529):

- protective laws for employees (Protection against Dismissal Act, Act on Payment of Wages during Sickness, Working Time Regulation, Company Pension Act,

Occupational Safety Act, Workplace Ordinance, Employment Promotion Act, Labour Court Act, etc.);
- laws with protective order for especially endangered employee categories (Young Persons' Protection of Employment Act, Maternity Protection Act),
- sources of the collective industrial law (Collective Agreements Act, Codetermination Act, Works Constitution Act, labour dispute law, etc.).

Currently in Germany, industrial law is often said to be not able to keep up with the current structural change from an industrial society towards an information society. The main weakness is seen in traditionally centralised conflict solving processes, which are said to be no longer effective in solving conflicts in a more and more decentralised economy. Therefore various authors point out that time has come for a new decentralised industrial law (for example Oechsler, 1994, pp. 57–60).

Industrial relations

Social peace is an important competitive factor Germany so far could always enter on the credit side (Zinken, 1992, pp. 194ff). Nevertheless the call for a change towards individualisation and flexibility in terms of unions and works councils becomes louder.

The institutionalisation of conflicts between employers and employees is distinctive of the current situation in Germany. However, companies are confronted with dissimilar pressures to change, they have to meet different challenges – it becomes increasingly difficult to find standard solutions with an area-wide collective agreement. As a consequence in 1994 in several sectors (for example chemical industry and metal industry) an agreement about rules on working hours was reached that extended the companies' sphere of settlement. Agreements like this should be trend-setting: industrial relations in Germany needs to switch away from standard solutions towards company-specific solutions (Töpfer, 1994, p. 12).

The call for company-specific solutions leads to the role of works councils. Currently there is no other country in Europe with such powerful works councils as there are in Germany – works councils have comprehensive rights of codetermination (Böhm, 1995, p. 676; Weitbrecht, 1995, p. 200). They have no right to participate in decisions that refer to the company *itself* (for example how much capital the company should be issued with, or what the products/services of the company should be), but the more staff are concerned the more the works council becomes involved (Böhm, 1995, p. 677). It is important to replace in our minds the old role picture according to which the works council represents the interests of the employees, while the company management stands at the other side of the table. This picture does not represent reality any longer: first, more and more companies do not see their employees only as a cost factor, but as human capital which is a valuable resource of the company. Second, it becomes increasingly difficult to represent or protect the interests of the employees – these are not homogeneous, but are heterogeneous (Staehle, 1992, p. 146).

Works council and company management need to become interlocutors, who work together. A survey among 853 German personnel managers shows that the majority of these companies have already started to intensify communication (see Fig 13.2).

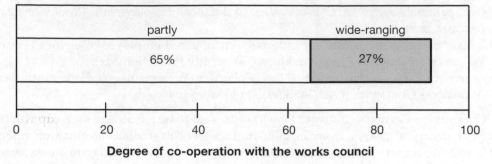

Source: Töpfer and Poersch (1989), p. 87.

Fig 13.2 Co-operation between company management and works councils in Germany

If the trend goes away from standard towards company-specific solutions – what will the role of unions be? It can be assumed that in Germany the symbiosis between unions and works councils will not be given up for the benefit of an increase of company-specific solutions. Currently works councils on the one hand draw near unions, but on the other hand they also become more independent. Especially qualification measures provided by unions cause this effect (Weitbrecht, 1995, p. 203). This indicates the role German unions might play in future: they will develop from an industrial dispute organisation to a service organisation for their members.

Key issues in HR strategy in Germany

The basic conditions we described so far set a frame for personnel functions in Germany. We will now take a closer look at some aspects of HR management that we believe to be the key issues of HR strategy in Germany.

Becoming international/globalising

It is not a secret that business has become an international, global affair. The growing international competition leads to cost pressure, the opening of new markets (regional and in terms of introducing new products and technologies) has a great influence on the growth of a company (Autenrieth and Domsch, 1994, p. 203). To understand the implications globalising has on HR strategies (and vice versa) in Germany, we first have to take a look at the current situation in terms of German companies acting globally. Looking at Fig 13.3, where six steps for globalisation are described, only very few German companies reach step 4, most companies remain on steps 1–3 (Henzler, 1992, pp. 90–92).

German companies are traditionally active in international business, but mainly in export, without direct presence in foreign markets with their own production sites, etc. Although direct investments have been increased during the last few years, these have been concentrated on Europe and the United States (Henzler, 1992, pp. 85–90), so German companies cannot really be called *globally* active. See Table 13.3.

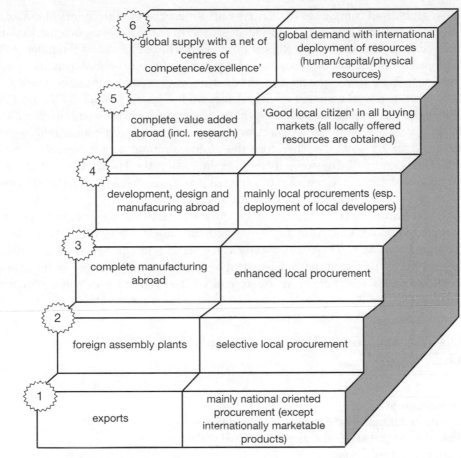

6	global supply with a net of 'centres of competence/excellence'	global demand with international deployment of resources (human/capital/physical resources)
5	complete value added abroad (incl. research)	'Good local citizen' in all buying markets (all locally offered resources are obtained)
4	development, design and manufacuring abroad	mainly local procurements (esp. deployment of local developers)
3	complete manufacturing abroad	enhanced local procurement
2	foreign assembly plants	selective local procurement
1	exports	mainly national oriented procurement (except internationally marketable products)

Source: modified from Henzler (1992), p. 85.

Fig 13.3   Six steps to becoming a global company

Table 13.3   German direct investments in foreign countries (in million DM)

Countries/regions	1989	1990	1991
total	194.908	221.794	248.945
EU[1]	84.229	109.083	128.452
USA	57.035	54.660	56.103
Japan	3.706	3.989	4.537
Eastern European reform states[2]	.286	.460	.711
former Czechoslovakia	data not available	data not available	.508
others	49.652	53.602	58.634

1 The EU countries included are: Belgium, Denmark, France, Great Britain, Greece, Ireland, Italy, Luxembourg, Netherlands, Portugal, Spain.

2 The Eastern European reform states included are: former Soviet Union, Hungary, Poland.

Source: own calculations, based on data from the Deutsche Bundesbank.

The most globalised companies in Germany are enterprises of the chemical industry, for example, Bayer AG, BASF AG and Hoechst AG. In some areas of production also companies such as Siemens AG or Robert Bosch GmbH are globalised (Henzler, 1992, p. 93). The medium-sized businesses were very successful on the global market with their strategy to keep development and production in Germany, while the marketing strategy covered the world market – with service on the spot (Henzler, 1992, p. 94). In the long term however, it can be assumed that at least large concerns will not be able to keep up their position in global markets by an export strategy (Henzler, 1992, p. 97), they will need to act globally. Therefore the global alignment of a company needs matching strategies in all divisions of the firm, including the HR division. It is a key issue in HR strategies in Germany to support the company's internationalisation strategy by developing an appropriate HR strategy.

German companies have to make a decision about how far they want to become international. In line with the company's internationalisation strategy, HR can build up an international strategy. There are mainly three basic strategies to decide between (Wunderer, 1992, p. 167; Kammel and Teichelmann, 1994, p. 30); a survey in 16 German enterprises shows the estimation of the spread of the utilisation of these strategies shown in Table 13.4.

Table 13.4 Dissemination of basic internationalisation strategies in German companies

	1990	2000
Ethnocentric concept (transfer of the philosophy of the company's headquarters to foreign branches; vacant key positions are only filled with managers of the mother company)	41%	31%
Polycentric concept (underlines the independence of foreign branches in consideration of differences in different countries; vacant positions are often filled with local managers)	37%	38%
Geocentric concept (seeks to integrate the ideas of the headquarters as well as those of foreign branches; nationality of applicants is no criterion for filling vacancies)	22%	31%

Source: data from Wunderer (1992), p. 167.

It seems that the tendency moves away from a clear domination of the mother company towards a consideration of the interests of daughter companies. According to the study, in the year 2000 all three strategies will be important for German companies, but the polycentric concept will be applied more often than the others.

International HR management is differentiated from national HR management by the following aspects, which are mainly related to specialised and executive staff (Wunderer, 1992, p. 162):

- *more functions and activities* – for example to find standardised arrangements for an international personnel development policy, remuneration policy and so on, or to offer support to expatriates in collecting information about the health system, schools, jobs for husbands/wives, etc.;

- *broader perspective* – for example HR has to deal with different cultures or economic systems;
- *higher involvement in the private life of employees* – for example support of expatriates and their families to reduce their special burden;
- *higher risk, higher costs* – for example costs of pay, personnel development, integration and so on. These costs are assumed to be three times as high as expenses for employees at home; and
- *extended external influences* – for example basic law, status of economy, trade practices and so on.

It would be beyond the scope of this chapter to explain these HR functions in full, so we will confine this part to a brief description of the situation of German companies investing in Eastern Europe. These companies find the special situation that most countries only started recently to open their markets towards western products and people used to live in a completely different economic system, so Eastern European countries and people are in a permanent process of transformation. Some aspects of this situation are especially important for HR management:

- East European employees not only have to become accustomed to new company policies, but at the same time they have to cope with the difficult economic conditions in their countries, for example with high unemployment rates (Domsch and Lieberum, 1995a, p. 507; Scherm, 1996, p. 221).
- German managers need to come to grips with the East European culture. Especially difficult are foreign languages, differences in mentality, an obstructing bureaucracy, a different perception of work itself and rapidly changing laws (Domsch and Lieberum 1995a, pp. 507–9; Scherm, 1996, p. 222).
- For personnel recruitment in Eastern Europe, companies should know that in the former economic system, where a right to work was guaranteed, companies only relied on personal applications from people who heard by word-of-mouth about the vacancy. Only in the last years has the dissemination of job advertisements increased. The usage of contacts to universities is to be recommended, because students as well as university professors build a pool of potential managers. The usage of personnel consultancies is increasing (Domsch and Lieberum, 1995a, p. 509).
- Although the opening of markets is the most important objective for companies investing in Eastern Europe, investments in their human resources (for example in personnel development measurements) should not be neglected. To introduce employees to the company's culture and know-how, personnel development is indispensable (Domsch and Lieberum, 1995a, p. 510).

Supporting 'new' management concepts

'The pursuit of quality is almost a given in today's marketplace. If your company isn't pursuing technical excellence, reductions in cycle time and increased profitability, then it's already on its way out of the game' (Caudron, 1993, p. 48A). In Germany mainly three concepts are used for finding a way to meet these requirements:

THE PRACTICE OF HUMAN RESOURCE STRATEGY

1. Total Quality Management (TQM), for example Robert Bosch GmbH (Euchner, 1996, pp. 16–20), Gerling Institut GmbH (Gipperich and Pane, 1996, pp. 22–5) and Volkswagen AG Wolfsburg;
2. Lean Management, for example VAW aluminium AG (Deppe, 1996, pp. 106–9) and Opel Eisenach AG (Haasen, 1996, pp. 80–5); and
3. Business Process Re-engineering (BPR), for example Deutsche Aerospace AG (Köhler, 1995, pp. 298–305) and F. Porsche AG (Der Betriebswirt, 1996, p. 38).

The following statements are taken from a study carried out by the IAO (Fraunhofer Institut für Arbeitswissenschaft und Organisation); they show the state of dissemination of BPR and customer orientation in German companies (IAO, 1995a, pp. 34–6):

- BPR projects have not been implemented in most German companies during the last years, but more than 50 per cent of the questioned companies conduct BPR projects at the moment or plan to implement them in the next three years.
- Of the companies, 80 per cent value the attainment of the customer's quality level as very important, but only 6 per cent believe they have already reached this objective. Here a big gap between demand and reality can be seen.
- Of the companies, 85 per cent believe it is very important that employees know their internal customers and their quality demands, but only 31 per cent can show an implementation of the 'internal customer principle'.

Obviously the 'new' management concepts have not been implemented completely in German companies yet. All these concepts imply new challenges for HR departments. This becomes obvious by taking a brief look at some central elements of these management philosophies:

- quality-orientation;
- process-orientation;
- customer-orientation;
- continuous improvements (KAIZEN); and
- teamwork.

A translation of these philosophies into regular practice is only possible if *all* employees are behind them, including all levels of the hierarchy. If only HR tries to announce these new guidelines, there is the danger that employees think 'Oh, so that's the flavour of the month!' – and continue working nearly the same way as before. So it should be as Ed Lawler puts it: 'Line management should lead the effort, but HR has to be involved as a partner from the beginning' (Ed Lawler, quoted from Caudron, 1993, p. 48A). The main tasks for HR are:

- to support line management with the reorganisation of work;
- to acquaint employees with the principles stated above;
- to invent incentives that support the principles stated above;
- to help increasing customer satisfaction by increasing employee satisfaction; and
- to align the HR department with the new philosophies, especially with customer needs.

To support line management with the reorganisation of work

HR works as a facilitator and moderator in the quality process and also in the process of restructuring the company's organisation according to Lean Management or Business Process Re-engineering. Companies that commit themselves to one of these management concepts need a structure that allows a decentralisation of responsibility, holistic processes and teamwork (Kierysch, 1995, p. 610). This leads to the following trends (Sarges, 1992, p. 345):

- The object principle makes up grounds on the functional division of labour/specialisation (Bleicher, 1990, p. 154).
- The organisational pyramid will become leaner by taking out management levels and limiting staff units to operational services (Sarges, 1992, p. 345).
- Organisational structures will become deformalised; this will be accompanied by an increasing orientation towards the individual, that means an increasing consideration of abilities, needs and values of employees (Wagner, 1989, p. 16).

Working in groups in some companies, for example Mannesmann–Demag AG (Hayn, 1996, pp. 766–70), Opel Eisenach AG (Haasen, 1996, pp. 80–5) and other car manufacturing companies, already is an essential element of the organisation of work, and in the future the dissemination of group work will increase; this can be presumed for blue-collar jobs as well as for white-collar jobs (Schusser, 1995, p. 128). There will be group work as a permanent form of organisation and temporary group work, for example in quality circles, project teams and so on. Obviously group work confronts employees with new challenges concerning qualification, responsibility and social competence (Schusser, 1995, p. 128).

To acquaint employees with the new philosophies

To acquaint employees with new keywords such as group work, quality, customer satisfaction and process orientation with continuous improvements, it is not enough to make them aware of these issues, it is also necessary to invest in training their skills: this means on the one hand to invent tools that enable employees to behave according to the new principles, for example problem-solving tools, and on the other hand it is also necessary to develop the behavioural skills of employees, such as ability for teamwork or communication skills and a sensitivity towards the needs of customers.

These management concepts lead to job enrichment and enlargement in all hierarchical levels. Superiors delegate some of their tasks to their followers, for example process control or quality control. Improving processes, quality or customer satisfaction becomes part of everyone's job – it is no longer left to managers or specialists (Schonberger, 1994, p. 110). 'Empowerment', meant as the delegation of responsibility top down to the level of hierarchy where the responsibility should rest, is going to be a key issue for all management functions in German companies (Anon, 1996a, p. 8). As a result of empowerment, employees can, for example, obtain the competence and power to stop the production line if the required 100 per cent quality is not given. To be prepared to meet the challenges the new management concepts imply employees need:

- broader qualification;
- social competence (for example for solving conflicts); and
- ability to accept responsibility (for example for continuous improvements, organisation of work).

In this context also the keyword 'organisational learning' should be mentioned – if 'change' is seen as a standard and a permanent part of processes in a company, the individual learning of employees should become co-ordinated by open communication, so that collective knowledge can be developed (Schreyögg and Noss, 1995, quoted from Chrobok, 1996, p. 52). HR's task is to develop the required skills and make sure that employee decisions are lead by the same criteria for success as management's: quality, time, costs (A. Töpfer, 1995, p. 14).

Former managers' jobs get enriched and enlarged too, although they delegate some of their tasks and responsibilities. They now become facilitators – whereas their former modus operandi was based on superior education, expertise, position and so on, it is now based on such factors as willingness to share knowledge, egalitarian communication talents, common sense, consideration, empathy and kindness (Schonberger, 1994, p. 112). For example Audi describes in its requirements profile for managers the following tasks: managers should have vision and should function as integrators, makers, experts and promotors (Sohn, 1996).

To invent incentives that support the new philosophies

Incentives, such as new payment systems, are needed that support principles such as teamwork, care for high quality in products and processes or customer satisfaction. These new payment systems should be quality orientated: for example employees who have been paid by the piece should now be paid time wages combined with variable aspects. The variable part of the income should depend on so-called weak parameters such as teamwork or customer orientation, creativity or the willingness to aim for continuous improvement of quality. In some German companies such payment systems already exist, but in most companies they do not. And even if they exist, they often only do so 'on paper' – so although it is written down that teamwork gets rewarded, in reality it is the performance of the individual that does. A survey of the Wirtschaftswoche in 1994 even shows that managers who claim to be good teamworkers earn 13 per cent less than the average (Deutsch, 1995, p. 96). But if companies work with the above mentioned management concepts without renewing their incentive system, they risk demotivating their employees: motivation decreases, absenteeism increases. So building up new incentive systems/payment systems certainly is a key issue in HR strategy in Germany.

An important aspect of incentive systems that concentrate on weak variables is how to register these variables. This is only possible by judgement, not by accurate measurements. Communication between superiors and followers or among team members will therefore play an important role – HR needs to train whoever has to make a judgement based on these weak factors to do so!

To help increase customer satisfaction by increasing employee satisfaction

Customer satisfaction is one of the most important factors in today's competition and a valuable parameter for assessing quality. It can be differentiated between internal and external customers: *internal* customers are people or departments in an organisation that are receivers of somebody else's work – and their behaviour! For example: followers are customers of their leaders, and their satisfaction is a quality parameter for the fulfilment of the task 'leadership'.

Although empirical studies still cannot verify a relationship between employees' satisfaction and their willingness to perform in as engaged a manner as possible, the plausibility of a correlation is undoubted. So one thing leads to the other: satisfied employees are more motivated than dissatisfied employees, motivated employees perform better and are not occupied by thinking about their own situation, so that they can focus on quality and customer needs, and this finally leads to a higher customer satisfaction, which can have a positive influence back on the satisfaction of the employees (A. Töpfer, 1995, p. 10). See Fig 13.4.

'Rating your supervisor' and employee satisfaction surveys in general are important tools to measure the satisfaction of internal customers.

Employee satisfaction surveys   Although the importance of employee surveys nowadays is undoubted, a survey conducted in 1989 showed that only 10 per cent out of 853 responding companies used this instrument. During the last years, however, willingness to use employee surveys has increased (A. Töpfer, 1995, p. 11). Employee satisfaction surveys can include the following criteria (Domsch and Schneble, 1992, p. 1379):

- work/work organisation;
- working conditions;
- remuneration, social benefits;
- communication/information;
- teamwork;
- opportunities to act according to own initiative and ability for performance;
- chances for development (qualification/career);
- relationship to supervisor/behaviour of supervisor;
- image of the company/safety of jobs; and
- statistical information.

The inclusion of these criteria depend on the concrete objectives of an employee survey, the willingness of the questioned employees to fill in long questionnaires and of course the money a company is willing to invest in surveys. They can focus on certain aspects, for example on qualification needs, payment systems, behaviour of superiors, etc. But two things are always very important: to feed back the results of the survey to the ones who filled in the questionnaires, and to take suitable action. To increase the focus taken on employee satisfaction and therefore to implement employee satisfaction surveys on a regular basis is a key issue of HR strategies in Germany. For about fifteen years a group of companies active in this sector have met regularly to interchange know-how concerning this subject, for example IBM Deutschland GmbH, W. Bertelsmann KG, BASF AG and many more.

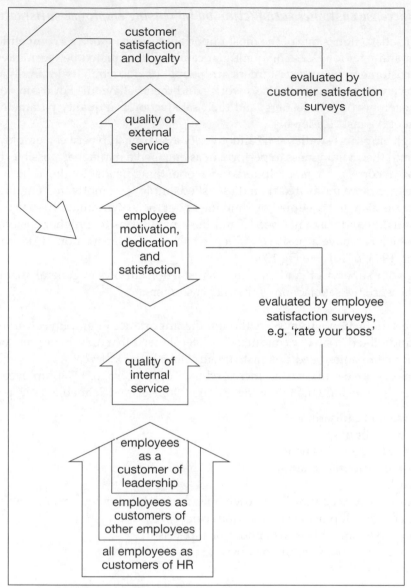

Source: modified from A. Töpfer (1995), p. 10.

Fig 13.4   The relationship between the quality of (internal and external) service and (employees' and customers') satisfaction

Rating your supervisor   The behaviour of superiors or the relationship somebody has to his or her supervisor often is an aspect of employee satisfaction surveys as described above. However, this is an *indirect* way of rating superiors, because only leadership behaviour of a *group of supervisors* is rated, not the behaviour of an individual superior (Domsch, 1992, p. 265). Direct methods to rate supervisors do also exist, but they are not used very often by German companies (Herbst and Heimbrock, 1995, p. 1068); the above mentioned group of companies which meets regularly to interchange know-how on employee quesionnaires also discuss experience in this field. Direct rating of supervisors means that employees give their opinion about the leadership behaviour of their direct superior, and this superior gets his or her own individual result, not only a group result. Examples for the objectives of such ratings are (Domsch, 1992, pp. 257–8):

- to get a diagnosis, to what extent employees as the customers of leadership accept their leader's behaviour, and in what way they would prefer him or her to change behaviour;
- to examine to what extent a change in leadership behaviour has been noticeable for the employees;
- to let the employees participate in the process of leadership by giving feedback to their superior;
- to develop leadership behaviour;
- to increase employee satisfaction;
- to increase performance concerning the relationship between superior and followers.

Employees of Daimler-Benz Aerospace Airbus had the chance in 1995 to rate their supervisors, provided that these supervisors agreed to the survey (nearly 100 per cent of the superiors did). Seventy-three per cent of the employees participated in the survey – it becomes obvious that employees are highly interested in rating their supervisors (Herbst and Heimbrock, 1995, p. 1072). However, as with employee satisfaction surveys in general, only doing the analysis is not enough. Concepts are needed that show how to deal with the results. As a first step the superior who was rated should get the results. Often the superior is asked to give his or her opinion on the items the followers were questioned about, too, so that a comparison between their own results and the results of the followers is possible. A next step is to inform the followers about the results. Then followers and superiors together should try to find measures that make a positive change possible. To find and to evaluate the success of these measures should be the responsibility of the team superior and followers (Domsch, 1992, p. 276).

By supporting the usage of such ratings HR can play an important role in increasing communication among leaders and followers and, by this, in improving satisfaction of internal and in the end also of external customers.

To align the HR department with the new management philosophies, especially with customer needs

Just as all other departments, the HR division should focus on satisfying its customers, too. But who are the customers of HR? The answer is every employee on every hierarchical level. HR departments need to become service departments (Autenrieth and Domsch, 1994, p. 213). Some tasks of HRM shift towards line management, for example some parts of personnel development. In line with the idea of a 'learning company' superiors will be integrated in qualification measures as facilitators, as training on the job becomes more important. This leads to a role change of HR departments, who need to become change agents, because otherwise their scope of duties will get reduced and (in the end) they will lose power (Töpfer, 1994, p. 11).

HR has to analyse and consider the required adaptation processes. The main objective of all HR activities should be to support company goals: this means that HR activities become judged on a result and success: oriented basis. This underlines the necessity of building up an effective personnel control system (Töpfer, 1994, p. 11). For being able to support a company's goals, HR strategies need to become aligned with company strategies. Currently, however, in the majority of German companies personnel management is not or only little integrated in the corporate strategy, so that fruitful teamwork is difficult (Böhm, in Wächter and Metz, 1995, p. 46).

To recognise and take over best process ideas by benchmarking processes

Benchmarking in HR is an important tool that enables companies to recognise and to take over the best process ideas, but in Germany so far only a small number of companies are known that use this instrument, for example Volkswagen AG Wolfsburg (Mollet and Egger, 1995, pp. 18–20), Daimler-Benz AG, Deutsche Aerospace AG, MTU GmbH (Maurer, 1996, pp. 232–6; Osten and Sander, 1996, pp. 26–31), Henkel KGaA (Wolffgang, 1996, pp. 288–91) and Commerzbank AG (Hillen, 1995, pp. 748–62).

Benchmarking can be defined as an objective, comparing assessment of organisational structures, costs, technologies, performance key indicators and processes by indicators that result from a direct analysis of data and information of a representative group of similar or competing companies that are considered as the worlds best (A.T. Kearney in Kreuz, 1994, p. 86). Therefore, benchmarking is a valuable instrument to support management concepts such as TQM, BPR or Lean Management (Kreuz, 1994, p. 99; Pieske, 1995, p. 28) – but it is an inconvenient one. In the United States there is a drop rate of 80 per cent (Burckhardt, 1995, p.17). There is no data about drop rates in Germany, but informally it is known that a lot of companies stop the benchmarking process as soon as they get information about the 'best in class', or companies discover such a big potential for improvements that they immediately start with partial improvements – without exhausting the whole potential for improvements by going through the entire benchmarking process (Burckhardt, 1995, p.17).

HR becomes an increasingly important competitive factor; therefore HR processes should also be compared among companies, so that the best processes can be identified. To illustrate the outcome of HR benchmarking processes we give two examples:

1. An interesting HR benchmarking was carried out by the IAO with seven companies of different branches. An example of this HR benchmarking is the number of employees needed to process the payroll of 1000 employees: the span reaches from 0.6 to 7.7 employees (IAO, 1995b, p. 23). In the benchmarking they also tried to find reasons for these differences.
2. As a result of another benchmarking exercise at Volkswagen the following new projects have already begun or will soon start (Mollet and Egger, 1995, p. 20; Hartz, 1996, p. 94):
   – decrease of absenteeism;
   – optimising foreign assignments;
   – optimising management planning;
   – improvement of communication between the sales department and the distribution network; and
   – process improvements in mechanical engineering.

A condition for successful benchmarking processes in all departments of a company is motivated employees who are willing to learn with and from others, who are courageous enough to admit weak points and start to develop themselves and who take responsibility (Mollet and Egger, 1995, p.19). Benchmarking requires process orientation, employee motivation and empowerment – as described earlier it is HR management's task to make employees aware of these issues and train their skills.

Taking up economically and socially important issues

In order to keep/exceed their competitiveness, companies need to recognise economically and socially important issues and have to decide whether they should act according to these issues. This claim is directly evident for, for example, marketing departments of R&D, but also for HR divisions there are some issues they should pay attention to, for example the demographic development, the change of values and ecological/technological trends (as we stated earlier). In the next paragraphs some important conclusions from these trends will be drawn.

To support new technologies

It can be taken for granted that new technologies will play an important role on the way from industrial society towards the information society or the service society. To see the impact technological development has on HR strategies in Germany we have to look at it from different points of view.

First, production nowadays relies more and more on the usage of technologies. We do not know what consequences this will have for both the quantity of staff needed and the qualifications needed. Concerning the *quantity* of employees, different effects are possible (Domsch, 1993b, p. 3160). On the one hand technologies lead to an increasing productivity by process innovation – this often leads to a reduction in the workforce (Cantzler, 1990, p. 77). On the other hand, the usage of new technologies is often followed by product innovations with expansive influences on employment. Concerning the *qualifications* there are mainly four theories about the impact of technological change on qualification standards (*dequalification*, *polarisation*, *higher* qualification and *different* qualification); none of them has been verified as yet. However, there is an agreement on some qualification requirements for the future (Domsch, 1993b, pp. 3161–3). These include:

- basic computer knowledge;
- the ability to think in a 'systemic', that is, an interdisciplinary logical-analytical, way; and
- subject-overlapping, non-technical capabilities.

In future, initial training will not be enough to meet these requirements, and even if job starters have these required qualifications, the number of job starters is decreasing while the number of older employees is increasing. Therefore the permanent development of personnel is a very important aspect of HR strategy in Germany.

The second influence new technologies have on HR can be described by the keyword 'telework'. Estimates of how many employees in Germany already earn their money as teleworkers at home vary from 150 000 (estimation of the institute 'Empirica', in Lenz, 1996, p. 4) to 300 000 (estimation of Kitty de Bruin, EU-co-ordinator for telework, in Sobull, 1996, p. 1) people; in Europe about 1.25 million teleworkers exist, in the USA about nine million employees work on-line at home (estimation of Kitty de Bruin, EU-co-ordinator for telework, in Sobull, 1996, p. 1). Telework is possible in many different professions: programmers, clerks, fieldworkers, and so on, and has a lot of advantages for the company as well as for the teleworking employee. IBM was one of the first companies that introduced telework in Germany (in 1991); since then IBM noticed an increase in productivity of 20 per cent (Gerd Kirchhoff, IBM, quoted from Sobull, 1996, p. 1). Another advantage for companies is lower rental costs (because less offices are needed). Advantages for employees can be seen in an increase in flexibility and freedom in design of living. As a general advantage, a reduction of traffic on roads and railways should also be mentioned.

There is consensus that the number of teleworkers will increase, although resistance also is noticeable: superiors are used to being able to have direct contact with their subordinates, to be able to look over their shoulder while they work. HR can do its part to overcome this resistance by starting a campaign of enlightenment, not only for superiors. There are more disadvantages of telework to overcome:

- the missing separation of work and home leads to a decrease in identification of employees with their employer and therefore to a lower motivation;
- teleworkers need to have distinct performance consciousness and self-discipline, otherwise they will be too costly;
- teleworkers get less information, especially informal information;
- teleworkers have less social contacts at their workplace, they might get socially isolated; and
- teleworkers fear to injure their prospects.

To find ways to overcome these disadvantages (for example by working out concepts that mix telework with normal office work, for example one day per week the teleworker has to come to his or her company office as IBM teleworkers have to) is a key issue of HR department's work – in Germany there is an estimated potential of 2.5 million jobs for teleworkers.

To support environmentally conscious behaviour

Earlier we pointed out why protection of the environment is an objective to which companies should attach importance. Protection of the environment should become one of the company goals (see among others Seidel, 1989, p. 75). To reach this objective all functions of a company have to contribute to it, including HR management. According to the opinion of 16 members of managing boards of German companies (15 of them in charge of personnel affairs), work organisation and personnel management are especially strategically important starting points for an ecological HR management, followed by personnel development and appropriate incentive systems (Wunderer and Kuhn, 1993, p. 100). The same managers are of the opinion that ecological HR management has been realised in German companies only to a little extent (average rating of 2.0 on a scale of 5). So the question is: how can HR support the objective 'environment protection'?

Work organisation Central issues are the institutionalisation of environmental activities, the definition of competences and the organisational incorporation of environment protection into all levels of the hierarchy (Strunz, 1990, p. 56). Although environment protection should be a task of every employee, nevertheless there are experts needed who are responsible for finding solutions to more complex problems. A plant inspector in charge of environment protection is presumably the most popular organisational unit for environment protection in Germany (Steinle et al., 1994, p. 422; Strunz, 1990, p. 56). According to law his or her function mainly is to support official control by being something like a corporate environmental conscience. However, equipped with no or only little command authority the fulfilment of this duty can be quite difficult (Steinle et al., 1994, p. 422). This and the complexity of environmental problems are arguments for having a decentralised organisation of environment protection, for example by interdisciplinary project groups or environment circles (Wunderer and Kuhn, 1993, p. 100; Steger, 1995, p. 769).

Personnel management/leadership   Environment protection as a strategic company goal should be supported openly by all hierarchical levels, so that employees can believe that ecology is really wanted by the company. Top management can do its part by writing environment protection down as one of the company goals. All management levels have to contribute by acting as role models and by appealing to the environment-consciousness of employees, for example at staff dialogues (Wunderer and Kuhn, 1993, p. 99; Steger, 1995, p. 771). The willingness of employees to act environment-consciously depends very much on the reaction of direct superiors to suggestions for environmental improvements (Steger, 1995, p. 771).

Personnel development   'Education and training to raise awareness about environmental problems, to change attitudes and behaviour and to provide the necessary skills to act in an environmentally responsible manner are important components of environmental management which concern staff as well as management' (North, 1992, p. 30). Thereby it is not enough only to give information about hard facts – if employees want to behave in an environmentally conscious way, they will have to communicate with colleagues or superiors (and that might sometimes lead to conflicts), therefore also social competence is an important content of qualification measures (Hopfenbeck and Willig, 1995, p. 79).

Incentive systems   Environment-conscious behaviour and the invention of ways to reduce environmental pollution should become rewarded. To do so environmental behaviour could become a criterion in personnel appraisal, and/or suggestions to reduce environmental damage could be valued in employee suggestion schemes (Steger, 1995, p. 768; Wunderer and Kuhn, 1993, p. 99).

Personnel planning/personnel selection   Ecological motivation and qualification could be taken as one of the criteria for personnel selection and personnel planning (Wunderer and Kuhn, 1993, p. 99).

It is envisaged that environment protection will become a more and more important objective of society and companies.

To support health by operational health promotion programmes

An increasing number of German companies nowadays demonstrate a sensibility for the health of their employees and implement health promotion programmes, for example Volkswagen AG Wolfsburg, Beiersdorf AG. These programmes exceed hitherto existing labour protection by taking the following disadvantages of the traditional labour protection into account:

- The traditional labour protection depends on such a variety of regulations that, first, the company's experts are completely occupied by controlling the execution of these rules – areas that are not ruled by regulations remain without control (Heese, 1991, pp. 28f). Second, employees themselves only have a few chances to influence labour protection, because mostly they are not familiar with the regulations.
- The traditional labour protection concentrates on areas that allow a direct connection between cause and effect, for example prevention of work accidents or occupational illness. However, these illnesses explain only about 1 per cent of all illnesses (Voigt, 1992, p. 508)!
- The activities of the experts for health in a company (occupational safety specialist, company physician, social institution and so on) were not co-ordinated, so possible synergies – were not used (Brinkmann, 1993, pp. 11f).

Despite these disadvantages the traditional labour protection system in Germany was very successful. There are mainly three reasons that finally made additional *new* concepts necessary (Nieder and Harms, 1995, p. 418):

1. The perception that illness is not a consequence of only one, but of the concerted acting of a variety of reasons (Vester, 1989, p. 243) lead from one-dimensional to comprehensive concepts of health promotion (Brinkmann, 1993, p. 12).
2. Occupational load factors have shifted from physical strains to stress (Kuhn, 1992, p. 146) – the traditional labour protection system was not sufficiently able to deal with these strains.
3. Nearly 70 per cent of all sick days are caused by circulatory disturbance, indigestion, illness of the respiratory tract or illness of the skeleton/restricted mobility (Voß, 1990, p. 100). These chronic illnesses are characterised by long-term progression without visible symptoms – traditional medicine that only acts when illness is already visible here often comes too late (Eberle, 1990, p. 24).

All these facts lead to a new concept: occupational health promotion. (In the USA such health programmes are known for several years by now, but in Germany it was only in the late 1980s/the beginning of the 1990s that companies started to run comprehensive health programmes.) Within the narrow bounds of this chapter it is impossible to describe occupational health programmes in full detail, so at this place a short description must be enough (for further details see Nieder and Harms, 1995, pp. 417ff).

Occupational health promotion does not only start to act when illness is already there, but tries to be preventive. Therefore health promotion projects normally start with a stock-taking of the actual status of health in the company and of ways to reduce unhealthy conditions and improve health-giving conditions. For this stock-taking, for example, experts are interviewed, employee surveys are conducted and data of health insurance funds becomes evaluated. All this data together gives a first impression of the actual state of health in a company. The second step is to intervene – that means on the one hand to offer a variety of measures to the employees that aim at making them aware of health issues and try to support a health-conscious behaviour, and on the other hand it also means to improve working conditions in a way that they do not endanger the health of employees any longer. An important instrument that combines the elements 'stock-taking/analysis' and 'improvement/action' is the health circle (a kind of quality circle in which employees discuss their working situation and try to find measures to improve it; for further explanation see: Westermayer and Bähr, 1994; Harms and Homp, 1995). Beside analysis and intervention the third element of occupational health programmes should be a permanent evaluation of health.

For companies and particularly for HR departments there are especially the following reasons for treating operational health promotion as a key issue:

- by improving the health of employees, absenteeism can be reduced;
- by aiming at an improvement of their health companies can satisfy and motivate employees; this could lead to a reduction of fluctuation in performance;
- health promotion projects have a positive influence on the (internal and external) company image, so the attractiveness of the company for actual and potential employees increases; and
- work places will become suitable also for older employees; because of the demographic development this is increasingly important.

To support equality

Despite the ongoing social discussion about equality of women in professional life and the increasing dispute also at plant level, a stock-taking on the theme 'women in the working life' demonstrates disadvantages for this employee group. One should distinguish between Eastern and Western Germany. It would be beyond the scope of this chapter to describe the different situation of women in Eastern and Western Germany in detail (for further information see Engelbrech et al., 1994; Domsch et al., 1995); however, a consideration of the unemployment rate of 1995 initially points to an equality of men and women in Western Germany: while the unemployment rate of women totals 9.2 per cent, the quota of the men is 9.3 per cent. For Eastern Germany we find a completely different picture: the unemployment rate of women in the new federal states, at 19.3 per cent, nearly twice as high as the men's rate of 10.7 per cent (data from the Bundesanstalt für Arbeit in Nürnberg, yearly average in 1995).

This can be seen as a first indication of an unequal treatment of men and women in terms of entrance to companies. If one considers additionally the situation of employed women within enterprises, in this area also unequal chances at the expense of the women can be noticed. First, there is a sex-specific segmentation of the labour market according to branches of industry and professions (Damm-Rüdiger, 1994; Osterloh and Oberholzer, 1994). Beside that, a segmentation of professional positions within the enterprises can be noticed. Despite different data for Eastern and Western Germany for both parts the following tendency is valid:

- women work in hierarchically lower positions – there is not only a very low average representation of women in management positions in general, the number of women

THE PRACTICE OF HUMAN RESOURCE STRATEGY

even decreases with increasing hierarchical level (Cornelsen, 1989, 1991, 1993; quoted from Domsch et al., 1994a, p. 12);

- women have lower chances for personal development in the enterprise, for example by participation in measures of ongoing education;
- men find better working conditions than women, for example women get a lower income than men: according to Stephan and Wiedemann (1990) in West Germany there is a sex-specific difference in income of 30 per cent. (In the former GDR there were also immense differences in pay of men and women. According to Schwarze et al. (1990) women earned in 1988 on average 16 per cent less than men.)

However, there are some good reasons for companies to improve the situation of women in the working life:

- *The demographic development* – as we described earlier the demographic developments lead to an increasing need for female workers.
- *The qualification and professional orientation of women* – a comparison of the qualifications of women in 1980 and 1989 shows a clear rise in their formal qualifications (Holst and Schupp, 1994, p. 158). In terms of a professional orientation of women it can be stated particularly for women in the new federal states – at times of the GDR their employment rate was about 90 per cent (Schenk, 1990) – professional activity is a firm element of the life concept (Domsch et al., 1995). But also in the old federal states an increasing profession orientation on the part of women can be recorded and also forecast for the future.
- *Company image/gender audits* – Enterprises need to adjust themselves to the fact that equal opportunities and promotion systems will have an essential influence on the image of the enterprise and might therefore also influence the behaviour of customers. Data like the woman quota of an enterprise or the share of female executives will become more and more important as factors that influence the enterprise´s image. Positive data might be very useful and valuable for the company. In this context the development of audits has to be mentioned. From 1996 onwards German companies that assume the obligation to maintain and continue measures to promote equal opportunities can apply for a 'Total E-quality' certificate, which will be valid for two years. This 'Total E-quality' certificate can be used for internal and external marketing. The assessment of companies by such audits will probably gain in importance in future, so for HR departments it is important to deal with such assessment instruments.

The above factors/developments speak for an increasing labour force participation of women in the Federal Republic of Germany. But although enterprises will be forced for competition reasons alone to use increasingly the work potential of women, equal opportunities are not self-starting. HR departments need to act. Companies that are already active in this field are for example Schering AG, Audi AG, Commerzbank AG or Hoechst AG.

There is concrete need for action on the part of the human resources departments to be able to 'cope with' the gender audits and therefore to improve the area of *personnel selection*. Beside the introduction of neutrally formulated employment advertisements (already prescribed by German law) improvements in aptitude diagnostics are especially necessary. In particular, selection processes for executives are often geared to male conduct and male value scales (Küpper, 1994). Research conducted by the IPA shows that out of 13 026 job advertisements 41 per cent were formulated in the male form, 6 per cent were formulated in a hidden male form, 50 per cent had a neutral formulation and 3 per cent were formulated female – although law demands a neutral formulation (Domsch and Lieberum, 1995b).

Concepts for promotion of women in working life remain important. By these plans and also by organisation agreements it would be possible to improve the share of women in management positions. Conceivable – though not undisputed – would be the introduction of quotas. Flexible working hours and the assumed increase of men working part-time will additionally contribute to a dissolution of traditional career patterns. Nevertheless because of the dissemination of traditional thinking it can be reckoned that the development towards equal opportunities for women and men concerning the filling of managerial positions will happen rather slowly. It is a key issue in HR strategies in Germany to contribute to the acceleration of this development.

However, the main responsibility for the family still lies as always with women. It can be assumed that this will not change in the near future. The increasing dissemination of telework will provide an essential contribution to the better compatibility of family and profession.

One essential task of the human resources department is to find ways to integrate female workers after an interruption of their employment. Even if women increasingly participate in working life, we can presume that the classic three-phases model of Myrdal (Myrdal and Klein, 1971) will remain valid. Here what matters on the part of HR departments is to find adequate rules, so that contact with the company and qualifications can be kept up also during career breaks.

Providing competent employees for the company

The key issues in HR strategies in Germany we described so far all have one thing in common: they require qualified and motivated staff. Fig 13.5 sums up the main influences on employees' qualifications.

It goes without saying that professional qualifications are also needed in addition to computer knowledge, systemic thinking, and non-technical capabilities to meet the requirements of today. Surveys even underline their growing importance: the number of employees without completion of their education decreases; in 1976 there were 35 per cent of all employees in Germany without a completed education, in 1987 there were only 23 per cent – that is a reduction of 2.6 million employees (Buttler and Tessaring, 1992, p. 290). Buttler and Tessaring estimate an ongoing decline to 13 per cent in the year 2010. However, professional qualifications *alone* are not enough, *key qualifications* are also needed. There are many definitions of key qualifications (among others: Buttler and Tessaring, 1992, p. 85; Grunwald, 1989, p. 31; Stabenau, 1995, p. 347); most of them cover the following aspects:

- *social competence* – ability to communicate/to co-operate/to resolve conflicts/to delegate, capacity for teamwork, self-assertion, and so on; and
- *methodical competence* – ability to deal with information/to make decisions, to identify interdependencies to solve problems, to reflect on the environment, discernment, creativity, willingness to learn, and so on.

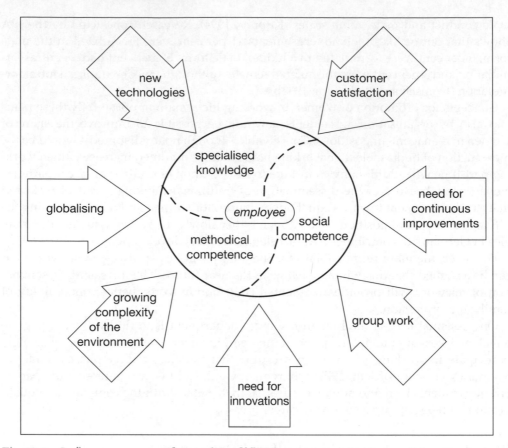

Fig 13.5   Influences on employees' qualifications

This is not a complete list of required key qualifications – but it already gives an impression of the variety of abilities needed. As mentioned before, initial training is obviously not enough to meet these requirements, lifelong learning is necessary. Companies therefore need to gain the best qualified employees from the labour market (for example by personnel marketing activities) – and need to qualify employees by personnel development measures and creating an atmosphere of a 'learning company'. These are the ways to provide competent employees for the company. Employee potential will more and more become a strategic factor of a company's performance, therefore firms need to increase their investments in personnel marketing and development. Companies that only pay lip-service to these issues will fail in the long term (Domsch, 1995a, p. 447).

Personnel marketing – only for managers?

Skilled staff and managerial staff are an important target group of personnel marketing (PM). There are mainly two reasons for this:

1. Highly qualified employees are an expensive investment in human capital. If a company can recruit highly qualified employees it can save time and money for qualification measures. And if the opposite happens (a highly qualified employee leaves the company), the investment in human capital is lost and the new vacancy must be filled either from the internal or the external labour market (Staffelbach, 1995, p. 147).

2. Although we still have high unemployment rates various authors believe that the often forecast manpower shortage (concerning skilled and managerial staff) will sooner or later come (among others Regnet, 1995, p. 47; Scholz, 1994, p. 14). The reason can mainly be seen in a growing need for university graduates. Buttler and Tessaring (1992, pp. 297ff) estimate for Germany:

   - the demand for managerial staff will increase from 1.5 million in 1987 to 2.4 million in 2000 and 2.7 million in 2010. Managerial staff will cover 10 per cent of the labour force (1987: 6 per cent).
   - the portion of managers who hold a degree will increase from 30 per cent in 1987 to 35 per cent in 2000 and 40 per cent in 2010;
   - that means for Germany to satisfy the estimated demand for managers with academic qualifications every fourth university graduate has to become a manager.

This increase of demand for skilled and managerial staff leads to competition between companies for qualified staff – a current trend which is likely to continue (Buttler and Tessaring, 1992, p. 291).

Among others these are two very important reasons for PM activities concerning skilled and managerial staff. *But is it enough to concentrate PM only on superiors?* Before we answer this headline question we have to define personnel marketing. The definitions of different authors vary (an overview of different definitions can be found in Dietmann, 1993, pp. 102ff; Staffelbach, 1995, p. 148). Perhaps the easiest way to explain PM is by comparing it with product marketing (see Table 13.5).

Table 13.5 Comparison between product marketing and personnel marketing

	Product marketing	Personnel marketing
Object	• product; in parts also the producing/supplying company	• work place, especially work opportunities in a specific company
Target group	• new customers • old customers	• future employees • current employees
Methods	• product-market research • image campaign • product marketing mix • after sales service	• labour-market research • personnel image advertisement • personnel marketing mix • staff dialogues
Action	• product related placement • market strategies	• placement in the labour market • personnel image strategies

Source: Scholz (1994), p. 603.

Personnel marketing is more than an originally designed job advertisement; it goes along with activities on the *internal and external* labour market; present and future employees have to be considered as partners. They are people who have as different needs and expectations as customers; employees can be seen as a kind of 'established clientele' (Staffelbach, 1995, p. 144).

To analyse the spreading of PM activities in Germany we take a survey conducted by Scholz in 1990/1991 among 83 companies of different size and branches (Scholz, 1994, pp. 605–9). According to this study 22 per cent of the companies have an established post for PM, 28 per cent plan to establish PM, and 22 per cent do not have or plan to establish PM. The instruments of PM used are shown in Table 13.6.

Table 13.6 The usage of personnel marketing instruments in German companies

		Established post for PM			Company size		
Instrument	*total* n=83	*yes* n=18	*planned* n=24	*no* n=18	*small* n=28	*medium* n=31	*large* n=24
contacts to universities and other schools	46%	56%	25%	56%	25%	45%	77%
internal measures (e.g. staff development)	36%	28%	46%	44%	46%	29%	36%
(image-) advertisement/PR	33%	39%	42%	28%	29%	29%	45%
company presentations on fairs	25%	33%	13%	39%	18%	23%	41%
internships/holiday jobs	21%	22%	13%	17%	14%	19%	32%
junior staff planning	11%	6%	13%	11%	11%	10%	14%

Source: Scholz (1994), p. 607.

The survey of Scholz confirms the estimation of Staffelbach that so far the majority of PM activities have been focussed on the external labour market – the internal market is often neglected (Staffelbach, 1995, p. 147). But the internal labour market is as important as the external! It is not only important to be able to recruit new employees from the labour market, it is also important to retain the employees already working for your company. Thereby the described change of values plays an important role. The expectations of employees towards their work have changed. As discussed earlier companies have to react to this change by adjusting the working conditions they offer. Therefore they need to evaluate needs and expectations of their employees (for example by employee satisfaction surveys). It is surprising to see how many companies go without instruments such as employee satisfaction surveys, image analyses or workshops concerning corporate culture (Scholz, 1994, p. 607).

We now can give an answer to the headline's question – PM only for managers? – it must be 'no'. At least *internal* PM activities have to cover all employees of all hierarchical levels – corporate culture and corporate success are both designed by the interaction of *all* employees.

To intensify PM activities certainly is a key issue of HR strategies in Germany. Thereby in our opinion it is not important whether a company has a special post for PM or not. Personnel marketing stands for a certain attitude towards employees as customers, which has to be lived by all functions and hierarchical levels. That is the important issue of personnel marketing no company should ignore.

Personnel development

A survey conducted by Töpfer and Poersch among 853 German personnel managers shows the current status quo of personnel development (PD) in Germany. An interesting result of this survey is the estimation of the importance of PD: on a scale from 0 (not important) to 100 (very important) PD reaches an average score of 91 points – that is the highest score of all personnel activities (Töpfer and Poersch, 1989, p. 75). In this survey personnel managers were also asked about the target groups of PD measures and who the trainers are. It was found out that:

- 44 per cent of the companies invest in comprehensive PD measures for executive staff, 54 per cent do so in parts;
- 44 per cent of the companies invest in comprehensive PD measures for prospective managers, 51 per cent do so in parts;
- Only 17 per cent of the companies include non-managerial staff in their PD activities, 74 per cent do so in parts; and
- Only 13 per cent of the companies do not only use internal or external trainers, but also their own managerial staff, 74 per cent do so in parts (p. 104).

This survey shows that German managers have realised that qualified and motivated employees are important assets and therefore investments in PD measures are investments in the future of a company. But still the main target group of PD measures are executives – although in line with TQM concepts *all* employees should be involved in PD measures. KAIZEN not only means continuous improvements – it also includes the development of all employees: for being able to improve processes and products employees need qualifications. According to the study of Töpfer and Poersch, German companies seem not to be totally aware of the PD potential in training on-the-job by leadership.

In another survey conducted by Wunderer and Kuhn 16 members of Managing Boards were asked about the current and future importance of PD on-the-job, near-the-job, into-the-job, off-the-job and out-of-the-job (classification according to Conradi, 1983, pp. 37ff). Table 13.7 shows the scores the different PD measures gained on a scale of 5.

According to this survey PD on-the-job will become very decisive in future; also important are PD near-the-job and PD into-the-job. The most important on-the-job measures will be (Wunderer and Kuhn, 1993, p. 138):

- to participate in/lead project groups;
- job enrichment;
- job enlargement; and
- a delegative leadership style.

While the importance of PD measures concerning special knowledge will decrease, the importance of social development will increase. Self-development will become more important than extraneous development (Wunderer and Kuhn, 1993, pp. 138–9).

The results of this survey underline the necessity of continuous learning for continuous improvements. Personnel development should no longer be a task only of PD departments – it has to become a task of every employee.

Table 13.7   Comparison of the usage of personnel development concepts (on scale of 5)

	In 1990	In 2000
PD on-the-job		
for example job enlargement, job enrichment, job rotation, semi-autonomous work groups, project work	3.3	4.8
PD near-the-job		
measures that are closely related to the job (in terms of time, content and geographical proximity)	2.6	3.7
PD into-the-job		
measures that prepare someone for a new job	3.9	3.6
PD off-the-job		
for example professional conferences, leadership training, personality training, congresses, etc.	3.1	2.6
PD out-of-the-job		
measures that prepare employees for their retirement	1.6	2.3

Source: data from Wunderer and Kuhn (1993), p. 136.

This leads again to the 'learning company' – a management model that is intensely discussed by the academic and the corporate world, mainly because knowledge becomes an increasingly important factor on the way towards the information society. Thereby a variety of definitions of organisational learning and the learning company exist, which we are not going to reflect here. Instead we will present in Table 13.8 the preliminary results of a qualitative-empirical research project that addresses the issue (Güldenberg and Eschenbach, 1996, pp. 4ff).

If 'learning' becomes so important that even new management concepts have grown up around it, this can be treated as a hint towards an increasing importance of brain power. With the growing portion of knowledge work also the number of qualified knowledge workers increases – while at the same time companies try to reduce their hierarchical levels in order to become a lean company. This makes career development a difficult task for HR management. One way out of this dilemma is to define parallel hierarchies (Domsch, 1993a, p. 564). Another way is the introduction of horizontal promotion. Therefore a new perception of superiors and followers is needed. Sarges suggests a break with the old idea according to which the manager is the 'boss' and his followers are inferiors. Qualified knowledge workers should be seen and valued as 'bosses', while their manager supports them by planning, co-ordinating and coaching (Sarges, 1992, p. 358). Therefore jobs need to become more challenging, so that horizontal promotion is seen as something valuable for employees as well as for companies.

Harmonising individualisation with flexibility

Individualisation and flexibility – on first sight these words seem to point to the same direction, but taking a closer look it becomes obvious that beside conformity also a conflict of interests is possible.

Table 13.8   Impediments and supportive measures for a learning company

Organisational learning			
The most important impediments	*The most important measures to support individual learning*	*The most important measures to support collective learning*	*The most important measures to support an institutionalisation of knowledge*
• fear of changes, initiated by passing on knowledge • lack of ability to realise knowledge-benefits for others than oneself • power politics	• decentralisation • delegation of authority • organisational culture which supports learning • areas of freedom	• continuous improvements in learning teams • self-organising project and production teams • co-ordination circles • group-oriented company suggestion scheme • removal of hierarchical, functional and personal barriers • support of formal and informal communication	• libraries, databases, expert systems • visualisation • coaching • transparent information systems • mutual, internal training

Source: data from Güldenberg and Eschenbach (1996), pp. 7–8.

Individualisation focusses on the employee's interests.   The change of values we have described leads to an increasing need of employees for individualisation. People's willingness to subordinate their individual needs and interests to company interests is decreasing, employees want to be able to have an influence on their work, for example in terms of working hours, work place, work content, personnel development, and so on (Schanz, 1992, p. 260; Scholz, 1994, p. 36; Wunderer and Kuhn, 1993, p. 83). Leadership styles can also become influenced by this development: employees tend to prefer an individually suitable leadership style.

Flexibility focusses on the company's interests.   The described change of values not only refers to employees, but also to customers: companies increasingly need to react to individual customer needs. This leads to an individualisation of products and services, which in return leads to a growing need for flexible working conditions – in general the same working conditions that employees also want to become individualised.

Fig 13.6 outlines context parameters of individualisation and flexibility.

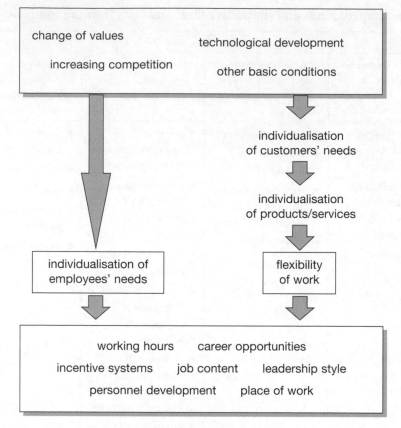

Fig 13.6   Context parameters of individualisation and flexibility

Although both parties, employees and company, head for an individualisation of the same working conditions, there *can* be conflicts. A typical example to explain the different interests of the company and its employees are capacity-oriented working hours; to be able to react as flexibly as possible to the market's requirements a company might like to organise the working hours in a capacity oriented way – in many cases this might not conform with the employees' needs for an individually shaped working time and spare time.

It is a key issue of HR strategies in Germany to find ways to harmonise the employees' need for individualisation with the company's need for flexibility. A survey found out the strategically most important fields for individualisation and flexibility in German companies (according to 16 German personnel managers, in Wunderer and Kuhn, 1993, p. 88) and these are shown in Fig 13.7.

Some of these areas for individualisation and flexibility have already been covered in this chapter. Flexible working hours and incentive systems is now discussed.

Incentive systems

Incentive systems include all deliberately designed working conditions that reinforce a certain behaviour/certain practices by positive incentives and diminish the probability

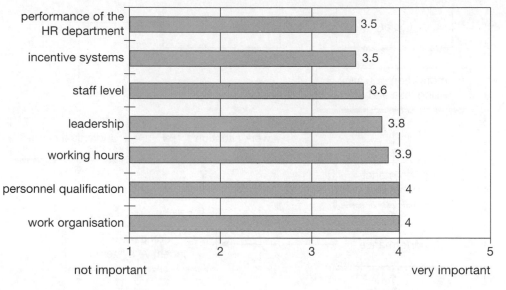

Source: Wunderer and Kuhn (1993), p. 88.

Fig 13.7 Strategic importance of some areas for individualisation and flexibility

of occurrence of other practices by sanctions (Becker, 1991, p. 280; Becker, 1995, p. 186). If employees are the most valuable resource of companies, the whole potential of this resource should be used. Therefore companies need to motivate their employees: there should be a fair exchange of performance offered by employees and (material and non-material) incentives offered by the company.

Fig 13.8 shows the place of the company's incentive system within the context parameters of HR management (Autenrieth and Domsch, 1994, p. 208).

Material incentives are, despite a generally high prosperity level, still top priority incentives of employees (Evers, 1992, p. 394). They consist mainly of the following components (Evers, 1992, p. 388):

- fixed and variable parts of the income; thereby it can be postulated that the income functions as a permanent incentive only if the variable part is high enough. In general the variable part of the income of managers should sum up to at least 25 per cent of the basic salary (Becker, 1991, p. 287). Furthermore it is important to consider that satisfaction with the income is more related to its *relative* amount (social comparison) than to its absolute amount (Rosenstiel, 1995, p. 177);
- employee profit-sharing scheme;
- company pension scheme;
- continued payment of salary in case of illness or death;
- company car (also for private usage);
- accident insurance;
- holiday;
- fringe benefits.

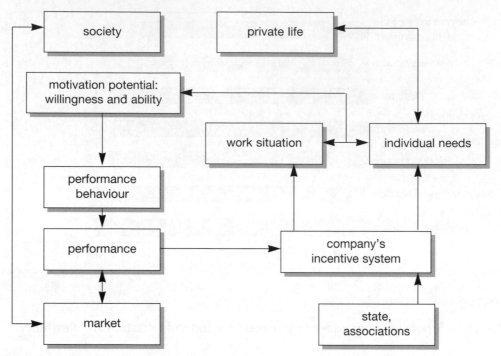

Source: Autenrieth and Domsch (1994), p. 208.

Fig 13.8   The incentive system within the context parameters of HR management

Lately so-called 'cafeteria systems' are discussed in Germany (Dycke and Schulte, 1986; Wagner, 1986, quoted from Domsch, 1993a, p. 551). This means that employees can choose from a variety of incentives their individual package, for example while an older employee might prefer the financing of his or her retirement, a younger employee might prefer a financing of his or her separate home (Scholz, 1994, p. 36).

Non material incentives in German companies are only seldom perceived as parts of incentive systems, although they also influence the employees' motivation and performance – they are basic conditions for employees' performance. Examples of non material incentives are (Becker, 1991, pp. 295f; Becker, 1991, p. 198; Evers, 1992, p. 388; Rosenstiel, 1995, pp. 176ff):

- job content;
- leadership style;
- range of competence/scope;
- status/recognition;
- personal development;
- career prospects;
- information/communication;
- job security;
- working conditions;
- rules on working hours;
- working atmosphere;
- corporate culture;

- company image;
- company location.

Although some of the material components are determined by collective agreements, at least concerning members of exempt staff there is enough liberty of action to use them deliberately as incentives. As to non material incentives there is enough freedom of action concerning both, exempt staff and non-exempt staff. German companies do not sufficiently use this liberty of action, neither concerning material nor non material incentives (Evers, 1992, p. 389). To develop company specific incentive systems is a key issue in HR strategy in Germany that should be of a high priority not only to HR departments, but also to the company management. Fig 13.9 shows the spread of incentives in 853 German companies.

The current incentive systems in Germany give occasion to criticism; the most important aspects are (Becker, 1995, p. 187):

- Incentives often motivate managers to reach operative short-term objectives, and strategic issues are neglected. This is mainly because strategic achievements often come about only after several years, so only then is it possible to evaluate the success. But motivation theories show that there should be only a short time between action and reward, otherwise incentives are not very stimulating.
- There seems to be no direct connection between the performance of managers and incentives: the operating profit of most companies hardly increased during the last few years, very much in opposition to the increasing incomes of managers.

So what are the requirements incentive systems in general have to meet? Becker names the following (Becker, 1991, p. 285): performance orientation (including reaching strategic objectives), transparence, flexibility, economic efficiency, covering the performance of individuals and groups, motivating.

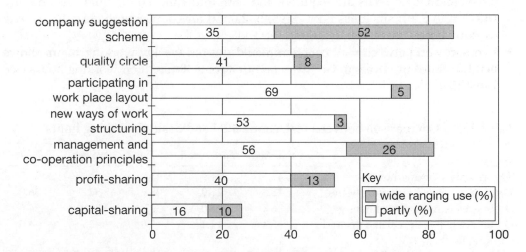

Source: Töpfer and Poersch (1989), p. 107.

Fig 13.9   How German companies motivate their employees

It is a key issue in HR strategies in Germany to develop incentive systems that cover operative *and* strategic issues by using material *and* non material incentives. To find out what motivates employees most, employee satisfaction surveys can be very useful. Finally the whole company should be seen as a holistic incentive system.

Flexible working hours

'Employees who work overtime are more engaged and more interested in their job' – this seems to be a common attitude towards overtime in Germany (Domsch, 1995b, p. 28; Weidinger, 1995a, p. 40). Overtime is often seen as a status symbol or an important criterion for promotion, so it is common knowledge that the working time that is most valuable for making a career starts at 5 p.m. (Born, 1995, p. 41).

This attitude towards overtime – although very common – is inconsistent with the needs of today's employees as well as with the needs of today's companies. New concepts for flexible working hours are needed, which exceed the common extra working hours. Those working extra hours have an attitude as stated above – they are time-oriented (aiming at collecting minutes), not result-oriented. The same phenomenon can be diagnosed for some shift schedules: their construction is lead by the question how to use the available working time. The result is manning provided by working time – not by the amount of work (Herrmann, 1995, p. 577).

New concepts for flexible working hours have to take the following aspects into consideration:

On the part of employees:

- the change of values;
- the necessity to co-ordinate family's and company's requirements (Schramm and Schlese, 1995, p. 571); according to American studies the daily time spent on a single child family amounts to 4.6 hours, a family with two children needs 6.5 hours, with three children 7.6 hours are required, and with four children the time needed daily adds up to 9.9 hours (Süssmuth, 1995, p. 23). So for couples with children flexible working hours are especially important; and
- a comparison between real, contractual and desired weekly working hours shows that full-time employees in Germany favour a reduction of their working hours (see Table 13.9).

Table 13.9 Comparison between real, contractual and desired working hours

	Full-time	Part-time	Men	Women	Total
Real weekly working hours	41.5	21.9	41.8	33.6	38.5
Contractual weekly working hours	38.3	21.9	38.2	32.7	36.0
Desired weekly working hours	36.1	23.0	36.8	30.9	34.5
Difference between real and desired working hours	–5.4	+1.1	–5.0	–2.7	–4.0

Source: ISO (1994), p. 116, quoted from Strümpel et al. (1995), p. 816.

On the part of companies:

- companies need to prolong the operating hours (Schramm and Schlese, 1995, p. 571), for example because customers demand longer service hours (Herrmann, 1995, p. 577);
- flexible working hours can support continuous improvements, because figuring out time schedules requires an ongoing reconsideration of processes (Herrmann, 1995, p. 579);
- because of a growing international competition companies need to avoid downtimes (Schramm and Schlese, 1995, p. 571);
- a reduction of working hours reduces the employees' appearance of fatigue, so that performance per reduced time is increasing. Although on the other hand also the personal set-up time and the time needed for communication, leadership and organisation is increasing, a study conducted by McKinsey shows that positive effects exceed the negatives: McKinsey found a 10 per cent increase in productivity (McKinsey & Company, 1994, quoted from Barth and Zika, 1995, p. 580);
- by offering flexible working hours companies are able to hold qualified employees even in a period of life with restrained availability, who otherwise might look for a new employer (Weidinger, 1995b, p. 831).

On the part of the economy:

- The current economic situation in Germany can be characterised by such keywords as mass unemployment, personnel reduction, loss of income and an increasing tax burden. A reduction of working hours can save jobs: Seifert estimates that from 1985 to 1990 by reduction of working hours 385 000–514 000 jobs have been saved or newly created (Hartmut Seifert, 1993, quoted from Barth and Zika, 1995, p. 582). 'It is better to have a part-time job than no job' (Domsch, 1995b, p. 27).

Obviously all involved parties can benefit from flexible working hours, but still there is resistance to overcome: on the one hand some employees might not want to give up working overtime, because they do not want to lose the additional income, or they have adjusted their private life with their working hours and therefore do not want a change. Another reason why employees might not want flexible working hours is that they might fear exploitation – in the factory gossip, stories circulate about employees getting paid for four days of work with a workload that doesn't differ from a full-time employee's (Domsch, 1995b, p. 28). And also executives are sometimes reluctant to support flexible working hours, because such models require a great deal of leadership ability (Anon, 1996c). It is not enough then to control employees by their attendance time, flexible working hours require performance-oriented leadership and control.

To overcome this resistance it could already help to explain to employees and their superiors what 'flexible working hours' really mean. Working hours can be flexible in terms of the duration (chronometrically flexible) and in terms of the position of the working time (chronologically flexible). If at least one of these two dimensions is permanently variable, it can be called flexible working hours. There are different models of flexible working hours, for example

- part-time work;
- annual working time;

- overtime;
- single tasks with free timetable;
- job sharing;
- sabbatical; and
- capacity orientated variable working hours.

(For further explanation see Domsch et al., 1994b, pp. 34ff; Domsch and Ladwig, 1995, pp. 839ff; Scholz, 1994, pp. 339ff; Weidinger, 1995b, pp. 828ff).

Research shows that flexible working hours are classed by prospective managers as a criterion for choosing a company directly behind salary level, career prospects and personnel development opportunities (Autenrieth et al., 1993, p. 98). So there is a demand for flexible working hours also among (prospective) managers in Germany. However, on behalf of the companies reluctance is noticeable; studies conducted by the IPA (Institut für Personalwesen und Arbeitswissenschaft) among companies in Hamburg shows the spread of flexible working hours for executive and specialised staff shown in Table 13.10.

Table 13.10 Spread of flexible working hours for executive and specialised staff

	Companies offering the time pattern to executives	Companies offering the time pattern to specialised staff
Flexible working hours	34.7%	58 %
Single tasks with free time-table	6.3%	17.8%
Capacitiy orientated variable working hours	5.6%	26 %
Daily reduction of working hours	26.4%	78.8%
Job sharing	6.9%	43.2%

Source: Domsch et al. (1994a), pp. 89ff.

The majority of German companies are of the opinion that managers' jobs cannot be done part-time (Autenrieth et al., 1993, pp. 111f). They mainly see the risks of flexible working hours (for example lack of continuity, higher personnel costs) without noticing the opportunities (for example increasing efficiency, creativity, decreasing absenteeism). Obviously, especially part-time work for executives has to be well planned before it is implemented, but successful examples – although still rare in German companies – show that flexible working hours are also possible for executives (see among others Domsch and Ladwig, 1995, pp. 843ff; Domsch et al., 1994b, p. 112).

In view of the advantages of flexible working hours for employees, companies and the economy in general, it is a key issue of HR strategies in Germany to support and implement models for flexible working hours. There are already examples to learn from, for example, Volkswagen, Opel Eisenach AG and Bayerische Motoren Werke AG (see among others Bihl and Gaßner, 1996, pp. 118–121; Domsch et al., 1994b; Hanisch, 1995, pp. 46ff; Hebler, 1995, pp. 43ff; Prieß, 1995, pp. 48ff; Roemheld, 1995, pp. 641–2; Weidinger, 1995b, pp. 827ff).

Special key issues in HR strategy in the new federal states in Germany

The issues in HR strategy we described so far are important for all federal states in Germany – for the new ones as well as for the old ones. But in the new federal states we find circumstances that bring also other key issues into focus.

The reunion of Germany was followed by an immense structural change in the new federal states. The political system changed rapidly from one day to the next, the planned economy was turned into a market economy. Obviously such a change made some problems unavoidable, but many people underestimated the heaviness of these problems, for example mass unemployment, short-time working and compulsory early retirements as a result of corporate liquidation (Wunderer and Kuhn, 1993, p. 90). No wonder that Eastern Germans lost their faith in HR departments, if they only got to know them as (in the former GDR) communist party spies and (in the reunited FRG) as dismissal departments! (Becker and Ganslmeier, 1995, p. 730).

For an upswing in Eastern Germany the efficient usage of all factors of production is needed – labour productivity must increase. Human resources can be seen as the key to success. At the moment the often mentioned tasks of HR management in the former GDR are staff reduction, short-time working and cost saving. The strategically important issues, however, are personnel management and personnel development (Wunderer and Kuhn, 1993, p. 90). Considering that people in Western and Eastern Germany have been living in different economic and political systems for 40 years it is obvious that HR instruments that work successfully in the old federal states have to be adapted before they are used in the new federal states. To be able to do so it is important to know about some of the main differences, especially concerning values.

Referring to different authors Lang figured out some characteristics of HR management in the GDR (Lang, 1995, p. 90), of which the most important ones are:

- accentuation of hierarchies and functional division of labour;
- only little autonomy of operating units;
- centralised decisions;
- specialisation and normalisation of a company's internal processes;
- employment for life, importance of socialisation within the company;
- on higher hierarchical levels there were authoritarian-patriarchal or patriarchal-benevolent leadership styles dominating, leaders on lower levels only had a weak position; a trend to informal labour relations was noticeable;
- on the one hand there was a bureaucratic culture that was oriented towards the rigid adherence to instructions and blocking of creativity, on the other hand there was the necessity to find ways to evade hierarchy and regulation; and
- on the one hand there was a ritualisation of participation in groups, but on the other hand a simultaneous decrease in abilities to take responsibility as an individual.

Especially the abolition of the right to work has had an important impact on the values of employees in Eastern Germany. In the GDR, government had taken over responsibility for jobs and promoted a working atmosphere in which team spirit was very important. Employees got the impression that socially they could not really fail (Walz, 1995, p. 590). Now, after the reunion, everybody is responsible for himself or herself.

269

Qualifications, performance and behaviour are important criteria for finding and keeping jobs. The relation between workers and salaried employees has been turned round; the apparent equality of the incomes policy in the GDR was replaced by a differentiated wage-scale policy. This policy is accompanied by the fact that many people perceive the newly created differences between the lowest wage rate bracket and top earners as unbelievably high (Walz, 1995, p. 591). If functionaries of the former GDR became managers, they often became very aware of their status – more than they used to at GDR-times (Walz, 1995, p. 592), so they even strengthened the differences among hierarchical levels.

To sum up, Table 13.11 gives a general overview of the main differences between official values in the former GDR and FRG.

Table 13.11   Comparison of official values in the GDR and the FRG

Official values	
GDR	*FRG*
authority	initiative
patriarchal values	adaptability
planning	ambition
mutual support	performance
co-operation	(material) pay
solidarity	personal prosperity
friendship	self-fulfilment
social ties	

Source: Bresser and Dunbar (1995), p. 34.

The neglect of these different values is an important reason for the protest, irritation and insecurity that are typical of the present relationship between Eastern and Western Germany (Bresser and Dunbar, 1995, p. 34). To support overcoming these differences is a key issue of HR management in Germany – and 'overcoming' is not only meant as replacing the Eastern values by Western values. There are also Eastern values, for example co-operation, which Western employees should take over! As a way to overcome the different values Bresser and Dunbar recommend the implementation of 'integration-circles'. These are a kind of quality circle in which Eastern and Western employees meet on a regular basis within working hours. The objectives of these integration circles are to increase job satisfaction and to contribute to overcoming the differences between values in the old and new federal states (Bresser and Dunbar, 1995, p. 37).

The situation in Germany after the reunion provides many challenges for HR management, of which we only could give a very short overview in this chapter. Apart from the key issues described previously that are important issues for both Eastern and Western Germany, especially important issues of HR strategies in the new federal states of Germany are:

- to win back the trust of employees in HR management;
- to overcome the different values (not only by taking over the Western values);
- to develop necessary qualifications; and
- to establish appropriate leadership styles.

Summary and conclusions

Human resources play an increasingly important role in today's business; they are one of the companies' most important assets. Therefore an appropriate HR management is needed. In this chapter the basic conditions for HR management in Germany have been described. Then the text concentrated on key issues in German HR strategies. Obviously it was beyond the scope of this chapter to describe them in full detail, but a brief overview over some of the most important issues has been given:

- globalising;
- supporting new management concepts;
- taking up economically and socially important issues;
- providing competent employees for the company; and
- harmonising individualization with flexibility.

Looking at these issues it becomes obvious that they could have expressed by one single sentence: *HR strategy needs to support company goals by finding ways to harmonise employees' and companies' needs.* To be able to do so human resources have to be accepted as an important asset by company management as well as line management, so that fruitful teamwork between the HR department, other company divisions and the company management is possible. In Germany this is not the case, although a survey among 853 German personnel managers shows the following estimation: 72 per cent of the questioned personnel managers value the importance of HR management in Germany as high, 80 per cent even believe that it will also be high in future (Töpfer and Poersch, 1989, p. 58).

Another survey (Table 13.12) shows the status of integration of HR aspects in strategic management decisions.

Table 13.12   Integration of the HR function into company management

In the year 1990		In the year 2000	
optimal	0	increasing integration	15
enough	5	no change	0
too little	10	decreasing integration	0
not enough	0		

Source: Wunderer and Kuhn (1993), p. 197.

So it is expected that the situation will change towards an increasing consideration of HR aspects.

But not only company management needs to increase their consideration of HR issues. HR departments themselves also need to increase their strategic efforts, as they are currently mainly occupied with personnel administration, neglecting strategic issues (Wunderer and Kuhn, 1993, p. 193). This has to change. Last but not least it has to be mentioned again that parts of the responsibility for human resources will shift from HR departments to line managers, so it is also important to bring HR issues into their focus.

Key issues in HR strategies in Germany can only be successfully pursued if they are considered as an important factor not only by HR departments, but also by line management and company management.

REFERENCES

Antes, R., Steger, U. and Tiebler, P. (1992) 'Umweltorientiertes Unternehmensverhalten – Ergebnisse aus einem Forschungsprojekt', in Steger (ed.) *Handbuch des Umweltmanagements*, München.

Autenrieth, C. and Domsch, M.E. (1994) 'Personalmanagement in Zeiten unternehmerischen Umbruchs', in Albach, H. (ed.) *Globale soziale Marktwirtschaft; Ziele – Wege – Akteure*, Wiesbaden.

Autenrieth, C., Chemnitzer, K. and Domsch, M. (1993) *Personalauswahl und -entwicklung von weiblichen Führungskräften*, Frankfurt am Main.

Badura, B. (1993) 'Die Gesundheitsförderung erschließt Humanressourcen', speech at the conference 'Gesundheit am Arbeitsplatz, Wohlbefinden und Leistung steigern – Kosten reduzieren', 23–24 December 1993 in Frankfurt am Main (organiser: Blick durch die Wirtschaft und Institut für Medienentwicklung und Kommunikation).

Barth, A. and Zika, G. (1995) 'Volkswirtschaftliche Effekte der Arbeitszeitverkürzung', *Personal*, 11/95.

Becker, F. (1991) 'Strategische Anreizsysteme – Mitarbeiter zukunftsorientiert motivieren', in Ackermann, K.-F. and Scholz, H. (eds) *Personalmanagement für die 90er Jahre*, Stuttgart.

Becker, F. (1995) 'Strategische Anreizsysteme (Überblick)', in Scholz, C. and Djarrahzadeh, M. (eds) *Strategisches Personalmanagement, Konzeptionen und Realisationen*, Stuttgart.

Becker, F.G. and Ganslmeier, H. (1995) 'Personalstrategien in den neuen Bundesländern', in Rosenstiel, L. von, Regnet, E. and Domsch, M. (eds) *Führung von Mitarbeitern, Handbuch für erfolgreiches Personalmanagement*, 3, revised and enlarged edn, Stuttgart.

Bihl, G. and Gaßner, P. (1996) 'Auf dem Weg zur ergebnisorientierten Arbeitszeit, Beispiel BMW AG', *Personalführung*, 2/96.

Bleicher, K. (1990) 'Zukunftsperspektiven organisatorischer Entwicklung – Von strukturellen zu human-zentrierten Ansätzen', *zfo (Zeitschrift für Führung und Organisation)*, 59.

Böhm, W. (1995) 'Zusammenarbeit mit dem Betriebsrat', in Rosenstiel, L. von, Regnet, E. and Domsch, M. (eds) *Führung von Mitarbeitern, Handbuch für erfolgreiches Personalmanagement*, 3, revised and enlarged edn, Stuttgart.

Born, J. (1995) 'Teilzeit oder Übervollzeit?', *Personalwirtschaft*, 10/95.

Bresser, R.K. and Dunbar, R.L.M. (1995) 'Zirkel', *Personalwirtschaft*, 10/95.

Brinkmann, R. (1993) *Personalpflege: Gesundheit, Wohlbefinden und Arbeitszufriedenheit als strategische Größen im Personalmanagement*, Heidelberg.

Burckhardt, W. (1995) 'Kunden begeistern, Mitarbeiter motivieren', *Gablers Magazin*, 2/95.

Buttler, F. and Tessaring, M. (1992) '"Arbeitslandschaft 2010" – Folgerungen für die Ausbildung und Beschäftigung von Führungskräften', in Kienbaum, J. (ed.) *Visionäres Personalmanagement*, Stuttgart.

Cantzler, F. (1990) *Quantitative und qualitative Beschäftigungswirkungen neuer Technologien*, München.

Caudron, S. (1993) 'How HR drives TQM', *Personnel Journal*, Vol. 72, 8/1993.

Chrobok, R. (1996) 'Organisationales Lernen', *zfo (Zeitschrift für Führung und Organisation)*, 1/96.

Conradi, W. (1983) *Personalentwicklung*, Stuttgart.

Cornelsen, C. (1989) 'Erwerbstätige mit Hochschulabschluß nach Hauptfachrichtungen', *Wirtschaft und Statistik*, No. 2.

Cornelsen, C. (1991) 'Erwerbstätige mit Hochschulabschluß nach Hauptfachrichtungen', *Wirtschaft und Statistik*, No. 5.

Cornelsen, C. (1993) 'Ergebnisse des Mikrozensus Mai 1992', *Wirtschaft und Statistik*, No. 10.

Damm-Rüdiger, S. (1994) *Ausbildung und Berufssituation von Frauen und Männern in Ost und West*, edited by the Bundesinstitut für Berufsbildung; Berlin, Bonn.

Deppe, J. (1996) 'Organisations und Personalentwicklung in der Praxis', *zfo*, 2/1996.

Deutsch, C. (1995) 'Heißes Eisen: Schlankere Organisationen bedingen neue Formen der Entlohnung', *Wirtschaftswoche*, No. 6, 2 February 1995.

Dietmann, E. (1993) *Personalmarketing – Ein Ansatz zielgruppenorientierter Personalpolitik*, Wiesbaden.

Domsch, M. (1992) 'Vorgesetztenbeurteilung', in Selbach, R. and Pullig, K.-K. (eds) *Handbuch Mitarbeiterbeurteilung*, Wiesbaden.

Domsch, M. (1993a) 'Personal', in Bitz, M., Dellmann, K., Domsch, M. and Egner, H. (eds) *Vahlens Kompendium der Betriebswirtschaftslehre*, Vol. 1, third edn, München.

Domsch, M.E. (1993b) 'Personalwesen und technologischer Wandel', in Wittmann, W., Kern, W., Köhler, R., Küpper, H.-U. and Wysocki, K. von (eds) *Handwörterbuch der Betriebswirtschaft*, Vol. 2, fifth revised and enlarged edn, Stuttgart.

Domsch, M. (1995a) 'Personalplanung und Personalentwicklung für Fach- und Führungskräfte', in Rosenstiel, L. von, Regnet, E. and Domsch, M. (eds) *Führung von Mitarbeitern, Handbuch für erfolgreiches Personalmanagement*, third revised and enlarged edn, Stuttgart.

Domsch, M. (1995b) 'Variable Arbeitszeiten: Sind Frauen und Familie die Verlierer?', speech at the conference 'Flexibilisierung der Arbeitszeit: Patentlösung für die Zukunft?', 31 August 1995 in Göttingen (organiser: Gothaer Versicherungen).

Domsch, M.E. and Ladwig, D. (1995) 'Arbeitszeitflexibilisierung für Führungskräfte', in Rosenstiel, L. von, Regnet, E. and Domsch, M. (eds) *Führung von Mitarbeitern, Handbuch für erfolgreiches Personalmanagement*, third revised and enlarged edn, Stuttgart.

Domsch, M. and Lieberum, U. (1995a) 'Joint-ventures in Osteuropa – personalpolitische Konsequenzen', in Rosenstiel, L. von, Regnet, E. and Domsch, M. (eds) *Führung von Mitarbeitern, Handbuch für erfolgreiches Personalmanagement*, third revised and enlarged edn, Stuttgart.

Domsch, M.E. and Lieberum, U. (1995b) 'Frauen als Fach- und Führungskräfte: Eine empirische Anzeigenanalyse', *Personalführung*, 5/1995.

Domsch, M. and Schneble, A. (1992) 'Mitarbeiterbefragungen', in Gaugler, E. and Weber, W. (eds) *Handwörterbuch des Personalwesens*, Stuttgart.

Domsch, M.E., Hadler, A. and Krüger, D. (1994a) *Personalmanagement und Chancengleichheit, Betriebliche Maßnahmen zur Verbesserung beruflicher Chancen von Frauen in Hamburg*, edited by the Senatsamt für die Gleichstellung; München, Mering.

Domsch, M.E., Kleiminger, K., Ladwig, D.H. and Strasse, C. (1994b) *Teilzeitarbeit für Führungskräfte; Eine empirische Analyse am Beispiel des hamburgischen öffentlichen Dienstes*; edited by the Senatsamt für die Gleichstellung; München, Mering.

Domsch, M.E., Macke, H. and Schöne, K. (1995) 'Weibliche Angestellte im Transformationsprozeß', unpublished study, Hamburg.

Dycke, A. and Schulte, C. (1986) 'Cafeteria-Systeme. Ziele, Gestaltungsformen, Beispiele und Aspekte der Implementierung', *DBW*, 46, 1986.

Eberle, G. (1990) *Leitfaden Prävention*, edited by the Wissenschaftliches Institut der Ortskrankenkassen, Sankt Augustin.

Engelbrech, G., Schenk, S. and Wagner, P. (eds) (1994) 'Bedingungen der Frauenerwerbsarbeit im deutsch-deutschen Einigungsprozeß', in *Beiträge zur Arbeitsmarkt- und Berufsforschung* (BeitrAB 167).

Euchner, W. (1996) 'TQM als Weg zur Optimierung der Personalarbeit', *Personalführung*, 1/96.

Evers, H. (1992) 'Zukunftsweisende Anreizsysteme für Führungskräfte', in Kienbaum, J. (ed.) *Visionäres Personalmanagement*, Stuttgart.

Franke, H. (1991) 'Arbeitsmarkt 2000: weiblicher, älter, qualifizierter', in Feix, W.E. (ed.) *Personal 2000: Visionen und Strategien erfolgreicher Personalarbeit*, Frankfurt am Main.

Gipperich, A. and Pane, H. (1996) 'Der Kunde im Mittelpunkt', *Personalführung*, 1/96.

Grunwald, W. (1989) 'Schlüsselqualifikationen von Führungskräften', *Personalwirtschaft*, 8/89.

Güldenbach, S. and Eschenbach, Rolf (1996) 'Organisatorisches Wissen und Lernen – erste Ergebnisse einer qualitativ-empirischen Erhebung', *zfo (Zeitschrift für Führung und Organisation)*, 1/1996.

Haasen, A. (1996) 'Opel Eisenach GmbH – Creating a High-Productivity Workplace', *Organisational Dynamics*, Spring 1996.

Hanisch, J. (1995) 'Langzeitkonten', speech at the conference 'Flexibilisierung der Arbeitszeit: Patentlösung für die Zukunft?', 31 August 1995 in Göttingen (organiser: Gothaer Versicherungen).

Harms, M. and Homp, K. (1995) 'Das Konzept "Gesundheitszirkel": Erfahrungen aus dem Gemeinschaftsprojekt der AOK Hamburg und der Beiersdorf AG', *Personalführung*, 11/95.

Hartz, P. (1996) *Das atmende Unternehmen, Jeder Arbeitsplatz hat einen Kunden*, Frankfurt.

Hayn, J. (1996) 'Audit Teamarbeit', *Personalführung*, 9/96.

Hebler, M. (1995) 'Teilzeit für Führungskräfte', speech at the conference 'Flexibilisierung der Arbeitszeit: Patentlösung für die Zukunft?', 31 August 1995 in Göttingen (organiser: Gothaer Versicherungen).

Heese, A. (1991) 'Zukunft der Arbeit – Gesundheit in Betrieben und Unternehmen', in Bundesverband der Betriebskrankenkassen (ed.) *Zukunft der Arbeit – Gesundheit in Betrieben und Unternehmen*, documentation of the opening conference of the European Information Centre 'Gesundheitsförderung im Betrieb' at the Bundesverband der Betriebskassen, 30–31 October 1991 in Essen.

Henzler, H.A. (1992) 'Die Globalisierung von Unternehmen im internationalen Vergleich', *ZfB-Ergänzungsheft*, 2/92.

Herbst, A. and Heimbrock, K.J. (1995) 'Führungskräfte im Spiegelbild ihrer Mitarbeiter', *Personalführung*, 12/95.

Herrmann, L. (1995) 'Arbeitszeitflexibilisierung – Wegbereiter für die Organisationsentwicklung?', *Personal*, 11/95.

Hillen, J. (1995) 'Durchführung von Benchmarking-Projekten', *Die Bank*, 12/95.

Holst, E. and Schupp, J. (1994) 'Erwerbsbeteiligung und Erwerbsorientierung von Frauen in West- und Ostdeutschland 1990–1993', Diskussionspapier Nr 90, edited by the DIW, Berlin.

Hopfenbeck, W. and Willig, M. (1995) *Umweltorientiertes Personalmanagement: Umweltbildung, Motivation, Mitarbeiterkommunikation*, Landsberg am Lech.

IAO (Fraunhofer Institut für Arbeitswissenschaft und Organisation) (1995a) 'Business Reengineering steht an erster Stelle', *Personalwirtschaft*, 8/95.

IAO (Fraunhofer Institut für Arbeitswirtschaft und Organisation) (1995b) 'Best in Class – Personalarbeit', *Personalwirtschaft*, 10/95.

ISO (Institut zur Erforschung sozialer Chancen) (1994) *Arbeitszeit 93. Arbeitszeiten und Arbeitszeitwünsche*, Köln.

IW (Institut der deutschen Wirtschaft) (ed.) (1995) *Zahlen zur wirtschaftlichen Entwicklung der Bundesrepublik Deutschland*, Köln.

Kammel, A. and Teichelmann, D. (1994) *Internationaler Personaleinsatz*, München, Wien.

Kierysch, P.V. (1995) 'Prozeßoptimierung – Veränderungen der Organisationsstrukturen', in Rosenstiel, L. von., Regnet, E. and Domsch, M. (eds) *Führung von Mitarbeitern, Handbuch für erfolgreiches Personalmanagement*, third revised and enlarged edn, Stuttgart.

Kobel, G. (1991) *Die Interdependenz zwischen Wirtschaft und Technik*, Ludwigsburg, Berlin.

Köhler, A. (1995) 'Re-engineering der Auftragsabwicklung bei der Deutschen Aerospace AG', *CONTROLLING*, September/October 1995.

Kreuz, W. (1994) 'Benchmarking: Voraussetzung für den Erfolg von TQM', in Mehdorn, H. and Töpfer, A. (eds) *Besser – schneller – schlanker: TQM-Konzepte in der Unternehmenspraxis*, Neuwied, Kriftel, Berlin.

Küpper, G. (1994) 'Personalentwicklung für weibliche Führungskräfte', *Zeitschrift für Personal* 2/1994.

Kuhn, K. (1992) 'Betriebliche Gesundheitsförderung – Stand und Perspektiven', in Trojan, A. and Stumm, B. (eds) *Gesundheit fördern statt kontrollieren. Eine Absage an den Mustermenschen* Frankfurt/Main.

Lang, R. (1995) 'Personalwesen im Osten vor und nach der Wende', in Wächter, H. and Metz, T. (eds) *Professionalisierte Personalarbeit? Perspektiven der Professionalisierung des Personalwesens*, München, Mering.

Lenz, F. (1996) 'Deutschland hinkt bei der Telearbeit hinterher', in *Weser Kurier*, 10 February 1996.

Maurer, R. (1996) 'Personalarbeit im welweiten Verleich', in *Personalführung*, 3/96.

McKinsey & Company (1994) *Zusammenhänge, Teilen und Gewinnen. Das Potential der flexiblen Arbeitszeitverkürzung*, München.

Mollet, G.S. and Egger, P. (1995) 'Das VW-Konzept', in *Personalwirtschaft*, 10/95.

Myrdal, A. and Klein, V. (1971) *Die Doppelrolle der Frau in Familie und Beruf*, Köln, Bonn.

Nieder, P. and Harms, M. (1995) *Betriebliche Gesundheitsförderung; Anforderungen, Umsetzung, Erfolgsfaktoren*, in *Personalführung*, 5/95.

Niejahr, E. (1995) 'Eine unheilige Allianz. Mancher Unternehmer ist umweltbewußter als Bonns Regierende', in Spiegel special, 2/1995.

n.n. (1995a) 'Re-engineering unter der Lupe', in Der Betriebswit, 1/95.

n.n. (1995b) 'Countdown für Deutschland', in Der Spiegel, 51/1995.

n.n. (1996a) 'Schlagwort des Monats: Empowerment', in management and seminar 1/96.

n.n. (1996b) 'Das TOTAL E-QUALITY Prädikat', *Newsletter of the European Commission – Positive Action Co-ordinating Group*, No. 3, 2/1996.

n.n. (1996c) 'Unteres Management skeptisch gegenüber flexiblen Arbeitszeiten', *Handelsblatt*, 19.01.96.

North, K. (1992) 'Environmental Business Management: An Introduction', *Management Development Series* No. 30, Geneva, ILO.

Oechsler, W.A. (1994) 'Das Arbeitsrecht steckt in der Krise', *Personalwirtschaft*, Jubiläumsheft 1994.

Opaschowski, H.W. (1993) 'Von der Pflichterfüllung zur Lebenserfüllung', *Personalführung*, 3/93.

Osten, M. and Sander, P. (1996) 'Benchmarking – ein Erfahrungsbericht', *REFA-Nachrichten* 3/1996.

Osterloh, M. and Oberholzer, K. (1994) 'Der geschlechtsspezifische Arbeitsmarkt: Ökonomische und soziologische Erklärungsansätze', *Aus Politik und Zeitgeschichte*, Vol. 6.

Pauwels, A. (1993) 'Maßgeschneiderte Gesundheitsprogramme', speech at the conference 'Gesundheit am Arbeitsplatz, Wohlbefinden und Leistung steigern – Kosten reduzieren', 23–24 November 1993 in Frankfurt am Main (organiser: Blick durch die Wirtschaft/Institut für Medienentwicklung und Kommunikation).

Pieske, R. (1995) 'Den besten Wettbewerber finden', *Gablers Magazin*, 2/95.

Prieß, J. (1995) 'Unpräzise Regelung der Arbeitszeit', speech at the conference 'Flexibilisierung der Arbeitszeit: Patentlösung für die Zukunft?', 31 August 1995 in Göttingen (organiser: Gothaer Versicherungen).

Regnet, E. (1995) 'Der Weg in die Zukunft – Neue Anforderungen an die Führungskraft', in Rosenstiel, L. von, Regnet, E. and Domsch, M. (eds) *Führung von Mitarbeitern, Handbuch für erfolgreiches Personalmanagement*, third revised and enlarged edn, Stuttgart.

Roemheld, B. (1995) 'Flexible Arbeitszeiten, Das Beispiel Open', *WiST*, 12/95.

Rosenstiel, L. von (1993) 'Wandel in der Karrieremotivation – Neuorientierungen in den 90er Jahren', in Rosenstiel, L. von, Djarrahzadeh, M., Einsiedler, H.E. and Streich, R.K. (eds) *Wertewandel, Herausforderung für die Unternehmenspolitik in den 90er Jahren*, second revised edn, Stuttgart.

Rosenstiel, L. von (1995) 'Motivation von Mitarbeitern', in Rosenstiel, L. von, Regnet, E. and Domsch, M. (eds) *Führung von Mitarbeitern, Handbuch für erfolgreiches Personalmanagement*, third revised and enlarged edn, Stuttgart.

Sarges, W. (1992) 'Veränderungen von Organisationsstrukturen und ihr Einfluß auf das Personalmanagement', in Kienbaum, J. (ed.) (1992) *Visionäres Personalmanagement*, Stuttgart.

Schanz, G. (1992) 'Flexibilisierung und Individualisierung als strategische Elemente der Personalpolitik', in Kienbaum, J. (ed.) (1992) *Visionäres Personalmanagement*, Stuttgart.

Schenk, S. (1990) 'Die Situation erwerbstätiger Frauen in der DDR', *Sozialer Fortschritt*, 6/1990.

Scherm, E. (1996) 'Sonderprobleme des Führungskräfte-Transfers in osteuropäische Reformländer', in Marchazina, K. and Wolf, J. (eds) *Handbuch Internationales Führungskräfte-Management*, Stuttgart, Berlin, Bonn.

Schnelldienst 3/96 *Stärken und Schwächen Deutschlands im internationalen Wettbewerb um Einkommen und Arbeitsplätze*.

Scholz, C. (1994) *Personalmanagement*, fourth revised edn, München.

Scholz, C. and Djarrahzadeh, M. (eds) (1995) *Strategisches Personalmanagement, Konzeptionen und Realisationen*, Stuttgart.

Schonberger, R.J. (1994) 'Human Resource Management: Lessons from a Decade of Total Quality Management and Re-engineering', *California Management Review*, 4/1994, Vol. 36.

Schramm, F. and Schlese, M. (1995) 'Beschäftigte wünschen auch in den Neunziger Jahren kürzere Arbeitszeiten', *Personal*, 11/95.

Schreyögg, G. and Noss, C. (1995) 'Organisatorischer Wandel: Von der Organisationsentwicklung zur lernenden Organisation', *Die Betriebswirtschaft*, 55, 2/1995.

Schusser, W.H. (1995) 'Mitarbeiter – Unternehmen im Unternehmen', in Heidack, C. (ed.) *Arbeitsstrukturen im Umbruch*, Festschrift für Prof. Dr. h.c. Friedrich Fürstenberg, München.

Schwarze, J., Gornig, M. and Steinhöfel, M. (1990) 'Die Bedeutung der Frauenerwerbstätigkeit für die Einkommensverteilung in beiden deutschen Staaten', *Arbeit und Sozialpolitik*, 6/1990.

Seidel, E. (1989) '"Wollen" und "Können" – Auf dem Wege zu einer ökologisch verpflichteten Unternehmensführung', *zfo (Zeitschrift für Führung und Organisation)* 2/1989.

Sobull, D. (1996) 'Mitarbeiter auf der Datenautobahn stehen nicht im Stau', *Die Welt (Berufswelt)*, 13 January 1996.

Sohn, G. (1996) 'Erfolgs- und Mißerfolgsindikatoren für Führungsnachwuchs – Woran sollten wir uns orientieren? – am Beispiel der AUDI AG, Ingolstadt', speech at the conference 'Analytik' in Hamburg, 25–26 January 1996 (organiser: Consulectra Unternehmensberatung GmbH).

Stabenau, H.-J. (1995) 'Schlüsselqualifikationen als Schlüssel zum Lean-Learning (am Beispiel eines betrieblichen Verhaltenstrainings für Jungingenieure)', in Geißler, H. (1995) (ed.) *Lean Management und PE*, Frankfurt.

Staehle, W.H. (1992) 'Das Bild vom Arbeitnehmer im Wandel der Arbeitgeber-Arbeitnehmer-Beziehungen', *ZfB*, 2/92.

Staffelbach, B. (1995) 'Strategisches Personalmarketing (Überblick)', in Scholz, C. and Djarrahzadeh, M. (eds) *Strategisches Personalmanagement*, Stuttgart.

Steger, U. (1995) 'Umweltorientierung von Unternehmen – Aufgaben für die Personalführung', in Rosenstiel, L. von, Regnet, E. and Domsch, M. (eds) *Führung von Mitarbeitern, Handbuch für erfolgreiches Personalmanagement*, third revised and enlarged edn, Stuttgart.

Steinle, C., Lawa, D. and Schollenberg, A. (1994) 'Ökologieorientierte Unternehmensführung – Ansätze, Integrationskonzept und Entwicklungsperspektiven', *ZfU*, 4/94.

Stengel, M. (1995) 'Wertewandel', in Rosenstiel, L. von, Regnet, E. and Domsch, M. (eds) *Führung von Mitarbeitern, Handbuch für erfolgreiches Personalmanagement*, third revised and enlarged edn, Stuttgart.

Stephan, H. and Wiedemann, E. (1990) 'Lohnstruktur und Lohndifferenz in der DDR: Ergebnisse der Lohndatenerfassung vom September 1988', *Mitteilungen zur Arbeitsmarkt- und Berufsforschung*, 4/1990.

Strümpel, B., Wilkens, U. and Pawlowski, P. (1995) 'Arbeitszeitflexibilisierung durch Teilzeit', in Rosenstiel, L. von, Regnet, E. and Domsch, M. (eds), *Führung von Mitarbeitern, Handbuch für erfolgreiches Personalmanagement*, third revised and enlarged edn, Stuttgart.

Strunz, H. (1990) 'Ökologieorientierte Unternehmensführung', *io Management Zeitschrift* 59/1990, No. 7/8.

Süssmuth, R. (1995) 'Variable Arbeitszeiten: Sind Frauen und Familie die Verlierer?', speech at the conference 'Flexibilisierung der Arbeitszeit: Patentlösung für die Zukunft?', 31 August 1995 in Göttingen (organiser: Gothaer Versicherungen).

Töpfer, A. (1994) 'Personalmanagement 2004', *Personalwirtschaft*, Jubiläumsheft 1994.

Töpfer, A. (1995) 'Kunden-Zufriedenheit durch Mitarbeiter-Zufriedenheit', *Personalwirtschaft*, 8/95.

Töpfer, A. and Poersch, M. (1989) *Aufgabenfelder des betrieblichen Personalwesens für die 90er Jahre*, Neuwied/Frankfurt.

Töpfer, K. (1995) 'Vorsorge als Leitlinie, Umweltschutz muß alle Lebensbereiche durchdringen', *Spiegel special*, 2/1995.

Vester, F. (1989) *Leitmotiv vernetztes Denken, Für einen besseren Umgang mit der Welt*, second edn, München.

Voigt, B. (1992) 'Betriebliche Gesundheitsvorsorge, Aktuelle Aspekte der Arbeits- und Präventivmedizin im Betrieb', *Personalführung*, 7/1992.

Voß, K.-D. (1990) 'Voraussetzung und Organisationsformen einer betrieblichen Gesundheits-förderpolitik', in *Gesundheitsförderung – Investition für die Zukunft*, international conference, supplementary Vol. 1 to the conference report, Bonn.

Wächter, H. and Metz, T. (1995) 'Die DGFP zwischen Wissenschaft und Praxis. Interview mit dem Geschäftsführer der DGFP, Dr Hans Böhm', in Wächter, H. and Metz, T. (eds) *Professionalisierte Personalarbeit? Perspektiven der Professionalisierung des Personalwesens*, München, Mering.

Wagner, D. (1986) 'Möglichkeiten und Grenzen von Cafeteria-Systemen in der Bundesrepublik Deutschland', *BFuP*, 37, 1986.

Wagner, D. (1989) *Organisation, Führung und Personalmanagement – Neue Perspektiven durch Flexibilisierung und Individualisierung*, Freiburg.

Walz, D. (1995) 'Der schwierige Weg bis zur Jahrtausendwende', *Personalführung*, 7/95.

Weidinger, M. (1995a) 'Arbeitszeitmodelle in der Praxis: Wettbewerbsverbesserung oder ökonomischer Hemmschuh?', speech at the conference 'Flexibilisierung der Arbeitszeit: Patentlösung für die Zukunft?', 31 August 1995 in Göttingen (organiser: Gothaer Versicherungen).

Weidinger, M. (1995b) 'Strategien zur Arbeitszeitflexibilisierung', in Rosenstiel, L. von, Regnet, E. and Domsch, M. (eds) *Führung von Mitarbeitern, Handbuch für erfolgreiches Personalmanagement*, third revised and enlarged edition, Stuttgart.

Weitbrecht, H (1995) 'Entwicklungstendenzen betrieblicher Arbeitsbezichungen in Deutschland, Heidack, Clemens (ed.): *Arbeitsstruktwen in Umbruch – Festschrift für Friedrich Fürstenberg*, München.

Westermayer, G. and Bähr, B. (eds) (1994) *Betriebliche Gesundheitszirkel*, Göttingen.

Winter, G. (1995) 'Verblüffende Chancen. Der Umweltschutz schafft neue Märkte', *Spiegel special*, 2/1995.

Wolffgang, R. (1996) 'Mit Personalcontrolling zur effektiven. Personalarbeit', *Personalführung*, 4/96.

Wunderer, R. (1992) 'Internationalisierung als strategische Herausforderung für das Personalmanagement', *ZfB-Ergänzungsheft*, 2/92.

Wunderer, R. and Kuhn, T. (1993) *Unternehmerisches Personalmanagement – Konzepte, Prognosen und Strategien für das Jahr 2000*, Frankfurt am Main.

Zinken, H. (ed) (1992) *High Tech Atlas: Märkte, Branche, Programme*, Düsseldorf.

STRATEGIC HUMAN RESOURCES MANAGEMENT IN FRANCE: KEY ISSUES

Frank Bournois

Over the last 20 years France has ranked higher in the world economy, in fourth place for its overall economy and also in the fourth place as exporter. The country's per capita wealth has also increased considerably, as is shown in Table 14.1. France is also the number 2 investor in the world, just behind the United States; it was equal with Germany in 1992 and with the United Kingdom in 1993. French companies employ more than 2.3 million people abroad, within 14 000 subsidiaries.

Table 14.1 Gross domestic product per capita (in constant dollars)

	1960		1991	
1	United States	9983	United States	22 130
2	Switzerland	9313	Switzerland	21 780
3	Canada	7758	Luxembourg	20 800
4	New Zealand	7222	Germany	19 770
5	Australia	7204	Japan	19 390
6	Luxembourg	6970	Canada	19 320
7	Sweden	6483	**France**	18 430
8	United Kingdom	6370	Denmark	17 880
9	Germany	6038	Austria	17 690
10	Denmark	5900	Belgium	17 510
11	The Netherlands	5587	Sweden	17 490
12	Norway	5443	Iceland	17 480
13	Iceland	5352	Norway	17 170
14	**France**	5344	Italy	17 040
15	Belgium	5207	The Netherlands	16 820
16	Finland	4718	Australia	16 680
17	Austria	4476	United Kingdom	16 340
18	Italy	4375	Finland	16 130
19	Israel	3958	New Zealand	13 970
20	Ireland	3214	Israel	13 460

But essentially, France is still an industrialised country, which means that abroad more than two employees out of three work in industry and the ten groups in Table 14.2 employ one-third of this total number.

Table 14.2   Ten biggest French companies/groups abroad

Ranking at 31.12.92	Employees abroad (in thousands)
1 Alcaltel-Alsthom	120
2 Accor	108
3 Michelin	92
4 Lyonnaise des Eaux-Dumez	85
5 Saint-Gobain	67
6 Générale des Eaux	64
7 Thomson	64
8 Suez	55
9 Schneider	46
10 Rhône-Poulenc	46
Total	747

In this chapter, I focus on the way human energies are mobilised within French companies by investigating certain specific characteristics of their management. After a bout of recession towards the middle of 1990, striking later than it did in Great Britain, France was shaken by an unemployment rate of 12.3 per cent in the spring of 1994, a level that had never been reached before. Since the summer of 1994, business activity has stepped up greatly and fewer small and medium-sized firms have gone to the wall while large groups have improved their results and merger and acquisition operations have been much more frequent. All this points to increasing economic prosperity. All the same, it would be naive to believe that all our unemployment problems have been solved, even though there has been a staunching of the wound. The recovery of companies which have used the recession to free themselves from debt is wholly dependent on a rise in the investment rate which reached an all-time low in 1993 of less than 16 per cent. According to a detailed study carried out by two economists to define the economic status of France, it is regrettable that 'the emphasis placed by French conventions and institutions on breaking into the industrial world may well have made it more difficult for them to break into other possible worlds' (Salais and Storper, 1994) and particularly into the world of services with its 8.9 million employees, which is a sector that does create jobs – more than 52 700 during the first quarter of 1994.

In this relatively concise chapter meant for those who are not specialists in human resource management in France, I analyse the interface between human resource management/corporate strategy, and highlight specifically French characteristics.

The arguments presented in this chapter are backed up with authentic illustrations taken from actual social and economic business situations experienced by top managers, as reported particularly in the specialised pages of the newspaper *Le Monde*.

It will be shown that certain laws recently enacted lay down the rules of the social game more than seems obvious at first sight. While fully covering the essential contribution provided by the law, care has been taken not to founder and drown in the murky waters of legalism.

An ongoing vision of strategic human resource management

It was during the 1980s that the business world gained in prestige in the eyes of the French and this, curiously enough, took place under a socialist government in an atmosphere which dismayed businessmen (particularly in 1982) with nationalisations, reducing the working week to 39 hours, the mandatory granting of a fifth week of paid holidays, the pegging of prices, the significant re-evaluation of the SMIC (the legal minimum wage paid across the board), and so on. Once the country had got clear of the rigours of the years 1984/1985 and after the employers had obtained three liberties – the freedom to fix their own prices, the unpegging of exchange rates and the freedom to hire and fire which came when compulsory government authorisation for all cases of dismissal was done away with – economic growth surged ahead and the overall financial situation proved to be very satisfactory.

Does a French form of management exist?

Just as a European management *gestalt* exists (Brewster and Bournois, 1992) which is relatively distinct from the American one, so it is possible to distinguish different *gestalts* or different forms typical of French management (Barsoux and Lawrence, 1991). A study carried out in 1994 by the very well-known firm Bernard Brunhes Consultants aims to explain the world of work in Europe or how other countries faced up to the shocks and tremors in their economies. The analyses are based on 57 large companies, 17 professional and trade union organisations and 18 survey and research institutions which agreed to grant us detailed interviews. These organisations are to be found in six countries of the European Union (Germany, Spain, France, Great Britain, Italy and Holland) and they represent six different fields of business activity: banking and insurance, the automobile, the chemical and the electronic industries, as well as agribusiness and large-scale retailing. In fact, the authors maintain that job management systems and methods resemble each other even when the industrial relations systems are extremely different. Faced with economic constraints and similar problems, such as the transnational integration of production units within large groups, subcontracting different activities, homeworking, the wild enthusiasm for working time 'à la carte' (*temps choisi* in French), the involvement of the company in the local social context and so on, the upshot of it all is that the German model gives proof of its innate capacity to adapt more readily than the French system which is still fraught with inadequate internal flexibility and lack of new, more supple management techniques in a system of institutions, laws and social relationships which finds it very difficult to free itself from its traditional values. The case of Air France discussed later in the chapter is an excellent illustration of this.

In short, the strategic management of resources and employment may be characterised by the following statements for the six countries under consideration:

- Germany or 'the advantages of a model passing through a period of structural mutation';
- Spain or 'a world in which human resources management is weighed down with constraints';

281

- Italy or 'a labour market which is loosening up steadily and growing gradually more flexible';
- Holland or 'flexibility already achieved';
- Great Britain or 'the ultimate limits of flexibility and the appearance of a certain precariousness'; and
- France or 'the difficult quest for internal flexibility' since the law exerts a great influence on social change (cf. our discussion of the Five-Year Law, pp. 292–5).

Other research has clearly revealed the specificity of French management in a large number of ways (Barsoux and Lawrence, 1990; Bournois, 1992a) and a style of management which may be generally characterised by the term 'employee consultation', thus situating the country half way between the German codetermination and the extreme liberalism/voluntarism of the British (Roussillon and Bournois, 1993). And it is surely not by chance that Jacques Delors, the former President of the European Commission, when dealing with social policy referred continually to 'social dialogue', a concept which involves acquiring information and consulting with the different social partners. Later, the state of mind underlying the decision-making processes of French management is discussed more fully.

HRM is now fully recognised in France

Human resource management really came into its own in France towards the end of the 1980s. Before this, one spoke of staff management and the function of the personnel manager was essentially concerned with administration and social relations; it hardly existed as a discipline in management schools and one of the very first books to link this field with management dates from 1978 and is *Monsieur Personnel et le développement des hommes (Mister Personnel and Human Development)* (Laufer et al., 1978).

As time went by, the role of the human resources manager gained in importance, or at least lip-service was paid to it. In fact, when strategic management developed in the 1980s in contrast to the traditional planning tendency and began to take into account environmental considerations, those involved tried to link up their staff management tools and techniques to the corporate strategy, without always paying attention to its coherence with other aspects of the HRM function (Wright and McMahan, 1992, p. 298); hence the emergence of strategic recruiting, strategic training and strategic career management.

In 1987 there appeared in France, at the same time as Tyson (1987) in Great Britain was writing about the strategic mutations of the function of staff management, the first book on strategic resources management in which my colleague Ch-H. Besseyre des Horts suggested that business leaders should adapt their HRM practices to the type of strategy being adopted (see Table 14.3).

The roles of human resources managers grow progressively more important and an increasing number of them take their place on the board of directors. The statistics for 1992, revealed in the research published by Professor Brewster of Cranfield, give France as being the country where the highest percentage of HRM belong to the board of directors (Table 14.4).

But what does this motivation towards strategic management really indicate? An article (Bournois and Derr, 1994) published in the *Revue française de gestion* (the leading

Table 14.3   HRM practices according to type of strategy adopted

Type of strategy	Human resources needs	Adapted HRM measures
Entrepreneurial	• innovative personnel • flexible staff	• young employees, informal performance appraisal, attractive pay
Dynamic growth	• committed staff • co-operation within teams	• good potentials • career possibilities
Profit	• low cost personnel • giving priority to short term	• lowly qualified, equitable pay • specialised training
Divestment	• fewer workers • not necessarily faithful	• few recruitments • no appraisal, little training
Turnaround, redeployment	• flexible staff • involvement for the future	• departure of older employees • motivating pay linked to results

Source: adapted from Besseyre des Horts, 1987.

Table 14.4   Percentage of human resource directors belonging to the board of directors

in %	F	S	E	N	FIN	DK	UK	P	IRL	NL	T	D
HRD belongs to board of directors	84	84	73	71	61	49	49	46	44	42	37	30
HRD does not belong	12	15	23	24	38	39	47	46	38	54	60	67

French management review) with the provocative title of 'Les DRH ont-ils un avenir?' ('Is there any future for Human Resource Managers?') highlights the giant strides that the function of HRM has made. In France, as in other countries, each in its own specific way, the role of the human resource manager is developing from a functional role into a strategic-type role of which the main features are listed in Table 14.5.

However, human resource managers should think about the different paths they could choose in the future. Several possibilities are open to them:

a allow HRM to become more and more integrated into line management which will lead to its losing its specialised organisational function;
b develop their competence in technical areas in which line management's expertise will never be very strong, for example labour law, etc.;
c seize the opportunity offered by internal and external transformations described here and concentrate their efforts in such areas as complex project management where their regulation organisational skills will be appreciated. In this case, new types of work will be expected of them: human resource managers will be entrusted with projects leading to change; they will have clearly defined assignments to be carried out within time limits. Having become internal consultants, their dependence on the company will continue to grow, and it may well come about, in certain cases where knowledge of the company is not essential, that human resource managers (a designation which will have lost all relevance) will simply turn into external consultants to a number of companies.

Table 14.5   Developments noticed in the roles of human resource managers during the 1990s

	The 'functional' human resource manager	The HRM incorporated into the supposedly 'strategic' level
Specific priority actions	Recruitment, training, remuneration, industrial relations, and so on	Corporate strategy, corporate culture, internationalisation, staffing adjustments
Focus	Control of resource costs	Flexibility of resources . . . but cost control at the profit centre level
Orientation	Tactical action at the micro-organisational level	Strategic action at the macro-organisational level
The HRM's customers	The employees and line management	Line managers and outside customers
Power/status	Rather weak	Rather strong (due to assimilation to top management)
Training/background of the HRM	Specialised in HRM embracing other functions	General management-type HRM with operational experience or a line manager with significant experience in HRM
Profile	Specialist in management tools and systems	Generalist concerned with line management
Time-scale of activities	Short term	Medium or long term
Management style based on	Transactions	Organisational change/transformation

Source: Bournois and Derr, 1994.

The permeability of the internal and external boundaries of the company that they themselves have advocated will create awkward political difficulties as far as role definition is concerned. Having so emphasised flexibility at all costs, will human resource managers still retain control in certain ambivalent areas? In Michel Crozier's country, it may well be asked what powers managers will still retain! It is important to stress the fact that the possibilities listed above will not be identical in each European country. In countries where there is a strong tradition of negotiating with employees (in Germany and in the Scandinavian countries for example), it is more likely that the traditional role of the human resource manager will be maintained: compared to the English and German models, for instance, France is in an intermediary position.

Employment, that unknown quantity

Since 1990, HRM has left the beaten track and given more attention to employment problems. It is no longer merely a question of setting up the right tools and techniques to help the managers do their job or analysing management situations with reference to some particular sociological grid, but rather of helping all the members of the organisation to understand and resolve complex problems (Brabet, 1994). And this is no simple task. Some human resource managers 'have the blues', to use the title of an article that appeared in the press (*Le Monde*, 8 April 1994).

Several Parisian human resource managers met together, almost like a group of conspirators, in the suite of the chairman of a famous French group and confessed their doubts and misgivings to each other. No one was to know that they had met together. As Alain Lebaube, the business reporter of *Le Monde*, put it, they were 'almost schizophrenic'; having constantly to reduce staffing levels, they were greatly concerned by the catastrophic rise in unemployment. Logically, human resource managers should be rather more in favour of part-time working or the four-day week, but, at the same time, people who want to work less always seem a little suspect: 'his motivation is put into doubt and he is considered rather negatively because the system imposes that kind of reasoning'. And yet, they are the ones who are supposed to create the system. And it is difficult to remain confident when there are just so many doubts and dilemmas: individualisation or globalisation, flexibility or planning, involvement or exclusion and so on.

Liberty, equality, fraternity and other French paradoxes

Republican values – the basis of it all

The motto of the French Republic is 'Liberty, Equality, Fraternity'; it is seen on coins, on official documents, on everything. These basic values indelibly mark the history of the nation; they are quoted when times are hard. But yet, as we shall see, there are certain snags that seem like contradictions to the foreign observer.

In the world of work, the value 'liberty' shows through clearly for the employer in his freedom to do business, to organise his company, to choose his management team; and for the employee, there is freedom of expression, both individual and collective, with the employer through an elected representative group, without necessarily passing through the trade unions (due to the Auroux Laws passed in 1982).

The liberty and respect of one's private life is also assured by the Law Informatique et Liberté passed in 1978 which makes it obligatory to declare all official files, computerised or not, to the Commission Nationale Informatique et Liberté, including all personnel management files.

There are many examples of the value 'Equality' which shows up clearly in the life of the French people, be it in their free education system including university level studies, or in their taxation system which does away with inequalities by means of a tax on family fortunes of more than 4 million francs.

The value 'Fraternity' which implies mutual support is also evident in the life of the firm. Very early on, General de Gaulle wanted the employees to benefit from the profits made by the firm. And so a law was passed, making profit-sharing schemes compulsory in all firms with more than 50 employees. This law typified the prevailing spirit of sharing in common the fruits of everyone's labour. Contractual optional profit-sharing schemes, a typically French phenomenon, may be signed at the local level by employers and the representatives of the employees. These schemes allow the extra profits over and above the common participation to be shared out and define the objectives which have been agreed upon and which will be renegotiated as time goes on. Such objectives are the improvement of productivity, product quality, reducing waste of raw materials, and so on. These schemes, if well thought through and in keeping with the strategic objectives of the firm and if clearly explained to the employees, can prove to be an excellent means of motivation, above all in small and medium-sized companies. Recent statistics show that among the firms of more than 50 employees where employee participation is obligatory, it is those that are the most productive and that occupy the most confident places in their markets that have the greatest chance of setting up contractual profit-sharing agreements. On the other hand, in firms where employee participation is not obligatory, such agreements tend to be set up in less productive firms whose competitive position is more risky.

This spirit of solidarity (in France there is a Ministry of Social Affairs and Solidarity), which militates against social exclusion, is most evident in such measures as the common social service tax (*contribution sociale généralisée* in French) which is levied on all salaries and wages in order to finance, among other things, unemployment benefits and a portion of the Social Security deficit. Another example of this same tendency is when the employees of certain firms vote for their wages to be frozen or even reduced in exchange for maintaining staffing levels. The broadcasting of a TV Job Programme for three weeks during the spring of 1994 was part of the same spirit and set out to be a link between employment information and job seekers. The word 'link' implied friendship and commitment. And so the indignation felt by the nation as a whole can be easily understood when certain dismissal procedures used by HRM became known.

SKF with 1100 employees, a French subsidiary of a Swedish firm manufacturing ball-bearings, summoned 33 employees to inform them of their immediate dismissal and their obligation to leave the firm within the hour. They claimed that they had adopted this method of dismissal 'to avoid causing psychological disturbances' [sic]. The management had even gone to the extent of ordering taxis to take the dismissed workers to the state outplacement centre. Even if the legal requirements had been respected, the procedure adopted was so shocking that the Prime Minister, Edouard Balladur, expressed his disapproval. Since then, the court has ordered damages to be paid to the employees, even though the dismissal orders have not been cancelled. This method of dismissal has given rise to a great deal of discussion about the spirit of fraternity and what is inadmissible treatment of people; the affair recently hit the headlines again when the same firm had to take on another 23 people to meet the increase in orders – without calling upon any of those dismissed so abruptly. The management claimed that none of them had the required qualities or qualifications. Part of the agitation was also due to the fact that during 1994 business activity revived and the firm made its expected annual net result of 76 million by the end of September.

Other cases just as spectacular and unheard-of in a French context have taken place. For example, a subsidiary of Bosch, the CPAOC, a tool-making plant decided to close down a site employing 145 people. The management called up the union representative to inform him of this, and in the following few minutes, the information was broadcast by loudspeaker with an interpreter to all the workshops. The message also stated that the employees could be redeployed in another factory 60 kilometres away and that refusal to accept this offer would lead to dismissal for economic reasons.

Going against these deep-seated values only served to tarnish the image of the human resource department: now no one considers himself or herself safe. The same thing happened when Uniroyal France, a subsidiary of the German firm Continental, lost in production more than 200 000 tyres because of a strike in spite of a recovery, with their employees exasperated by the flexibility which had got out of control. One member of the strike picket described the situation in a nutshell: 'For years they have been asking us to tighten our belts. Till now we have kept our mouths shut to keep our jobs going. But now it seems business is picking up! Alright then, but we want our share, and not in any old way they want to give it to us!' Many human resource managers will have to manoeuvre very skilfully to get clear of this crisis and resolve this very tricky dilemma. When you come to the end of a planned redundancy scheme, how do you relaunch business activity to meet the so-called one-off orders without offering considerable compensation and without giving employees the impression that they have been taken in?

There are sometimes surprises

In spite of these sound values, French society also has certain characteristics that appear as almost contradictory. French companies are well known for being hierarchical and stratified – so where is the equality here? Authority is linked to the individual and to the post he or she holds but not necessarily to his or her competence. Laurent (1986) covers all this when he writes: 'being an efficient executive in France means managing power relationships and playing the system'.

The highly stratified education system tacitly encourages this attitude – as with the entrance examinations to the Grandes Ecoles, the professions and the categories laid down by the press. Within the field of HRM, all the weight given to the concept of managerial potential is immediately obvious (Roussillon and Bournois, 1993).

France is one of the few countries which distinguishes so clearly between the executive and the non-executive (Bournois, 1991, 1992b), to the extent that everyone can be placed precisely in one category or the other. The executive category corresponds to a kind of 'nobility'; for certain supervisory staff to reach executive status is a lifelong ambition. For the first time since its creation 60 years ago, this executive category is suffering unemployment and its numbers even decreased by almost 1 per cent in 1993. What is worse, the unemployment rate in this category has increased threefold in four years and to become a member is now more and more difficult. Marie-Odile Paulet, the General Secretary of the Confederated Union of Executives of the CFDT, one of the five large trade union groups, made this point very well when she said: 'Whereas half of the executives now working did not begin their professional life as executives, the young people entering the labour market now must have done at least four years of university level to qualify for this category.' The conclusion to be drawn from this is that on-the-job promotion has come to a standstill (*Le Monde*, 10 February 1994).

Because of these inequalities in practice, the great national principles are called upon to justify and regulate the day-to-day situations: among the most obvious of these principles are honour (cf. the work of Iribarne mentioned further on), meritocracy and the exceptional case principle (which only confirms the rule). For example, elitist, non-egalitarian practices are justified on the basis of merit, which is supported by the fact that competition assures an equality of opportunity. To deal with a sense of injustice that is sometimes felt, there is often a back way in for a certain limited number of border-line cases, which proves that the system is not as ruthless as it looks! A certain very limited number of places in the very prestigious, highly selective Grandes Ecoles like l'ENA (The National School of Administration) or Polytechnique are reserved for a few extra-muros candidates. Thus at l'ENA certain trade union officials, heads of associations or elected representatives have in theory a certain number of places allotted to them, though they are rarely filled in practice.

Sometimes the tensions built up can lead to serious public demonstrations when the basic principles seem threatened.

> The Balladur government passed two decrees in February 1994 defining the 'contrat d'insertion professionnelle (CIP)' which was a measure taken to encourage the drawing up of short-term work contracts for young people less than 26 years of age, who would be trained in the company by a tutor and paid 80 per cent of the SMIC (the minimum legal wage). This decree was to apply to young graduates with a two-year degree who had been unemployed for at least six months. By this measure the government meant to set up a system of job creation, presuming that firms would offer full-time employment to those who proved themselves worthwhile. This project had to be withdrawn by the government after a great deal of public demonstration. The symbolic significance of this scheme can be very easily understood, since a lot of French people identified themselves with these young people. They saw it as a young people's SMIC. The scheme was interpreted as a means of paying lower-than-legal wages. Furthermore, the CIP concerned young graduates, which represented a break with the traditional social structure; how, indeed, could society accept that young people with a diploma be less well treated than those without any qualification? The government's counter-argument that the company was investing in training and supplying a tutor was met with taunts and sarcastic remarks about the lack of training of the tutors!

Let us take, as a final example, a proposal rather astute in itself but probably doomed to failure before it gets off the ground. In the French town and country planning context, where economic forces are unequally distributed, the employers' association have made quite a number of proposals to the government. They have suggested doing away with the idea of a uniform minimum salary (SMIC), since, they claim, it guarantees a uniform purchasing power, and since the purchasing power varies with the place of residence, the fact that labour costs are the same throughout the country is an absurdity. The violent protestations in the name of the sacrosanct equality among Frenchmen that such a measure would meet with can well be imagined!

In short, while emphasising the important role played by the rules (the legal codes), we must insist upon the significance of the informal and instinctive level of behaviour which alone can provide the necessary flexibility when the rules weigh too heavily: labour laws are legion, but firms rarely commit their HRM policies to paper (Brewster and Hegewisch, 1994).

The world in which Iribarne's principle of honour (1994) prevails is a comfortable world to live in. And though the French have disgarded the notion of an inherited aristocracy (like the one that existed before the Revolution of 1789), they are so profoundly attached to an aristocracy of merit and talent that the state rewards with its numerous decorations, such as the Légion d'honneur and le Mérite National. According to

Philippe d'Iribarne (1994), the driving force behind people's actions and behaviour patterns is this principle of honour, which Montesquieu wrote about as early as the middle of the eighteenth century. He claims also that these frames of reference cannot be interpreted as the consequence of institutional specificities, but rather as the source of such specificities (Iribarne, 1994, p. 94). And so it is important when dealing with a Frenchman to understand what to him and to the social group he belongs to is considered noble and what is considered less noble. Certain subtle observers have even suggested that it is possible to manipulate the Frenchman by playing upon these principles if they are well understood. In Table 14.6 several noble and less noble features have been suggested.

Table 14.6 Behaviour considered noble and less noble

Noble	Less noble
• reflection, analysis	• action, construction
• rapid professional career (young achiever)	• slow professional career (routine promotion)
• prestige from diplomas	• self-made man
• references from well-known top managers	
• technical functions (for an engineer)	• administrative functions
• scientific studies	
• verbal eloquence	• factual communication
• being at the centre (for example in Paris)	• being at the periphery (for example, in the provinces)

Thus, it is easy to understand the cultural shock that would be experienced if a foreign firm appointed as Head of its French subsidiary a self-made man or woman who had proved his or her worth in a provincial factory . . . .

To complete this discussion on how profoundly the French feel their national identity emphasis is given to a final characteristic: their very real national pride, but at the same time, their strong feeling of belonging in Europe. An extensive study sponsored by the European Commission (see Fig 14.1) shows clearly that the French, like the Italians, are among those who feel their European identity most strongly. The British feel the least European.

The place of the state and the importance of the law

A rapid or careless reading of the following text could lead to misunderstanding. This was not a human resource manager addressing the employees of his or her firm; it was the then President of the French Republic, François Mitterrand, expressing his seasonal greetings to the French people. This text in itself is sufficient to understand the role that the state attributes to itself in the economic and social life of the country.

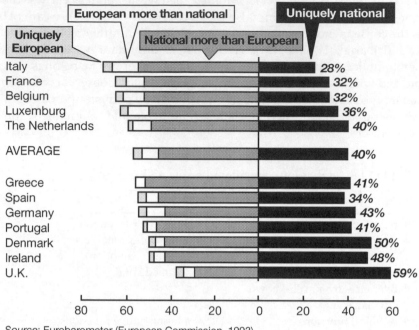

% of respondents who see themselves with an identity that is:

Source: Eurobarometer (European Commission, 1993)

Fig 14.1   European identity of the various EU countries

> My dear Fellow-Citizens, 1993 is almost over. . . . How dearly I should like to see so much effort rewarded in 1994 in such areas as unemployment, working conditions and organisation, housing and social security. These are the areas that cause so much worry and suffering to so many French people – these, and the fight against AIDS. And is it not unbearable to see powerful companies making vast profits, which in itself is not a bad thing, while the workers and the executives who have created these profits, may be at any moment suddenly laid off? No national economy is sound if there is no social cohesion. Will the economic recovery that is predicted lead to a fall in unemployment? We cannot be sure of this. The time has now come for employers' associations and trade unions to work out together as quickly as possible the foundations of a new social contract to guarantee employment. The State must lend its support. I hope that one of its main concerns will be to put an end to this tragic increase in loss of jobs to which more and more wage and salary earners are falling victim. . . .
>
> François Mitterrand, Paris, 31 December 1993

When President Chirac (right wing) was elected in May 1995 he fought with the same energy as President Mitterand, Monsieur Alain Juppé (in place since Chirac's election) even created a special Ministry for Employment.

The state as the great arbiter

Since Louis XI who in the second half of the fifteenth century began to centralise the national administration, the state has played a leading role. A second fillip was given during the First Empire by Napoleon who founded a number of great institutions, such as the Civil Code, the University, and the Supreme Court of Appeal (Cour de Cassation).

France is one of the few countries to develop a national strategy by means of a Five-Year Plan. Even Jean Gandois, who is currently the President of the CNPF (the National Confederation of French Employers) wrote in the preface to the report 'Compétitivité française' on the eleventh Five-Year Plan (1993–7): 'It would be futile for a country to have individually keenly competitive companies, if they were to be then crushed directly or indirectly by social charges to sustain the retired and the out-of-work.'

Since the end of the Second World War, the state has wanted to stimulate the economy by nationalising companies in certain sensitive sectors, such as energy, transport, the chemical industry, armament, banking and insurance, among others. The presence of the state makes itself felt there largely through its being a shareholder, but also through the appointing of high-ranking public servants to posts of responsibility, even though changes of appointment corresponding to changes of government require a certain getting used to. In those companies which are in a competitive sector, HRM is by and large similar to what it is in private companies where job security is fairly certain. As well as public companies, the great public services such as EDF-GDF (the Electricity and Gas Company of France), the SNCF (the French National Railway Organisation) and la Poste (the Post Office with 270 000 employees) must be taken into account. In this second category of organisations, HRM has not passed the crawling stage: cultural change is extremely difficult to bring about and there have been countless attempts at reform that have failed. The third category concerns state administered organisations (the Treasury, the University, Defence and Justice) as well as Health which is assimilated to the state. Also there are the local government bodies at regional, departmental and commune level. Human resource management observes the tenets of the public service statute – job security, appointment by competitive examination, promotion by competitive examination and seniority; remuneration is hardly ever based on performance and for identical qualifications remuneration is considerably less than in the private sector. It must also be noted that public servants do not come under the standard labour law code. All these organisations linked directly or indirectly to the state must observe all the points of social legislation punctiliously and often serve as testing-grounds for the government in office.

The number of privatisations increased under the Balladur government. A vast series of privatisations which recently took place was so appealing to the French that there were maximum amounts of shares that one could buy as an individual every time the state sold off a company. In all, 21 French groups in various sectors of the economy such as industry, banking and insurance, transport, and so on were sold off to the public in the two years between 1993 and 1995. All this is happening calmly and steadily without appointing a Monsieur Privatisation as Great Britain did with Peter Levene at the head of the Efficiency Unit. A law passed in July 1993 provides specific protection for national investment – non-European Union investors cannot hold more than 20 per cent of the capital of privatised companies. In selling these companies, more than 77 billion francs will go to the state. Among the companies sold, we find (in chronological order): CLF (Crédit Local de France), Banque Nationale de Paris, Rhône-Poulenc, Elf Aquitaine and AGF (Assurances Générales de France).

Another characteristic of the French system is seen in the management of the large firms. Two French academics, Michel Bauer and Bénédicte Bertin-Mourot, speak in terms of an exclusive managerial caste and the results of their research are most interesting. There are three ways of reaching the higher management echalons of a company be it public or private:

1. by owning capital;
2. by making one's career within the company;
3. by passing through the right channels in the state which are the important decision-making bodies and the appropriate ministries.

Many foreigners find it surprising that this third way in is the most common in France. Out of the 100 leading firms, 44 per cent have recruited their top managers from the state, 33 per cent were appointed because of the capital they hold and for about 20 per cent it was the culmination of their career. It is obvious that this fact has great influence on the development of strategy and in particular on the knowledge that the leader has or has not of that particular area, as far as management is concerned.

A 1993 government commission, proposed a reform of the functioning of the state, emphasised this point clearly: 'In France, today, there is a real demand for State involvement [...] We need this form of spiritual unity which is necessary for a people to survive in History and in keeping with our own peculiar tradition, we expect this unity to come, above all, from the State.'

Major changes in legislation in 1994: the Five-Year Law for employment

Legal enactments are often condemned for their ponderousness. They can quickly lose their relevance for the firm, so varied and unstable business situations tend to be. But it must be admitted that such laws serve the important purpose of regulating and binding the society together. They enable problems to be broached, to be discussed in Parliament, to take into account the opinions of labour and management, to get reports written, and, in short, to see to the maturing and perfecting of projects in hand. The French greatly value the referendum process; in the case of the Treaty of Maastricht, each elector received a complete copy at his home address.

The Five-Year Law is an enormous undertaking which is meant to relaunch the economy and the job market. It is called the Five-Year Law ('loi quinquennale') because it is supposed to redeploy employment with objectives over a period of five years (confirming the planning attitude of the French).

This law, passed on 20 December 1993, contains approximately 80 decrees. For a summary of the measures presented by the government, see the report presented by M. Balladur after one year in office (Balladur, 1994). The main measures are the following:

1. A policy to deal with unemployment: a five-year law conceived to make 'the mechanisms and the regulations more flexible, while maintaining the essential rights of the employee'. It is presented as a most important attempt at modernisation without threatening the rights of the wage and salary earner.
2. A special tax on salaries was increased in order to compensate for the deficit of the Social Security Fund; the Generalised Social Contribution (CSG) was increased by 1.3 per cent.
3. Helping small businesses and boosting their development. Also helping to start up

new businesses by granting aid – especially if it is an unemployed person setting up a business.

4. Reducing social contributions paid by employers for wages up to 1.2 times the minimum wage. Employers' contributions to family allowance grants have been done away with or decreased in the case of these same wage levels. Employers' contributions are no longer required for a first employee and there has also been an easing in corporation contributions.

5. Special measures are provided for training, especially of young staff. Substantial budgets have been made available
   - to encourage the training of young unqualified people: the orientation contract, the qualification contract and the adaptation contract;
   - to maintain employment by increasing the number of hours and the hourly rate paid by the state during short-time working; and
   - to combat chronic cases of unemployment with more than 650 000 job-solidarity contracts in 1993, which represented a financial effort of 8 billion francs.

6. To create a 'service-cheque' system which enables anyone to hire any short-term employee for household work. Instead of using undeclared people, you buy a book of cheques corresponding to hours of work and you give the cheque to the employee who can cash it very easily. In this case, everything is legal and easy for all concerned: the employee is declared, social contributions are paid in advance, the service is attractive, unskilled employment is boosted. Since the system deals with the social contributions, the employee can be paid without forms and pay slips.

7. Boosting professional insertion by means of
   - the return to work contract which enables the long-term unemployed to find a job exempt from employers' social charges for the first nine months; and
   - gradually transferring the administrative responsibility for apprenticeships and professional training to the Regional Authorities by 1999.

8. Changing the conception of working time
   - encouraging employers and labour through consultation to organise work differently, which could bring about new developments such as the annualisation of working time. Since the spring of 1994, the employer can vary working time over all or part of the year with one single condition that the maximum daily and weekly working periods as laid down by labour legislation be respected (10 hours per day, 48 hours per week, and 46 hours on average per week over 12 weeks);
   - the development of part-time work;
   - reconsidering the injunctions against working on Sundays in tourist areas; and
   - the LRILD (compensated reduction in working time) shows up well the impact that the flexibility paradigm has had. This aid aims at preserving employees' work contracts in firms that have been suffering from a fall off in business activity over a long period. This particular measure, which completes the consideration given to part-time unemployment, contains a proviso that the state and UNEDIC (the unemployment fund) will be responsible for allowances paid to employees whose working time has been reduced by at least 1200 hours per year over a maximum period of 18 months.

9. A time-training package is proposed. The employee can alternate training and business activity. For reasons of flexibility, employers like making people work more than their standard amount. Instead of claiming extra pay, individuals may claim

more free time, which is consistent with new values in the workplace! They may add up all their overtime and change it into 'time-capital' of six months for instance and use it as a sabbatical or time for retraining in whatever they wish. This time-training capital, which is considered as work time, will have to be defined by national agreements within each sector after negotiations between management and labour. Let us mention also the desire to explore new areas for job creation, in particular in the environmental field, caretaking, safety surveillance in public transport, the hotel trade, fuel delivery, and so on.

Besides the Five-Year Law, measures for social protection have been taken and it was decided that

- the number of quarters worked would be increased from 150 to 160 – one quarter a year over ten years – for claiming a full pension (by decree on 27 August 1993);
- the basis for calculating a pension will now be the best 25 years of pay instead of the best 10. This change will be applied progressively – one more year will be added per year over 15 years.

So, the laws governing society are in a perpetual state of change. These examples illustrate both the reshuffling and readjustments necessitated by the unemployment crisis as well as the fact that these rather considerable changes are well structured by the law, while yet permitting local negotiations and adaptations within the individual company. A human resource manager operating in France is well aware of the driving force of the state and of the law. An example of the direct application of the Five-Year Law is given by the case of the fruit juice factory, Sunnyland.

A third of the employees of a factory will work half-time
(adapted from an article in *Le Monde*, 5 August 1994)

To avoid losing their jobs, a third of the hundred or so employees of the fruit juice factory Sunnyland (a subsidiary of the Canadian Group McCain) in a town in the south-east of France have just accepted half-time work for two years. The 32 people benefiting from this adapted work schedule made possible by the Five-Year Law will receive 90 per cent of their gross wages the first year and 80 per cent the second year, which corresponds to much more than their half-time work schedule. This extra pay will be met during the first year equally by the state and by the company.

This flexi-time work schedule is the result of an agreement signed by the management of the firm and the CFDT which is the only trade union represented. This procedure was ratified by 93 per cent of the staff by referendum and enabled the number of lay-offs necessitated by a reduction in the production capacity of the factory to be reduced from 36 to 4. Sunnyland has included in its restructuration project an investment plan of 30 million francs to modernise its installations. The local political authorities have also signed an agreement to participate in the construction of a sewage plant. The mayor of the town sees this agreement as a means of promoting business activity in the area.

The case of Sunnyland highlights the positive influence of the law and the negotiation process within the firm. It also takes account of the stakeholders outside the firm – the politicians, the environmental aspects and so on. It is obvious that a successful operation like this has positive effects at various levels of the firm, internal motivation, subsidies from outside and so on. It is relevant at this point to mention Shaun Tyson's work which so much emphasises *practical strategy* and the necessity to audit carefully the environmental influences developed by Johnson and Scholes (1988) (see Fig 14.2).

All this is not at all the preserve of small companies. The large bank Crédit Lyonnais in the same way decided to adopt a series of measures inspired by the Five-Year Law with the theme 'every job can be a part-time job'. Its aim was to increase the proportion of part-time staff from 8.5 per cent to 17 per cent and to plan for 1300 cases of progressive early retirement. France is lagging behind other European countries in this respect. The overall cost to the Crédit Lyonnais of this operation amounted to 250 million francs over three years and the pay-off was about a billion francs.

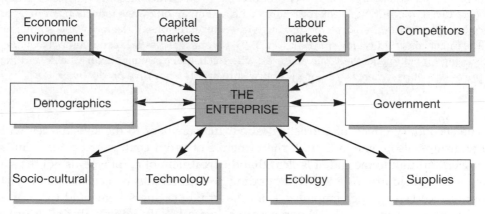

Source: Adapted from Johnson and Scholes, 1988, pp. 56–7.

Fig 14.2   Environmental influences on the firm

French trade unions in the 1990s

The traditional principles of collective bargaining

A few brief outlines suffice to characterise industrial relations in France that certain books or articles treat in detail (Goetschy and Rozenblatt, 1992; Rojot, 1987):

- The typical model is one of consultation; it is an absolute necessity for employers to inform, consult and negotiate with the different interested bodies, the works council, the trade union representatives, the staff delegates, and so on. But they are not forced to arrive at an agreement. The legal requirements have been fulfilled when a consultation has taken place.
- The trade union influence has lessened considerably in the last few years and its membership rate has now reached a stable level of about 9 per cent, which represents the lowest rate in Europe.
- Five trade unions are said to be representative and employers are bound to recognise them as soon as an employee claims to be an official representative of one of them.

The beginning of the 1990s saw serious social discontent, even in the firms traditionally considered to be peaceful and in the vanguard of social innovation.

In 1994 for the first time the trade unions set up a common front at Danone, even though the President of the Group, Antoine Riboud, is well known for his advanced social attitudes. This firm, the leader in the agribusiness field, is not exempt from the productivity rat-race in its biscuit branch with an exchange rate of approximately 9 French Francs to the Pound it went from 666 francs to 995 francs per employee between 1987 and 1992). And what is more, it is undergoing restructuration, though not profoundly – 90 per cent of its staff have been redeployed within or outside the group and the trade unions are complaining of an intolerable case of 'job blackmail'. They are protesting against such decisions as the one taken in a unit of Belin, a subsidiary of Danone which produces biscuits, in which 145 job losses were avoided by reducing the working week to 30 hours with accompanying wage reductions from 6 per cent to 12 per cent. In this sector, productivity seems to be one of the few viable solutions. The financial periodical *Investir* (February, 1994) reports that Nestlé, a competitor of Danone, is being forced to take the same measures: where consumer buying remains stable and the prices do not rise, there is only one way to assure profits – improve productivity.

The secondary effects of entrusting labour management to the subsidiaries within large groups also come to light. If the principle of profit centres or business units is followed through to the end, it is clear that the treatment of employees is not the same from one subsidiary to another; according to the results of each subsidiary, the amount received by each employee from the profit-sharing scheme and the working conditions can vary greatly. Differences that were hardly noticed during a growth period can later stand out alarmingly and can lead to trade union action and so united industrial action begins to appear. Business leaders with the reputation for being as socially aware as Riboud of Danone will have to come up with really novel solutions if they mean to stick to their claims that social considerations should mould economic action.

Trade unions and the rule of flexibility

Encouraged by the government, both labour and the employers must seek out new paths to take. All the interested groups within the company must work together, the trade union representatives, the staff delegates and all other influences. Many observers consider that we have missed our great chance by not taking significant action during the prosperous years from 1987 to 1990.

The trade unions are becoming more and more vigilant while the workers are being made increasingly vulnerable because of the growth of flexibility. Three examples that occurred recently in the social context may serve as an illustration. Two firms of American origin ran into trouble with their employees and with the law because, as they put it, they were trying to introduce 'flexibility'; the employees and the law, however, claimed that it was 'exploitation'. The third complicated example was Air France in which management finally withdrew its case.

The flexible remuneration project in IBM France

There is no end to the different social schemes that this company has put forward; out of the 24 000 employees they had in 1986, only 13 500 remained at the end of 1993; the general management is proposing a further reduction of 3000 jobs in 1994, of which 1700 will be voluntary departures (early retirement and progressive departures allowed by the trade unions) and 1300 equivalent departures representing a saving of 300 million francs by reducing wages; part of all wages will be indexed to the company's turnover and the granting of the thirteenth month will be reconsidered. All trade unions except the in-house one have rejected the management's proposal claiming that the efforts required were not justified by the firm's results indeed another wave of lay-offs struck in 1995. The Chairman and Managing Director of IBM France, Claude Andreuzza, sees this measure as a means of focussing the attention of all the staff of IBM on increasing the turnover. The trade unions are against this change in the employment contract and have filed a suit since the management, confident in the support they have from the company's own trade union, have decided to incorporate an additional clause into the contract, stipulating that refusal to comply will lead to dismissal. The courts have sided with the employees who condemn this action as 'far-west social justice' and they have pronounced null and void the agreement signed with the in-house trade union and have instructed the firm to pay 20 000 francs to the five trade union organisations; management has acknowledged the decision and has 'deplored the fact that it is very difficult to innovate in the present social environment'. The implied injunction is quite obvious: internal previsional flexibility is to be preferred to external flexibility.

Limits are being set to ruthless attempts to increase flexibility and productivity. Certain observers are quite outspoken: the drop in purchasing power is due to poverty and the United Kingdom's example of extreme flexibility serves as a foil. An article in *Le Monde* of 30 July 1994 headed 'The failure of a rich country in which poverty is increasing' depicts Great Britain, with facts and figures, perhaps to an exaggerated degree, as the country of the 'near poor' in which more than one child in three lives in poverty and in which 40 per cent of school children have undeclared part-time jobs contravening labour legislation which forbids under 13s from having any paid activity.

McDonalds' problems with the law

The case which shook McDonald's in France is another illustration of the same thing. This fast-food chain boasts 24 000 employees, 315 outlets and for 1994 planned to open 60 or so restaurants, create 4000 jobs and invest about 800 million francs. But basically the chain works on a franchising system, in which each franchise holder carries all responsibility and is an independent entity in the eyes of the law. It is obvious that this scattered type structure makes it difficult to protect the interests of staff who are mainly part-time workers with a very rapid turnover; the term used for this by this kind of flexible company is 'peripheral employees'. In July 1993, certain conflicts broke out in the McDonalds of the Lyon region. Local managers appeared before the court after employees had condemned what they called a 'system of blackmail and exploitation' with unfair dismissals and unbearable, even illegal working conditions. In fact, there are very few shops where the number of permanent employees is enough to justify the election of staff representatives and the setting up of works councils. Yet, in July 1993, the magistrates' court in Lyon ruled that since the McDonalds in that area employed 1000 people, mostly young and on part-time contracts, they should be considered as a single economic entity and as such should set up one overall works council.

Le Monde reports other affairs concerning McDonald's which perhaps would not have arisen in another national culture:

Ludovic Legris is 23 years old and hasn't much to lose since he is waiting for his national service call-up and so found a fill-in job at McDonald's. Trouble began when he claimed among other things some retrospective pay owing to him and certain bonuses awarded in the collective agreement. Being a militant member of the CFDT (one of the five large trade union bodies in France) he was dismissed 'for serious misconduct, falsifying his working time, rowdy behaviour and insubordination'. This was the shop that Mr A., the main McDonald franchisee of the Lyon area, who runs a dozen or so fast-food restaurants, invited us to visit to show his good faith. And it was also in this shop that the most embarrassing situation for McDonald's arose. A manager of this shop appealed to the CFDT after being dismissed by her employer on the rather doubtful grounds that there had been too high a percentage of her employees who had voted in the June works council elections. She threatened to make certain revelations.

In Paris, employees have condemned the exploitation of young, foreign staff, being constantly blackmailed by the threat of dismissal and many other types of pressure used to stifle all complaints. McDonald's central management plays down the importance of these charges: 'this sort of conflict is part and parcel of the daily life of the company', explains George B. Brown, the deputy Chairman responsible for Human Resources management.

Le Monde, 19 July 1994

Though it is in no way our intention to pass judgement on the basic charges in question, this McDonald case does deserve a twofold comment. The world of labour relations in France is built up on a certain number of rules which must be respected. If these rules are ignored or tampered with, it can lead to increasing problems with the labour force. And furthermore, there are certain arguments that are unacceptable to society at large. It was, therefore, quite inappropriate for the Human Resources manager for France to reply that 'he finds it regrettable that McDonalds has been victimised in this way, when it is contributing just so much to the fight against unemployment in France'.

These two examples dealt with here show clearly that, paradoxically enough, if they feel they are being cheated and deprived of their rights, workers can react more strongly and call upon the trade unions to defend them in spite of the very bleak economic situation. Before engaging in legal battles that always leave their mark on both parties concerned, it is so much more advisable to analyse the situation strategically and to do everything possible to inform and negotiate. Otherwise the whole of the labour force will become embittered and demotivated.

The case of Air France

After several serious strikes had led to the resignation of its CEO, the nationalised firm embarked on a rescue operation in the spring of 1994 under the guidance of its new CEO, Christian Blanc. A diagnosis of its strategy is very revealing: the company with its 42 000 employees is staggering under the weight of its excessively bureaucratic and hierarchical structure. Even though the general air-transport problem is one of overcapacity, Air France had quality as its main strategic specificity, whereas the competitors were filling their planes as much as they could. Hence the 36 billion franc debt, ongoing since 1990. As a union representative remarked bitterly, 'if they decided not to pay all the employees for a year, that still would not have us breaking even'! In such a critical situation, the CEO devised a rescue plan with severe social repercussions: 5000 jobs lost but no dismissals, a wage and salary freeze for three years, all promotion suspended and the working week going from 38 to 39 hours for the ground staff, with a resulting productivity increase of 30 per cent. He stated that he required the agreement of all the 14 trade unions represented in the company, and failing this he would organise a referendum for all employees and put his own resignation on the line in case of refusal.

The referendum, though acknowledged as having no legal value, was organised and this new social regime, denounced by the unions as being a reshuffling and bypassing manoeuvre, has put all the various bodies concerned at loggerheads just when their validity as representatives is being challenged. Only six trade unions were in favour of the plan, though the others did not call on their members to vote against it. Following are the results: 83.55 per cent of the labour force voted, and 81.26 per cent were in favour of the CEO's rescue plan. Since then, 10 trade unions have signed and the social agreement came into force on 1 September 1994. The whole work structure was reviewed and did not seem to be following the profit centre culture set up by British Airways more than ten years ago.

It is obvious that Blanc's method is open to criticism since the referendum cannot replace traditional labour relations management practices. But we do have here an example of situational management: danger and panic have broken out on board, certain trade unions are in favour and the employees support the CEO's emergency plan. The Air France plan really does represent a change of direction in management/trade union/employee/state relationships. In spite of what may be said, France is moving towards a system of greater flexibility, even if not quite of its own free will.

In March 1997, when Renault (automobile) decided to close their Belgian production site, the CEO was strongly disapproved by the Head of State, Prime Minister and leading right wing politicians; this showed clearly that productivity can be objective but not at all costs to the expense of quality in communication and employee relations.

One of the traditional main issues: training and personal development

Training as part of a tradition

A promise was made to the French that in the year 2000, 80 per cent of the candidates every year would obtain the baccalauréat. Considering the way employment has developed both qualitatively and quantitatively, it is obvious that the diploma will no longer lead to the labour market and this means that the French will have to understand that the purpose of the diploma is no longer to open the door to a qualified job. How could it be when INSEE (Institut National des Statistiques et Etudes Ecomoniques) shows that between 1982 and 1990 ten of the twelve occupations which have most increased their numbers do not require the baccalauréat (nursing assistants, secretaries, cleaners, café waiters, and so on).

Training and developing the individual as solutions to the employment problem

A study carried out by CERC (the Research Centre on Income and Costs) is alarming: 5 million people are in a precarious position as far as employment is concerned either because they are jobless or because they are finding it difficult to readapt. It is also stated that about 850 000 persons are on long-term unemployment and so close to losing all their social assistance, even if they still qualify for the RMI (Minimum Unemployment Allowance) which saves them from total social exclusion by giving them about 2300 francs per month for one single person. Tribute must be paid to the important role played since 1987 by 'intermediary associations' which have made available to individuals, associations or firms, certain people who are excluded from the labour market to do work that is not covered by the commercial sector. It is most gratifying to see that these intermediary associations enable 27 per cent of the long-term unemployed to become reinstated by on-the-job training. In-house training in France is a basic principle of HRM and, let it not be forgotten, every firm with more than six employees is obliged by law to devote a minimum of 1.5 per cent of its payroll to staff training (0.15 per cent if fewer than 10 people are employed).

INSEE statistics are eloquent: between 1988 and 1993, 5.5 million people followed at least one training course in comparison with 2 million from 1980 to 1985; in most sectors, 20 per cent of the employees followed a training course during the 18 months during which the survey was taking place with all the attendant differences due to the size of the companies.

President Mitterrand himself addressed the young business leaders in the following terms: 'Could it not be envisaged that every employee could devote 10 per cent of his time throughout his working life to training so as to be better prepared to face the economic challenges?' (message delivered in January 1994).

This suggestion could greatly worry those who advocate an extreme degree of flexibility which burns out competence without investing in training; but it does make certain political choices in business in the field of HRM more comprehensible.

Training and recruiting

As a direct consequence of the levelling out of the recession, a lot has been said about social plans. Growth and recruitment in businesses is now considered.

The falling off in values as far as employment is concerned, particularly in the case of the young, is seen by some firms as a cultural change providing an opportunity to achieve different objectives, with a whole variety of consequences:

- to introduce new skills and new blood while rejuvenating the age pyramid, which often has a rugby ball shape, by using early retirement and restricted hiring;
- to introduce flexibility;
- to get control of the payroll; and
- to remodel the corporate culture, to change mentalities in the light of new management practices.

The UAP, one of the leading insurance companies recently privatised, signed an agreement concerning its 9250 administrative personnel. The volunteers from all of the different professional categories are encouraged to work part-time. Those who work 80 per cent of the time will be paid 105 per cent of the 80 per cent which makes in fact 84 per cent. Those working only 60 per cent of their time (specially recommended for mothers), will be paid 110 per cent of their full-time time which works out at 66 per cent. Finally, those choosing half-time work will be paid on the basis of 115 per cent which works out at 57 per cent. General management expects this scheme to attract 300 people for the first year, or else the possibility of hiring 150 people. It must be emphasised that this objective applies to all categories including the executives. The firm does not hide the fact that it would like to see 20 per cent of the young executives adopt a formula in keeping with their lifestyle, that is to say to avoid wasting all their life trying to earn a living, caught up in an eat-sleep-work routine.

Training/quality/career for workers

Over and above recruitment and work-time arrangements, the necessity to be competitive has forced firms to set up training schemes leading to qualifications which can increase the quality of the products, while keeping jobs going.

The experience of Citroën's Normandy factory deserves some attention. The Chairman of the Group PSA (Peugeot, Citroën Automobiles) has taken as his number one priority continuous growth in productivity and yet it was while respecting the injunction of 12 per cent annual increase in productivity that the experience took place: the managers of the Caen site, 2280 employees of which 1760 are workers, had to choose between dismissing unskilled workers and taking on more suitably skilled staff or else setting up an in-house training scheme. The factory manager explained that an imbalance had come to light between 'our overall staffing level and our specific staff needs in each type of activity and category of employee, considering future developments in production volume'. The problem could be defined as a shortage of a hundred or so skilled workers and a surplus of 181 persons in very unskilled jobs. What was to be done? (i) there was no point in waiting for the situation to grow worse; (ii) taking on more staff would have reduced productivity; (iii) gradually training 300 volunteer workers to fill more skilled posts. Without delay, four groups of fifteen workers followed training sessions one week per month in their working time where they were replaced by temps. The management was quite satisfied by this operation which cost 11 million francs for 96 000 hours of training over three years. They emphasized the fact that 'the faculty of absorption of practical knowledge by workers considered to be, a priori, unskilled is more impressive than most people realise'. (*Le Monde*, 29 September 1993)

Training and career development for executives

This topic of training cannot be left without quoting some experiences in combining career development, reduction of unemployment and 'transmitting the memory' within the organisation. With the number of early retirements steadily growing, certain line managers complain of the loss of know-how which disappears along with the retiring staff. The large insurance company Axa with its 8500 employees has just set up a very clever system which consists in letting 250 executives of more than 55 years of age take their retirement. These 'reservist' executives receive 70 per cent of their gross annual pay, but if there is an emergency, they can be recalled by the firm for a period of from four to eight months according to the case, to give a temporary hand or to act as instructors. The firm undertakes to take on one person for every three 'reservist' executives that go on retirement.

Conclusion

All these different points relevant to different specificities within HRM in France reveal that periods of upheaval and social difficulty can also be times of real innovation. And perhaps we have not yet had time to analyse all this adequately.

Certain obvious tendencies can be clearly defined, such as the loss in prestige of the 'work ethic'; and it becomes clear that French employees are really hoping for new kinds of work. We have also seen that French firms are becoming more open to flexibility even if there is still a certain degree of reticence. But workers and executives are realising that they can be the victims of productivity propaganda for which they have sometimes made considerable sacrifices without reaping any rewards. They have sometimes experienced any number of restructuration projects and are now no longer so keen to commit themselves unreservedly. Bernard Perret and Guy Roustang's 1993 book *L'Economie contre la société* (*The Adverse Effect of the Economy on Society*) illustrates all these aspects quite well.

And finally, since the human resource manager is becoming a more and more important member of the board of directors, his or her role of introducing change will become increasingly crucial.

With an employment level of 13 per cent (1997), French Human Resources Managers have to contribute not only to productivity but also to the introduction of *'amémagement du temps de travail'* (working time modulations), that is to more flexibility with working time, a really important challenge for French companies in the years to come.

REFERENCES

Balladur, E. (1994) 'Une année de redressement – mars 1993/mars 1994', *La Lettre de Matignon – Service d'information du Premier Ministre*.

Barsoux, J-L. and Lawrence, P. (1991) *Management in France*, London: Cassell Educational Ltd.

Bernard Brunhes Consultants (1994) *L'Europe de l'emploi ou comment font les autres*, Editions d'organisation.

Besseyre des Horts, Ch-H. (1987) 'Typologies des pratiques de gestion des ressources humaines', *Revue française de gestion*, novembre–décembre, pp. 149–55.

Bournois, F. (1991) *La gestio des cadres en Europe*, Paris, Eyrolles.

Bournois, F. (1992a) 'Human Resource Management in France', in Brewster, C. (ed.) *International Guide to Human Resource Management*, London, Academic Press.

Bournois, F. (1992b) 'The Impact of 1993 on Management Development in Europe', *Journal of International Studies of Management and Organization*, Spring, Vol. 22, No. 1, pp. 7–29.

Bournois, F. and Derr, C.B. (1994) 'Les DRH ont-ils un avenir?', *Revue française de gestion*, mars–avril–mai 1994, pp. 64–78.

Brabet, J. (coord) (1993), 'Repenser la GRH ?', *Economica*.

Brewster, C. and Bournois, F. (1991) 'Human Resource Management: A European Perspective', *Personnel Review*, Vol. 20, No. 6, pp. 4–13.

Brewster, C. and Hegewisch, A. (1994) *Policy and Practice in European Human Resource Management – The Price Waterhouse Cranfield Survey*, London: Routledge.

Brewster, C. and Mayne, L. (1994) 'The Changing Relationship between Personnel and Line Management: The European Dimension', a report for the Institute of Personnel Management, University of Cranfield, May.

Brewster et al., The European HRM Guide, Academic Press, London, 1992.

Goetschy, J. and Rozenblatt, P. (1992) 'The Industrial Relations System at a Turning Point', in Ferner, A. and Hyman, R. (eds) *Industrial Relations in the New Europe*, Oxford, Blackwell.

Iribarne, P. d' (1994) 'The Honour Principle in the "Bureaucratic Phenomenon", *Organization Studies*, Vol. 15, No. 1, pp. 81–97.

Johnson, G. and Scholes, K. (1988) *Exploring Corporate Strategy*, second edn, London: Prentice Hall.

Laufer, J., Amado, G. and Trepo, R. (1978) *Monsieur Personnel et le développement des hommes*, Paris, Flammarion.

Laurent, A. (1986) 'The Cross-Cultural Puzzle of International Human Resource Management', *Human Resource Management*, Spring, Vol. 25, No. 1, pp. 91–102.

Perret, B. and Roustang, G. (1993) *L'Economie contre la société*, Paris, Seuil.

Rojot, J. (1987) 'Les syndicats et les entreprises face au nouvel environnement des relations de travail', *Revue française de gestion*, November/December.

Roussillon, S. and Bournois, F. (1993) 'Nouveaux points de repères d'identification Europe', *Revue Personnel*, October, pp. 33–40.

Salais, R. and Storper, M. (1994) *Les mondes de production – enquête sur l'identité économique de la France*, Editions de l'Ecole des hautes études en sciences sociales.

Tyson, S. (1987) 'The Management of the Personnel Function', *Journal of Management Studies*, Vol. 24, No. 5, pp. 523–32.

Tyson, S. (1995) *Strategic Prospects for HRM*, Institute of Personnel and Development, London.

Wright, P. and McMahan, G. (1992) 'Theoretical Perspectives for Strategic Human Resource Management', *Journal of Management*, Vol. 18, No. 2, pp. 295–320.

KEY ISSUES IN STRATEGIC HUMAN RESOURCE MANAGEMENT IN THE NETHERLANDS*

Jaap Paauwe

This chapter gives an overview of key issues in strategic human resource management (SHRM) in the Netherlands. The experiences and needs of practitioners act as a starting point for this analysis. Based on an inventory of recent publications in the professional journals and conferences for practitioners the following key issues were selected:

- linking HRM policies and practices to corporate strategy;
- from specialist staff to regular line management and external agencies;
- improving quality;
- monitoring/measuring the performance of HRM activities; and
- redesigning HRM tools: from flows thinking to competency building.

These themes are discussed below. For each key issue empirical data is presented and examples and experiences drawn from the practice of Dutch trade and industry are discussed, with an eye to contributing to the interaction of theory and practice.

Each theme begins with a presentation of the present state of the art in each of these areas based on evidence (mainly survey data) drawn from a number of different sources. This is followed by an analysis which attempts to discern underlying causes and factors which can account for the present tendencies in that area. Finally possible future perspectives are presented, inspired by case study evidence from leading companies in the area of SHRM.

Before the key issues are described the scene is set by way of a brief review of the major trends over the past ten to fifteen years in Dutch personnel management and industrial relations.

In the author's evaluation the underlying rationalities in strategic HRM and the possible (negative) outcomes for 'human resources' themselves and the personnel

---

* This chapter is partially based upon a previous article in *Human Resources Management Journal*, Vol. 6, No. 3, pp. 76–93, 1995.

function are discussed. The so-called (human) resource based theory might offer a useful 'escape' out of the one-sidedness of SHRM, that too often seems to be exclusively linked to the strategic demands of the marketplace. The human resource based theory of the firm seems to offer better possibilities for reconciling both strategic and humane aspects by taking into account the specific nature and complexities of human resources.

Setting the scene

The selected key issues are not separate islands. They are expressly part and parcel of the historical development of the personnel function; they relate to current themes in the area of management and organisation and, naturally, to the socio-economic context in general and that of industrial relations in particular.

Personnel management

Personnel management in the Netherlands is of long standing. It is probable that the first personnel manager was appointed by the Yeast and Methylated Spirits Works in Delft (1880). This company took the lead in experimenting with industrial democracy in the form of so-called nuclear units. These may be seen as precursors of the works councils which were eventually introduced across the Netherlands by statute.

Personnel management itself developed from personnel administration in the post Second World War years to a period when social issues, such as industrial democracy, job consultation and job structuring moved centre stage. This period ended rather abruptly with the advent of what is known as the no-nonsense phase, prompted by the economic recession towards the end of the 1970s and the early 1980s. This trend was modified by the rise of the idea of human resource management (HRM), which stressed integration with corporate strategy and with line management, and sought to contribute to flexibility, quality and customer orientation.

Nearly 50 per cent of the personnel officers are members of the NVP, the Dutch Association for Personnel Management. The association has been flourishing since the end of the 1980s; its membership (1996: 4800 members) is expanding and much attention is given to the issue of professionalising. This leads to greater concern with the quality of the personnel function and with interaction between theory and practice.

Management and organization

Recent developments in the area of management and organisation are not very different from those taking place elsewhere in Western Europe, in the United States and in south-east Asia. At most one may note a certain time lag.

CEOs, managers and consultants are eager to gain inspiration through new developments in management as presented in Anglo-Saxon business and professional journals. In the Netherlands, too, there is tension between, on the one hand, the demand to counter increasing complexity by way of greater autonomy at every level in the organisation and, on the other hand, the need to retain overall control. A first line of current development, therefore, consists in seeking alternatives for the bureaucratic, large-scale organisation, based on Taylorism. Examples of that kind of widely applied alternative include delayering, decentralisation and the creation of entrepreneurial internal market systems like unit-management (Paauwe, 1994, p. 17; Van Hoof, 1995, p. 6).

However, structural adjustments in themselves are useful but insufficient. Management and employees need to be equipped with greater autonomy, which is reflected in a second current line of development aimed at expanding tasks and increasing competencies and responsibilities at every level of the organisation. More specifically we refer to (more or less fashionable) approaches like empowerment, policy deployment, self-managing teams and the introduction of socio-technical measures and improvements in order to enhance the quality of working life.

The two organisational trends mentioned above have one thing in common, namely that – within the framework of strategic policy – they aim at bringing about an increase in the self-regulating capacity of managers and employees. At the same time they intensify mutual dependence. Exchange of information and ready access to it for everyone is necessary in order to establish co-ordination, both in a formal and an informal way. It goes without saying that the manner in which human resources are treated is crucial in bringing about this self-autonomy of managers and employees.

Industrial relations

This chapter need not cover all relevant developments over the past ten to fifteen years. Visser (1992, pp. 323ff) is an excellent reference for this purpose. But a brief review (abridged from Smit et al., 1995) of the most prominent developments – at least from the point of view of developing HRM in the Netherlands – will be helpful.

Dutch industrial relations are traditionally characterised by neo-corporatist arrangements (Visser, 1992, pp. 323ff; Smit et al., 1995). Organised interest groups were much involved in governmental decision making, and the federations of trade unions used to be centralised and hierarchically structured. The trade union movement opted for legal enactment and participation in neo-corporatist policy, which had several consequences for labour unionism. A first consequence was that trade unions used to be weakly represented at the company and plant level. The company level is the domain of works councils, whereas collective bargaining was located outside the company. Second, the organisation of production used to be kept separate from wage bargaining. The unions concentrated on the determination of the terms and conditions of employment and never questioned the Tayloristic mode of organisation. Third, the government had an enormous influence on wage policies. However – according to Schilstra and Smit (1994, p. 3) – the national bilateral agreement of 1982 meant a watershed in Dutch industrial relations and began the decline of national concertation. Confronted with high unemployment, trade unions and employers' organisations agreed on wage moderation, job-sharing and reduction of working hours. As Visser (1992) notes, for the first time since 1945 collective bargaining at the meso-level (industries and large corporations) had become legally and factually liberalised from nationwide controls. Employers and trade unions both recognised the worth of collective agreements, but pursued larger potentialities for choices. This implied a development in the direction of more general sectoral agreements, which allow firm-specific arrangements to be negotiated by either union or works council.

Some well-known developments formed the backdrop for these decentralising tendencies in industrial relations. First, the neo-liberal policies of deregulation became dominant in the 1980s. Second, European unity and economic internationalisation renders the national level increasingly more obsolete, which promotes willingness to accept USA- or Japanese-based elements into industrial relations practices. Third, employers increasingly seek flexibility and tailor-made terms of employment – standard clauses in collective agreements discourage this. For this reason Bolweg (1989) concludes that industrial relations, which had previously been kept outside the firm, now is becoming increasingly internalised. At the same time personnel management is becoming more subject to processes of 'political debate' among the various parties involved, such as top and line management, the personnel department itself, and the employees, primarily represented by the works council.

There are at least two reasons why the works council assumed greater importance at company level. First, legislation extended its responsibilities in 1979. Second, the tendency towards decentralisation of collective bargaining implies that unions are reassessing the standard character of labour contracts. They have taken initiatives to propose two-tier models of industry-wide collective labour agreements which leave room for company- and works-specific arrangements and/or individual differentiation. Naturally, works councils are involved in this process especially since trade unions were unable to develop strong roots within the companies. At present the tide is turning, but from the end of the 1970s the rate of unionisation was dropping sharply from 35 per cent in 1980 to 25 per cent in 1990. On account of this, trade unions lack manpower to staff their labour-intensive decentralisation policies and to strengthen their visibility at shop floor level. Increasingly, therefore, trade unions co-operate closely with their trade union representatives in the works council.

Most works councils (70 per cent) are dominated by union members, who constitute a majority. In fact, works councils appear to have developed into the primary form of union activity at company level.

Linking HRM policies and practices to corporate strategy

An essential feature of the HRM approach is the integration of personnel management and corporate policy. Following Golden and Ramanujam (1985) administrative linkage, one-way linkage, two-way linkage and full integration are distinguished.

Empirical data

Integration of personnel management into the strategic-organisational context is a fairly popular topic in Dutch research (57 out of 392 research projects, or 14.5 per cent; source: van Maenhout and van Hoof, 1993, p. 192). One of these projects is a survey by Scheurer et al. (1993, p. 38), which is based on 58 medium-sized organisations in industry, trade and services. The findings show that in 40 per cent of the cases there is no linkage at all; 29 per cent of the cases show a one-way linkage and in 31 per cent the linkage is two-way. The survey information was provided by personnel managers. It is likely, therefore, that 'wishful thinking' encouraged some distortion in favour of supposed integration.

Extended research among 600 industrial companies by Ten Have (1993) dealing with the relation between production structure, job characteristics and workforce profile leads to two noteworthy conclusions. First, there is a strong connection between the typology of the market and the typology of the production structure, including the workforce profile. Second, there is no systematic integration of job characteristics, workforce profile (including mobility, qualification and social policy) and job continuity. Human resource management is 'good practice' rather than a reflection of job characteristics, production structure and the marketplace. There is a connection with company size in the sense that larger companies feature a more elaborate HRM and greater continuity in labour relations.

> The larger a company, the greater the differentiation in personnel function, but integration with company objectives diminishes. When the personnel function is disentangled from general management – which in itself would promote more specific personnel policies – there are no complementary integration mechanisms. (Ten Have, 1993, p. 183)

In short, personnel management in larger companies tends to follow its own leads and is hardly related to corporate strategy (cf. Kluytmans and Van Sluijs, 1995, pp. 34ff). In addition, Ten Have notes that lack of fit (that is a linkage between corporate strategy and personnel management) does not affect company performance. The conclusion therefore must be that personnel management has a fair amount of leeway in shaping itself. This conclusion was drawn earlier by Paauwe (1991) on the basis of longitudinal case studies.

Closer analysis

Summarising the above we can say that in practice there is little integration of personnel management and corporate policy. Should this disappoint us? We need to look more closely at the research undertaken.

First, research has not been very extensive (Scheurer, et al.), or was based on data gathered towards the end of the 1980s (Ten Have, 1993 and Paauwe, 1991). In the Netherlands, however, HRM thinking did not really take hold until the 1980s and only became well established at the end of that decade and the early 1990s. Second, are these findings really all that disappointing? After all, the practice of personnel management is typically embedded in the system of institutional labour relations as it has grown historically. An important role in this falls upon the industrial relations parties via collective bargaining and collective measures. Even more important perhaps is the role of the works council, which has legal competency in matters relating to personnel. The limited room to manoeuvre means that, apart from strategic objectives, personnel policy is in part shaped by the power relations among the parties concerned, each with their own objectives and interests. In the practice of Dutch industry, therefore, we meet with a variety of approaches, at least in those cases where companies are seriously seeking to integrate personnel management and corporate strategy. These approaches, or experiments, have discarded the prescriptive/theoretical line in the manner of Schuler and Jackson (1987), who tie a straightforward strategy in the area of quality, cost-effectiveness and innovation to preformatted HRM practices (the so-called HRM menus). Based on a unique mixture of three different dimensions (administrative heritage, product/market/technology combinations and the institutional setting of the various actors involved (including trade unions and works councils) SHRM policies are developed that fit the situation of the company (see examples below).

Perspective and examples

In this connection the analytical models based on the resource-based theory of the firm (Flood et al, 1996; Paauwe, 1994) are likely to be more promising. The theory explains how a competitive edge may be based on matters such as a unique constellation of resources. In the case of HR this would mean a governance structure which is valuable, scarce, and difficult to reproduce, imitate or replace. This would enhance durability of the competitive advantage, while others will find it hard to copy this specific configuration. Case studies in the Netherlands (Paauwe, 1994) provide examples of this. These serve to illustrate unique configurations and ways of strengthening competitive advantage. Up till now we have carried out 12 case studies; an additional 5 are still in progress. Below are some examples which illustrate 'unique approaches'.

- A shipping company where employees are given the opportunity to move up through the entire job-classification scheme (a series of ten job functions), both in terms of required training and the necessary experience. In this way the company arrives at a unique optimum of multi-deployability, which yields an independent, and possibly decisive, competitive edge when flexible and high-quality personnel is needed. These employees are rewarded on the basis of these qualifications, regardless of the function they are actually performing.
- A large municipal organisation which takes the lead in linking job evaluation and performance evaluation to output-related objectives and criteria.
- A leading international publishing company which, via an extensive system of monthly ratios and critical success factors, monitors workforce developments (size, costs, structure, qualifications) in each business unit, in order that head office can take initiatives to improve efficiency and effectiveness.
- An internationally well known brewery company, where all available methods to manage and empower personnel are reviewed in a critical way and adjusted in terms of mutual consistency (horizontal interaction) and their contribution to strategic objectives (vertical integration).

From specialist staff to regular line management and external agencies

Next to closer alignment with business is the shift from staff to line ('internalisation'), the second core characteristic of SHRM. 'Internalising' refers to the shift from specialist staff departments or sections to regular line management and/or workers. In its extreme form this shift or 'downloading' of activities – possibly in combination with contracting-out – may yield a personnel management without personnel managers (see Paauwe in Flood et al., 1996). Along with the shift from staff to line greater emphasis may be placed on contracting-out or externalising. Externalising implies a shift from the in-house 'make' option to the 'buy' option (outsourcing).

To match this trend an increasing number of agencies are making themselves available. Obviously, the decision to make or buy is subject to a whole range of considerations including effectiveness, quality, efficiency, accessibility, speed of delivery and associated costs of monitoring. Williamson's transaction-costs theory (1985) offers a very useful framework for this kind of decision. In this section, however, we concentrate ourselves on the shift from specialist personnel department to line management.

Empirical data

There are no survey based data which would present a precise indication of the size and scope of this shift from staff to 'line'. There are, however, a number of examples of companies (such as Shell and Rank Xerox) which reduced recently (in the last five years) the number of active personnel specialists per 100 employees, and which have simultaneously begun to download personnel activities to line management. These companies also raised their budget for outsourcing. In addition, some indications may be distilled from a survey of organisations conducted by a project group of the Erasmus University. However, the number of participating companies was 127, overall response: 15 per cent, which implies that the data need to be interpreted with a certain degree of reservation. In terms of time invested, the HRM department spent some 60 per cent of its available time on line management advice and support; actual personnel activities for the line took up 35.6 per cent of the available time (Project group 'Personnel management in strategic perspective', 1993, p. 18). Of the recommendations issued by the HRM department, 53 per cent were in response to line management requests. The Dutch contribution to the Cranfield/Price Waterhouse project, implemented in 1992 (Hoogendoorn et al., 1992), showed that the issue of professionalising and decentralising, defined as a shift of responsibilities and competencies from staff to line, was among the first five priority objectives for the next three years (Hoogendoorn et al., 1992, p. 7 and p. 11). The repeated Cranfield Survey in 1995 (Hoogendoorn et al., 1995) reconfirms the tendency of a noticeable increase of responsibilities for line management in areas such as training, health and safety, workforce fluctuations, recruitment and selection (Hoogendoorn et al., 1992, p. 12; Hoogendoorn et al., 1995, p. 7).

In summary, the survey showed that 59 per cent of the organisations surveyed were moving towards decentralisation (such as downloading of tasks to line management); among 34 per cent the situation remained unchanged, and in 7 per cent the tendency was towards centralisation rather than decentralisation.

Closer analysis

From the HR professional point of view the shift of tasks and competencies from staff to line can be assessed either positively or negatively. The assessment depends on the type of explanation used to clarify the shift. Beginning with the positive view:

- Growing recognition among line managers that Human Resources and the management of them are crucially important in connection with gaining and retaining a durable competitive advantage.
- Growing consensus regarding the concepts of integral management and unit management, on the basis of which every line manager assumes responsibility on his or her level for all processes, including accounting, quality control and personnel management.
- As a result the profile of the Human Resource manager changes and is enhanced:

- *delegator*: in order to enable line management to serve as primary implementors of HRM systems;
- *technical expert*: encompassing a number of highly specific HR-related skills, which relate to the needs of line management; and
- *innovator*: recommending new approaches in order to solve HRM-related problems like productivity (Carroll, 1991, p. 208).

A more critical or negative point of view may suggest other explanations when personnel tasks are assumed by regular line management:

- (Top) management may not be convinced that the personnel section contributes to the bottom-line process.
- Regular line management is critical of the degree of professionalism, quality, timeliness and applicability of personnel services.
- Personnel officers are insufficiently able to empathise with the specific characteristics of the unit.
- Outside consultants render services that are more up to date and of higher quality.

Perspectives and examples

Following John Storey's 1992 project and Shaun Tyson's 1995 project, the author carried out a case study oriented research project in leading Dutch companies, very often operating at an international level, with regard to the degree of strategic integration of HRM into corporate policy and its contribution to company performance. The companies included among others: retail, food, leisure, building and construction, publishing, trade and furniture. Interviews included CEO, Director of Personnel, Director of Finance and Control and Works Council Representatives. At the time of writing the author had carried out 12 case studies; an additional 5 are still in progress (Paauwe, 1994). If we disaggregate the 'average' and often superficial survey data and base our analysis on this case study evidence of leading companies in the Netherlands the following picture emerges:

- highly qualified personnel staff and specialists often:
- limited in number but highly ranking in professional expertise; with:
- ample budgetary means at their disposal being:
- well integrated in line management both at strategic, managerial and operational level; and
- seeing themselves as part of strategic policy making bodies; and, mainly concerned with the following activities:
  - corporate culture and communication;
  - organisational change and development in order to improve commitment;
  - training and management development;
  - outside lobbying and internal advice;
  - consultancy/mediation;
  - remuneration systems that are geared to the specific needs of the different business units;
  - modifying collective bargaining agreements in order to get more leeway for company – and business unit specific arrangements.

What the core activities listed above (see also Purcell, 1985, p. 29) have in common is that they can be achieved only when the personnel function can operate in close consultation and co-operation with top and line management. This requires credibility which, in turn, must be earned via adequate implementation of the more traditional personnel management tasks (cf. Bolweg, 1994, p. 24).

The relation with line management depends wholly on the quality of the services delivered – this is true for virtually every professional staff function. By simply making the relationship with management subject to the forces of the marketplace and/or (internal) competition, we can undoubtedly expect initiatives to improve quality. The following are examples of this. A more extensive discussion of this key issue follows later.

> **AKZO Coatings is a subsidiary of one of the leading Dutch multinational chemical companies, AKZO. AKZO Coatings employs about 2400 people. Organisationally it is made up of business units. Its personnel department is considered to be a profit centre and is located at corporate level. Every line manager in charge of one of the business units buys the services of the personnel unit on the basis of a previously negotiated contract. This means that the business unit manager is confronted with forced shopping. However, for some activities like training and development or a specific consultancy assignment a manager can turn elsewhere.** (Uijlen and Paauwe, 1994)

> **PTT Post (Mail) is a good example of a recently privatised company, that has introduced 'contract management' in order to restructure its personnel services/activities. It employs about 60 000 people in the Netherlands. At corporate level it still has a corporate personnel department, however at business unit level the line managers in charge of the unit and the decentralised personnel staff departments are subject to the principles of contract management. So every budget year it negotiates a number of services and activities.** (Uylen and Paauwe, 1994)

Improving quality

The third central theme has to do with the quality of the personnel function. As briefly noted above, part of the reason why personnel tasks are being downloaded to the line or contracted out is the degree of quality as perceived by the customers of personnel services. These stakeholders or customers are line managers, employees and works council members. Quality as a concept is subject to some confusion, though. Sometimes it is used in relation to the contribution of the personnel function to the implementation of 'total quality management' (as in Wilkinson et al., 1993). In the present context we mean the quality of the personnel function itself and the scope for its improvement. This does not, of course, exclude the possibility that total quality management is applied to the personnel function. A number of companies do just that – successfully, as we shall see below.

Definition

The concept of quality – related to a service department such as personnel – can be defined as the extent to which the services are perceived by customers as meeting their requirements and expectations. On the basis of Zeithaml et al. (1990) quality so defined can be assessed by customers in terms of the following dimensions:

1. Tangibles: these are the evident products of the personnel function, such as procedures, evaluation systems, ratios, training and development facilities.
2. Reliability: the capacity to implement the services in adequate ways.
3. Responsiveness: the preparedness to provide rapid and certainly timely assistance.
4. Assurance: the ability to convince the customer that the department can handle things because expertise and hence credibility is readily apparent and perceived.
5. Empathy: the ability to perceive and understand the customer's situation.

In short, at issue are not only actual products and services, but also their effectiveness, timeliness, and, in the customer-supplier relationship, the ability to evoke confidence and display empathy. Following Soin (1992) the approach to quality management can be described as

an effort of continuous quality improvement of all processes, products and services through universal participation and services, that results in increasing customer satisfaction and loyalty, and improved business results.

Empirical data

A recent survey – conducted by the Association of Personnel Management professionals itself – among 240 personnel managers and 60 line managers, evaluated the quality of personnel and organisation officers, the department itself, the instruments used and the degree of customer-orientation. The survey awarded average performance with a score of 7 on a scale ranging from 0 (negative) to 10 (positive) (KVM, 1994).

Closer inspection reveals, however, that the strong points in personnel and organisation relate to personnel administration, with the traditional tasks of planning, recruitment and selection, labour conditions, appraisal and training. On the other hand the most prominent weak areas are these five:

- professional process skills like intervening, consultancy, and counselling;
- organisational development;
- management, planning and control of own work processes and systems;
- policy-making and issues; and
- professional attitude especially with respect to the building up of an effective relationship with management and the ability to express/to embody sincere customer orientation.

Moreover, more than 80 per cent of the survey participants suggested that changes in the content of the personnel function were overdue. This is an alarmingly high figure, which certainly puts a different slant on the satisfactory score awarded by personnel managers and line managers. Specifically, the relation with line management requires a major overhaul, as do personnel managers' knowledge and skills in the area of organisation development and corporate restructuring.

Research by Tissen (1991, p. 92) among line managers confirms this picture. More than 50 per cent of the managers hold that the quality of the personnel function is below or far below the desired level. (However, Tissen's survey among managers saw a response rate of 7.8 per cent, which again implies the necessary reservation; n = 246.)

Closer analysis

The quality profile that emerges is that of a personnel function which does well in 'tangibles' in the traditional areas of personnel management. Things are less rosy in areas relating to strategic and organisational action and the accompanying demand for contributions to processes of change and competency building. In these areas the personnel function is still unsatisfactory on the quality dimensions of reliability, assurance and empathy. Personnel professionals have been aware of this for some time. The above shortcomings were first pointed out by various authors as early as the middle of the 1980s, and we can wonder why little improvement can be seen, and why the expectations among parties concerned (customers) are not being met, or at least met in part. There are four possible explanations for this:

1. The very broad scope of tasks of the traditional personnel manager makes it difficult for him or her to prioritise those genuinely important tasks which will strengthen his or her credibility and image among customers.
2. The influx and career of those who occupy specialised personnel staff positions: their background is still quite disparate, while senior positions can still be filled by people who have no specific training or experience in the area of personnel management (Cranfield/Price Waterhouse Project, Dutch part, Hoogendoorn et al., 1992, p. 6). About 25 per cent of the respondents fulfilling a personnel function at the highest possible hierarchical level do not have a background in personnel management. There is a lack of a professional personnel career.
3. The professional specialist education for personnel management provides insufficient attention to the linkage with corporate strategy and the contribution of the personnel function to incisive processes of change.
4. There is a lack of application of planning and control mechanisms to the performance and processes of the personnel department itself. This is recognised by personnel managers. Little use is made of deadlines, management by objectives and principles of project management. Many organisations neglect systematic evaluation of the disparity between objectives as planned and objectives as realised (Project group 'Personnel management in strategic perspective', 1993, p. 15, Table 3.5; p. 20, Table 4.3 and p. 38). The effects of such inadequate progress control obviously result in poor scores on quality dimensions like reliability, responsiveness and assurance. (The author would like to thank his colleague Job Hoogendoorn (Erasmus University) for his stimulating contribution in our discussion about the various explanations, which account for the lack of not meeting expectations and the lagging behind of the personnel function.)

Perspectives and examples

Nevertheless, there are exceptions to the picture drawn above. A number of companies (mostly larger ones) certainly do well on quality-dimension scores. This is true, for example, for Ahold, Heineken, KBB, Reed Elsevier, Shell and Unilever. Each of these are companies where the personnel function is, just like line management, used to working to clear targets. Rank Xerox is an example of such an integrated approach to management by objectives and quality management. In this company management initiatives in areas such as policy deployment and total quality management have long been implemented. Secondary objectives are derived from strategic objectives such as customer orientation and a persistent drive for continuous quality improvement. These derived objectives are reviewed for each section and for every individual in the assessment of performance and performance-related pay. The personnel department itself is subject to the same procedure and, like sales and production, is confronted with challenging assignments which, year after year, seek to enhance HRM outcomes like employee satisfaction, turnover and flexibility. A growing number of quantitative indicators are available to measure these outcomes such as personnel surveys measuring organisational climate and job satisfaction.

One might wonder why this kind of approach is not widespread among the majority of organisations. A reason why the above mentioned companies apply principles as described above is the drive to excel as a dominant element in their company culture. A drive to excel in areas such as sales, brand reputation, quality, customer satisfaction is very often linked to the objective of increasing shareholders' value in a consistent and stable way. A dominant cultural pattern exists that imbues every aspect of running the business, inclusive of specialist staff departments like personnel.

Monitoring and measuring the performance of HRM activities

As mentioned above, one possible explanation for the lack of quality and the less than optimal image in the eyes of line management rests on insufficient utilization of planning and control mechanisms on the part of the personnel department itself. Interest in this is growing as evidenced by publications in professional journals and the popularity of a recent book on the use of personnel ratios (Baarda et al., 1994).

In more tangible terms this implies the development of measurable objectives, the use of personnel information systems for purposes of steering and adjustment, the development of a set of ratios and/or critical success factors, which may be useful in performance monitoring and benchmarking, and development of measurements (preferably quantified) of the value added.

Survey indications

The survey conducted by the association of professionals (KVM, 1994) notes a strong preference among respondents for development of an auditing instrument to assess the quality of the personnel function. The Cranfield/Price Waterhouse survey (Dutch part, Hoogendoorn et al., 1992, p. 10) shows that the use of computerised personnel information systems is widespread, but that its use is largely restricted to administrative tasks such as wage and salary administration, keeping track of sick days and days off, and data on individual employees. Utilisation of the system for the purpose of 'managing' and the department's own planning and control cycle is less widespread.

Any evaluation of personnel management policies is mainly done by comparison with previous years' results in the same firm and to pre-established target figures.

Comparison with statistical averages (national or industrial sector) is far less common, while only 11 per cent reports use of benchmarking (Project group 'Personnel management in strategic perspective', 1993, p. 15). The Cranfield survey (Dutch part, carried out in 1994/1995, Hoogendoorn et al., 1995, p. 5) does not allow us to conclude that the situation is improving.

Perspective

Current reluctance to monitor and evaluate own performance obviously does not contribute to strengthening the image towards other specialist staff departments and line management. Performance of, for example, a department of finance and accounting is monitored critically throughout in the sense that financial information (monthly and quarterly figures) must be sound and timely. The marketing department is assessed in terms of increasing or diminishing brand reputation, or whether an advertising campaign results in greater turnover. Line managers must take into account targets and budgets for their planning and control cycles. They are assessed, evaluated in the sense that their income tends to reflect their performance. So how about the perspective for the personnel management department? Our case studies in leading Dutch companies (Paauwe, 1994) showed that best practice was for the work processes of the personnel function to be subject to the same principles and forces that are typical for the work processes of line managers/entrepreneurs. Based on our case studies these characteristics and their implications can be outlined as shown by Table 15.1.

Table 15.1 Principles and forces typical for work processes of line managers and the personnel function

Characteristics of line management	Implications for personnel
entrepreneurial	risk
set tasks/objectives	vulnerability
have market awareness	customer orientation
have insight into the production process	overall view
expect visible results (key factors)	recognition
expect accountability	performance related pay

Translated to the personnel function in our case studies the aspect of an entrepreneurial approach manifested itself in developing clear objectives for the coming budget period and consecutive assignments. Those targets were subject to discussion and approval by top management when being established. In the majority of cases the chief personnel manager reported directly to the CEO. Following this process of target setting and writing it down as part of the strategy development and budgeting procedure, it implied an increase in vulnerability. This increase was strengthened by the more or less logical consequence of introducing performance related pay (at least part of it) for all the professional personnel specialists. In this way the personnel department committed itself to realising – in a visible way – the stated and agreed upon objectives. Moreover these objectives clearly represented a strong sense of awareness of the wishes of the (internal) customers and its subsequent contribution to overall business goals in the area of quality, cost-cutting and/or improving commitment and productivity.

Redesigning HRM tools: from flows thinking to competency building

A fifth central theme is the retooling of the various techniques and instruments used by personnel like recruitment, appraisal, rewarding and training, in order to fulfil the promised contribution to strategic objectives. For the most part the available instruments contribute mainly to management of human resource flows (cf. Beer et al., 1984) as shown in resource flow charts (see Fig 15.1).

The required redirection/reshaping in the context of SHRM is especially aimed at the capability of the various personnel instruments to develop, build up and strengthen HR competencies in the areas of quality (both of products/services and of working life), innovation, flexibility, commitment, willingness to change and cost effectiveness. This requires the personnel department, and especially the senior people working with their line colleagues to redefine these resource flow instruments so that the contribution of each technique to strategic objectives of quality, flexibility, willingness to change and participation/commitment is determined and the instruments redesigned.

A redirection of this kind implies the need to review critically each and every instrument. This demand comes at a time when most personnel departments are still working hard at recalibrating instruments, formerly meant to evaluate and keep track of personnel data, to make them useful for the managing of HR flows (in-, through-, and outflow). This is a step in the right direction, to be sure. But it does not go far enough.

Phase	Inflow	Throughflow	Outflow
Personnel activities 'tools'	recruitment selection staffing	appraisal rewards training job rotation management development	retirement outplacement downsizing

Time scale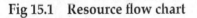

Fig 15.1   Resource flow chart

Empirical indications

The various surveys mentioned earlier are not really sufficiently specific to assess/evaluate the nature of the different instruments. The surveys do bring out quite strongly the importance of improvement of the strategic contribution, the intensification of the relation with line management, and the focus on topics such as quality, flexibility, cost awareness and investment in employees via training and development. This is expressed, for example, in a conclusion formulated in the 1994 survey by the professional association Kooimans & Van Mill Consultants B.V.

> Our conclusion is that, while the instruments of the personnel management department are technically reasonably sound, they take on a life of their own. The line experiences

> them as an obligation decreed by the HRM department, and less as means to manage and monitor the personnel function. A closer linkage of the instruments to be used and the specific objectives of the organization seems desirable. (KVM, 1994, p. 26)

As such, we may assume that the redirection from administration via the managing of personnel flows to building HR competencies is very much in the picture and will be an important development theme in the years to come.

Taking up the challenge

A last central theme is the room which may or may not be left for a HR policy in its own right. In other words: can we say that, in the midst of the swell of SHRM and its banners of effectiveness, efficiency, flexibility and quality, there is room for other considerations and criteria? Or must we conclude that management and its dominant, economic and rationality-directed criteria has become the sole stakeholder and hence the last remaining customer for the HRM department as is being frequently expressed in USA- and UK-based MBA textbooks on HRM?

Recent HRM literature frequently advocates the role of the HR manager as being that of a business person or business manager. See, for example, Schuler, 1990; and see Shipton and McAuley, 1994 for an overview of role prescriptions in this respect. Shipton and McAuley refer to the following role prescriptions:

- seeing themselves as business managers;
- identifying closely with management;
- viewing people as resources;
- describing their roles in ways that other managers can understand;
- seeing the rest of the organisation, and particularly managers of the senior echelons, as 'customers'; and
- being able to identify the core values of the organisation and being centrally involved in gaining organisation-wide acceptance of them.

These roles in fact imply that the personnel manager acquires a power base by conforming to the dominant culture and principles of the line management. Legge (1978) refers to the 'conformist innovator' who accepts the dominant utilitarian values and bureaucratic relationships within the organisation and tries to demonstrate the value added (contribution to the bottom line) of his or her activities within this framework. This is an approach which holds a number of evident risks, such as the eventual inability to differentiate HRM from the regular line manager contribution or expertise, so that the option of personnel management without personnel managers is on the horizon.

An alternative way of acquiring power – or rather influence – is the 'deviant innovator' approach, whereby the personnel specialist identifies with a set of norms that are distinct from, but not necessarily in conflict with, the norms of organisational success (Legge, 1978). In this connection Shipton and McAuley (1994, p. 9) refer to the need for an 'organisational fool, who without danger to himself can take non-consensual stances. . . . personnel people are perhaps uniquely fitted for this role because they frequently have the key responsibility for exploring, with members of the organisation in which they work, the issues surrounding the management of change and the factors that make it work'.

In the end it all comes down to the fact that HRM specialists cannot focus only on criteria such as efficiency, effectiveness and flexibility. Other appropriate criteria are those of fairness (in the exchange relation between the individual and the organisation) and legitimacy (the relation between society and organisation). A staff specialist in the area of personnel and organisation would be the right person to counter or correct an extreme economic rationality, so that the long-term interests of the various organisational members are kept in mind and the outcomes of organisational effectiveness will benefit the various stakeholders of the firm.

In this respect Kamoche (1994) underlines the inherent paradoxes of strategic HRM, as a concept encompassing both the issues of 'strategy' and 'human'. On the one hand SHRM is characterised by the dominant organisational imperative for performance and productivity, which according to Kamoche draws from an industry-based view of the firm and is informed by a rationalistic view of human action. On the other hand HRM is concerned with meeting the complex and often ambiguous needs and expectations of employees, the humanising of work and a concern with 'equitable' or 'fair' practices.

A promising way of reconciling both strategic and human aspects is to use the resource-based theory of the firm (Barney, 1991; Wernerfelt, 1984) as a starting point, because it takes into account the competencies and capabilities of the (human) resources instead of focussing on dominant business-like criteria as being dictated by the industry-based demands of the specific product/market combination. Kamoche strongly advocates this view because in this way it has more potential to take into account the specific nature and complexities of human resources:

> this paradigm emphasises that the skills of employees are conceived of as a vital resource, which the firm is able to build upon rather than simply to exploit rationally and ideologically. Therefore the full potential of HRM can be realised and can be a key determinant in a firm's performance, without the *a priori* imposition of the organisational imperative.
> (Kamoche, 1994, p. 41)

For HRM professionals this paradigm implies a focus on using multi-dimensional/ multi-faceted approaches in the development and rendering of specialist personnel services. Especially within a Western European social-economic setting it is important to do full justice to the claims of the various stakeholders involved in management of human resources. Contrary to USA and UK approaches in which personnel management is increasingly seen as just representing the line management perspective in meeting strategic demands, the Dutch and continental Western European perspective sees the personnel manager as the only expert who can reconcile both the strategic demands of the marketplace and the justified claims from the 'human resources' themselves in terms of fairness and legitimation often expressed by the members of the works council who – in combination with local trade union activists – play an increasingly important role in shaping industrial relations and HRM policies and practices at local plant and office level.

The following conceptual framework (see Fig 15.2) brings these two forces – next to the administrative heritage of the organisation – in relation to the dominant coalition in order to bring about a unique synthesis of strategic demands and the characteristics and aspirations of the workforce itself. On the one hand HRM is to a large degree deter-

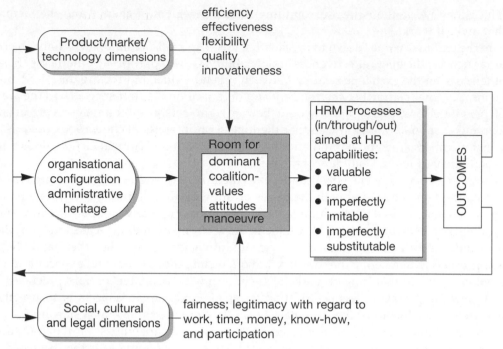

Source: Paauwe, 1994, p. 32.

Fig 15.2   The human resource based theory of the firm

mined by demands arising from relevant product/market combinations and the appropriate technology (P-M-T dimension). These demands are usually expressed in terms of
criteria such as efficiency, effectiveness, flexibility, quality and innovativeness. This
dimension represents the tough economic rationality of national and international competition. On the other hand it is important to remember that the so-called 'free market'
is embedded in a social, cultural and legal context (S-C-L dimension). Prevailing values
and norms and their institutionalisation channel the outcomes of the market process in
ways that simultaneously do justice to the dictates of fairness and legitimacy. By *fairness*
(see also Watson, 1977) we refer to a 'fair' arrangement in the agreed exchange between
the individual as an employee and the organisation as employer. Elements in this
exchange are not only time, money and labour, but information, know-how, and voice
as well. *Legitimacy* refers to the same elements, but collectively, whereby the parties
involved are interest groups (employees, unions, government through legislation)
rather than individuals.

   In addition to the above-described two dimensions, historically grown configurations of firms also have their bearing on the structuring of HRM. The concept of administrative heritage (Bartlett and Ghoshal, 1989) refers to the influence of structures,
methods, competencies, values and so on, which originated in the past and can still be
considered as an important influential factor (for better or worse) in continued organisation structuring, including the structuring of HRM (Flood et al., 1996, p. 317).
Together with the two dimensions these three forces have an impact upon the so-called
dominant coalition and its room for manoeuvre. From a pluralistic perspective the

dominant coalition is made up of a number of key actors. Examples of these are the various executive and governing boards, the works council and the HR department. These actors all have their own norms and values, shared with others to a greater or lesser degree. Whether the human resource department is really part of this dominant coalition, however, depends upon its perceived credibility and professional capabilities in the eyes of its main stakeholders as outlined earlier in this chapter. The shaded area in Fig 15.2 represents the available room for the dominant coalition to manoeuvre in shaping HRM. Depending on the situation this leeway may be expansive or restricted. Examples of relevant circumstances are the market position, the degree of unionisation, labour-capital ratio, and the financial health of the company (see for a more extended treatment of contingencies governing the degree of leeway, Paauwe, 1991). Based on the available room for manoeuvre actors involved in the dominant coalition develop initiatives to shape HR policies that will further or strengthen a sustainable competitive advantage. Important in this respect are initiatives that are unique and thus firm specific. This unicity is valuable, scarce, virtually inimitable, and difficult to replace in the short run (Mahoney and Pandian, 1992).

The resource based approach, of which we have given some examples earlier, focusses on the key success factors of individual firm behaviour which are a portfolio of differential core skills and routines, coherence across skills and unique proprietary know-how and values. Important in this respect is the role that can be fulfilled by HR professionals. Amidst all the pressures for profit maximising they are able to emphasize the long-term perspective in building commitment by taking into account not only justified claims in the areas of fairness and legitimacy as put forward by interest groups, but also the capabilities and specific characteristics of the human resources and their possibilities for training and development. Emphasising these elements offers insights in competitive strategies that are unique, firm specific and difficult to imitate by competitors. Without such an expanded vision the power of the HRM specialists within a Western European social economic context will decline. Moreover presenting the specific characteristics and capabilities of human resources and offering a developmental perspective for them implies a unique contribution from the personnel function – a unique contribution based on criteria that are 'deviant' from the line manager's perspective and which provide a continuous and limitless source of offering added value in a wider sense than the strict economic rational meaning of that concept.

The works council can as well play an important role in this whole process of strategy development. Based on its legally prescribed twofold task of representing both the interests of the sound functioning of the enterprise in all its objectives and the interests of workers it can help to reconcile different claims put forward by for example management and unions. In this way it can help to bring about a unique synthesis of strategic demands and the characteristics and aspirations of the workforce itself. In this respect it is not surprising that in our case studies among leading Dutch companies we very often encountered a co-operative and creative – albeit sometimes due to conflicts and diverging opinions – working relationship between HRM specialists and representatives of the works council.

Summary

In this chapter a number of key issues that are all relevant in the area of strategic integration have been discussed – integration with respect to corporate strategy, line management, quality, planning, control and performance and finally the integration of the different tools and instruments in order to achieve HR competencies. Based on case study evidence we were able to give perspective to the average and sometimes gloomy image that arises out of the available survey data. Although the Dutch image presented here might not be very rosy we have no reason to be pessimistic about the future. There is a high degree of consciousness that things need to change and a number of companies demonstrate progress in different areas of strategic integration. This aim of strategic integration does not imply that HRM is being condemned to the simple one-sidedness of fulfilling business managers' needs exclusively based on strategic demands of the marketplace. On the contrary, the reputation and credibility of the HR professionals will be at stake if they solely offer added value in that narrow sense. The Dutch and continental Western European social-economic setting with all the different parties involved offers unique possibilities for developing HR strategies that take into account the specific characteristics of the workforce and its potential for development. The conceptual framework of the HR based theory of the firm gives a clear overview of the different dimensions and parties involved. Moreover it emphasises both co-operation and 'creative conflict' between the parties involved in the dominant coalition in order to bring about unique propositions for competitive advantage in the long run.

REFERENCES

Baarda, P.R., Kouwenhoven, C.P.M., and Werkhoven, J.A. (1994) *Ken- en stuurgetallen voor personeelsmanagement*, Kluwer Bedrijfswetenschappen/NVP, Deventer.

Barney, J.B. (1991) 'Firm Resources and Sustained Competitive Advantage', *Journal of Management*, 17, pp. 99–120.

Bartlett, C. and Ghoshal, S. (1989) *Managing across Borders: Transnational Solutions*, Boston, MA, Harvard Business School Press.

Beer, M., Spector, B., Lawrence, P.R., Mills, D.Q. and Walton, R.E. (1984) *Managing Human Assets*, New York: The Free Press.

Bolweg, J. (1989) 'Internalisering van de arbeidsverhoudingen en politisering van het personeelsmanagement', in Bolweg, J.F., and Kluytmans, F., *De noodzaak van nieuwe verhoudingen*, Deventer.

Bolweg, J. (1994) 'De beste plek is midden in de organisatie', *Personeelsbeleid*, 30/1994, Nos. 7/8, pp. 24–5.

Carroll, S.J. (1991) 'The New HRM Roles, Responsibilities, and Structures', in *Managing Human Resource in the Information Age*, Washington, DC, Bureau of National Affairs, pp. 204–26.

Flood, P., Cannon, M., and Paauwe, J. (1996) *Managing without Traditional Methods: International Innovations in Strategic Human Resource Management*, London, Addison-Wesley.

Golden, K.A. and Ramanujam, V. (1985) 'Between a Dream and a Nightmare. On the Integration of the Human Resource Management and Strategic Business Planning Process', *Human Resource Management*, winter, No. 4, pp. 429–52.

Hoof, Van, F.F. (1985) Arbeidsbestel op een Keerpunt. In: Faase, L., Ott, M. and Vos, C.J., *Nievure breukslakken in het Arbeidsbestel*, Tijdstroom.

Hoogendoorn, J., Sirks, J. and Haima van der Wal, T. (1992) *Het Price Waterhouse Cranfield Project over Internationaal Strategisch Human Resource Management*, voorlopig verslag van de Nederlandse resultaten (Erasmus Universiteit Rotterdam, Faculteit Bedrijfskunde).

Hoogendoorn, J., Laumans, M., van Stiphout, J. and Sirks, J. (1995) *Het Cranfield Onderzoek naar Internationaal Strategisch Human Resource Management*, 1994/1995, Erasmus Universiteit Rotterdam, Faculteit Bedrijfskunde, mei/1995.

Kamoche, K. (1994) 'A Critique and a Proposed Reformulation of Strategic Human Resource Management', *Human Resource Management Journal*, Vol. 4, No. 4, pp. 29–43.

Kluytmans, F., van Sluijs, E. (1995) 'De relatie tussen bedrijfsbeleid en personeelsmanagement', *Tijdschrift voor arbeidsvraagstukken*, 11e jrg, nr 1, pp. 34–44.

(KVM) Kooimans and Van Mill Consultants B.V. (1994) *P&O op waarde geschat*, rapportage naar aanleiding van het onderzoek naar de ontwikkelingen van de kwaliteit en klantgerichtheid van P&O, Rotterdam, September 1994.

Legge, K. (1978) *Power, Innovation and Problem-Solving in Personnel Management*, London, McGraw-Hill.

Maenhout, J.M.M. van and Hoof, J.J. van (1993) *Personeelsresearch in Kaart gebracht*, SISWO-informatief nr. 1.

Mahoney, J.T. and Pandian, J.R. (1992) 'The Resource Base View within the Conversation of Strategic Management', *Strategic Management Journal*, 13, pp. 363–80.

Paauwe, J. (1991) 'Limitations to Freedom: Is there a Choice for Human Resource Management?', *British Journal of Management*, Vol. 2, pp. 103–119.

Paauwe, J. (1994) *Organiseren: Een grensoverschrijdende passie*, Oratie, Samsom Bedrijfswetenschappen, Alphen aan den Rijn.

Paauwe, J. (1996) 'Personnel management without personnel managers: varying degrees of outsourcing the personnel function', in Flood et al., *Managing without traditional methods: International innovations in strategic HRM*, London, Addison Wesley, 1996, Chapter 6.

Project group 'Personnel management in strategic perspective' (1993) *Enquete resultaten strategische P&O-beleid*, Rotterdam School of Business Administration, Erasmus University, September (43pp.).

Purcell, J. (1985) 'Is Anybody Listening to the Corporate Personnel Department?', *Personnel Management*, September 1985, pp. 28–31.

Scheurer, L., Krancher, F., and Manders, F. (1993) 'Human Resource Management is géén vanzelfsprekendheid', *Gids voor Personeelsmanagement*, 1, pp. 31–69.

Schilstra, K.M., and Smit, E.J. (1994) 'Changing Forms of Interest Representation in the Netherlands', paper presented at The IIRA Regional European Conference, Helsinki, August 1994.

Schuler, R.A. (1990) 'Repositioning the Human Resource Function: Transformation or Demise?', *Academy of Management Executive*, Vol. 4, No. 3, pp. 49–60.

Schuler, R.A. and Jackson, S.E. (1987) 'Linking Competitive Strategies with Human Resource Management Practices', *Academy of Management Executive*, 1, 3.

Shipton, J. and McAuley, J. (1994) 'Issues of Power and Marginality in Personnel', *Human Resource Management Journal*, Vol. 4, No.1, pp. 1–13.

Smit, E., Schilstra, K. and Paauwe, J. (1995) *Belangenbehartiging van werknemers: een toekomstverkenning*, VUGA uitgevery B.V., 's Gravenhage.

Soin, S.S. (1992) *Total Quality Control Essentials: Key Elements, Methodologies, and Managing for Success*, New York, McGraw-Hill, Inc.

Storey, J. (1992) *Developments in the Management of Human Resources*, Oxford, Blackwell.

Ten Have, K. (1993) *Markt, Organisatie en personeel in de industrie*, Tilburg University Press, Tilburg.

Tissen, R.J. (1991) *Mensen beter managen in theorie en praktijk: een exploratieve studie*, Proefschrift d.d. 23 mei 1991, Kluwer Bedrijfswetenschappen, Deventer.

Tyson, S. (1995) *Human Resource Strategy*, London, Pitman Publishing.

Uijlen, Y. and Paauwe, J. (1994) Internal Research Memorandum on personnel management and unit management, HRS-RU, Rotterdam: Erasmus University, 12 pp.

Visser, J. (1992) 'The Coming Divergence in Dutch Industrial Relations', in Gladstone, A. et al. (eds) *Labour Relations in a Changing Environment*, Berlin.

Watson, T.J. (1977) *The Personnel Manager: A Study in the Sociology of Work and Employment*, London, Routledge and Kegan Paul.

Wernerfelt, B. (1984) 'A Resource-Based View of the Firm', *Strategic Management Journal*, 5, pp. 171–80.

Wilkinson, A., Marchington, M. and Dale, B. (1993) 'Human Resource's Function', *Total Quality Management*, June 1993, pp. 31–5.

Williamson, O. (1985) Markets and Hierarchies, New York: Macmillan.

Zeithaml, V.A., Parasuraman, A. and Berry, U. (1990) *Delivering Quality Services: Balancing Customer Perceptions and Expectations*, New York, The Free Press.

16 HRM IN SWEDEN – A STRATEGIC CHALLENGE OR A STRUGGLE FOR SURVIVAL?

Magnus Söderström

Personnel management in Sweden has a long and well established history. But its importance and status have changed considerably since the early 1920s, reflecting the political, economic and social developments of the country. Now the Swedish economy and labour market is rapidly shifting from manufacturing towards a service- and knowledge-based society. Since 1995 Sweden has also entered the European Union. The aim of this chapter is to discuss the opportunities and challenges to HRM in Sweden in the future (see also Söderström, 1993; Söderström and Syrén, 1992).

Economy and the labour market

In the middle of the nineteenth century Sweden still was a rural, decentralised and poor country. The last quarter of the nineteenth century, however, witnessed economic change, as manufacturing expanded rapidly. A new infrastructure was developed and a number of successful manufacturing companies were soon established.

At this time, and despite its small size, Sweden had the benefit of a number of strong technological innovations, such as Dahlén's automatic lighthouse, Ericsson's telephone system, de Laval's milk separator, Ljungström's turbine wheels and Winquist's ball bearings. It has often been pointed out that an unusual abundance of natural resources, together with creative innovators, were the main preconditions for the expanding Swedish export industry.

The Swedish economy has been based on large reserves of resources such as timber, minerals and water power. Due to technological progress in iron and steel production and new chemical processes for turning wood fibre into paper pulp, the metal and forest product industries became very strong and dominated the business sector for many years. Swedish car, aircraft, electronic and drug manufacturing achieved international renown. In addition to this, shipbuilding and textile industry for a long time played an important role in the economy.

An essential part of the Swedish economy, therefore, has been export sales and manufacturing. On the other hand, however, there has been a long and powerful co-operation between employers, employees and the government, often known as the 'Swedish Model' (*Svenska Modellen*). This model was originally based on five national agreements during 1938–48, which then became the framework for economic development and industrial relations for the next 25 years. The annual increase in GNP was extremely high during this period, more than 3 per cent on average, a situation that created social development and welfare improvements for a long time.

Today the picture has changed totally. Facing increased competition on the international markets since the 1970s a great deal of the traditional manufacturing has been restructured or closed down, especially in the forest sector, mechanical engineering, shipbuilding and textiles. Further on, a number of service industries have replaced the role of manufacturing in the Swedish economy and labour market, particularly in retail, catering, hotels, banking, finance, insurance, transport, computing, consultancy and tourism. Even the public sector has grown in volume and importance.

A significant trend during the 1980s and the 1990s has been towards *increasing specialisation and high value added products*, particularly within electronics, telecommunications, chemicals and drugs. Another obvious trend has been *developing new services and service concepts* as well as integrating advanced physical products with different kinds of services, such as maintenance systems, computer software, training programmes or financial support.

Sweden has now mainly become a service- and knowledge-based economy, where about 60 per cent of the annual GNP is derived from private and public services (including building and construction). About 75 per cent of the labour market will be defined as private or public services and less than 20 per cent as manufacturing work.

The present economic crisis in Sweden, therefore, might be explained as a function of increasing international competition, a structural change from manufacturing towards services, increasing public sector costs and a declining internal productivity. Unfortunately unemployment has also risen from a level of 2–3 per cent during the 1970s and 1980s to about 9–10 per cent in 1997 and is predicted to remain on this level for at least two to three years.

Four periods in Swedish HRM

Regarding this general background four different periods in the history of Swedish HRM can be identified. The first three were the 'individual' period 1921–45; the post-1945 expansion; and the period of structural transition and change during the 1970s to the early 1980s. Today we are approaching a 'fateful period', which to the HRM functions could either mean an active strategic orientation or a struggle for survival.

The early history of personnel management in Sweden is also the history of one single woman, Ms Kerstin Hesselgren, a liberal MP and our first female inspector of work environment. In 1921 she established the SAIA association (Social Workers within Industry and Business), which later became the SPF (Sveriges Personaladministrativa Forening, Sweden's equivalent of the IPD – Institute of Personnel & Development). By the late 1930s SAIA had grown into a powerful unit with about 1000 members, mainly women working with health and safety on an individual level in a variety of companies. At this time operational personnel issues were handled by middle management and supervisors.

After 1945 personnel departments were gradually founded, first in manufacturing sites and, some years later, in the public sector. During this time new managerial principles heading for large-scale production, centralisation and specialised staff departments were introduced. The now expanding economy also underlined the need for professional efforts concerning recruitment, training, manpower planning and reward systems. Another important task was to transform the national agreements of the *Svenska Modellen* framework to local activities on company level. For the next 25 years industrial relations became the overall keyword.

The first personnel managers came from a varying background, for example psychologists, technicians, accountants, union officials and retired army officers. They mainly became specialists in administrative procedures, negotiations and planning, rather than being real professionals of the whole HRM field. Mirroring this the personnel function of the line managers now became obviously restricted. Instead, a functional line management was introduced where line managers took the responsibility for operations and technical issues only, while most planning and administration duties lay upon the new personnel departments.

The third period in Swedish personnel management then came during the 1970s with an emphasis on two particular areas; labour market law and structural change. During this time several new laws were introduced, leading to a radical change in industrial relations policies and creating new demands on employers and personnel departments. The centralised model therefore became reinforced for a number of years, where line management still did not take very much part in the HRM process. The increase in legislation coincided with a structural crisis, mainly reflecting the energy crisis and, not the least, increased international competition. As already mentioned lots of manufacturing sites were closed, particularly mechanical workshops, saw mills, textile units and shipyards.

In these years, personnel managers had to spend a lot of time on negotiations with local unions as well as on dismissals, early retirements and retraining. Unemployment was then increasing, for the first time since 1945, although it was still not high compared to today's figures.

However, things changed. In the 1980s the transition in the labour market from manufacturing to service industries accelerated rapidly, which meant a new managerial context and other demands to many HRM professionals. New ideas for strategy and organisation strategies were introduced and HRM now had a more complicated and sometimes blurred role.

The new service strategies meant an emphasis on customer relations and quality but also on staff training, corporate culture, motivation and work organisation (see, for example, Jones, 1989; Voss et al., 1985). The well-known SAS (Scandinavian Airlines) launch of a new service strategy took place in 1981–2, an approach which was then followed by hundreds of other companies and public bodies in Sweden. As part of the new strategies, market orientation, decentralisation and deregulation became the overall trends which meant a new interplay between HRM departments and line management.

The general basis for the new strategies is to be found in for example Thompson (1967), Ansoff (1978) and Argyris and Schön (1978) and, more specifically, from for example Peters and Waterman (1980). From the Nordic perspective especially could be mentioned, above all, Normann (1983) and Grönroos (1983) who have developed the ideas of service management, Beckérus and Edström (1987), who explain the ideas as a new 'doctrine of management' and Arvonen (1989) who introduced the term 'management by ideas'.

In practice line management now received a more powerful responsibility for operational HRM issues, a trend which has been observed in the current Cranfield and Price Waterhouse study (Brewster and Söderström, 1993). This pattern of course varies considerably reflecting different kinds of business and operations, but three models now could be identified in Swedish HRM.

The first model means that line managers on different levels have taken over daily HRM procedures such as recruitment, training, assessment, determination of wages and salaries (within the frames of local agreements), work environment and so on. HRM departments then seem to adapt by focussing on policy issues, management development, co-ordination and administrative support.

Another model which apparently has become quite popular, particularly in big companies and public bodies such as hospitals and health care, is where line managers now often have their own 'barefoot HRM' assistants, mainly young personnel all-rounders, professionals with a qualified background in HRM.

The third model simply means that personnel departments have been reduced or closed down, most HRM staff have been dismissed and the main HRM issues have been taken over by line management and, to some extent, accountants.

Although there is a lack of empirical evidence, all three models could be observed in Swedish companies and public bodies today. The interpretation of this might be that personnel departments and HRM professionals have faced the new demands in very different ways, from very active and enterprising measures to attitudes of denial or defence. The history up to now can be shortly summarised by Table 16.1.

The situation 1995 and forward – at the cross roads

As in many other western countries, traditional personnel policies in Scandinavia are now gradually being replaced by a wider concept of human resource management (Beardwell and Holden, 1994; Beer et al, 1985; Brewster and Hegewisch, 1994; Guest, 1989; Storey, 1989; Tyson and Fell, 1986).

To a country like Sweden with its strong traditions of industrial relations, based on national agreements, collective models, equality between all parts of the labour market and social welfare, this shift seems not to be just a 'game of words' but also an important ideological shift. As Sweden now has entered the European Union this tradition has to be related to, and requested in, a wider European perspective.

Therefore the future of HRM in Sweden, of course, is discussed a lot. One way would be the professional, strategic path; the alternative would be non-professional and non-strategic, something like an administrative support function in the backyard. There seems to be a number of opinions on this.

The first one is simply about economy and cost/benefit analysis: does the professional HRM function in fact contribute to business and operations in such a valuable way that it will be worth its own costs in the future?

Another question is about strategy and development: How should a professional HRM function respond to a changing external environment? Will the HRM professionals be able to provide organisations with relevant competence for the future? And, in

Table 16.1 Different periods and main characteristics in the history of Swedish HRM

Period	Time	Level	Main tasks and characteristics
The pioneers	1921–45	Individual	Health and safety, counselling
Expansion	1945–75	Organisation	Industrial relations Centralised personnel management Manpower planning Application of the 'Swedish Model'
Transition	1975–85	Organisation and individual	New labour legislation Crisis management Outplacement and retraining
Strategic (?)	1985–	Organisation	Strategic and organisational development Economics, quality and ethics Value conflicts The European Union

which way could HRM face critical strategic demands for customer service and quality, flexible work patterns and internal productivity?

A third question is perhaps more complicated. It is about national values and beliefs. As an important part of the Swedish social history, personnel management has always focussed on human values and social welfare. Do the structural changes and economic crises mean that we have to throw this tradition away and replace national values by short-term accountancy and maybe accelerating social conflicts? What kind of renewal in thinking and compromises have to be carried out in the near future?

Having these questions in mind HRM obviously has to become more clear about its own core areas but also more integrated with other functions in organisations. According to the literature, and empirical studies carried out at IPF Institute (Frank and Vejbrink, 1994) in the current debate it seems possible to discern the following five areas of strategic demands to HRM in the near future, namely:

1. the *economic* perspective – accountancy and HRM;
2. *new markets and quality concepts* – quality management and HRM;
3. new *organisational roles* – HRM in another organisational context;
4. the *ideological* dilemma – from industrial relations towards HRM; and
5. the *ethical* perspective – the growing demand for ethical consciousness.

A discussion of the contents and implications of these demands follows, then some final comments and conclusions.

The economic perspective

As pointed out a noticeable overall trend of the late 1900s will be the continuing shift in the labour force of most industrialised countries, Sweden not the least, from manufacturing towards companies and other organisations working with services, competence and information as organisation-determining factors.

A dramatic change is, therefore, occurring in the relative importance of various production factors in most organisations, from traditional variables such as raw materials, financial capital, labour force and energy towards competence (or, more traditionally, know-how) and corporate culture. Drucker (1993) says, for example, that competence is no longer a resource, it has rapidly become *the* resource!

It is reasonable to assume that competence will become even more interesting from an economic and investment point of view and that various forms of the human capital approach will be more widely used (Brewster and Connock, 1985; Lundmark and Söderström, 1992; Tyson and Fell, 1986). From an HRM perspective, different ways of developing, using and maintaining competence seem to be of an increasing strategic and economic interest. Or, as Barbara Morris points out (1985, p. 81):

> Obviously, using people effectively and making the most of their skills and abilities is important in any organization, whatever its type, but in service operations human resources have an added importance for a variety of reasons ...

In front of all, the following questions will be of great importance to most organisations (see also Lundmark and Söderström, 1992):

- What competence will be needed to develop and implement new business ideas or strategies, today and in the immediate future?
- What alternatives are available as regards obtaining, developing, retaining and using critical competence for a certain period of time?
- What are the economic consequences, in terms of costs and pay-off, of the different alternatives from an investment point of view?

Although defined as a production factor of increasing value, competence, as well as corporate culture, cannot always be estimated and handled in the same quantitative way as traditional factors such as financial capital, raw materials and labour force. Tyson and Fell (1986) particularly emphasise two problems concerning investment judgements which are important to notice, namely:

> (1) ... Finding a layer of costs that is valid for all personnel decisions is extremely difficult, but unless comparability of costs is achieved, the analysis will be biased, and hence as irrational as any other method ...
> (2) ... There is frequently no 'objective' benefit for personnel policies, therefore there is not only the question of *who* benefits, but also the question of *who says who benefits*. (1986, p. 106)

Not too much research has been done in this field up to now. There are, however, some promising approaches to manage an encounter between accountancy and HRM. A human capital approach to training, as well as to HRM in general, has appeared in the literature from time to time, for example in terms of cost–benefit analysis of training (Sandberg, 1974; Thomas et al., 1969); the view of 'social accounts' (Gröjer and Stark, 1978); evaluating the personnel function (Tyson and Fell, 1986); a wider look at 'the economics of personnel management' (Brewster and Connock, 1985; Cannon, 1979; Johansson, 1987); or the 'economics of competence' (Lundmark and Söderström, 1987, 1992). Regarding the varying approaches here the following statements ought to be made:

- compared to manufacturing, the cost structure is different in service operations, as competence and labour force most often are the dominant costs, and the most expensive resource (often something like 60–90 per cent of the total costs);
- employees do not only represent costs, they also generate incomes and revenue as they are part of the service and therefore will have a great impact on the customers;
- by affecting the most expensive resource HRM policies and measures will be expected to contribute to the outcome of the operations in most organisations; and
- consequently it seems desirable to integrate cost/benefit analysis and HRM measures in order to show the real economic aspects, in terms of revenue and costs, of varying HRM efforts.

New markets and quality concepts

Research on service organisations has emphasised important differences compared with traditional manufacturing in terms of operations, markets, quality, customer relations and the role of the employees (Brown et al., 1991, Grönroos, 1983; Grönroos and Gummesson, 1985; Jones, 1989; Normann, 1983; Voss et al., 1985).

In the classical industrial market, physical goods are sold. Traditionally, factors such as price, technical quality and delivery time have played a decisive role. Within the service sector, on the other hand, services are produced that, to a great extent, possess subjective elements and cannot be produced until there is an interplay between producer and consumer: often it may be said that the service is created jointly. Furthermore, today it is common for physical goods to be sold together with services, a 'combined service'. The completeness of the combination, or the service part of the product, is often what makes the product unique and competitive.

The new markets therefore work differently than goods markets. Now factors such as image, relationships, functional quality, competence and flexibility have become of particular importance, in addition to price and technical standards. These are factors that are primarily qualitative, abstract and difficult to measure in the usual way. Also, they are mainly defined by the customer. Quality is shaped by an interactive process in which both producer and customer take part. Value is then created during every single encounter with the customer, which clearly puts the competence and involvement of the front-line staff in a key position in most service industries.

The success in the new markets obviously very much depends on the performance of the front-line staff, in the context of HR measures such as first-line management, corporate culture, training, team spirit and relations, reward and work-time systems, work environment (as well as available technical support systems). If economic success depends on investments in these factors, consequently a professional HRM function may contribute directly to income and revenue for the company (given appropriate services in relation to the market).

This situation creates a strategic opportunity for an interesting co-operation between the market function, line management and the HRM professionals. As discussed in the previous section it will also become necessary to look at various HRM activities from a cost/benefit point of view, where the professional task will be to find the right measures for development, such as training programmes, reward systems or work environment improvements, and to show a convincing correlation between those investments and operational pay-off.

New organisational roles

A general observation seems to be that decentralisation in general means new roles *both* for previous staff departments and for line management. Further, decentralisation obviously is a dynamic process rather than a shift from one situation to another (Södergren, 1992).

Responding to decentralisation and deregulation the former HRM departments in Sweden have become organised in a new way, focussing on three different roles: the *strategic* role, the *consultancy* role and the *internal service* role. However, although varying in detail, this model has been introduced during the last years in manufacturing and service industries as well as in the public sector (see Table 16.2; see also Brewster and Söderström, 1994, p. 55).

Sometimes all roles and functions could be organised in the same department, other times there will be for example a small strategic group close to top management and other units for consultancy and administrative services. The role of line management in this model will primarily be as an 'internal customer' who demands services from the HR function according to their own operations, needs and conditions. As decentralisation gathers speed only a few tasks tend to survive centrally, for example HR policies and frames, crucial negotiations, management development, career planning models, reward systems and international aspects.

According to empirical studies which have been carried out at the Swedish IPF institute (Frank and Vejbrink, 1994; Hedlund et al., 1990) there is an obvious trend from an administrative and centralised HRM role towards more strategy and consultancy work for the HRM professionals in general. As already mentioned the daily HRM work has, on the other hand, become more integrated in line operations and business.

In another Swedish study, decentralisation in 40 big private companies was analysed (Södergren, 1992). The most conscious and explicit changes that took place in the decentralisation process were changes in structures, formal responsibilities and control systems. Less evident, but even more important, says Södergren, were changes in working roles and competence patterns, factors that have not very often been observed in earlier

Table 16.2   Roles for the HRM function in decentralised and deregulated organisations

Role	Related to	Contents
Strategic	Top management, other companies.	Strategic planning, co-ordination and support
Consultancy	Line management	Non-standardised consultancy services
Service/admin. support	Line management All employees	Standardised services, for example training, health care, salaries and pensions

studies. The strongest pressure for change was reported for local managers who were responsible for the local business level. They met an increasing amount of 'indirect work' such as planning, HRM issues and administration; 'Frequent examples were the budgets and accounting of the unit, human resource management, marketing and customer contacts, quality control, rationalizations, and business development' (Södergren, 1992, p. 324).

Consequently this meant a considerable change in role expectations and demands for new competence to most line managers. This also illuminates the statement made in this chapter that HRM is still becoming more integrated with operations and business in general. From this point of view it might be possible to look at the HRM function as 'a company in the company' with different internal 'markets' and services, such as top management (for the strategic role), line managers (for the consultancy role), and both line management and employees in general (for the administrative support role). In its turn it means that the same kind of demands on quality, discussed in the previous section, will be as important to obtain for the HRM function in relation to its internal customers.

The ideological dilemma – from IR towards HRM

To illuminate the current debate in Sweden it seems possible to compare traditional personnel and industrial relations (IR) policies and the new HRM principles (see also Söderström and Lindström, 1994 and Söderström and Syrén, 1992) as shown in Table 16.3.

Although the new principles have not fully replaced traditional personnel policies, the direction is obvious in Swedish work life today. A number of steps have been taken, from time to time, on the path towards HRM, such as decentralised negotiations on trade or company level, individual salaries, assessment centres, career planning, cost/benefit analysis on training efforts, flexible work time and task flexibility.

Table 16.3   Comparison of traditional personnel management policies and the new principles for HRM

Traditional personnel policies	The new concept of HRM principles
Internal perspective (defined in terms of administration, equality and justice)	External perspective (defined from the market and business point of view)
Centralised organisational forms, which are managed by formal plans, rules and control systems	Decentralised and deregulated organisational forms, managed by visions, objectives and shared values
Focus on the relationship between employer and employee	Focus on the relationship to business and operations
Rights and obligations	Contribution to business
An approach for distribution of rights and obligations	An approach for investment and development
Labour force	Competence
Mainly a static concept	Mainly a dynamic concept

However, national negotiations as well as industrial actions during the last few years show that there is still a potential, and sometimes apparent, disagreement between the employers' federations and the main unions concerning the direction and speed of the change towards the HRM principles. As already underlined, it is not too easy to replace the strong traditions and beliefs of the once so successful 'Swedish Model' by the new market-oriented and individualistic ideas. Maybe it is not possible in a lifetime. Reflecting Swedish traditions, a professional HRM function in the future, therefore, has to manage step by step, avoiding too many disputes on the way.

Many voices are heard in Sweden today asking for a 'new Swedish Model', responding to the changing demands of the service economy and the need for European co-operation, but also trying to keep up the main ideas of the previous model. A first step has been taken in 1995 by forming a new government commission to look at the labour market laws from two points of view, (a) the 'need for increasing flexibility in companies and public bodies' and (b) 'every single employee's right to fair treatment and security'.

The ethical perspective

For a number of reasons, questions are often being asked in the Swedish debate about ethics and morals in relation to business operations in general and HRM in particular (see for example Brytting et al., 1993; Hansson, 1985; Hermerén, 1990).

In fact there are different reasons for this current trend. One reflects the above mentioned structural change in the Swedish economy and labour market, which has emphasised problems and principles concerning dismissal, outplacement and the transfer of employees. The second reason is that the managerial principles of decentralisation and deregulation open up possibilities for more individual responsibility and judgement within organisations. To managers as well as employees this in its turn means uncertainty and an increasing need for advice on ethical issues.

A third reason, apparently, is connected to the development of service quality, as discussed above, where there will be an ethical dimension as part of the encounter between the customer and the producer in many services, for example, banking, health care or public administration.

In this section we will therefore briefly discuss the implications of this challenge to HRM in Sweden today and in the future. According to the *Cambridge International Dictionary* (1995) ethics means 'a system of accepted beliefs which control behaviour, . . . such a system based on morals'. Hansson (1985) defines ethics as the 'study of principles of moral action and moral values'. Furthermore, he observes that the word 'moral' is sometimes used as a synonym but usually refers to the application of technical principles. Moral also has to do with instrumental values, with characteristics that contribute to people's ability to live and work well together.

Koskinen (1993) differentiates between two approaches to ethics. On the one hand there are *descriptive* ethics, which describe and analyse notions of good and evil, right and wrong, and so on. On the other hand there are *normative* ethics, which question what actions are morally correct or reprehensible, what values should be desirable or should be rejected, and so on.

Brytting et al. (1993) hold a similar view, claiming that the term 'morals' has come to refer to actions or practice, while the term 'ethics' is used for the thinking and reasoning process. In addition to the differentiation between descriptive and normative ethics, there is a further distinction between ethical value theory and constructive theory, as well as between the ethics of expedience and the ethics of duty. Brytting et al. point out that actions taken in business can be judged from various perspectives, including an ethical one, defined as follows:

> **By an ethical perspective we mean that reason, empathy, and conscience assume a central role in decisions and emphasize a moral dimension when evaluated.** (1993, p. 67)

Brytting et al. also distinguish between common ethics, based on our common culture, and specialised ethics that originate from the ambitions of various occupational groups to formulate and live up to special codes of occupational ethics. In their view it should be possible to express common ethics in the following four points (see also Hermerén, 1990), namely:

- the right to autonomy;
- the right to fair treatment;
- the obligation to do the right thing; and
- the obligation not to cause harm.

When the debate about quality in the business world started Peter Drucker (1981) wrote a noteworthy article on the then-current debate about business ethics. His main premise was that ethics always depends on relationships, just as the roles may change in various relationships. Drucker recognised that systems of rules alone do not create ethics or morals; rather, the starting point should be the reciprocal obligations that traditionally apply to various relationships. Drucker goes on to say that there are no real differences between public and private organisations; rather, every business that creates relationships and interdependence also gives birth to moral demands, although the type of demand may vary.

A recurring idea in the literature about work-life ethics seems to be that one's consciousness should be raised about ethical questions, and one should strive for dialogue and develop a moral understanding to a higher degree than normally takes place on a daily basis (Brytting et al., 1993; Hermerén, 1990). Examples of questions that should then be answered follow immediately from the different ways of regarding ethics and morals. One way of taking responsibility for one's actions is to contemplate, writes Wahlund (1994). Bergquist et al. (1994) emphasise in the conclusion of the same book (p. 129):

> **The reader who has come this far in the book must have realized that the authors describe ethical questions as intellectual problems. They are easier to solve, or at least they can be solved, if they are made conscious and become the object of thought and reflection.**

As Grönroos (1983) points out, functional quality is often the most critical part of the total quality of different services. It is also here that the ethical dimension comes in; it is quite simply part of the considerations that should be taken by the producer *before* every service is delivered, and it is also part of the interplay between producer and consumer. Ethical aspects therefore become part of the front-line staff's daily work, particularly in decentralised and deregulated organisations.

In addition to this the parallel to HRM seems obvious; in any relationship between employer and employee, as well as between employers and unions, ethical, or moral, issues will appear from time to time. Consequently the HRM function, as well as line management, ought to be prepared for this, by training, by dialogues and, perhaps, also by some kind of ethical codes etc.

In situations in which a service is created and produced, either externally or internally, various kinds of ethical questions may very well arise. On a qualitative basis, we think it is possible for the HRM function to distinguish the following *ethical categories* (see also Söderström and Wåglund, 1994):

- ethics that arise from *laws and other legal systems* (reflecting a democratic process at some point);
- ethics that traditionally (and for religious reasons) deal with *protection of life, health and safety*;
- ethics that deal with *individual respect and integrity*;
- ethics that are based on *professional practice, rules of ethics*, and the like (this may also include 'sound business practice' and so on); and
- ethics that are based on *'common sense' and cultural codes* (pertaining to different national cultures and so on).

One way to illustrate ethical views of HRM would be to analyse real situations in operations and daily work, of a type designated 'critical incidents', in terms of one or more of these categories. Then it would be possible to discuss the right measures or the need for corporate policies. Irrespective of organisational context, it is obvious that these categories will influence HRM responsibilities and policies, as a consequence of market-orientation, decentralisation and deregulation not the least.

Conclusions and a short look ahead

We have now discussed five areas of demand on the HRM function in the future. The discussion can be summarised by Table 16.4, with keywords and possible measures referring to each area of demand (the table should just be seen as an example, not a detailed conclusion).

As illustrated in the table there are some strategic areas of demand to which the HRM function has to respond in a professional way. Referring to e.g. Thompson (1967) or Handy (1989) it then will be most important to the organization to *develop and maintain its core* but also to adapt to a changing environment by flexible methods and practices. We think this is very much the case for HRM in Sweden today, as well as in other countries with a similar economic and social context.

The core of expertise and professionalism in HRM in the future consequently seems to be to integrate 'good personnel management practice' with human capital theory (economy), service management (quality), strategy and organisational theory (new organisations), HR principles (ideology) and ethical understanding (ethics). This integration then might be the unique contribution to business and operations tomorrow.

As discussed here a look ahead also reflects, of course, the links between the political and economic mainstream and the labour market on one hand and HRM on the other. Unclear values and strategies make for unclear HRM, a declining economy means short-term decisions, cost cutting and less welfare; a changing environment demands renewal, creativity and new strategies. The map for the future of choices about HRM in

Table 16.4 Strategic demands, keywords and possible measures for the HRM function in the future

Area of demand	Keywords	Measures (examples)
The economic perspective	Managing the most expensive resource; new cost structure Competence as main production factor Cost/benefit analysis Employees generating income/revenue	Integration of economy and HRM Developing 'economic models' for HRM measures/activities Appropriate inventions in, for example, training, reward systems, work organisation Systematic evaluation
New markets and quality	New market dynamics Interactive customer relations Functional quality Interplay producer/customer Front-line staff part of the product/service	Co-operation with market function and line management Integration between service development, training and support systems Reward systems reflecting customers' satisfaction
New organisational roles	Three main roles; strategic, consultancy and administrative support (more or less separated) 'A company in the company'	Clarified demands with possible contributions in the various roles The new concept of service quality applied to HRM
The ideological dilemma	Shift from traditional personnel management towards HRM Potential value conflicts	Step-by-step strategy Clarified values and beliefs Looking for a new 'Swedish Model'
The ethical perspective	Ethics and morals more crucial in services Decentralisation and deregulation means demand for ethical advice and support	Ethical consciousness needed, for example by training/dialogue Empirical situations (analysed by ethical categories) basis for HRM policies Ethical codes for HRM

Sweden seems clear; however, HRM in Sweden is at the cross roads, and the right choices have to be made.

REFERENCES

Ansoff, S. (1978) *Strategic Management*, London, Macmillan.

Argyris, C. and Schön, D. (1978) *Organizational Learning*, Reading, MA., Addison-Wesley.

Arvonen, J. (1989) *Att leda via idéer*, Lund, Studentlitt.

Beardwell, I. and Holden, L. (1994) *Human Resource Management. A Contemporary Perspective*, London, Pitman.

Beckérus, Å. and Edström, A. (1987) *Doktrinskiftet. Stockholm*, FA-rådet.

Beer, M. et al. (1985) *Human Resources Management: A General Managers' Perspective*, New York, The Free Press.

Bergquist, L. et al. (1994) *Etik och finanser*, Stockholm, SNS.

Brewster, C. and Connock, S. (1985) *Industrial Relations: Cost-Effective Strategies*, London, Hutchinson.

Brewster, C. and Hegewisch, A. (ed.) (1994) *Policy and Practice in European Human Resource Management*, The Price Waterhouse/Cranfield Survey, London, Routledge.

Brewster, C. and Söderström, M. (1993) *Human Resources and Line Management*, in Brewster et al., pp. 51–67.

Brewster, C. and Söderström, M. (1994) 'Human resources and line management', in Brewster and Hegewisch 1994, pp. 51–67.

Brewster, C. et al. (1992) *The European Human Resource Management Guide*, London, Academic Press.

Brown, S. et al. (1991) *Service Quality: Multidisciplinary and Multinational Perspectives*, Toronto, Lexington.

Brytting, T. et al. (1993) *Moral I verksamhet. Ett etsikt perspektiv på företag och arbete*, Stockholm, Natur & Kultur.

Cannon, J. (1979) *Cost Effective Personnel Decisions*, London, IPM.

Drucker, P. (1981) 'What is Business Ethics?', *McKinsey Quarterley*, Autumn.

Drucker, P. (1993) *Post-Capitalist Society*, London, Butterworth-Heinemann.

Frank, C. and Vejbrink, K. (1994) *Framtidens personalarbete*, Stockholm, SSR.

Gröjer, J.E. and Stark, A. (1978) *Social Redovisning*, Stockholm, SNS.

Grönroos, C. (1983) *Strategic Management and Marketing in the Service Sector*, Lund, Studentlitt.

Grönroos, C. (1992) *Service Management, Ledning, strategi och marknadsföring I servicekonkurrens*, Göteborg, ISL förlag.

Grönroos, C. and Gummesson, E. (1985) *Service Marketing – Nordic School Perspectives*, Stockholm University, Dept. of Business Administration.

Guest, D. (1989), in Storey, J. (ed.) (1989) *New Perspectives on Human Resources Management*, London, Routledge.

Handy, C. (1989) *The Age of Unreason*, London, Arrow Books.

Hansson, H.I. (1985) *Affärsliv och moral*, Stockholm, Liber.

Hedlund, E. et al. (1990) *Personalfrågor I tredje vågen*, Uppsala, IPF.

Hermerén, G. (1990) *Det goda företaget. Om etik och moral I företag*, Stockholm, SAF.

Johansson, U. (1987) *Utveckla det mänskliga kapitalet*, Stockholm, SPF.

Jones, P. (ed.) (1989), *Management in Service Industries*, London, Pitman.

Kanawaty, G. et al. (1989) 'Adjustment at the Micro Level', *International Labour Review*, 1989, 3.

Koskinen, L. (1993), *Vad är rätt? Handbok I etik*, Stockholm, Prisma.

Lundmark, A. and Söderström, M. (1987) 'Personalutbildning och ekonomi'. Arbetsrapporter från Pedagogiska institutionen, Uppsala universitet, 109.

Lundmark, A. and Söderström, M. (1992) 'Economics of Training and Personnel Development in Organizations', *Scandinavian Journal of Educational Research*, 36, 1.

Morris, B. (1985), in Voss et al., 1985.

Normann, R. (1983) *Service Management*, Stockholm, Liber.

Peters, T. and Waterman, R. (1980) *In Search of Excellence – Lessons from America's Best Run Companies*, New York, Harper & Row.

Sandberg, B. (1974) *Företagsutbildningen coh dess ekonomiska problem*, Stockholm, RTI.

Södergren, B. (1992) *Decentralisering, Förändring I företag och arbetsliv*, Stockholm School of Economics.

Söderström, M. (1990) 'Det svårfångade kompetensbegreppet', *Pedagogisk Forskning i Uppsala*, 94.

Söderstrom, M. (1993) 'Personnel Management in Sweden. An HRM Role Struggling for Survival,' *Personnel Management*, pp. 28–33.

Söderström, M. and Lindström, K. (1994) *Från IR till HRM. Två synsätt på personalfråg*, Uppsala, IPF.

Söderström, M. and Syrén, S. (1992) 'Sweden', in Brewster et al., 1992, pp. 483–523.

Söderström, M. and Wåglund, M. (1994) *Service Quality, Value-Creating Processes and Ethics: Unified Vision or Incompatible Concepts?*, Uppsala, IPF (in print).

Storey, J. (ed.) (1989) *New Perspectives on Human Resources Management*, London, Routledge.

Thomas, B. et al. (1969) 'A Cost-Benefit Analysis of Industrial Training', *British Journal of Industrial Relations*, 1.

Thompson, J.D. (1967) *Organizations in Action*, New York, McGraw-Hill.

Tyson, S. and Fell, A. (1986) *Evaluating the Personnel Function*, London, Hutchinson.

Voss, C. et al. (1985) *Operations Management in Service Industries and the Public Sector*, Chichester, John Wiley and Sons.

Wahlund, R. (1994), in Bergquist et al., 1994.

CHAPTER 17

THE THEORY AND PRACTICE OF HUMAN RESOURCE MANAGEMENT

Shaun Tyson

All the chapters in this book have shown the integration between business and human resource strategy as a practical necessity. At work, it is the self-evident benefit of arranging management processes to achieve agreed objectives, and to do so as cost effectively as possible, which occupies management thinking. One may ascribe to practical 'common sense' the managers' desire to incorporate people management strategies into their actions, rather than any attention to theoretical concerns they may have. What then is the place of theory in understanding HRM?

Theories of HRM – science or common sense?

The well known theories of HRM have been produced from the assumption that HRM is a sub-set of economically rational actions, directed on behalf of shareholders or other stakeholders, to protect and increase the value in the business. There is usually in these framework descriptions also a feedback loop from the organisation's output back to society, which in turn provides the labour and capital input (through the education system and capital markets) to the organisation (Beer et al., 1984; Fombrun et al., 1984; Hendry and Pettigrew, 1990). These rather cosy systemic structures express the underlying belief that HRM performs a societal function. However, the purpose of HRM, in the theories mentioned above, derive from three assumptions:

1. that the organisation itself is performing a valued service for society;
2. that the interests of all the stakeholders (especially those of shareholders and of employees) are identical; and
3. that people in the organisation act on a basis of economic rationality.

From these assumptions we can see that such HRM theories are management theories within a restricted compass, the intentions of which are to describe the effects of management policies, rather than to be concerned with what management is, of itself. While we would accept that HRM has a societal role, the systems perspective of the functionalist theories so commonly applied to HRM move from the system of HRM as a part of the wider social system quickly to a position which accepts HRM as societal phenomenon without questioning the legitimacy of HRM as an act of managerial authority. Such a view strongly supports a unitary frame of reference, where all employees are believed to be working towards a common set of goals. The co-operation between people is not seen to be problematic, and the fundamental issue addressed by sociological inquiry 'how is social life possible?' is not raised.

In part, the answer to this question resides in the common sense theorising of managers themselves. They trade on norms, and on their 'common sense' understandings of what is a common basis for action. Theories about the behaviours of others are a way of producing to the managers themselves a reality from which they can act, in the belief that they can predict the likely reactions of those with whom they are engaged in their roles.

> Schutz argues that our knowledge of the world is organised in a series of typifications which structure our understanding of settings and actions by allowing us to infer the unknown parts of others' motives. According to our understanding of 'what is really happening', we bring to bear what Schutz calls 'cook-book' knowledge, using tried recipes for success to achieve our purposes. Common-sense knowledge, then, defines our relevancies and our attribution of relevancies to others. (Silverman, 1972, p. 7)

Such attentions to common-sense theorising as derived from the phenomenologist Alfred Schutz can be found in the works of ethnomethodologists (Douglas, 1971; Garfinkel, 1967) whose approach to understanding the 'natural attitude' is helpful in showing how managers interpret and reinterpret meanings within organisations. While we might regard the negotiation of meaning as part of everyday social interaction (Berger and Luckman, 1966), the significance of the negotiation for managers is the special role they perform in organisations of converting employee meanings to be broadly in agreement with management meanings. For managers, common-sense theorising entails addressing questions about the motivation and commitment of their staff, for example, which is management for all 'practical purposes' to managers.

A general theory of HRM

This position on the way organisational reality is negotiated informed the general theory of HRM set out in Tyson (1995), and which was outlined in Chapter 1. According to this view, HRM is concerned to reinterpret societal and managerial meanings into the organisational context, and to reconcile these with the perceptions of organisation members. The framework for this theory seeks to explain the way these three levels of analysis interact (Fig 17.1).

At the level of the organisation, meanings are under continuous negotiation; the outcome from this process enables the interests of the various groups, the pluralities of power resources, to be sufficiently accommodated and reconciled to make working life possible. This was the process described in Chapter 2 where the perceptions of professional groups such as engineers, pilots, medical practitioners and consultants were noted to be critically important in managing change.

In the chapter on 'downsizing' the interests of the 'survivors' of change were discussed, along with the difficulties managers experienced in reconciling different

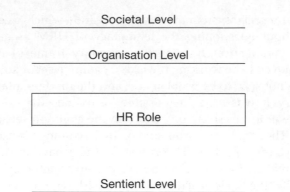

Source: after Tyson (1995).

Fig 17.1　Framework for the general theory of HRM

interests when the harsh realities of redundancy intrude. In the Burton Group case study we saw how employment contracts between the company and employees incorporated benefits to the employees and accommodated the needs of customers as well as staff. The ability to reconcile the interests of the three key groups – management, employees and customers – was a prerequisite for the HR strategy to be successful – a theme also found in the chapters which examine key HRM trends internationally in the other major economies.

The formal collective bargaining processes in the UK which were originally intended as mechanisms for reconciling competing interests have now been superseded by company and local level employee relations strategies, and employment laws which stress individual rights and obligations. Reward strategies are thus adopted which seek to build the psychological contract around individual rewards, or team based rewards, with objectives tied into organisational requirements. The opportunity to involve employees in creating their own reward packages and through share holding schemes is evidence of this trend towards individualism, and also of a strategy to engage employees to internalise the attitude change.

A more direct attempt at converting employee perceptions towards managerial perspectives is possible through employee and management development strategies. The management development and business education initiatives described here show how, as part of a coherent package of measures, management development in its widest sense can be the chief lever for organisation development. The process of the intervention itself, for example the analysis of the interpersonal processes taking place as part of an ethnographic study, can perform a developmental function by uncovering hidden agendas, and by penetrating to a deeper level, thus facilitate behavioural change. Change management is almost universally described in the management literature in terms of changing behaviours, attitudes, or values even, so that employees come to espouse managerially acceptable or preferred behaviours, attitudes and values. There is often also a further, long-term purpose to development: to sensitise employees to the need to change, and to encourage flexibility and a preparedness to accept future changes. Staff development policies and business education therefore are significant facilitators for managers to help create and prepare people for a new reality.

The theoretical view of HRM as an integrative mechanism is supported throughout this book. Integration between each of the three levels of analysis – the societal, organisational and sentient levels – is necessary, according to this argument, in order to implement strategies. Integration entails a negotiation over the meanings of managerial actions and interventions (which may be different at each hierarchical level) and over employee responses (which could equally vary between occupational groups and over time). The change management strategies described here were all attempts to bring the disparate interest groups within organisations to a point where change became accepted and defined in a way which would encourage the new behaviours required by management.

Managerial work as a practical activity

We have here put together a book which emphasises the need for practical strategies because managerial work ultimately is practical work: buying, selling, making or giving various kinds of service can only be achieved if such work is practically conceived and executed. Strategies must be 'practical' in the sense that they must, in the eyes of employees, including managers, be capable of implementation. Management is action oriented.

The paradox is that in order to implement strategies we must have a theory about the responses of others (customers, suppliers, employees and colleagues), and that while we may rely upon common-sense theorising and our experience of others when we attribute motives and forecast reactions we can never be sure what will actually happen until we do act. Thus we ourselves must be able to react appropriately in different and often complex organisational settings.

In these circumstances, predictions assume great significance. In part the rationale for a specialist HR function is its ability to make accurate predictions about employee responses to policies. Theories which managers rely upon are often models of, for example, decision making under economically rational conditions, or predictive theories for example on motivation, job satisfaction, and communication. One fruitful area for future research would be to attempt to understand how managers use formal theories in their predictive work.

HRM as a societal phenomenon

However, as Willmott (1996) reminds us, managerial 'knowledge' and theories are a product of the power relationships in organisations, and as suggested in our earlier critique of HRM theories, when we accept knowledge as 'objective' we make assumptions about the legitimacy of managerial authority:

> Knowledge that represents management as a set of technical roles, tasks or functions is a very powerful way of ignoring or delaying the political and problematic nature of management. (Willmott, 1996, p. 325)

But management knowledge, with all its assumptions, has been socially constructed, and is centred on the employment relationship. The production of this knowledge presents managers with a set of preconceived choices, and well established ways to negotiate new meanings, with employees, and to translate social norms and trends into organisational realities, through the perceptions of employees.

> It is no exaggeration to say that the employee is the subject of knowledge about work in industrial society. Since it is this society which has produced management as a practice and management knowledge as a body of academic teaching and research, one might say that what is available as knowledge about managing workers is knowledge of l'employé.
> (Jacques, 1996, p. 94)

From the society we might expect different educational systems, different industrial relations systems and different approaches to management to have an effect on how HRM is defined and on what constitutes HR knowledge (Tyson and Wikander, 1994). Societal influences remind us of the significance of context, and that changes to HRM are contingent upon cultural, political, legal and technological influences, and economic changes, especially to the labour market. The international comparisons we have in this book show the way societal changes influence HRM.

In the chapter on Japan, we can see an example of how multinationals were seeking to adjust their policies to fit the new business environment. The redefinition of 'lifetime' employment, and the 'hollowing out' of the economy – the loss of full-time, permanent jobs in Japan are consequences of these adjustments. Policy adjustments, for example through the changes to job evaluation schemes, and the end to seniority based pay, are part of the redefinition of the situation by management.

By the same token, the chapters on Germany and France show how new laws and the sensitivity of organisations to societal values are influences on HR functions in those two countries. Unwritten societal norms are just as important as official laws, so for example general concern on ecological matters in Germany, and in France the way redundancies were handled, produced pressure on managements to react positively in response. The notion of society is thereby given meaning in the workplace. But as we saw in the chapter by Frank Bournois there are no changes without conflict. These reflect the processes of organisational negotiation and adjustment.

When making broad statements on key issues in whole countries, inevitably an institutional approach has to be taken, in order to explain how national laws, customs and economic and social trends at a country level influence organisation level HRM. These chapters show how useful this approach can be, when as in the examples and cases quoted, the additional corporate level variations are added.

HRM and organisational performance: the theoretical base for HRM

Because new approaches to management have emerged, with new organisation structures, new technologies and new economic and social trends, the extra demands to make the most effective use of the human resource have been translated into new HR roles. The strands in the changing HRM role have been analysed in the chapters by Paauwe and Söderström, where we can see a widespread convergence in the extent and the direction of the changes, confirming the evidence from the UK, USA, Japan, Germany and France. The five key US issues discussed by Schuler and Huselid summarise these common concerns: what are described as the needs to 'align people with the business, to link HR with business needs, to facilitate global operations, to reconceptualise the HR function and to reorganise the HR Department'.

The underlying theme behind these questions centres on the contribution of HRM to organisational performance, and has prompted the thinking in every chapter of this book. The link between HRM and business needs can be seen in one of five main theoretical positions which have been elucidated in various forms in the preceding chapters. These theoretical positions are set out in the chart shown in Table 17.1. These theoretical positions are not mutually exclusive, rather there are implicit associations between them.

Institutional theories place the main source of competitive advantage in the way varying forms of capitalism are operated with different corporate governance structures ('insider' versus 'outsider' structures, for example), and the HR response via the way managers use and adapt to the business environment. Resource based theory gives HR a direct role through the way the whole mixture of variables within the organisation are operated. Contingency theory informs the resourced based view (the control of uncertainty granted through the inimitable mixture), and has two variants – first, setting out how bundles of policies are able to bring together the 'fit' between business strategy and the people responses required; on the other hand, from the same stable, the contribution of HR by means of change management grants HRM an OD (Organisation Development) role, helping to achieve the fit by aligning motivations and competencies with organisational needs (contingencies). The knowledge worker of the future will be the main source of competitive advantage, it is often argued. This would provide a

Table 17.1 Theoretical interpretations of sources of contribution of HRM to organisational performance

Theoretical linkage	Source of contribution	HR function activities
1. Institutional	Government policies, educational systems, social norms. Operation of capital markets, banks, investors, and shareholders	Exploits environment. Adapts societal processes. Organisation structures, corporate governance short term versus long term
2. Resource based theory	Employee competencies, product knowledge, organisational structure, management process creates inimitable mixture, delivers competitive advantage	Develops people, climate, skill base, retention policies
3. Contingency or 'fit' school	Direct contribution through bundles of policies. Integration of policies delivers performance	Analyses, creates policy solutions. 'Fit' through an HR strategy
4. Contingency or strategic change school	Process contribution: management of the process, co-ordination of activities according to context	Changing people to align their motivation, competencies with the business
5. New labour market structures	Knowledge workers – brain power equals main source of competitive advantage	Discover, develop, nurture, reward and value, talent

prime role for HRM in the contribution to organisational performance, since the retention and development of knowledge in the organisation would be the redefined HR role, according to this scenario.

The 'internalisation' or shift to line management of many formerly HRM specialist activities has produced the resultant focus on the quality of HRM and what the specialist function adds to the business. Changing models of HRM have been noted throughout the text. Magnus Söderström summarised the options now most frequently taken up – a 'strategic role', a 'consultancy role' and a service/administrative role. Clearly the first two such roles offer the most likely area for contribution to the business. There is evidence that a split is occurring between a strategic role advising senior line management on HR strategy on the one hand, and a routine administrative service conducted at operational level, on the other.

Conclusion

This chapter has argued that the processes of adjustment at organistional level is a process by which societal norms, economic and political trends are reinterpreted, by common-sense theorising, into meanings on which managers and employees can act. If we accept that the level of theorising should be at the same level as the phenomenon to be explained, we may say there is a separate sociological theory of the purpose of HRM, as an adaptive mechanism in society. However, the processes of adjustment and the negotiation of meaning are best explained by the common-sense theorising among managers. It is within organisations that the practice of HRM takes place, and this is where the contribution to organisational performance can be assessed, therefore. The framework suggested in Fig. 17.1 is intended to show how the different levels of theorising and managerial actions interact. The practical activities undertaken by managers have an adaptive purpose: flexibility policies, change management initiatives, new management education schemes, for example, are practical theorising, with a wider organisational purpose of adaptation.

Our book has been devoted to exploring these practical managerial purposes. Each chapter has set out activities managers perform to adapt organisations to the business needs. It has been our intention to show how, without losing sight of the meanings which can be found in organisations on the contribution of HR to organisational performance, we can also interpret the activities of HRM in a variety of theoretical ways. We hope therefore our book will assist those whose inquiries as practising managers or as students of management have taken them down this path – in the hope that the journey will bring benefits to all those who wish to understand how to make practical strategies, and who see the contribution of HRM in the widest sense, to society.

REFERENCES

Beer, M., Spencer, B., Lawrence, P.R., Quinn Mills, D. and Walton, R.E. (1984) *Managing Human Assets*, New York, Free Press.

Berger, P.L., and Luckmann, T. (1966) *The Social Construction of Reality: A Treatise in the Sociology of Knowledge*, New York, Doubleday.

Douglas, J.D. (1971) *Understanding Everyday Life*, London, Routledge and Kegan Paul.

Fombrun, C.J., Tichy, N.M. and Devanna, M.A. (1984) *Strategic Human Resource Management*, New York, Wiley.

Garfinkel, H. (1967) *Studies in Ethnomethodology*, New York, Prentice Hall.

Gröjer, J.E. & Stark, A. (1978) *Social Redovisning*, Stockholm: SNS.

Hendry, C. and Pettigrew, A. (1990) 'Human Resource Management: an Agenda for the 1990s', *International Journal of Human Resource Management*, 1, (1), pp. 7–44.

Jacques, R. (1996) *Manufacturing the Employee*, London, Sage.

Peters, T. & Waterman, R. (1980) *In Search of Excellence – Lessons from America's Best-Run Companies*, New York, Harper & Row.

Silverman, D. (1972) Introductory comments in *New Directions in Sociological Theory*, Filmer, P., Philipson, M., Silverman, D. and Walsh, D., London, Collier-Macmillan, pp. 1–14.

Söderström, M. (1993) Personnel Management in Sweden. An HRM Role Struggling for Survival. Personnel Management, June 1993, pp. 28–33.

Tyson, S. (1995) *Human Resource Strategy: Towards a General Theory of Human Resource Management*, London, Pitman.

Tyson, S. and Wikander, L. (1994) 'The Education and Training of Human Resource Managers in Europe', in Brewster, C. and Hegewisch, A. (eds) *Policy and Practice in European HRM*, London, Routledge, pp. 36–50.

Willmott, H. (1996) 'A Metatheory of Management: Ommiscience or Obfuscation? A Comment', *British Journal of Management*, Vol. 7, No. 4, pp. 232–327.

INDEX

348